Constitutions and Conflict Management in Africa

NATIONAL AND ETHNIC CONFLICT
IN THE TWENTY-FIRST CENTURY

Brendan O'Leary, Series Editor

Constitutions and Conflict Management in Africa

Preventing Civil War Through Institutional Design

Edited by
Alan J. Kuperman

PENN

UNIVERSITY OF PENNSYLVANIA PRESS

PHILADELPHIA

Copyright © 2015 University of Pennsylvania Press

All rights reserved. Except for brief quotations used
for purposes of review or scholarly citation, none of this book
may be reproduced in any form by any means without
written permission from the publisher.

Published by
University of Pennsylvania Press
Philadelphia, Pennsylvania 19104-4112

Printed in the United States of America on acid-free paper
1 3 5 7 9 10 8 6 4 2

Library of Congress Cataloging-in-Publication Data
ISBN 978-0-8122-4658-2

CONTENTS

1. Designing Constitutions to Reduce Domestic Conflict   1
   Alan J. Kuperman

ACCOMMODATION IS RISKY

2. Burundi: Institutionalizing Ethnicity to Bridge the Ethnic Divide   27
   Filip Reyntjens

3. Kenya: Gradual Pluralization Fails to Buffer Shocks   51
   Gilbert M. Khadiagala

4. Nigeria: Devolution to Mitigate Conflict in the Niger Delta   71
   Eghosa E. Osaghae

5. Sudan: "Successful" Constitutional Reform Spurs Localized Violence   96
   Karly Kupferberg and Stefan Wolff

INTEGRATION CAN WORK

6. Ghana: The Complements of Successful Centralization: Checks, Balances, and Informal Accommodation   117
   Justin Orlando Frosini

7. Senegal: The Limits of Hyper-Centralization   135
   I. William Zartman, Hillary Thomas-Lake, and Arame Tall

8. Zimbabwe: The Unintended Consequences
   of Authoritarian Institutions   158
   Andrew Reynolds

APPLYING THE LESSONS

9. Africa's Domestic Institutions of Integration
   and Accommodation: A New Database   183
   Eli Poupko

10. Rethinking Constitutional Reform for Democracy and Stability   226
    Alan J. Kuperman

Notes   237

List of Contributors   273

Index   275

Acknowledgments   293

CHAPTER 1

Designing Constitutions to Reduce Domestic Conflict

Alan J. Kuperman

Can deadly internal conflict be prevented, or at least significantly reduced, by changing a country's domestic political institutions? This might seem an obvious and important question, especially for Africa, which recently has suffered the most such violence—in Rwanda, Congo, Darfur, and elsewhere. Yet, this continental puzzle has never before been addressed in a rigorous, comparative manner.

This volume, by the Constitutional Design and Conflict Management (CDCM) project, is the first such effort. As with any initial attempt to address a question of such enormous scope, the methodological challenges are substantial and the findings can be only tentative—but they are nevertheless intriguing. The book approaches the subject in three steps. First, it assembles seven of the world's leading experts on constitutional design, conflict management, and African politics. Each of these scholars presents a detailed case study of an African country, identifying how at key turning points the domestic political institutions either mitigated—or exacerbated—political instability and violence. These studies provide vital lessons about the types of domestic political institutions—or "constitutional design"—that are best for peacefully managing conflict. Second, the book presents the first database of constitutional design in all African countries. This new resource reveals that most African countries have highly centralized and integrative political institutions, which many experts previously have said fosters conflict. Third, the book brings together these two pieces of the puzzle—comparing the political institutions that Africa currently has to the type that might reduce violence—to develop policy prescriptions for foreign aid aimed at promoting democracy and good governance.

Counterintuitively, this chapter does not recommend promoting the constitutional design typically prescribed by academics for ethnically divided societies—which is based on decentralization and other explicit accommodation of ethnoregional groups—because it would be too different from what currently exists. Attempting such radical change, this chapter argues, would likely result in half measures that could backfire by exacerbating political instability and violence, contrary to their intent. Instead, this chapter recommends promoting gradual reform of Africa's existing, integrative constitutional designs by counterbalancing them with liberal institutions, especially the separation of powers—including a strong parliament, independent electoral commission, and judicial review. The case studies and database suggest that such evolutionary reform of constitutional design could both promote democracy and reduce the incidence of political instability and deadly conflict in Africa.

What We Know

The previous relevant scholarly literature can be broken into three categories: comparative African studies, comparative global studies, and specific African studies.[1] In the first category there is one, relatively old, comparative statistical analysis of African countries, suggesting that parliamentary systems of proportional representation may reduce conflict in multiethnic states.[2] However, the only qualitative comparative studies of the continent, focusing on southern Africa, fail to reach consensus on that question.[3]

This book aims to engage the debate, among both academics and practitioners, regarding two opposing strategies of constitutional design.[4] The first, "accommodation," provides guarantees to societal groups based on their distinct identity or geographic location, via mechanisms such as proportional representation, federalism, autonomy, quotas, economic redistribution, and veto power. The opposing strategy, "integration," aims to erode the political salience of groups that are distinguished by identity or location and instead promote a single, unifying nationality through more centralized institutions.[5] The difference between the two approaches is not merely the degree of government centralization, but also the extent to which state institutions aim to reinforce or erode substate, ethnoregional identities.[6] Between these two ideal-

Single ←		IDENTITY PROMOTION		→ Multiple
Assimilation	**Integration**	**Centripetalism**	**Accommodation**	**Secession**
Coercive imposition of unifying nationality, erasing separate identities based on ethnicity/geography.	Promotion of unified nationality and governance, eroding separate identities based on ethnicity/geography.	Incentives for cross-group appeals during elections, promoting both national and separate identities.	Guarantees to groups based on ethnicity/geography, reinforcing separate identitites.	Partition providing independence to areas of country asserting separate identity.

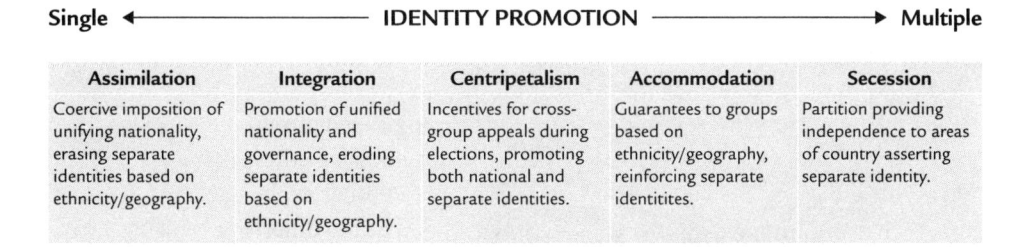

Figure 1.1. Spectrum of constitutional design.

types, integration and accommodation, lies a spectrum of constitutional design strategies (see Figure 1.1).[7]

Consensus is elusive on the best approach for conflict management. Arend Lijphart famously advocates the accommodation approach of "consociational" democracy that guarantees each major identity group a share of executive power, some autonomy, proportional representation and benefits, and a veto over fundamental decisions.[8] Donald Horowitz criticizes such arrangements both for being inefficient and for reinforcing identity divides, and instead advocates "centripetalism," the somewhat more integrative strategy of providing electoral incentives for political candidates to appeal across identity lines, an approach that might erode such divisions over time.[9] Lake and Rothchild criticize the specific accommodative approach of territorial decentralization on the grounds that it is an unstable outcome, destined to devolve into secession or reintegration, often entailing violence. By their reasoning, the integrationist approach of territorial centralization is the only stable alternative to secessionist dissolution of the state.[10] Recent scholarship suggests that conflict management is best fostered by flexibility of constitutional design over time, a hypothesis that has yet to be tested rigorously.[11] Existing case studies of African countries provide a rich evidentiary base for future scholarship,[12] but to date they have lacked a common methodology, which is essential to drawing reliable and broadly applicable lessons. (For further discussion of the relevant literature, please see this book's final chapter.)

A New Research Strategy: Shocks and Outcomes

Figuring out which constitutional designs are better or worse for conflict management in Africa is harder than might appear. At first, one might be tempted

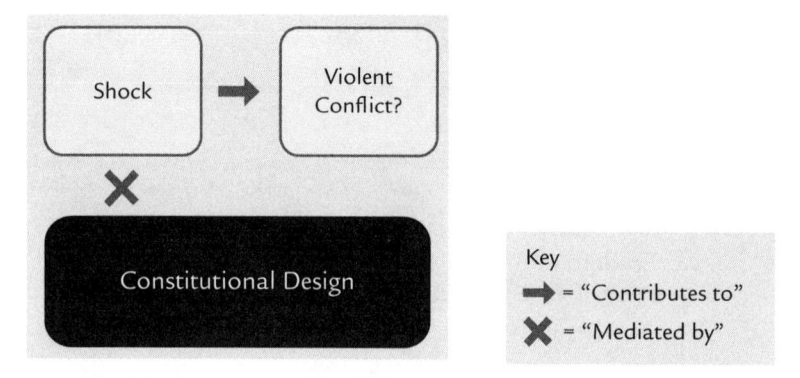

Figure 1.2. Innovative methodology.

simply to examine the correlation between domestic political institutions and violence across the continent. This could be misleading, however, because African countries face a wide variation in the extent of the challenges they confront, so that some may remain peaceful not because of beneficial constitutional design but rather the good fortune of facing few stresses. Contrarily, other countries may succumb to violence despite beneficial domestic political institutions because they have the misfortune to be overwhelmed by events, such as the spillover of war from a neighboring country.

To control somewhat for this variation, and thereby increase the validity of comparisons between cases, the authors agreed to focus on moments when each country faced particularly difficult challenges—"shocks"—and how constitutional design mediated the impact. The project does not aim to explain all domestic violence, but rather the role of constitutional design in mediating between shocks and the potential outcome of violence. In methodological terms, shocks are the "independent variable" that causes violence (the "dependent variable"), if not buffered adequately by constitutional design (the "condition variable"), as illustrated in Figure 1.2.

Shocks are defined by the book as relatively sudden—or more gradual, but especially large—changes that affect the distribution of resources and power in a country, whether arising from economic, political, demographic, or environmental dynamics (see Figure 1.3).[13] Each shock creates societal winners and losers, which scholars say can lead to violence via various mechanisms, including grievance,[14] opportunities for predation,[15] state weakness,[16] or insecurity.[17] The case studies explore how constitutional design interacts with such causal mechanisms to increase or reduce the likelihood of a vio-

> **Economic:**
> - Dramatic changes in "terms of trade."
> - Resource windfalls.
>
> **Demographic:**
> - Immigration, emigration, or internal migration.
> - Epidemics of disease.
>
> **Environmental:**
> - Drought, flood, and resulting famine.
> - Rapid environmental degradation.
>
> **Political:**
> - Disputed Elections.
> - Land redistribution.

Figure 1.3. Examples of shocks.

lent outcome. Economic shocks include sharp changes in terms of trade, as well as resource windfalls or shortages. Political shocks include disputed elections, term-limit violations, land redistribution, assassinations, or other momentous political events—typically domestic but potentially foreign—that affect the distribution of power in the country. Demographic shocks include sudden migration flows and epidemics. Environmental shocks include floods, droughts, famine, and rapid environmental degradation.

Shocks can have complex causes and consequences. A shock may affect only one region of a country, but the results of that shock and the implications for constitutional design can implicate the entire country. In some instances, a shock may lead to an outcome that serves as yet another shock, in a domino effect. In other cases, a single structural factor—such as poor governance, inadequate infrastructure, or economic dependence on a single export—may lead to multiple shocks over time. Constitutional reform, analyzed in this book mainly as a way to help buffer shocks, may also affect the structural factors that cause shocks.[18]

Admittedly, this book's common focus on shocks is an imperfect means of controlling for the magnitude of the challenge confronting each country's

Components of Constitutional Design:
Accommodation, such as quotas, vetoes, or autonomy for identity groups
Integration, typified by a strong presidency
Election rules, including proportional representation in legislatures and qualified-majority voting by legislatures
Devolution of authority to sub-national territories
Mandated transfer payments or other redistribution to sub-national territories
Separation of powers provisions for the judiciary, legislature, and/or opposition to challenge the executive
Informal elements of constitutional design, including norms and pacts
Legitimacy of constitutional design among the populace
Procedures for modifying and interpreting constitutional design—whether formally by supreme courts or amendments, or informally via deals among parties
Transitional justice mechanisms

Figure 1.4. Constitutional design.

domestic political institutions, given the wide variation in the type and intensity of shocks. However, by focusing on shocks, this methodology does at least avoid lumping together data from easy and hard times—and thus represents a useful first step in aggregating and comparing the evidence between cases.

"Constitutional design" is defined by the book as the formal and informal structures of countrywide governance (see Figure 1.4). Most obviously, this comprises institutions of integration and accommodation—including election rules, the nature of the executive, the extent of decentralization, and any guarantees to identity groups. It also includes the separation of powers—that is, provisions for the judiciary, legislature, or opposition to challenge the executive—and transitional justice for states emerging from autocracy or war. Additionally, it entails whether citizens accept the political institutions as legitimate, as well as any procedures for modification and interpretation of constitutional design, whether by courts, amendments, or informal pacts. The book examines not merely de jure institutions, but de facto implementation, finding that some codified institutions are not implemented, while other noncodified norms routinely are. This sheds important light on the need for and

	#1	#2	#3	#4
Burundi				
year:	1993	2005		
shock:	End minority rule	End minority rule		
outcome:	Genocide	Peace		
Ghana				
year:	1960s	1992	2000	2008
shock:	Volta Dam	Disputed elections	Incumbent defeat	Incumbent defeat
outcome:	Peace	Minor violence	Peace	Peace
Kenya				
year:	early-1990s	mid-1990s	mid-2000s	2007
shock:	Protests/Sanctions	Riots	Political turmoil	Electoral violence
outcome:	Multi-party politics	Temporary reforms	Ethnic polarization	New Constitution
Nigeria				
year:	1960s	1990s	2000s	
shock:	Oil windfall	Environmental Damage	Oil price spikes	
outcome:	Biafra genocide	Rebellion	Rebels escalate	
Senegal				
year:	1980s–1990s	2000s		
shock:	Secession	Flooding		
outcome:	Suppression	Minor protest		
Sudan				
year:	2005	2011		
shock:	Power-sharing	Secession		
outcome:	Implementation	Civil (not N-S) war		
Zimbabwe				
year:	1980s	2000	2008	
shock:	Ethnic tensions	Referendum fails	Opposition victory	
outcome:	Massacres	White farms seized	Electoral reversal	

Figure 1.5. Shocks and outcomes in seven African countries.

advisability of proposed reform of de jure institutions. Our definition of constitutional design does not, however, include the historical evolution of political institutions prior to each case study, because the initial constitutional design is treated as an independent condition variable.

Rather than mechanically assessing each of the above elements, the case studies highlight the aspects of constitutional design that have the greatest mediating role—whether beneficial or deleterious—in each country. (For a summary of the shocks and outcomes examined in each case, see Figure 1.5.) The case studies also explore whether various elements of constitutional

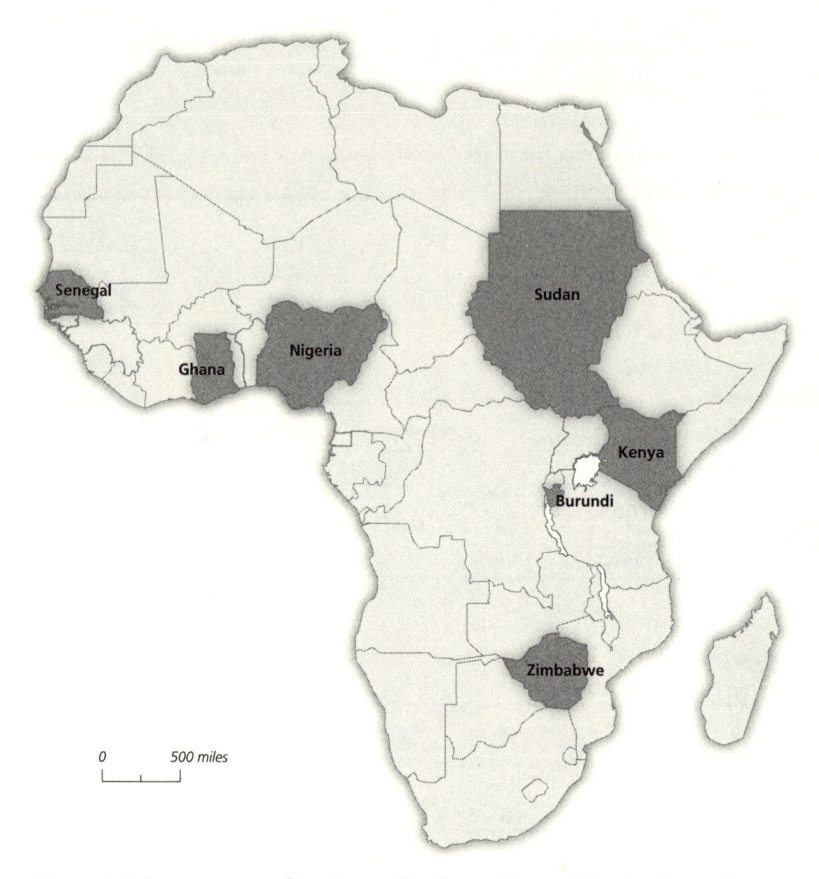

Figure 1.6. Seven case studies: Burundi, Ghana, Kenya, Nigeria, Senegal, Sudan, and Zimbabwe.

design interact with each other in ways that may alter their mediating effect. The book also recognizes that shocks may be mediated by factors other than constitutional design, including antecedent, proximate, structural, and individual characteristics in each country. Accordingly, the case studies report when such additional factors play an important mediating function, but the authors emphasize the role of constitutional design in accordance with the book's main research question.

To the extent possible, this book aims for detailed insight into the capacity and limitations of constitutional design to buffer shocks. It recognizes that such shocks vary along many dimensions, including rate of onset, magnitude, and duration. For example, a flood can arise in a matter of days, whereas desertification might take years to manifest but still would fit our definition of a shock. Some political institutions may be capable of buffering a gradually arising shock but not a sudden one, or a short shock but not a prolonged one. Moreover, constitutional design can mediate at various moments along the pathway from shock to violence. Some political institutions might prevent shocks from triggering rioting, while others could inhibit a subsequent escalation from rioting to full-blown civil war. The case studies highlight such nuanced lessons wherever possible.

Methodological Challenges and Choices

As the first rigorous study of its kind, this book faces formidable methodological challenges—regarding causal variables, outcome variables, endogeneity, omitted variables, selection effects, and degrees of freedom. In the future, as research expands and knowledge cumulates on the ways in which constitutional design may buffer or exacerbate shocks, such challenges should diminish. In the meantime, this book's methodological choices, justifications, and implications are explained below.

Outcome Variables

The outcome that this book focuses on is peace, not democracy. While that focus is commonplace in the field of conflict management, it is not in the study of constitutional design. Accordingly, this choice may be controversial because, for example, it could lead to coding a peaceful dictatorship as a success, despite that outcome being antithetical to many. The book makes this choice not because peace is more important than democracy—nor because constitutions necessarily are designed mainly to promote peace—but rather because peace is a valuable outcome whose determinants should be understood. Democracy is also an important outcome, yet a genocidal democracy would be viewed by many as a failure. The book starts from the assumption that any potential trade-off between peace and democracy should be informed by rigorous social scientific analysis of the causes of each.

Coding the outcome of peace is qualitative and relative to a country's history (see Figure 1.7 below). In some cases, the coding is obvious. For example,

Burundi's genocidal civil war starting in 1993 represents a failure, while Ghana's decades without major political violence is a success. In other cases, coding is more nuanced and relies partially on counterfactual analysis of the plausible alternative outcomes for each country. For example, Sudan is not coded as a total failure after 2005—despite subsequent fighting in its regions of Darfur, the Nuba Mountains, Blue Nile, and the secessionist South Sudan—because there has been no return of the genocidal wars fought between north and south until 2002 and in Darfur until 2004. Zimbabwe is coded largely as a failure after independence, in light of not only large-scale eruptions of killing—such as the massacre of 20,000 ethnic Ndebele in the 1980s—but also recurrent lower-level political violence. Senegal is coded mainly as successful, because urban protests and the attempted secession of Casamance have entailed little violence, yet the persistence of these disputes still represents a shortfall of conflict management. Kenya is coded as a partial failure because of its intermittent deadly riots surrounding elections, while Nigeria is coded as a somewhat larger failure because of the chronic nature of its ethnopolitical violence, including in the Niger Delta in the south and between Christians and Muslims in the north.

Causal Variables

This book codes "constitutional design" mainly along a spectrum from integration to accommodation in order to engage the above-cited debates among scholars and practitioners about the types of political institutions that should be promoted in the developing world. As noted, the authors assess these institutions not merely de jure but also de facto by looking at informal elements of constitutional design and the degree to which formal elements are implemented. The book regards constitutional design as a structural variable, but acknowledges that at times it can be modified or ignored, and thus may be viewed alternatively as a set of nonbinding norms that facilitate cooperation. In some instances, such as moments of military dictatorship, de jure constitutional design is effectively irrelevant, and the de facto design is coded most accurately, albeit imperfectly, as hyperintegration.

There exist many alternative ways to code constitutional design.[19] For example, a substantial literature on African politics explores forms of patrimonialism.[20] Regimes have also been coded on scales from democracy to autocracy.[21] Historical legacies have been explored by comparing the constitutions of former British, French, and Portuguese colonies. More recent scholarship assesses the inclusion and exclusion of ethnic groups from power.[22] The malleability of constitutional design—that is, the ease or difficulty of reforming political institutions—may in some cases be more important than the institutions themselves. The effect of each of these variables on the capacity of states to buffer shocks is worthy of focused exploration, but beyond the scope of this book.

We nominally label constitutional design as an "independent" condition variable, because our focus is on its mediating role between shocks and violence, but these relationships can be partially endogenous. Constitutional design is not applied to states as a random treatment, but rather evolves in part through self-selection. As illustrated by our case studies, constitutional design also can be both a cause and consequence of shocks, not merely a mediator of their impact. In some instances, there may be a spurious correlation between constitutional design and outcome, if both are caused by a third variable, such as interethnic animosities. Nevertheless, our case studies also confirm the mediating role of constitutional design, which has important implications for African countries contemplating institutional reform, and for international aid programs that promote democracy.

Shocks are categorized by this book into four groups: economic, demographic, political, and environmental. But they also could be differentiated by the extent of their endogeneity with constitutional design, into three categories.[23] The first type would be essentially exogenous, including extreme weather or sharp changes in world commodity prices. A second type of shock would result from the normal functioning of constitutional design, such as when a longtime incumbent loses reelection. The third type would stem from a violation of constitutional design—such as a coup, stolen election, or state violence. It is possible that the mediating role of constitutional design varies depending on the extent to which a shock is endogenous to that design, and this too could be explored in future research.

Other potentially important variables are excluded from our theoretical model for the sake of parsimony, as is common in the early stages of any research field. For example, ethnic demography may condition the ability of constitutional design to mediate shocks.[24] If so, it is possible that accommodative designs, such as consociational democracy, could help to buffer shocks in states with two or three polarized ethnic groups, but would be suboptimal in other situations. Likewise, some constitutional designs may be more beneficial in the immediate wake of a civil war than during times of sustained peace (as discussed further in this book's concluding chapter).[25] Such questions could be explored in future research by examining only shocks in states with accommodative constitutional designs, or only in the wake of civil war, and then investigating which other variables correlate with the variation in outcome.

Qualitative Method

If our methodology were statistical, this book would face hurdles stemming from "degrees of freedom." In other words, there are many potential explanatory variables for the relatively few outcomes to be explained. Constitutional design comprises more than a dozen components, and even the partially aggregated coding in this book's database includes five categories. Shocks are grouped into four categories but also vary further within each category by type and intensity. Yet, the case studies examine only seven countries, including the outcomes of just 20 shocks. No statistical method could overcome these challenges. It would be possible to further amalgamate some of the subcategories of constitutional design and shock, and to greatly expand the number of shocks under examination, but that could lump together disparate phenomena, creating more noise than signal and reducing the value of any inferences.

Pessimists might throw up their hands at these challenges, declaring that no lessons can be drawn to guide policymakers. Indeed, each of Africa's 53 countries (the total when we created our database) has a different constitutional design, faces different shocks, and is characterized by unique culture and history, so that facile generalizations should be avoided. But by moving beyond statistics, meaningful inferences are possible.

Qualitative methods are well suited for this book's research design. By employing the methodology of "process tracing,"[26] the case studies can identify with relative confidence the causal relationships between shocks, constitutional design, and violent outcomes. Even though no two shocks are identical, nor any two constitutional designs, qualitative methods can focus on the intervening variables, which may be quite similar. These include the sudden creation of societal winners and losers, the resulting demands on the political system, the capacity of the constitutional design to respond to those demands, and the consequences when constitutional design proves inadequate in this regard.

To help infer reliable lessons, the book deliberately picked case studies that provide variation on several key variables,[27] including the outcome (both comparatively between cases and longitudinally within cases), constitutional design,[28] and African subregion. Still, the book's findings are by no means the last word on constitutional design and conflict management in Africa. It is hoped that other scholars will evaluate and build upon the book's tentative findings, including by employing additional cases and methods. As detailed below, the book's first four cases illustrate that the constitutional design of accommodation—widely touted as a prescription for conflict management—is not without substantial risks in practice. By contrast, the last three cases suggest that the commonly denigrated constitutional design alternative, integration, may actually mitigate conflict under certain circumstances.

Accommodation Is Risky

Burundi: Incomplete Accommodation May Backfire

The chapter by Filip Reyntjens contrasts Burundi's two attempts at accommodative constitutional reform to help mediate the shock of ending minority rule, which produced starkly different outcomes. The first attempt, in 1993, tragically led to civil war and genocide. By contrast, the second attempt, in 2005, appears so far to have promoted relative peace, equity, and ethnic reconciliation. In each instance, the constitutional design aimed to accommodate both the traditionally dominant ethnic Tutsi minority, by providing security guarantees and representation, and the historically oppressed ethnic Hutu majority by transitioning to democracy.

The case study finds three main explanations for the far superior outcome of the latter effort. First, the revised accommodative institutions offered firmer guarantees of representation to the ethnic minority. Second, a regional peacekeeping force helped reduce the physical security concerns of that minority. Third, sufficient time had passed since the initial reform effort for the ethnic minority to be reconciled to its loss of political dominance. Although the case thus confirms the beneficial potential of accommodation, it also highlights an important caveat—that accommodation by itself cannot mitigate intense group insecurity. Accordingly, transitions of power should be implemented gradually and accompanied by third-party security guarantees, rather than relying solely on accommodative domestic institutions.

Burundi also illustrates the counterintuitive lesson that explicit acknowledgement of ethnic identity by government institutions can help reduce both the political salience of identity and the proclivity to interethnic violence. This may have important implications for neighboring Rwanda, whose government is attempting to mitigate a similar history of interethnic violence with the opposite strategy—denying the existence of group identities—which, unfortunately, seems to be heightening ethnic salience and tensions.

Kenya: Backsliding on Accommodation Perpetuates Electoral Violence

The chapter by Gilbert M. Khadiagala explores how, since the late 1980s, Kenya's constitutional design, characterized by partial accommodation, has failed to buffer four major shocks to its political system. The result of each shock typically has been midlevel violence, followed by only marginal constitutional reform, leaving the system vulnerable to the next shock. The shocks examined are as follows: (1) in the early 1990s, popular demands for a multiparty system, combined with donor aid cutbacks; (2) in the mid-1990s, violent riots and protests; (3) in 2003–2005, the combination of three successive tremors arising from the demise of incumbent parties and coalitions; and 4) in late 2007, accusations of a stolen election.

Three broad lessons emerge. First, the integrative aspects of the country's constitutional design, including a strong presidency, fostered and then failed adequately to buffer a series of economic and political shocks. Second, the constitutional design historically reinforced ethnic dominance, which contributed to a protracted national stalemate over that design. Third, endogenous and exogenous shocks eventually gave rise to a more substantial constitutional reform in 2010, but the robustness of these modified institutions will not be revealed until they are tested by future shocks.

Nigeria: Federalism Requires More Devolution

The chapter by Eghosa E. Osaghae examines the effects of three shocks arising from petroleum extraction in the Niger Delta region of southern Nigeria. The first shock was the discovery of oil in the 1960s, which created a major revenue windfall that spurred secession by the Biafra region (including the delta), leading to civil war and massive civilian victimization. The second shock was the oil industry's pervasive environmental degradation that became politically salient in the 1990s, spurring a new rebellion. The third shock was the oil price spike of the 2000s, which magnified both the resources available to militants and their demands, thereby escalating the rebellion.

Nigeria's constitutional design has long contained elements of accommodation, notably federalism and requirements for diverse regional representation in government institutions. This case study demonstrates, however, that such limited devolution has proved inadequate to address local grievances about oil revenue sharing and environmental justice in historically neglected areas populated by ethnic minorities. Except for federalism, the Nigerian government is highly centralized in its executive, legislative, and fiscal institutions, while lacking the resources to manage complex issues in the periphery. Osaghae concludes that prospective reforms to increase revenue sharing and to devolve political authority to the community level may offer the best hope of reducing grievance and the resulting persistent rebellion in the Niger Delta.

Sudan: The Hazards of Inequitable Accommodation

Sudan's 2005 Comprehensive Peace Agreement (CPA), which successfully ended a long-running north-south civil war, represented a major constitutional accommodation to the country's south, including a pledge (subsequently honored) to hold a secession referendum after six years. The chapter by Karly Kupferberg and Stefan Wolff explores the two main shocks entailed by implementation of the agreement: first, in 2005, the sharing of power between adversaries who had fought each other for more than two decades; second, in 2011, the south's vote to declare independence. Both events satisfy the project's definition of "shock"—because they represent a sudden change in the balance of power and resources—so it is important to examine how the agreement's constitutional design mediated each. Although there has been no recurrence of full-blown war between the north and south, local violence has erupted, not only in the disputed border area of Abyei, but also in other areas of the north (Blue Nile and South Kordofan states) and the south (Jonglei, Unity, Upper Nile, and Warrap states).

The case study finds that the CPA's institutions to regulate core north-south issues did successfully foster compromise and peaceful management of conflict *between* the two sides, with assistance from international engagement. But the implementation of the CPA failed to establish political institutions to mediate interactions among the contending groups *within* each region, thereby contributing to the outbreak of violence in both the north and south, some of which has been exacerbated by cross-border support to militants.

The case thus illustrates the dangers of *inequitable* accommodation. Although the 2005 agreement nominally pledged comprehensive reform, in practice it made significant concessions only to the most violent opponent of the government, while essentially ignoring other aggrieved groups. "Comprehensive" was thus a misnomer. The flawed design and implementation not only permitted the grievances of other groups to fester, but also aggravated them and encouraged these groups to resort to violence in hopes of earning similar accommodation. This experience suggests that accommodation must be equitable—not merely on paper, but in practice—if it is to buffer effectively against shocks.

Integration Can Work

Ghana: Liberal Institutions Mitigate Perils of Integration

The chapter by Justin Orlando Frosini explores how and why Ghana has remained peaceful in the face of repeated shocks, despite having a highly integrative constitutional design, which many scholars claim is suboptimal for conflict management. The four shocks under examination are the construction of the Volta Dam that displaced 80,000 people in the 1960s, and then the turbulent elections of 1992, 2000, and 2008, which entailed accusations of electoral fraud, boycotts by opposition parties, and the defeat of incumbent presidents. Although each shock produced some political conflict, none resulted in significant violence.

The beneficent effect of key individuals and culture cannot be excluded in Ghana, but several aspects of constitutional design also helped foster nonviolent outcomes. Since 1992, for example, the president has been limited to two terms, thereby offering political opponents hope that they can accede to the top office peacefully, rather than having to fight for it. Although the government's formal institutions are highly integrative, including first-past-the-post legislative elections, one informal aspect of constitutional design is highly accommodative: by tradition, cabinet posts and other executive positions are distributed to reflect the country's ethnoregional diversity. This may produce a stabilizing effect similar to that attributed to formal accommodative institutions, such as quotas or proportional representation. Perhaps most important, liberal institutions—including free media, an independent electoral commission, and courts with the power of judicial review—provide a separation of powers that can check abuses by the executive. Facilitated by these factors, Ghana's integrative institutions produce many of the benefits typically ascribed to centripetal constitutional design: namely, there is a two-party system in which politicians make cross-group appeals, coalitions are fluid, political power alternates between parties and among groups, and the political salience of group identity diminishes over time.

Senegal: Inefficiency of Hyper-Centralization

The chapter by I. William Zartman, Hillary Thomas-Lake, and Arame Tall explores how Senegal's highly centralized constitutional design has mediated two shocks: rain-induced flooding that has produced widespread population displacement around the capital of Dakar; and secessionist rebellion in the province of Casamance. It finds that the highly empowered office of the president has been able to take belated, unilateral action to address shocks superficially—thereby temporarily buffering their effects and averting large-scale violence—but has lacked the capacity for urgent action or for reform to address the underlying vulnerabilities. As a result, the country's populace remains persistently susceptible to shocks, and thus moderately aggrieved, but has not yet resorted to large-scale, extrasystemic violence.

To provide better protection against shocks, such a hypercentralized constitutional design requires one of two types of reform. The first option is accommodation, such as devolving authority to local officials who could be more responsive to local concerns. The alternative would be liberal institutional checks on the executive, such as a strong legislature and independent judiciary, to foster greater accountability to constituents.

Zimbabwe: Exclusionary Authoritarianism Exacerbates Shocks

The chapter by Andrew Reynolds assesses how Zimbabwe's increasingly centralized and authoritarian constitutional design over the past three decades has mediated the effect of three shocks on political stability and interethnic relations. At independence, the country's constitutional design contained aspects of accommodation, both formal and informal, for minorities. The small White community was constitutionally ensured representation in the legislature and the protection of its property. The main Black minority ethnic group, the Ndebele, had during the preceding war of independence been effectively accommodated within the ruling party that was led by the ethnic majority Shona.

The first shock, in the early 1980s, was the emergence of violence between the government and its former allies, the ethnic Ndebele paramilitaries. The outcome was the Gukurahundi massacres by the state of an estimated 20,000 Ndebele in the region of Matabeleland, eviscerating the informal accommodation toward this minority. The second shock, in the year 2000, was the defeat of the regime's constitutional referendum. The result was the Third Chimurenga—the seizure and occupation of White-owned farms—which led to a breakdown of law and order, out-migration of White farmers, economic decline, and the effective end of the formal accommodation of Whites. The third shock was the 2008 election victory by the opposition Movement for Democratic Change (MDC). This led to the regime's violent suppression of the opposition (Operation Ngatipedzenavo), followed by a nominal power-sharing agreement that effectively reversed the electoral outcome.

The case demonstrates, most obviously, that exclusionary authoritarianism can only temporarily succeed at using force to suppress the domestic opposition, because the government's violence exacerbates economic decline and other sources of unrest. Less obviously, the study reveals a potential silver lining. President Robert Mugabe's three decades of increasingly exclusionary and oppressive rule have helped unite his opponents across ethnic lines to forge perhaps the most inclusionary political alliance in any African country, comprising Shona, Ndebele, and Whites. This offers some hope for a future political transition in Zimbabwe.

Lessons Learned

The broad lesson from the case studies is that neither of the two opposing constitutional approaches—integration or accommodation—is necessary or sufficient for buffering against shocks, but that each may achieve this goal if institutionalized appropriately. (Indeed, as illustrated in Figure 1.7, the

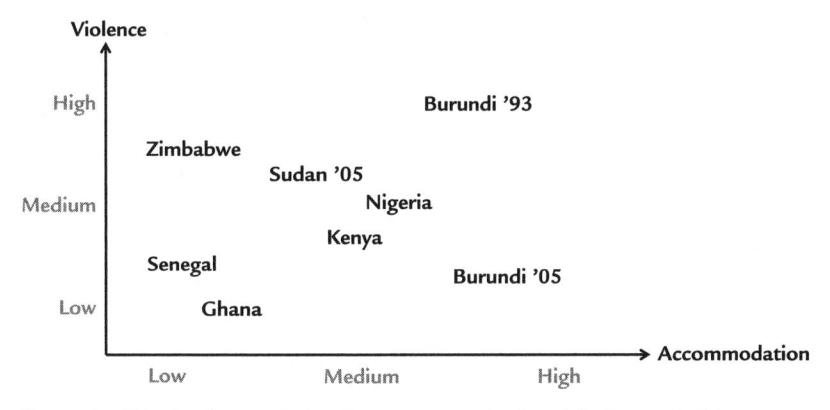

Figure 1.7. No simple correlation between constitutional design and violence. Note: Burundi appears twice because its two attempts at accommodation produced radically different outcomes. Countries listed without specific years are coded on the basis of overall post-independence experience.

two most successful constitutional designs in our case studies—Ghana and Burundi-2005—lie on opposite ends of the integration-accommodation spectrum.) If implemented poorly, however, either approach can leave a society highly fragile to shocks, which may trigger instability up to and including civil war and genocide. For each of the two approaches to constitutional design, the sources of fragility and the requirements of "appropriate" institutionalization are different, as discussed below.

The main danger of integration is that it tends to concentrate power in the hands of an executive that may be unaccountable, and therefore insufficiently responsive, to large segments of society. This can breed grievance among the neglected population, compelling the executive to rely on an even narrower base, which further exacerbates societal resentment, leading to an escalatory spiral. In such a situation, a shock can magnify grievance and create opportunities for offensive or preemptive violence by the government or its domestic opponents. Five of the seven cases—Kenya, Nigeria, Senegal, Sudan, and Zimbabwe—illustrate that pathology.

This hazard of integration can be mitigated in two very different ways, according to the case studies. One option is to promote accommodation, which runs substantial risks as detailed below. The other option is exemplified by Ghana, which balances its integrative design and strong executive with liberal institutions—including term-limits, courts with the power of judicial review, an independent electoral commission, and media freedom—which offer reassurance to the political opposition about a peaceful path to power.[29] In the context of these complementary liberal institutions, the country's integrative electoral mechanisms—including first-past-the-post elections—encourage cross-group appeals by politicians who cannot gain sufficient votes for victory from their own ethnic group alone. This also promotes fluid pre-election coalitions among societal groups as they aggregate into the two main political parties. Both dynamics help erode identity divisions and further encourage the expectation among opposition groups that they eventually can gain power through political rather than violent means, thereby promoting a virtuous rather than escalatory spiral.

The other option, accommodation, is the more obvious constitutional strategy for conflict management, because it addresses grievance through direct appeasement. This can work, but entails risks of backfiring gravely if not institutionalized appropriately. Three of the seven cases—Burundi, Kenya, and Sudan—illustrate the potential of accommodation. Burundi greatly reduced persistent interethnic tension and recurrent violence, and even the salience of identity, by accommodating both the Hutu majority and Tutsi minority in its 2005 constitution, providing guarantees and protections for each. Likewise, Kenya broke its cycle of election-related, inter-tribal violence—at least for one national vote in 2012—by adopting accommodative constitutional reforms in 2010. Sudan successfully ended decades of north-south civil war in 2005 by accommodating the south with a 2011 referendum on secession.

But two of these cases also illustrate the dangers of poorly implemented accommodation. Burundi, in its first attempted transition to democracy in 1993, made the error of accommodating the ethnic majority too quickly, without adequate protection or socialization of the traditionally dominant ethnic minority. The tragic result was that the minority resorted to lethal force to retain its security and prestige, culminating in genocide and civil war. The lesson is that accommodation should be pursued in an evolutionary rather than revolutionary manner, providing sufficient time and security guarantees to enable traditionally dominant groups to overcome their psychological obstacles to surrendering power.

Sudan made the error of accommodating only the country's best-armed opposition groups, in the south, by permitting a secession referendum in that region. This not only failed to accommodate other aggrieved groups in the north and south, but encouraged them to view violence as the path to accommodation. The consequence has been an escalation of civil war and civilian victimization in both rump Sudan and South Sudan. The lesson is that accommodation should be institutionalized in an equitable rather than selective and discriminatory manner, if it is to provide a buffer against shocks.

Patterns of Constitutional Design in Africa

The chapter by Eliezer Poupko presents the first database of constitutional design in all of Africa's countries, coded on a spectrum from integration to accommodation. That coding is based on three separate but interrelated institutional dimensions—executive, legislative, and administrative—including both de facto and de jure measures at the start of 2011. The executive is coded as integrative if there is a directly elected president and otherwise is coded as accommodative, except in rare cases where additional executive elements provide substantial counterbalance. For example, vote-pooling in a direct presidential election would make the executive more accommodative, while appointment of the president by a majoritarian parliament would make the executive more integrative. The legislature is coded as most accommodative if the lower (or only) house is selected by proportional representation with sizeable districts and minimal thresholds for representation, and as most integrative if there is plurality voting in single-member districts. Adjustments are made for mixed voting systems, quotas, bicameralism, and the power of the legislature in relation to the executive. The administrative dimension is coded as integrative in a unitary state, and as accommodative to the extent there is federalism or devolution to subnational entities, especially based on identity.

Each country as a whole is coded as hyperintegrative or hyperaccommodative if all three institutional dimensions point in the same direction. If two of the three dimensions point in the same direction, the coding is integrative or accommodative. The remaining countries are coded as balanced. These de jure codings are then adjusted, based on implementation, to determine the de facto codings. For example, if a legislature is formally accommodative and empowered, but in practice is dominated by an integrative executive, the de facto coding of the legislature is switched to integrative, potentially altering the overall country coding. (As discussed above, important roles may also be played by informal or extraconstitutional domestic institutions—such as traditional authorities, norms of regional distribution, militaries acting as guardians of stability, or political parties cooperating

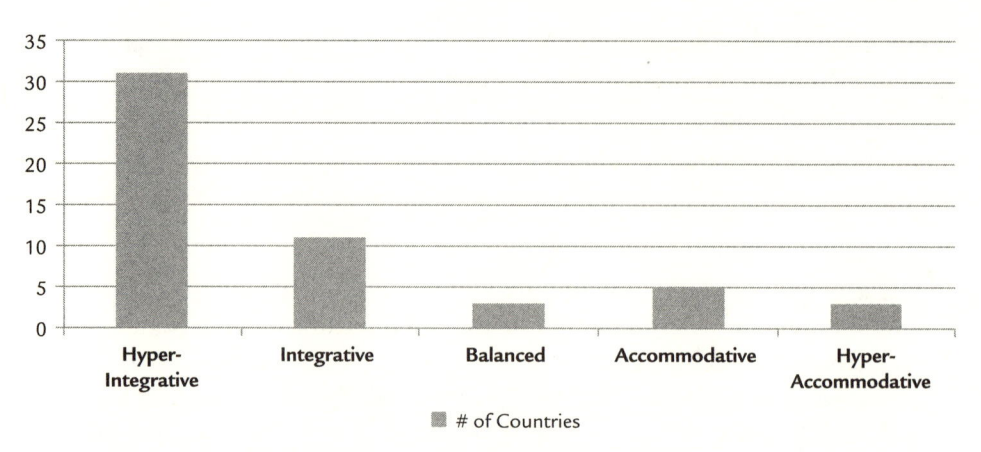

Figure 1.8. Accommodation is rare in constitutional design of African countries. Note: categories reflect constitutional design de facto coding, as of 1 January 2011; see Eliezer S. Poupko, this volume.

outside of government—but these are difficult to code and so are not incorporated in our database, although they are in our case studies.) As illustrated by a summary of the database (see Figure 1.8), Africa has a strong tendency toward integrative constitutional design, as nearly 80 percent of countries on the continent are coded as integrative or hyperintegrative.[30] The two most common elements of such integration are directly elected presidents and centralized administrative structures that limit identity-based politics.

Policy Implications

Given that most African countries have highly integrative constitutional designs—which leave them susceptible to shocks—foreign aid to promote democracy and good governance could follow either of the two strategies identified above. One option would be to promote a radical transformation of domestic institutions from integrative to equitably accommodative. The alternative would be to promote only marginal changes in constitutional design by complementing the existing integrative institutions with liberal elements—such as term limits, empowered legislatures, media freedom, and independent courts and electoral commissions—to counterbalance and thereby mitigate the pathologies of strong executives.

Designing Constitutions to Reduce Domestic Conflict 23

| Most African countries have integrative constitutional design | → | R_x: Promote liberal reform of existing integrative design, not radical replacement with accommodative design |

X

Foreign pressure for full accommodation would be resisted, leading to inequitable accommodation or inadequate guarantees

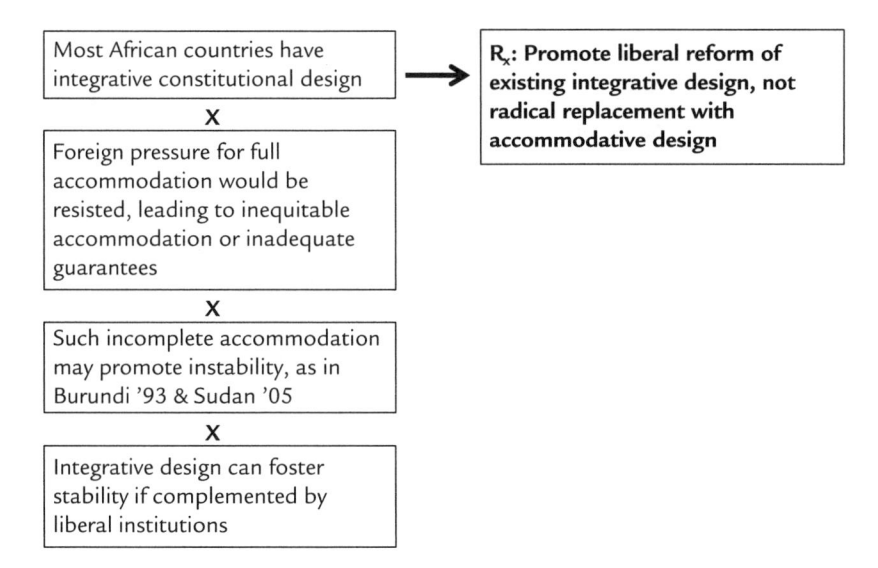

X

Such incomplete accommodation may promote instability, as in Burundi '93 & Sudan '05

X

Integrative design can foster stability if complemented by liberal institutions

Figure 1.9. Donors should promote reform, not replacement, of prevailing integrative design.

In theory, either pathway could work. In practice, however, it is difficult for outsiders to induce major changes in a country's constitutional design, due to countervailing dynamics of culture, politics, resistance to perceived neo-imperialism, and historically rooted path dependency.[31] As a result, foreign pressure to adopt full accommodation could well result in only partial reform that is inequitable or provides inadequate guarantees to insecure groups, raising the grave risks illustrated by Burundi and Sudan (see Figure 1.9). Accordingly, aid donors should consider instead promoting liberal reforms of Africa's existing, integrative constitutional designs—rather than their radical replacement with accommodative designs—despite the general academic preference for the latter, if they wish to foster both peace and democracy in Africa. The book's concluding chapter elucidates this policy recommendation and its rationale.

ACCOMMODATION IS RISKY

CHAPTER 2

Burundi: Institutionalizing Ethnicity to Bridge the Ethnic Divide

Filip Reyntjens

This chapter examines how changes in Burundi's constitutional design have helped buffer the shock of democratic elections, thereby contributing to a sharp reduction in ethnic violence. Inter-group conflict was the most important and lethal hallmark of Burundian politics starting at independence in 1962, and claimed hundreds of thousands of lives as recently as the 1990s, but has largely receded over the past decade. This chapter shows that constitutional engineering along consociational lines—explicitly accommodating ethnicity rather than attempting to suppress it—played a major part in reducing ethnic conflict and violence, in concert with other endogenous and exogenous factors. Only by looking at changes in constitutional design, together with these other factors, can we understand why the 1993 elections ended in disaster, while those of 2005 and 2010 were not followed by ethnic strife. Indeed, recognition and institutionalization of ethnicity have proved to be a powerful tool for pacification.

The rest of this chapter is organized as follows. After a brief historical outline, the chapter addresses the conditions under which the institutional recognition of the ethnic factor came about, after it had been neglected on purpose for nearly three decades. The next two sections examine the first attempt to bring peace through a consociational dispensation, its failure, and the negotiations that led to a second attempt a decade later. The following two sections analyze the implementation of the new arrangement, the reasons for its success in terms of ethnic pacification, and the consolidation of power by the winner of the 2005 elections. Lessons are drawn in the conclusion.

Methodologically, the chapter identifies ethnic conflict as the main dividing factor of Burundian politics, and explores how consociational mechanisms have been gradually introduced to tackle it. In terms of this book's analytical framework, the "shocks" in Burundi, from 1993 to the present, have been the democratic elections that confronted a society deeply divided between two ethnic groups. The chapter explores how constitutional design has mediated those shocks, contributing either to ethnic violence or to more peaceful outcomes. Additionally, the chapter illustrates how factors beyond constitutional design also have influenced the outcomes.

Because Burundi has been grossly under-researched, little literature is available on political developments during the last quarter of a century. I rely on Lemarchand for the period preceding the profound change that started at the end of the 1980s,[1] on Sullivan and Vandeginste for the application of power-sharing and other consociational mechanisms,[2] and on my own writings for most of the political transition in the 1990s and 2000s.

Roots of Conflict

Just like its northern neighbor Rwanda, Burundi's main political problem and source of violence has been ethnic strife. Open conflict between elites of the Hutu majority (85 percent) and the Tutsi minority (15 percent) started just prior to independence, when Prime Minister Louis Rwagasore was assassinated in January 1962. Although a Tutsi, he was widely respected among Hutu too, and his death was to prove a crucial event in the subsequent tragic history of the country. His disappearance led to ethnic divisions within the dominant political party, Union pour le Progrès National (UPRONA), and to the violent spiraling of the Hutu-Tutsi divide. Tensions reached a climax after another prime minister, a Hutu, Pierre Ngendandumwe, was assassinated in January 1965. During the ensuing political crisis, a faction of the Hutu-dominated *gendarmerie* (national police) attempted to seize power in October the same year. The state's repression of this abortive coup was extremely violent: virtually the entire Hutu political elite was massacred, together with thousands of rural Hutu who had supported the revolt; hundreds of Tutsi were killed too. These events effectively ended any significant participation by the Hutu in political life for many years. The Tutsi-dominated UPRONA became the single party.

Captain (later Lieutenant General) Michel Micombero, a Tutsi-Hima[3] from Bururi, took power in November 1966. Subsequent purges of Hutu officers and politicians, but also of Tutsi opponents, consolidated the supremacy of a group of Tutsi-Hima from Bururi province. In 1972, following an uprising by Hutu rebels who killed nearly a thousand Tutsi, retaliatory massacres of unprecedented magnitude and brutality were carried out by the Tutsi-dominated army and the youth wing of UPRONA. It is estimated that, out of a total Hutu population of about three million, 100,000–200,000 were killed, and a further 300,000 fled the country, mainly to Zaire, Tanzania, and Rwanda. Virtually all Hutu were eliminated from the armed forces.[4] This 1972 genocide was a major watershed in contemporary Burundian history. In addition to radicalizing the ethnic divide, it heralded a culture of impunity, as no one was prosecuted for massive human rights violations. In November 1976, Colonel Jean-Baptiste Bagaza, like Micombero a Tutsi-Hima from Bururi, seized power. In September 1987, he was in turn deposed by Maj. Pierre Buyoya, another Tutsi-Hima from Bururi. Constitutions adopted in 1974 and 1981 did not address the ethnic issue, but rather chose to ignore it; indeed, it was forbidden to mention ethnicity. "Ethnic amnesia"[5] served to hide the fact that power was exercised by the elite of an ethnic minority.

Acknowledging Ethnicity

Burundi only began to address the ethnic issue after new violence erupted in August 1988, less than a year after Buyoya came to power. During an operation aimed at "restoring order," following local confrontations between Hutu and Tutsi, the army randomly killed thousands of unarmed Hutu civilians in several northern municipalities, notably in Ntega and Marangara. The death toll may have been as high as 20,000, while another 60,000 Hutu fled to neighboring Rwanda.[6] Although initially the reactions of the authorities did not differ greatly from those of their predecessors, who routinely denied the occurrence of massacres and refused to draw lessons, these dramatic events helped trigger a new policy. Also influenced by considerable pressure from abroad, President Buyoya embarked on a program of reform aimed at breaking the cycle of violence. Without explicitly saying so, he introduced a quota system that enabled bringing the Hutu majority back onto the political scene. This was to be the beginning of the use of constitutional design to deal with the ethnic divide.

The first actions taken by Buyoya were of considerable psychological value. In October 1988 he set up a National Commission to Study the Question of

National Unity, comprising 12 Hutu and 12 Tutsi. He also appointed a Hutu, Adrien Sibomana, as prime minister, and put into place a cabinet with an equal number of Hutu and Tutsi. During the following years, this policy was further extended; by the end of 1990, a sizeable number of provincial governors and mayors, and even the general secretary of UPRONA, were Hutu. In addition, Hutu were increasingly represented equally with Tutsi in most bodies of the state. However, the armed forces and the police and intelligence services resisted change, remaining predominantly Tutsi.

Initiated in a single-party context, the process of reform was to continue in a more pluralistic environment in the early 1990s. After the Cold War, Western pressure on Africa eventually forced Buyoya to accept the introduction of multiparty democracy, with all the dangers it entailed for his efforts at ethnic reconciliation. Many Tutsi feared that ethnic voting in a competitive system would transform the Hutu demographic majority into a permanent political majority. When a constitutional commission started its work in April 1991, this concern was ever present in the proceedings. As a result, the report published by the commission in August 1991, and the constitution approved by referendum in March 1992, called repeatedly for broadly inclusive power-sharing. For example, the new constitution's Article 84 mandated that "the government be composed in a spirit of national unity, taking into account the diverse component parts of the Burundian population"—a reference mainly to the ethnic groups and to a lesser extent the regions.[7] Likewise, Article 101 mandated that each party's list of candidates for the parliamentary elections "shall be composed in a spirit of national unity." Such inclusivity requirements were incorporated in 12 of the 189 articles of the constitution.

Power-sharing techniques were particularly striking in the provisions on parliamentary elections. The requirement that party lists were to reflect the population's "component parts" was coupled with a closed-list voting system, which meant that a voter could choose only among parties, not their individual candidates. Nor could voters alter the proposed order of candidates on each party list, which had to include a sufficient number of Tutsi near the top. This power-sharing strategy aimed to avert the prospect of ethnic voting by Hutu at the expense of Tutsi, while also guaranteeing a sizeable representation of the latter in parliament. Also aiming to protect the minority, the constitution imposed obstacles to amendments, requiring an 80 percent parliamentary supermajority.

Although the terms Hutu and Tutsi were not used in the constitution, the above provisions clearly were consociational mechanisms aimed at reassuring the minority Tutsi by offering them over-representation. The effectiveness of this constitutional design was put to the test in the elections of June 1993, Burundi's first competitive ones since 1965. During the run-up, two realities soon emerged. First, the contest was a two-party affair. UPRONA was seriously challenged only by the Front pour la Démocratie au Burundi (FRODEBU), which had organizational ability, committed militants, successful campaign strategies, and a charismatic leader, Melchior Ndadaye. The second reality was the mounting salience of ethnicity in the electoral contest. Seeing the new party gaining ground, UPRONA embarked on a campaign that attempted to discredit FRODEBU by claiming that it was an ethnic organization of the Hutu. This tactic backfired by reinforcing the view that UPRONA was a party of the Tutsi minority, which, given the relative demographic weights of the ethnic groups, could only play into the hands of FRODEBU.

The Hutu candidate, Melchior Ndadaye, won the presidential election of 1 June 1993, with 65 percent of the vote, while the Tutsi incumbent, Pierre Buyoya, managed only 32 percent. The turnout was a massive 97 percent of registered voters, a clear indication of Burundians' interest in their first ever opportunity to determine who should be their head of state by means of a competitive election.[8] The outcome showed that voting was not merely along ethnic lines, as Ndadaye received significantly less support than the Hutu share of the population, while Buyoya obtained over double the Tutsi share.

By contrast, the parliamentary elections at the end of June 1993 were ethnically more polarized. Even though both parties had multiethnic party lists, FRODEBU was dominated by Hutu and UPRONA by Tutsi. FRODEBU won 71 percent (6 points more than Ndadaye) against 21 percent for UPRONA (11 points less than Buyoya). In terms of parliamentary seats, FRODEBU secured 65 of the 81 total. This was just above the 80 percent threshold required for amending the constitution. In ethnic terms, the membership of the Assembly was as follows: 69 Hutu (about 85 percent) and 12 Tutsi (about 15 percent). Of the Tutsi members, eight were FRODEBU and four were UPRONA, so ironically most of the elected Tutsi were from the "Hutu" party. This ethnic breakdown of parliament matched nearly perfectly the demographic composition of the population, confirming Tutsi fears that democracy would transform the Hutu demographic majority into ethnic political domination. It also meant that even across party lines the Tutsi members did not have a blocking minority of 20 percent should they feel that a constitutional amendment were to threaten their vital interests, so the consociational objective of reassuring the minority was not achieved.[9]

Civil War

After having ruled Burundi since 1965, UPRONA was significantly weakened by losing the presidency and obtaining only a politically useless minority of less than one-fifth in the national assembly. Such an end to one-party rule had transpired peacefully in other African countries, so there might have been a similarly benign outcome if not for Burundi's particular history of ethnic conflict and minority rule. Although some leading figures in UPRONA and FRODEBU crossed ethnic lines, the former was perceived as a Tutsi party and the latter as Hutu. The victory of FRODEBU was thus seen as the end of a long period of domination by the minority Tutsi, based on their control of both the former single party and the army. For many among the Tutsi elite, the long-feared specter of the Hutu demographic majority turning into a political majority had become reality. These concerns were openly expressed by Tutsi students who demonstrated in Bujumbura on 4 June 1993, proclaiming that the presidential election had become an "ethnic inventory of Burundi." Another of their slogans declared, "Yes to democracy, no to the ethnicization of power." A few days later, a Tutsi youth organization claimed that the "pseudo-democracy put in place automatically excludes the ethnic minority."[10]

A more serious threat came from the army, where Tutsi comprised most troops and nearly all officers. Two unsuccessful coups d'état were launched on 16–17 June and 2–3 July 1993. Although the number of military involved was small, and the attempts were unable to muster wider support, these incidents reflected the discontent felt by some members of the ousted politico-military elite. President Ndadaye understood this well and so took immediate steps to reassure the minority. For example, although FRODEBU enjoyed an 80 percent majority in parliament, the party took only 13 of 23 cabinet portfolios (57 percent), while UPRONA was given six ministries, including the post of prime minister. Looking at the cabinet from an ethnic standpoint, over one-third of its members were Tutsi. On the other hand, Ndadaye also engaged in housecleaning of the former elite, as no member of the outgoing cabinet was reappointed. All provincial governors also were replaced, with FRODEBU taking 14 of those 16 positions, as well as the chiefs of staff of the army and *gendarmerie*, and most ambassador slots. The party's members also filled many intermediate and lower positions in the civil service and local administration. Critics expressed fears of the "Frodebization" of the entire system.

For the new regime, the honeymoon was very brief. Ndadaye immediately faced considerable problems: the massive return of refugees and resulting land conflicts; the delicate process of making the civil service more inclusive of Hutu; the domination by UPRONA of the bureaucracy and the judiciary; the inertia of, and even sabotage by, the Tutsi-dominated army; the control of most of the economy by the ousted elite; and the hostility of a private-sector press corps that was generally very close to the former incumbents. A new recruiting system for the national police school, which capped the number of candidates from each province, caused anxiety among Tutsi, because it was viewed as a precedent for the recruitment of army troops scheduled for November 1993. In addition to diluting the power of the traditionally dominant Bururi province, the reform raised the fear that the provincial quota would soon be followed by ethnic ones. The government had a legitimate agenda, including some affirmative action to address past underrepresentation of Hutu, but it provoked great resistance. Things came to a head at the end of October 1993.

During the night of 20–21 October 1993, Bujumbura-based army units carried out a coup without encountering resistance in the capital. They assassinated President Ndadaye and some of his close associates, and drove others into hiding. As the coup unfolded in Bujumbura, violence erupted in the provinces. In many places Hutu residents, spontaneously or organized by local Hutu officials, resisted the army and perpetrated reprisals against Tutsi (and even Hutu) members of UPRONA. Elsewhere, the army and local Tutsi attacked FRODEBU members and Hutu generally. By the end of December, the death toll approached 50,000, divided roughly equally between Hutu and Tutsi victims. In the meantime, the coup collapsed after it was firmly condemned by the international community and local civil society. Political authority became vacant. The momentarily ousted, FRODEBU-led government went "into exile" in the French embassy, declaring that it did not trust the army and that its security could only be ensured by an international military force. Thus commenced a ten-year civil war—not detailed here for reasons of space—which killed thousands and sparked a humanitarian disaster with 650,000 Burundians internally displaced (see Figure 2.1) and hundreds of thousands more seeking refuge in neighboring states.[11]

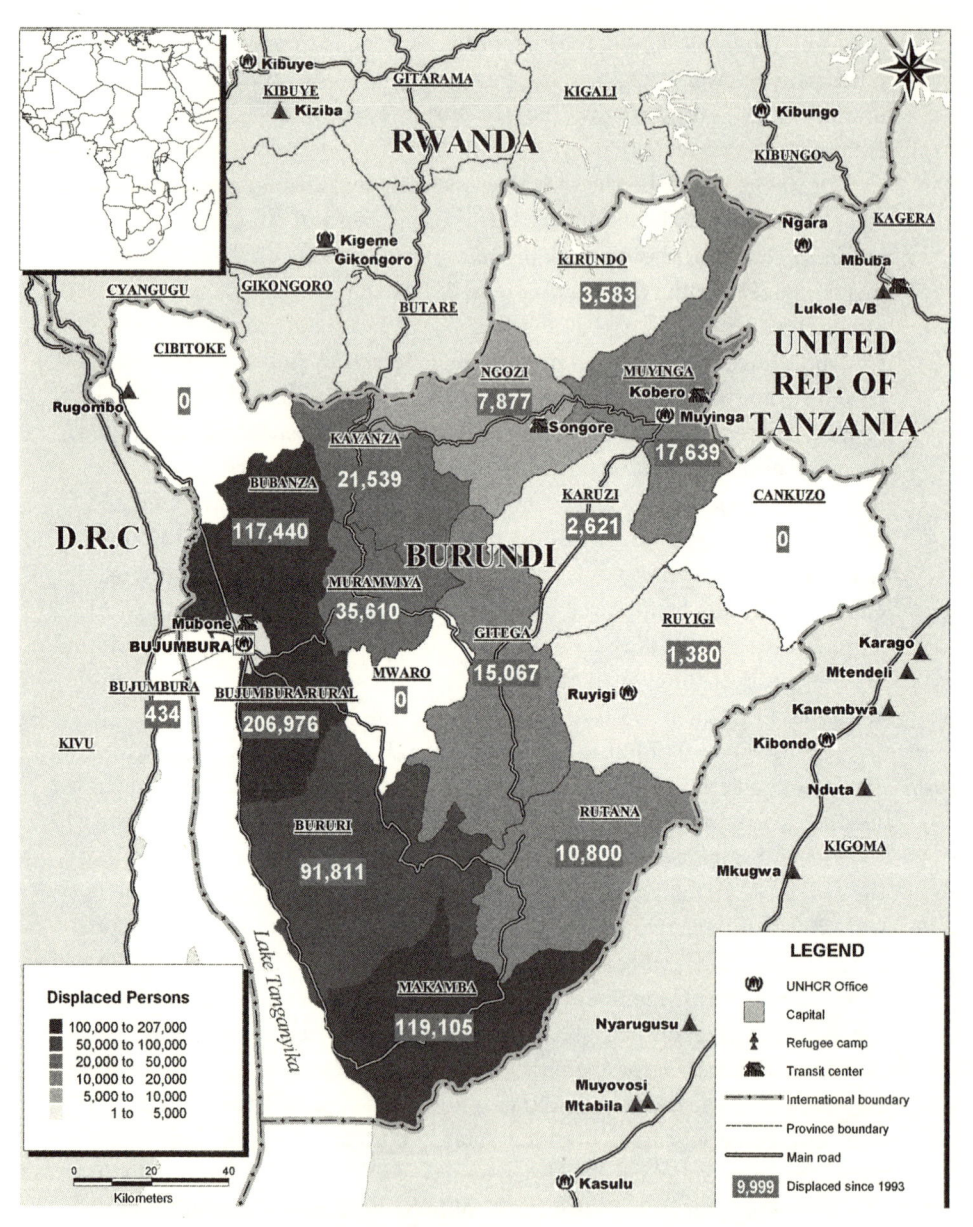

Figure 2.1. Failed accommodation of 1993 triggers civil war, prolonged displacement of 650,000. Note: numbers indicate Burundians still displaced in each province in June 2000. Source: UNHCR, 27 June 2000. http://www.unhcr.org/3ae6baf80.html.

Why did constitutional engineering fail to buffer the shock of the 1993 elections and avert the resulting ethnic violence? Buyoya's policy of "reconciliation"—meaning to get the Hutu into the system—was well-intentioned and a real break with the past, in that it effectively recognized ethnicity, even if not spelled out as such. But international events—mainly the end of the Cold War and the ensuing Western demand for political liberalization across Africa—forced Buyoya to accelerate into "democratization," resulting in an abrupt switch from minority Tutsi to majority Hutu rule. This transition was too sudden to permit the establishment of confidence between the elites of the two ethnic groups. Many Tutsi in the military and beyond were not yet ready to face the loss of power and privilege that likely would follow, considering Burundi's neo-patrimonial tradition. This explains the violent reaction, starting with the coup d'état of October 1993, and followed by the mutual ethnic massacres. Many Tutsi feared for their physical survival, while many Hutu were deeply frustrated by the erasure of their electoral gains. As civil war persisted, ethnic polarization and radicalization became rampant, blocking any prospect of negotiated settlement for many years.

Peace Negotiations

While some FRODEBU leaders engaged in peace talks in early 1994, others embraced armed rebellion. In June 1994, Léonard Nyangoma, until then minister of the interior, created the Conseil National pour la Défense de la Démocratie (CNDD) and its armed wing, the Forces pour la Défense de la Démocratie (FDD). Two older rebel movements—the Front pour la Libération Nationale (FROLINA), and the Forces Nationales de Libération (FNL), which was an armed faction of the Parti pour la Libération du Peuple Hutu (Palipehutu)—stepped up their actions. In September 1994, FRODEBU and UPRONA forged an agreement known as the "government convention," but it quickly broke down. The president and the national assembly were impotent, the cabinet was divided and unable to formulate or implement coherent policies, and the army effectively controlled what little state power remained. Then, on 25 July 1996, the army staged a new coup, restoring former president Buyoya to power.

Neighboring countries reacted by imposing an embargo on Burundi. So, Buyoya moved cautiously toward negotiations with the opposition that eventually started in June 1998, in Arusha, Tanzania, under the mediation of former Tanzanian president Julius Nyerere. The process was extremely difficult and slow, and the risk of failure ever present. After Nyerere's death in October 1999, former South African president Nelson Mandela reluctantly took over as mediator, but with a different style. More direct and impatient than his predecessor, Mandela insisted on the involvement of the rebel movements in the talks, and he challenged the Burundian political class to overcome its "inflexibility." Pressure from him and regional leaders eventually produced results in August 2000, when the Arusha Accord was signed. Its main provisions called for a consociational form of power-sharing and international security forces to alleviate the "physical" fears of both ethnic groups. Some "Tutsi" parties among the 19 signatories agreed only reluctantly and expressed reservations about key provisions. They signed the accord, but did not embrace it sincerely. The rebel movements, all of which were predominantly Hutu, did not take part in the talks and rejected the accord outright.

Implementation of this weakly supported accord took another three years. Nelson Mandela needed all his charisma and skills, as well as the support of the region, to avoid total breakdown. During a meeting of the regional initiative that brought together a number of neighboring countries under the leadership of Ugandan president Yoweri Museveni, in Arusha, on 23 July 2001, it was agreed that the transition would last for 36 months, with Buyoya (UPRONA) remaining as president for 18 months and Domitien Ndayizeye (FRODEBU) presiding over the second half. The summit also decided that army reform would start immediately and that an African peacekeeping force would be deployed—initiatives that previously had been resisted by Burundi's army and many of the country's Tutsi elites. After promulgation of a new, transitional constitution along the lines of the Arusha Accord, on 28 October, Buyoya took the oath of office on 1 November 2001, two days after the first South African peacekeeping contingent arrived in Bujumbura.

Although the transition remained very fragile, and stalemate was a constant threat, implementation did proceed, under heavy pressure of the regional leaders. In October 2002, two wings of the rebel movements signed ceasefire accords, and some of their leaders entered the government in early 2003. After a great deal of hesitation, Buyoya stepped down on 30 April 2003, in favor of Ndayizeye. This succeeded in attracting the most important rebel movement, the CNDD-FDD, into the peace process. After intense efforts by South African vice president Jacob Zuma, who replaced Mandela as the facilitator, the rebel CNDD-FDD and the government signed a Protocol on Political Power-Sharing, Defense and Security, on 8 October 2003, in Pretoria, South Africa. Pierre Nkurunziza, a Hutu of the CNDD-FDD, became minister of state in charge of good governance and the general inspection of the state.

The Arusha Accord and subsequent agreements provided for an end to the transition period on 1 November 2004, but this deadline was not met. Nevertheless, substantial progress was made throughout 2004. Pressure by regional heads of state and Zuma at a series of meetings led to the signing of the Pretoria Power Sharing Accord on 6 August 2004. It contained the outline of a post-transition political dispensation, which the transitional government translated into a new, draft constitution. The resulting constitution, described below, was adopted by parliament on 20 October 2004, but its approval by referendum was postponed on several occasions. Eventually, it was endorsed by over 90 percent of voters on 28 February 2005.

Tutsi-led parties, however, had opposed both the Pretoria Accord and the draft constitution. They feared that slots allotted to Tutsi in the cabinet and parliament would be filled all or mostly by Tutsi aligned with "Hutu" parties, and so insisted that party affiliation also be taken into account. In other words, they demanded that Tutsi in the legislature and executive must come from "Tutsi" parties. But the mediator generally resisted this demand—except regarding one vice-presidential slot—and he prevailed, with the support of regional leaders.

The new, post-transition constitution was markedly consociational,[12] attempting as it did to combine majority rule with minority protection. This was achieved by trademark instruments of consociationalism, such as quotas, minority over-representation, and minority veto. The president, likely to be a Hutu, was to be seconded by two vice presidents: one Hutu from a mainly "Hutu" party, and one Tutsi from a mainly "Tutsi" party. The cabinet was to contain 60 percent Hutu and 40 percent Tutsi, and 30 percent of its members were to be women. In light of Burundian history, the posts controlling defense and public order were particularly delicate. Therefore, the constitution required that the ministers for the army and the national police must be of different ethnic groups.

The national assembly was also to comprise 60 percent Hutu and 40 percent Tutsi. If this balance were not achieved as the result of the elections, the electoral commission would ensure it by creating additional parliamentary seats and filling them with members of the ethnic minority—a process known as "co-optation." In addition, a minimum of 30 percent of MPs were to be women, and three slots were reserved for Twa (a pygmoid group representing less than 1 percent of the population), both goals also to be ensured by co-optation if necessary. The senate was to be composed of an equal number of Hutu and Tutsi, as were the army and national police. At the local level, a maximum of 67 percent of mayors could belong to one ethnic group, presumably Hutu. Vandeginste points out that the notion of power-sharing negotiated in Arusha, and also in subsequent deals signed with rebel groups, "referred to the dividing of the cake between competing political elites and their networks, in particular the distribution of posts (at different political, military, senior administrative, diplomatic and economic levels)" between an incumbent government, the opposition, and eventually rebel groups.[13]

In contrast to Burundi's initial tragic failure of power-sharing in 1993, this second effort featured four major differences. First, while the electoral process in 1993 was bipolar in two senses—pitting FRODEBU vs. UPRONA and Hutu vs. Tutsi—the 2004–2005 political landscape was more diversified. Second, in the latter time period, both the political class and civil society adopted more conciliatory approaches. Although inter-party relations were not exempt from conflict, the parties refrained from taking positions likely to result in violent deadlock, and they used language conducive to keeping communication channels open. Civil society, including the media, avoided extremism. Independent radio stations funded from abroad developed into peace media, as opposed to the hate media so prevalent in 1993–1994.

Third, the army's role changed considerably. In the past, it was constantly lurking behind the scene, ready to intervene should the interest of Tutsi elites be threatened. This situation had now changed in two respects. The new Forces de Défense Nationale (FDN) stayed aloof from politics and overwhelmingly rejected the prospect of a return to war and instability. In addition, the army had successfully integrated the main rebel movement, CNDD-FDD. Command structures were unified, and former rebel units conducted joint patrols with their erstwhile enemies.

The final new element was a peacekeeping force led by capable South African troops, authorized initially in April 2003 by the African Union (a mission known as AMIB), and subsequently in May 2004 by the United Nations (known as ONUB), eventually growing to 5,500 troops. In the past, the Tutsi elite and the army had resisted such an international presence, but regional leaders now prevailed successfully on the government to accept it. This armed, international presence rendered a coup much less likely. Although the peacekeeping force was not especially large for the size of the population, it was sufficient because the civil war had decreased considerably in intensity by that time, since all but one of the rebel movements had signed agreements with the government and effectively ceased fighting.

The peaceful outcome in 2005 demonstrates that the international community can in some cases, unlike 1993, exercise leverage to promote conflict management. The regional leaders and South Africa played a major role in forcing the Burundian political and military players into finding an accommodation. Indeed, on several occasions, the region put Burundi under a de facto trusteeship, using leverage and persuasion to impose solutions. In 2000, Mandela prevailed on the reluctant Tutsi to accept the Arusha peace accord. Several years later, neighboring states persuaded Burundi's army and Tutsi elite to accept peacekeepers. Regional leaders blocked attempts by Tutsi parties to reject the draft constitution and by President Ndayizeye to amend its text and postpone the electoral process, although they eventually accepted a limited delay. The wider international community supported the regional Burundi peace initiative—for example, by offering financial and diplomatic backing and by converting the AU peacekeepers into a UN mission—but preferred to subcontract leadership to the region. Despite setbacks and delays, the political calendar finally took shape in 2005. On 22 April, a regional mini-summit in Entebbe set a final deadline for the transition. Four days later, President Ndayizeye announced the schedule for the vote, to be held in four stages: municipal elections on 3 June; elections for the national assembly on 4 July; indirect elections for the senate on 29 July; and, finally, the indirect election of the president by the national assembly and the senate on 19 August 2005.[14]

Electoral Marathon

The initial round of elections, at the municipal level, also had major national significance for three reasons. First, the municipal elections were the first electoral exercise in twelve years and thus were seen as a major test for the entire transition. Second, Article 180 of the new constitution provided that the elected municipal councilors would in turn elect the members of the national Senate—two per province. Third, the municipal councils were also empowered to elect mayors, who in the past had been appointed by the national government.

The 2005 electoral competition differed markedly from the 1993 experience, as noted above. Rather than pitting one Hutu party vs. one Tutsi party, the 2005 elections featured two main "Hutu" parties (CNDD-FDD and FRODEBU), and UPRONA was now challenged by other Tutsi parties like Parti pour le Redressement National (Parena) and the Mouvement de Réhabilitation du Citoyen (MRC). The new constitution also required all parties to field both Hutu and Tutsi candidates, so purely ethnic voting was inhibited. In practice, the electoral campaign mainly pitted the CNDD-FDD vs. FRODEBU, both "Hutu" parties. Although the latter took heart from its victory during the elections of 1993, it worried about the rapid progress the CNDD-FDD had made since abandoning rebellion for the political game. An ominous sign for FRODEBU was the defection in the spring of 2004 of over 50 of its MPs to the CNDD-FDD, until then unrepresented in parliament. Other parties also lost some of their members to the CNDD-FDD, though to a lesser extent. FRODEBU, in a bid to discredit its rival, highlighted human rights abuses by the former rebel movement. In desperation, FRODEBU also dangerously played the ethnic card by suggesting that the CNDD-FDD was a traitor to the Hutu cause, given the many Tutsi in its ranks.[15] Both of these gambits failed, and the CNDD-FDD won the municipal elections convincingly, as detailed in Table 2.1.

Three points must be highlighted. First, the handsome victory of the CNDD-FDD did not surprise close observers of Burundi. Although the party had not abandoned the military option and entered government institutions until the end of 2003, it derived a great deal of legitimacy from its years of armed struggle, its rejection of the ethnic discourse used by its main competitors, and its absence from the partnership between FRODEBU and

Table 2.1. Municipal Elections, 3 June 2005

Party	Percent of votes	Percent of seats
CNDD-FDD	63	55
FRODEBU	21	26
UPRONA	5	8
CNDD	4	4
MRC	2	3
Parena	1	2

Note: percentages do not total 100, due to rounding and exclusion of smaller parties.

UPRONA that had been at the helm during the preceding ten years of instability. These two establishment parties had become increasingly discredited and were seen by many Burundians as inept. The fact that the CNDD-FDD had succeeded, through its armed struggle, in compelling reform of the army and police, something FRODEBU had proved unable to achieve, further boosted its popularity with the Hutu electorate. For many Burundians, support for the CNDD-FDD also reflected their desire for peace, which they feared might be jeopardized if the party failed to win.

Second, only four parties achieved the two percent threshold of voter support that would be necessary to obtain seats in the forthcoming elections for the national assembly. Although some thirty parties participated in the municipal elections, the weakness of most was revealed.[16] A number of small Tutsi parties, which in the past had been able to impose their presence in government and at the Arusha talks on grounds that they were "protecting the Tutsi," also proved to have very little support—even among the Tutsi.[17]

Third, while the multiparty competition affected both main ethnic groups, it had more impact on the minority Tutsi, because dividing their smaller number of voters had more pronounced electoral consequences. Though "ethnic voting" was by no means universal, only about 9 percent of the electorate voted for "Tutsi" parties, and these votes were scattered over ten parties. As a consequence, only UPRONA crossed the 2 percent threshold, gaining support from a mere 5 percent of the voters, less than half the Tutsi share of the electorate.

Article 266 of the new constitution provided that no ethnic group was to have more than 67 percent of mayors, as already noted, so the Electoral Commission entered into consultations with the political parties.[18] In a remarkably smooth fashion, this led to two lists of communes: 86 to be headed by Hutu mayors, and 43 by Tutsi mayors. On 8 July, the municipal councils elected the mayors according to this ethnic distribution. In terms of political parties, the CNDD-FDD emerged as the big winner in mayoral representation, consistent with the results of the 3 June elections, obtaining 97 posts, while FRODEBU got 21 and the CNDD 5. Meanwhile, the "Tutsi" parties—UPRONA, MRC and Parena—gained only two mayoral seats each, totaling a mere six of 129 (less than 5 percent).

The electoral process was not wholly without controversy. FRODEBU, which was genuinely surprised by the scale of its defeat, proved a poor loser. On 7 June, it issued a statement accusing the CNDD-FDD of having used physical intimidation to coerce the electorate into voting for it and of victimizing those suspected of having voted for FRODEBU. It asked the electoral commission to annul the elections and organize fresh ones. A smaller losing party also dominated by Hutu, the CNDD (not to be confused with the victorious CNDD-FDD), on the same day denounced "irregularities never seen in the electoral history of Burundi." This party asked for the disarmament of the population before proceeding any further with the electoral process and, like FRODEBU, demanded new elections. The "Tutsi" parties, by contrast, reacted in a resigned fashion. In an interview, UPRONA leader and former president Buyoya said that "in 1993, the Tutsi were surprised [by the election results], but today they expected this to happen. So there is no tension that could be transmitted to the army."[19]

FRODEBU, frustrated and rudderless in the run-up to the national assembly elections the following month, escalated its ethnically tinged campaign of demonizing the CNDD-FDD for its inclusion of Tutsi. The party also spread rumors of impending violence and threatened to deploy its youth across the country to "protect the population against the pressures and aggressions exercised by the CNDD-FDD."[20] But this blatant attempt to disrupt the electoral process failed. Despite scattered violence during the campaign for the assembly, particularly between supporters of the CNDD-FDD and FRODEBU, resulting in a dozen deaths, the parliamentary elections took place in calm on 4 July. Domestic and international observers agreed that the polls were, by and large, free and fair.[21] In the first stage, 100 MPs were elected by proportional representation within the 17 provinces that served as electoral constituencies. The results are summarized in Table 2.2.

In addition to being the clear victor, the CNDD-FDD, generally portrayed as a "Hutu" party, emerged as the most inter-ethnic, because over 30 percent of its elected MPs were Tutsi. By contrast, UPRONA and the MRC seemed to confirm their "Tutsi" nature, as no Hutu were elected on their lists.

Table 2.2. Elections for National Assembly, 4 July 2005

Party	Seats	Seats by ethnicity Hutu	Tutsi
CNDD-FDD	59	41	18
FRODEBU	25	21	4
UPRONA	10	-	10
CNDD	4	3	1
MRC	2	-	2

But this apparent variation in the multiethnicity of the parties was actually a consequence of constitutional design. Article 168 of the constitution required that the lists of candidates proposed by the parties in each province "shall be multiethnic in nature and take into account gender balance. Of every three candidates proposed one after the other on a list, only two shall belong to the same ethnic group, and at least one out of every four shall be a woman." Thus, while all parties proposed lists with a mixed ethnicity, it was the absolute number of seats they won per province that determined the ultimate ethnic distribution of their seats. Because UPRONA failed to secure more than one seat in any province, it only could elect the top person on any provincial list, always a Tutsi, at the expense of Hutu placed lower on the lists. The two large "Hutu" parties—CNDD-FDD and FRODEBU—likewise typically listed Hutu at the top of their provincial lists (although the CNDD-FDD placed a Tutsi on top of its list in one of 17 provinces). Had these Hutu parties garnered only one seat per province, their parliamentary representation would have been almost exclusively Hutu. But because they won more seats per province, they had to delve deeper into their lists, which as required by the constitution included Tutsi. Thus, CNDD-FDD's parliamentary delegation emerged as the most multiethnic simply because the party gained the greatest electoral support. Its victory was by no means evidence that Burundians voted for a party that was inherently multiethnic. Indeed, the claim that Burundi's election hailed the "disappearance of the ethnic factor" was premature at best.

Because the electoral results did not satisfy the constitutional quota in terms of ethnic and gender balance, the electoral commission applied "co-optation" under Article 164.[22] The constitution required a 60–40 ethnic ratio, but the elections yielded 65 Hutu and 35 Tutsi. The elected women numbered only 24 of 100, but the constitution required a minimum 30 percent. Accordingly, in mid-July, the Electoral Commission appointed another four Hutu and eleven Tutsi members of parliament, of whom three were men and twelve women. The expanded membership of 115 now fit the constitutional requirements: 69 Hutu (60 percent), 46 Tutsi (40 percent), and 36 women (31 percent). The commission also appointed three Twa, for a total of 118.[23] The fully constituted assembly is summarized in Table 2.3.

Overall, the CNDD-FDD secured 54 percent of the seats. While this was a clear majority, it was by no means a blank check. Under the new constitution, a two-thirds majority was needed to pass legislation in a number of important areas, such as defense and security. Amending the constitution

Table 2.3. Full Composition of 2005 National Assembly

Party	Seats	Hutu	Tutsi	Twa
CNDD-FDD	64	43	21	–
FRODEBU	30	23	7	–
UPRONA	15	–	15	–
CNDD	4	3	1	–
MRC	2	–	2	–
Twa	3	–	–	3
Total	118	69	46	3

Seats by ethnicity shown in Hutu/Tutsi/Twa columns.

required a four-fifths super-majority. The CNDD-FDD would therefore need to develop post-election alliances across political and ethnic lines—an explicit goal of consociational constitutional design. Of course, by guaranteeing dispensations to various groups, consociational institutions may inhibit political innovation or cross-group appeals prior to elections, but these potential drawbacks were accepted as quid pro quo for ethnic pacification.

Despite—or likely because of—its overwhelming victory in the parliamentary elections, the CNDD-FDD quickly sent signals aimed to reassure those who feared its dominance. On 5 July, when the scale of its triumph became apparent, the party's spokesman stated that the CNDD-FDD was "not to govern alone," but rather would "open up to other political parties, except those that have indulged in blind militantism and division," a clear allusion to FRODEBU. He also announced three priorities for the five-year parliamentary term: reinforcing security, including by conducting serious negotiations with the last remaining rebel movement, the FNL; implementing a genuine policy of national reconciliation; and reconstructing the economy. While FRODEBU once again, as after the municipal elections, claimed that the polls had been fraught with irregularities, its criticism was much more moderate, and its chairman, Jean Minani, congratulated the CNDD-FDD and stated that he accepted and respected the verdict. Likewise, former President Buyoya of UPRONA sounded reassuring: "One must accept the result of democratic elections, and avoid tolling the bells of fear, and place trust in those who have won."[24]

The results of the municipal polls made the senatorial elections held on 29 July a foregone conclusion, because the senators were to be elected through indirect suffrage by the municipal councilors. Only seven parties participated, fielding a total of 142 candidates for the 34 available seats. The new constitution required the senate to comprise an equal number of Hutu and Tutsi, so the members of the electoral college each had two votes, one for a Hutu and the other for a Tutsi. The CNDD-FDD won 30 seats, while FRODEBU obtained three and the CNDD one. In addition, nine women were co-opted to achieve the 30 percent minimum,[25] as well as three Twa. Finally, the four former presidents were ex officio members of the senate.[26]

The new constitution mandated that the first post-transition president was to be selected by the national assembly and the senate sitting in joint congress, so this election too became a mere formality. The CNDD-FDD held 96 of 166 seats (58 percent), just 15 votes short of the two-thirds majority needed to elect the president, so it was the only party to propose a candidate: Pierre Nkurunziza, its chairman. On 19 August, he was elected by 151 votes. Although the vote was secret, this overwhelming support, representing 90 percent of the Congress, revealed that some members of UPRONA and most or all those of FRODEBU and the CNDD had voted for him. Nkurunziza took the oath of office on 26 August, formally completing Burundi's long transition to democracy.

In his inaugural speech, Nkurunziza again sought to project reassurance: "Today's victory is that of all Burundians, the great and the little folk alike." He pledged to "defend peace, tranquility and development for all" and to "combat the ideologies of ethnic division and genocide." He also vowed to engage the FNL, the last holdout rebels, in negotiations aimed at definitively ending civil violence. His initial personnel appointments also conveyed a message of inclusiveness. On 29 August, he appointed the two vice presidents who, as required by the constitution, belonged to different ethnic groups and political parties. Dr. Martin Nduwimana, a Tutsi from UPRONA, became first vice president, while Alice Nzomukunda, a Hutu from the CNDD-FDD, was appointed second vice president. When Nkurunziza announced his 20-member cabinet on 30 August, its female and minority ethnic representation actually exceeded the dictates of the constitution by including nine Tutsi (45 percent) and seven women (35 percent). The new cabinet also confirmed a changing of the guard in the political class, as only one minister had previous experience in the executive branch, and even then only briefly in the transitional government. By appointing young technocrats, Nkurunziza sidelined the traditional "party bosses," including those from his own CNDD-FDD. Women were not mere window dressing to achieve a quota, but held important portfolios, including foreign affairs and justice.

Peace by Design?

The peaceful nature of the 2005 transition, a stark contrast from the failed attempt of 1993, is explained by several factors. Constitutional design played a major role, as several political mechanisms alleviated fears among the Tutsi elites: quotas for minorities in the cabinet, in the municipalities, and in the two chambers of parliament; the closed-list proportional-representation voting system, requiring both Hutu and Tutsi to be near the top of each party's provincial candidate lists; and ethnic parity in the defense and national police forces. Partly as a result of these institutional guarantees, the Tutsi elites were now—in contrast to 1993—more reconciled to the victory of a "Hutu" party, in what was seen as a competition between the CNDD-FDD and FRODEBU. Indeed, as some Tutsi leaders told this author, the 2005 electoral contest "was not their concern, but that of the Hutu." The fact that pre-election violence occurred mainly between these two "Hutu" parties demonstrates how constitutional design contributed to a marked decrease in the salience of ethnicity.

But additional factors beyond constitutional design also help explain the peaceful outcome of the 2005 elections. In contrast to 1993, most leaders of the political parties and civil society in 2005 knew first-hand the cost of civil war and so were willing to accept compromise to avoid its resumption. These leaders also learned during the transition period to work together and acknowledge the "other" ethnic group's concerns. Finally, regional leaders and the international community played crucial roles. In particular, the preventive deployment of peacekeepers helped integrate former Hutu rebels into Burundi's army, while greatly reducing the risk of a violent backlash from the army's traditionally Tutsi officers and soldiers, thereby paving the way for implementation of the peace agreement.

Remaining Challenges

The CNDD-FDD consolidated its hold on power rapidly. Unfortunately, it did so by violating principles of good governance in ways that pervade Africa:

financial abuse, corruption, and suppressing the opposition, the press, and civil society.[27] Lacking experience in running a state, the party reflexively embraced such anti-democratic practices, despite and sometimes in response to criticism from Burundi's urban populace and the international community. Yet, the government retained popularity with its domestic rural constituents by providing social services, such as free primary education and health care for the needy. The former rebels' long experience in the bush had attuned them to the needs of ordinary Burundians.

Domestic politics became increasingly fragmented and partisan, often leading to institutional stalemate. The main schisms were not along ethnic lines, however, but between various Hutu factions, typically arising more from personal differences than from policy ones. Howard Wolpe, the late U.S. special envoy to the region, blamed all sides: "The CNDD-FDD never fully transitioned from its status as a rebel group to that of a democratic political party. It has therefore carried its historical paranoid and authoritarian tendencies into its style of governance—intimidating opponents, harassing opposition political parties, torturing its political enemies. At the same time, the opposition parties were simply unprepared to accept their electoral defeat, regardless of the broad international consensus that the elections were legitimate and an accurate reflection of popular sentiment."[28] Despite these stumbles in establishing a culture of democracy, Burundi's last rebel movement, the FNL, did register as a political party on 22 April 2009, belatedly formalizing the end of a civil war after more than fifteen years.

Political activities during the remainder of 2009, and the first half of 2010, focused on Burundi's forthcoming second round of post-Arusha elections—municipal, parliamentary, and presidential—slated for mid-2010. The results of those elections, peaceful but banal perpetuation of one-party dominance, highlighted again both the capabilities and limits of constitutional engineering. Consociational guarantees had successfully diminished ethnicity as an electoral issue—no small achievement in light of Burundi's genocidal history—but failed to produce better governance than in most African countries.

In the municipal elections of 24 May 2010, the CNDD-FDD received 64 percent support, with voter turnout at 91 percent. Although international and national observer missions noted a number of irregularities, they found the polls, by and large, to be free and fair. The CNDD-FDD had won just two percent more of the vote than in 2005, rather than a huge margin of victory that would have signaled manipulation. The geographic distribution of reported votes also was plausible, as other parties won strong support among disgruntled residents of Bujumbura, while the CNDD-FDD enjoyed a landslide in the rural areas that were its base. Nevertheless, the losing parties claimed that the municipal elections were riddled with massive fraud, and a dozen of them established an opposition front called ADC-Ikibiri, which boycotted the subsequent legislative and presidential elections.

Nkurunziza was thus the only candidate in the presidential poll of 28 June, a direct election by universal suffrage, unlike the indirect election by parliament in 2005. Nkurunziza won 92 percent of the vote, but the boycott suppressed turnout to only 77 percent, a sharp decline from the municipal elections. Voter apathy and perhaps the boycott grew even stronger during the parliamentary elections, on 23 July, when turnout fell to 67 percent, and the CNDD-FDD garnered 81 percent of the vote. Two of the other parties that had not boycotted also received nontrivial support: 11 percent for UPRONA, and 6 percent for FRODEBU-Nyakuri, a splinter from FRODEBU that was actually closer to the CNDD-FDD.[29] To satisfy constitutional quotas for Tutsi and women, additional appointments were made by co-optation, resulting in 81 seats for the CNDD-FDD, 17 for UPRONA, 5 for FRODEBU-Nyakuri, and 3 for Twa, totaling 106 seats.[30] Thanks to the boycott, the CNDD-FDD obtained 76 percent of the seats, exceeding the two-thirds super-majority needed for parliamentary votes on important issues of state. Even more significant, by teaming with the allied FRODEBU-Nyakuri, the dominant party could surpass the 80 percent threshold required for amending the constitution. Thus, the government now had the power to abolish legally the consociational guarantees for minority ethnic and political groups that were the basis of the Arusha peace accord. The electoral boycott had thus weakened the balances enshrined in the constitution, backfiring on the opposition.[31] Fortunately, the CNDD-FDD is unlikely to tamper with the constitution's essential guarantees, even though the party did not participate at the Arusha talks that produced the document. Indeed, the ruling party's own Tutsi MPs and senators would oppose any such change that could reignite ethnic tensions and end their political careers.

Surprising Lessons

A previous comparative study of constitutional design, by Basedau, expresses caution about generalizing any lessons:

> Empirical results are mostly inconclusive.... Often there are no robust results, or findings are confined to certain geographically or politically defined groups of countries.... [The effectiveness of institutional measures depends on] the exact nature of the institutional arrangement... in relation to the ethnic context of the country... and the [non-ethnic and non-institutional] surrounding conditions.[32]

Yet, with regard to Burundi's most important and lethal historical problem, the ethnic divide, constitutional engineering has been hugely effective. The situation since 2005 is a marked improvement over 1993 in many ways: the political landscape is no longer polarized into two opposing, ethnically based parties; the Tutsi minority is reconciled to its loss of political control;[33] the army's ethnic composition and attitude have been liberalized; and across ethnic lines civil society by and large supports democracy. This transition was facilitated by skillful constitutional design, regional pressure, an international security force, and the remarkable restraint of key domestic Hutu and Tutsi political leaders, who marginalized the more extremist forces on both sides of the ethnic divide. Successful ethnic pacification can thus be attributed both to endogenous factors—such as constitutional engineering and the moderation of elites—and exogenous factors, including pressure from regional leaders and deployment of peacekeepers. In light of Burundi's long history of ethnic violence, it seemed unlikely in 2005 that the fear and distrust accumulated over decades of conflict really had disappeared relatively quickly. Yet, subsequent events suggest that ethnicity indeed has been dramatically reduced as a defining factor of the country's politics.

Burundi's main divide is now between parties rather than ethnic groups, and when violence occurs it is political rather than ethnic. For instance, security forces controlled by the CNDD-FDD have killed members of the FNL, which is now the most significant opposition party but boycotted the 2010 elections, and FNL militants in turn have targeted local CNDD-FDD officials. Yet, both parties emerged from Hutu rebel groups. Similarly, the Hutu leaders of two parties, Léonard Nyangoma of the CNDD and Agathon Rwasa of the FNL, both went underground following the elections, citing fear for their lives from the Hutu-led, ruling CNDD-FDD. These dynamics reveal that while constitutional engineering has virtually eliminated Burundi's interethnic violence, it has not brought liberal democracy, good governance, or respect for human rights, and it has actually increased intra-ethnic tensions.

Insight also is offered by comparison to neighboring Rwanda, which has a similar demographic composition and history of ethnic violence, but a starkly different approach to ethnicity. The current Rwandan regime, born out of a Tutsi-led rebel victory in 1994, and still heavily dominated by Tutsi elites, imposes a policy of ethnic amnesia, outlawing any reference to ethnicity as "divisionism." But this Rwandan policy of officially ignoring ethnicity has failed to reduce ethnic tensions, and ironically has exacerbated them. By contrast, Burundi's consociational mechanisms that institutionalize the ethnic factor have paradoxically reduced ethnic fear and tension.

The two neighbors' differing ethnic strategies and degrees of ethnic tension also stem partly from the divergent nature of their most recent political transitions: unilateral seizure of power in Rwanda; political negotiations in Burundi.[34] Intuitively, Burundi's policy of institutionalizing ethnicity might be expected to rigidify the ethnic divide,[35] but the opposite appears to have happened. Indeed, Burundi's strategy appears to have dealt much more effectively with ethnicity, paving the way for a political system where more productive debates and less lethal divides can come to the fore.

This does not necessarily mean that Burundi's progress can be emulated in other divided societies. Burundi's engineering of relative ethnic peace occurred in a particular setting and under contingent circumstances, and could have failed, and indeed potentially still could. Bipolar ethnic divisions are especially difficult to manage over the long term, particularly if one group is substantially larger than the other, as in Burundi.[36] Consociational mechanisms have sometimes failed elsewhere, as in Lebanon and Cyprus, and they may be failing in Belgium today. Finally, despite the apparent success of constitutional design in ending Burundi's violent ethnic conflict, the question remains whether such constitutionally mandated power-sharing, with its inherent rigidities and less than fully democratic features, can or should be more than a temporary solution. When and if ethnic peace is ever confidently ensured in Burundi, the question must arise whether the country's power-sharing constitution should be replaced by majoritarianism—in the name of fairness, flexibility, efficiency, and democracy.

CHAPTER 3

Kenya: Gradual Pluralization Fails to Buffer Shocks

Gilbert M. Khadiagala

This chapter probes how Kenya's constitutional design has mediated shocks to the political system since the late 1980s. Shocks are major events that can affect the relative power of societal groups, produce new elites, and redefine state-society relationships. Four major shocks, and their consequences, are examined. (1) In the early 1990s, domestic protests combined with international donor aid cutbacks to produce a shock that compelled the government to reintroduce multiparty politics. (2) In the mid-1990s, the endogenous shock of riots and protests led to additional constitutional reforms that the government subsequently reversed. (3) Between 2001 and 2005, the combination of three successive domestic political tremors—the loss of power by the ruling Kenya African National Union (KANU) in 2002, the unraveling of the succeeding governmental alliance of the National Rainbow Coalition (NARC) in 2003, and the loss of a constitutional referendum by the government of President Mwai Kibaki in 2005—created a shock that disrupted political alliances and exacerbated ethnic polarization. (4) In 2007–2008, the shock of electoral violence spurred a national dialogue leading to adoption of a new constitution in 2010. At the heart of this analysis is the accretion and accumulation of shocks against a decrepit but resilient constitutional order, until a major political upheaval compelled substantial reform. Except for the first shock, when Kenya's constitutional design was a single-party presidential system, all the shocks occurred in the context of a semicompetitive, multiparty system.

The analysis contends that these political and economic shocks have had wide-ranging consequences for Kenya's political landscape. They demonstrated the weaknesses of existing constitutional design, triggered violent responses, and—most importantly—led eventually to changes in political institutions. The cyclical pattern of violence and incremental reform that started in the early 1990s culminated in the momentous electoral violence of 2007–2008, a shock that ultimately compelled major constitutional redesign. This repeated cycle—beginning with a shock, followed by violence, and then constitutional reform—stems from the fact that each reform effort also provoked countervailing pressures such as militarism, repression, human rights violations, and ethnic intolerance that undermined the progress toward constitutional re-design. Because of the backdrop of ethnic animosities, elite insulation, and regional and class divides, until recently the reforms were only incremental steps, often interspersed with profound reversals. Only the final shock was sufficient to compel the elite to fundamentally change the constitutional design to address the structural factors that had underpinned previous shocks.

The second section of this chapter provides a historical overview of Kenya's politics from independence until just prior to the shocks under examination. It highlights the major players and forces that have shaped Kenya's constitutional design and briefly reviews the literature on key trends in Kenya's politics during this time. Section three is a detailed process-tracing of the consequences from each of the four shocks, including the mediating role of constitutional design. The concluding section summarizes the findings and then situates the Kenya case in the context of comparative African experiences, suggesting conceptual lessons.

Historical Overview and Literature Review

In the lead-up to independence in 1963, Kenyan leaders and the British government negotiated the Lancaster House constitution that adopted the Westminster multiparty system of governance. The Westminster constitutional framework provided for the separation of powers among the executive, judiciary, and legislature, and promised fundamental freedoms for individuals and institutions. Kenya also inherited a competent bureaucracy, a mixed economy based primarily on agriculture, and a growing middle class. The major political parties in the immediate independence period were the Kenya African National Union (KANU)—led by the two major ethnic groups, the Kikuyu and Luo—and the Kenya African Democratic Union (KADU), a conglomeration of smaller ethnic groups. From the outset, elite contestation around the emerging fissures of ethnicity and regionalism focused on both succeeding within the existing constitutional design and modifying that design to alter the tilt of the political playing field.

The liberation triumphalism of independence dissipated quickly as the ruling party, KANU, transformed Kenya into a de facto single-party state. Consistent with broad African patterns, the government of President Jomo Kenyatta instituted this one-party dominance with the objectives of consolidating power, forging developmental nationalism, and checking the escalation of domestic conflicts over power and resources. The process of state consolidation around the president's fellow ethnic Kikuyu elite deepened in the late 1960s, when the state violently repressed challengers to KANU. In the 1960s and 1970s, five significant amendments to the 1963 constitution centralized power in the presidency, abolished opposition parties, created a rubber-stamp parliament, strengthened the repressive arms of the state, reduced elections to five-year ritualistic plebiscites, and whittled the role of the judiciary and parliament. At the same time, an intricate system of domestic ethnic balancing and patronage, combined with a fortuitously favorable global economic environment devoid of shocks, fostered order and stability during the Kenyatta regime (1963–1978). Under Kenyatta, economic growth was fueled by the export of agricultural commodities (coffee and tea), increasing revenues from tourism, and the consolidation of economic dominance by Kikuyu elites of the Central Province. From 1963 to 1973, gross domestic product (GDP) grew at an annual average rate of 6.6 percent. During the same period, agricultural production grew by 4.7 percent annually, stimulated by small-holder agricultural production.[1]

This era of economic growth and political stability ended in the late 1970s, when President Daniel Arap Moi (1978–2002) took power. In 1982 the Moi government changed the constitution to make Kenya a de jure one-party state. The transition from Kenyatta to Moi coincided with economic shocks that overwhelmed the conflict-management capacity of the existing constitutional mechanisms. The negative exogenous and endogenous shocks of the 1980s included mounting droughts in the subregion, the fall-out from the second oil crisis of 1979, and declining revenues from exports.

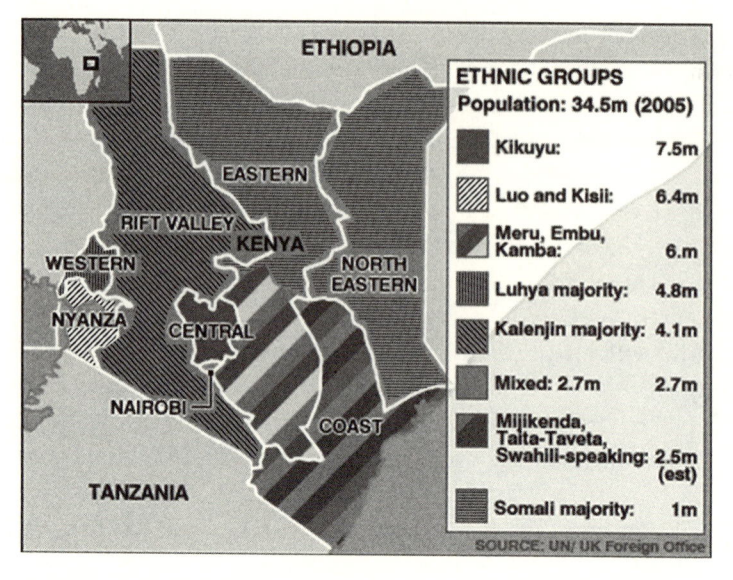

Figure 3.1. Map of Kenya—administrative and ethnic. Sources: UN, UK Foreign Office, and "Kenya stokes Tribalism Debate," BBC, 4 January 2008.

The government then compounded the economic troubles by adopting a policy of redistribution—ethnic and regional—that sacrificed growth. Benno Ndulu argues:

> With the ascension of Moi to the presidency in 1978 . . . attempts to address the imbalances in Kenyan society marked a significant change in policy, entailing a marked trade-off between equity and productivity. This policy of redistribution led to complaints that Moi had merely shifted resources from Central Province to the Rift Valley [see Figure 3.1], which was a significant if not central contributor to the upheavals of the 1990s centered on multiparty democracy.[2]

The shocking decline of Kenya's economy in the 1980s engendered new social and political groups that challenged Moi's authoritarian and exclusive government, which responded with more violent forms of authoritarianism.[3] In 1981, university students and lecturers led demonstrations demanding an end to presidential authoritarianism and the opening of political space. Taking advantage of the growing urban activism, a former MP created the first opposition party since the 1960s, the Kenya African Socialist Alliance (KASA), in May 1982. But the government preemptively forced through constitutional amendments in parliament, in June 1982, outlawing all opposition parties. By formalizing the merger of the state and party, the KANU government signaled determination to remove any vestiges of competition that had existed in the system. In August 1982, a faction of the Kenya Air Force attempted a coup against the government, invoking solidarity with the mounting protests against Moi's dictatorship and the skewed distribution of resources.[4]

Following the university protests and the attempted coup, the government resorted to a violent escalation, encompassing mass detentions, arrests, forced exiles, torture, and killings of opposition actors. Moreover, once KANU became the sole governing party, Moi used parliament and the judiciary to enact constitutional measures that criminalized dissent and fortified his stranglehold on power. Constitutional changes after the inauguration of the one-party state included the following: extending incarceration of political prisoners without judicial scrutiny, abolishing the constitutional guarantee of tenure for judges, and abolishing the secret ballot for the 1988 elections in favor of a system where voters queued behind their preferred candidates.[5]

Most scholars on Kenya have noted that the constitutional design in the postcolonial era was fragile because it lacked strong social anchorage and commanded little respect from the new elites.[6] Thus the consolidation of the imperial presidency and the decimation of participatory institutions were perhaps inevitable, given a context where elites preferred the use of informal rules and incentives rather than the formal institutions of government. Susanne Mueller argues:

> In situations comparable to those in Kenya, institutional checks and balances and rules concerning accountability may exist on paper. Often, however, they are overridden personally by politicians, civil servants, and others operating under an entirely different set of informal incentives, sanctions, and enforcement mechanisms. Public trust in institutions and the rule of law then dissipates.[7]

Rather than serving to mediate emerging stresses and shocks, Kenya's constitutional design throughout the 1990s became a source of strains that yielded violent shocks. Colin Kahl, Peter Kagwanja, and Jacqueline Klopp, among others, have documented how the multiple shocks of demography, environment, economic stagnation, and resource competition converged to overwhelm the ability of the constitutional framework to contain the resurgence of ethnic violence, including state-sponsored violence.[8]

Shock One: Pressures for Pluralism, 1991–1992

The initial shock entailed the convergence of internal and external pressure on the Moi government to relinquish single-party control. That shock was mediated by Kenya's highly centralized constitutional design, which enabled the president to grant ostensible concessions that had little practical effect as implemented. The outcome was a constitutional amendment that nominally restored political pluralism and, eventually, multiparty elections in December 1992, but without truly pluralizing political contestation.

The domestic root of this shock was pressure arising from new social actors in Kenya, who were motivated by the country's economic stagnation and political repression, and were inspired by the wave of democratization in Eastern Europe at the end of the 1980s. These groups launched violent protests against the government in 1990–1991, dubbed the Saba Saba (seven-seven) riots because they came to prominence on 7 July 1990. The riots marked the start of organized anti-Moi campaigns that by themselves would have represented a tremendous shock to the system. Within a few days of the Saba Saba riots in 1990, the government detained leading opposition figures, accusing them of attempting to take power by forceful means. During the riots, 13 people were shot dead and more injured. But the protesters were undeterred, and they demanded the legalization of political parties and the release of political detainees. Although Moi persisted in his resolve to defeat the Saba Saba movement, the government superficially compromised in August 1990, by appointing a KANU Review Committee to consider constitutional reforms. After countrywide tours in August and September 1990, the committee suggested cosmetic changes that would allow more openness in KANU, sidestepping the grievances that had animated the protests.[9]

KANU's reaction to these popular yearnings at the end of 1990 underscored the imperviousness of the Moi government to internal pressure, because of the centralized constitutional design. Accustomed to weathering political storms during his 12 years in power, Moi remained defiant. But opposition groups were emboldened by the Saba Saba riots, which gave them confidence in the collective will of the people to contest their grievances on the streets. Civic and opposition leaders also translated the street protests into political platforms. In August 1991, pro-democracy advocates amplified pressure on the government by forming an opposition party, the Forum for the Restoration of Democracy (FORD). Defying the regime's dire warnings of further arrests and detentions, protesters in Nairobi launched some of the country's largest ever mass rallies at the Kamukunji independence grounds in October and November 1991, paralyzing normal life. The police and paramilitary General Service Unit (GSU) fought pitched battles with the protesters, causing deaths and injuries. Moi infamously remarked that he would "crush the opposition like vermin."[10]

International outrage at KANU's obduracy triggered additional pressure from Kenya's aid donors, who had become less tolerant of autocracy by the 1990s as democracy spread in Eastern Europe and the developing world. This exacerbated the shock to Kenya's political system, as exogenous and endogenous forces combined to stress the existing constitutional design. François Grignon, Marcel Rutten and Alamin Mazrui observe:

> The pressures that forced Daniel Arap Moi and KANU to grant the opening of the political landscape came as much from the "third wave" of global democratization of the early 1990s as from the specific push of the international community at the end of 1991, as well as from the victims of the *Saba Saba* riots and the Kamukunji grounds of 1990 and 1991 who paid a price for what they hoped would be their second liberation.[11]

Donors initially had reacted cautiously to government repression of the opposition, but after the escalation of the attacks, some embassies offered protection to opposition leaders and became more assertive. At the forefront of Western pressure was U.S. ambassador Smith Hempstone, who, in July 1990, publicly warned the Moi government that the United States would begin to condition its aid to Africa on multiparty democracy.[12] In Washington, a public-interest lobby group, the Trans Africa Forum, took up the issue of repression in Kenya, asking Congress to impose economic sanctions.[13] As part of these efforts, members of Congress addressed a letter in October 1990 to U.S. secretary of state James Baker, requesting a freeze in aid unless Kenya's government stopped intimidating opposition leaders and moved toward political reforms.[14]

Similarly, during the street riots in 1991, international pressure mounted on Moi to address the worsening political situation. At the Commonwealth heads of state summit in Harare, Zimbabwe, in October 1991, Canadian Prime Minister Brian Mulroney singled out Kenya as a human rights offender and warned that future Canadian aid would be linked to Kenya's human rights record. Nordic countries—Norway, Sweden, Finland, Denmark, and Iceland—also expressed their displeasure over the mistreatment of those advocating political pluralism, releasing a statement in October 1991 that reminded the Kenyan government of Nordic support for democratic change.[15] These external pressures converged in the decision by the 12-donor Paris Club, in late November 1991, to suspend $350 million in multilateral aid to Kenya for six months, pending improvements in the country's political, economic, and human rights records. Specifically, the Paris Club predicated the resumption of donor assistance on "the early implementation of political reforms, including greater pluralism, the importance of the rule of law and respect for human rights, notably basic freedoms of expression and assembly and . . . firm action to deal with corruption."[16]

Analysts of constitutional change in Kenya have depicted the Paris Club decision as the key to unlocking the stalemate that had persisted since the mid-1980s. Imposing major stress on the aid-dependent Moi government, the funding suspension also coincided with other economic pressures—in particular, high unemployment, weak prices for tea and coffee, and a precipitous decline in tourism, which was the country's largest source of foreign exchange. In addition, poor rains, prolonged drought mainly in northern Kenya, and the mass influx of refugees from neighboring Sudan, Somalia, and Ethiopia worsened food shortages and contributed to high food prices. Indeed, in 1991–1992, Kenya was forced to import 500,000 tons of maize to address the shortfalls, further straining foreign reserves. The Kenya Economic Survey for 1991–1992 also revealed a severe budget deficit: total revenue collected was Ksh57.8 billion, while total expenditure was Ksh88 billion, leaving a deficit of Ksh30.2 billion (about $1 billion), or 13.6 per cent of Kenya's GDP of Ksh222 billion. Total external funding, including grants, was Ksh9.2 billion (about $300 million).[17] To fund the remaining Ksh21 billion of the deficit, the government was forced to borrow from local commercial banks, thereby reducing the funds available to the private sector and further contracting the domestic economy.[18]

Moi's concession to permit opposition parties in December 1991 resulted directly from the shock of sustained pressure from external and local actors. But he dragged his feet on implementation throughout the 1990s. Soon after the legalization of political parties, Moi warned that constitutional reforms would plunge Kenya into ethnic violence and political instability, in what became a self-fulfilling prophecy. Events during the one-year period between the legalization of political parties and the holding of the first multiparty elections, in December 1992, demonstrated KANU's new strategy of crippling the reform momentum through militarism and violent repression of opposition parties and their supporters. For this reason, the initial shock from local and external pressures also led ultimately to more violence, undermining its earlier benefits.

Opposition groups expected the reforms to produce broad political liberalization and early elections that would remove KANU from power, but Moi had only made tactical concessions that allowed KANU to reorganize itself and the state machinery to contain the opposition. Although the government did legalize opposition parties, it placed severe restrictions on their registration, public meetings, and access to the media. KANU also militarized the campaign process in the lead-up to the 1992 elections. Armed militias linked to Moi's ethnic Kalenjin group instigated ethnic cleansings that drove Gusii, Kikuyu, Luo, and Luhya populations out of the Rift Valley province, leading to disenfranchisement, displacement, and the killing of migrants. The raids began in November 1991, after KANU ethnic Kalenjin leaders addressed rallies in the region and appealed to their people to reject opposition parties and expel members of ethnic communities who supported the opposition. They declared the Rift Valley a "KANU Zone," where opposition parties were not permitted to organize.[19]

By June 1992, ethnic attacks had killed an estimated 800 people and displaced 60,000 in the Rift Valley and the neighboring Western province. This pro-government violence, along with splits within the opposition, assured KANU's victory in the elections of December 1992, as it won 100 of the 188 contested seats. Among the opposing parties, Raila Odinga's FORD-Kenya won 31 seats, as did Kenneth Matiba's FORD-Asili. Under the constitution, Moi then appointed an additional 12 members of parliament, giving KANU a clear majority: 112 of 200 seats. Following this victory, Moi co-opted opposition members, enticing and bribing them to rejoin KANU. The government also manipulated the judicial system to nullify opposition electoral victories, forcing constitutionally mandated by-elections in which KANU candidates won with massive state support. The government also continued to foment ethnic violence in the Rift Valley. The tone for renewed violence was set by government ministers, who announced that ethnic killings would continue until there was "respect for President Moi" from opposition communities.

They further instructed people in their constituencies to "lynch opposition members of parliament who speak ill of the KANU government."[20] By September 1993, the death toll had risen to 1,000, with another 300,000 internally displaced.

Shock Two: Pressure for Constitutional Reforms, 1995–1997

The second shock, in the mid-1990s, arose from the popular protests and riots in the streets of Nairobi, demanding a broadening of political space. Although the first shock had led to the legalization of political parties, Kenya retained the vestiges of authoritarianism, particularly a constitutional framework tilted toward KANU. In this new shock, civil society actors led the protests, putting considerable pressure on political parties and the government to negotiate constitutional revisions that would level the political playing field. This shock was mediated by a constitutional design that now was nominally more pluralistic, so that parliament and civil society played a marginally greater role, but the president could and did still act unilaterally to temporarily appease opponents without really sacrificing power. As in the first shock, the outcome was constitutional revisions, but now encompassed under the umbrella of the Inter-Party Parliamentary Group (IPPG). Again, this second time, the constitutional compromise failed to resolve the country's political stalemate for long.

The root of the second shock was KANU's effective reversal of the limited pluralism it had granted after the first shock. In response, civic groups constructed new alliances and tactics of engaging the state. Comprehensive constitutional change was called for by legal organizations such as the Kenya Human Rights Commission, the Law Society of Kenya, and the Kenya section of the International Commission of Jurists. The protests by civil society demanding a new constitution arose in part because KANU had reneged on a promise in early 1994 for constitutional reforms in response to demands from opposition parties and civic groups. Moi worried that a new constitution would alter the balance of power against KANU, so his main strategy was to stall.[21] The high point in the civic reform movement occurred in November 1994, when these organizations collaborated on a "Proposal for a Model Constitution" to stimulate national debate on institutional reforms. Its aims were to "establish genuine multiparty democracy . . . prevent the fragmentation of the country into uneconomic and tribal-based *majimbos* (federal states) and provide an alternative forum for constitutional reform other than parliament or government, which are the products of a defective constitution geared to support dictatorship."[22] The framers envisaged a two-year national debate that would end in a broad Constitutional Convention to approve a revised constitution before the 1997 elections.

As part of the new initiative on constitutional reforms, the legal groups invited opposition parties and religious groups to join a broad-based national reform conclave, the National Convention Assembly (NCA). In its first session, in April 1997, the NCA gathered 500 delegates from civic organizations and political parties (except KANU) to deliberate on a minimum set of constitutional and legal reforms in preparation for the elections. The reforms were as follows: constitutional amendments to reduce the power of the presidency, public funding of political parties, repeal of repressive laws, and inclusion of more women in parliament. Notably, the NCA also agreed to boycott the 1997 elections if the government refused to enact these reforms. Finally, the NCA created an organization to pursue its demands after the conclave, the National Convention Executive Council (NCEC). KANU rejected the NCA reform overtures, a response that sparked new street confrontations along the lines of the Saba Saba and Kamukunji riots of the early 1990s.[23]

From May to October 1997, the NCEC led violent mass demonstrations in Nairobi that were unprecedented in scope and intensity, provoking brutal repression by the police and the paramilitary force, the General Service Unit (GSU). On 7 July 1997 (the anniversary of the Saba Saba demonstrations), the NCEC called for mass action across Kenya; in the ensuing demonstrations, at least 14 people lost their lives. Mass looting and destruction of property accompanied the riots, raising the specter of generalized lawlessness. The demonstrations also dealt a severe blow to the economy. As the shilling fell against major currencies, the Central Bank was forced to inject $29 million into the market to stabilize the currency. The trade volume at the Nairobi Stock Exchange also fell by two-thirds, generating pressure from business groups on the government to negotiate with the opposition.[24]

The second NCA convention in August 1997 occurred against the backdrop of continued mass action and violence. Deep divisions, however, started to emerge between civic leaders and political parties on the modalities of achieving the overall constitutional objectives. While civic groups contemplated transforming the NCA into a parallel government and favored continued mass action to force reforms, political parties became more cautious, opting to engage the government in renewed talks on constitutional reforms. KANU moderates, meanwhile, sensing that the government's obduracy was leading inexorably toward anarchy, persuaded Moi to permit negotiations on minimum reforms. Thus, the shock of the mass demonstrations impelled both KANU and the opposition toward a mutual compromise of effecting some political changes, while preempting the radical agenda of the NCA. Mutua argues: "Moi, an astute political animal, knew that the political crisis over reforms could not be wished away, that, in fact, it could cost him political power. But he did not want to succumb to popular pressure of the NCEC. Instead he reached out to the opposition political parties, hoping to take the steam out of the NCEC."[25]

The political compromise led to formation of the Inter-Party Parliamentary Group (IPPG), a forum for negotiating minimum constitutional reforms. In meetings held from late August to mid-September 1997, the IPPG addressed a broad agenda: "the political crisis facing the economy and country, the search for peace and unity, the need for dialogue and trust, the specter of violence ... the constitutional and legal reform process, the role of Parliament and Civil Society in the reform process, and the forthcoming elections."[26]

At the conclusion of the negotiations, the IPPG agreed on the following reforms: creation of a bipartisan Electoral Commission; abolition of laws that impeded freedom of expression and association; registration of all unregistered political parties; fair treatment of competing views by the state media; and removal of legal barriers to multiparty representation in the cabinet.[27] But before the reforms could be debated comprehensively, Moi dissolved parliament in September 1997 and called elections, effectively preempting implementation of the reforms. Although the NCA still held a final convention in October 1997, which threatened to boycott the upcoming vote on the grounds of "No Reforms, No Elections," the dissolution of parliament demonstrated that Moi still had the upper hand in dictating the pace of change.

The 1997 elections were conducted in circumstances similar to those of 1992, with divisions among opposition parties and between them and civic groups.[28] Moreover, the state again deployed paramilitary forces and militias against civilians in almost all the provinces where the opposition parties enjoyed substantial support. As Kagwanja observed:

In the run-up to the elections, the culture of vigilantism reached a fever pitch. A month to the elections, Kenya was a cesspool of all genre of communal violence. In the Rift Valley, the regime used violence to intimidate and disenfranchise rival communities, and to suppress resistance within its own ethnic community. At the coast, it employed vigilantes to displace and disenfranchise inhabitants in such opposition strongholds with the aim to eliminate the demographic basis of a nation-wide political alliance between up-country and coastal groups.[29]

Vigilantism was the precursor to a fraudulent electoral process that confirmed the warnings and fears of the NCEC and its supporters about compromising with Moi on constitutional reform. Opposition parties alleged massive rigging by the Electoral Commission of Kenya (ECK) on behalf of KANU. Based on the official tally, KANU won the 1997 elections with 41 percent of the vote, which gave it a slim, four-seat majority over the combined opposition in parliament. This would have made it difficult to govern without support from one of the opposition parties. But after the elections, further schisms in the opposition allowed Moi to co-opt new defectors into KANU, most notably Raila Odinga's National Democratic Party (NDP), with its populous ethnic Luo base (see Figure 3.1). Moi tacitly gambled that expanding the long-established practice of neo-patrimonial co-optation would breathe new life into the faction-ridden KANU. The partnership between KANU and NDP was cemented in 1998, by inclusion into the cabinet of Odinga and other members of his party. Subsequently, in March 2002, to avert a looming succession crisis, NDP and KANU actually merged into a "New KANU."

Shock Three: Political Realignment, 2001–2005

The third shock arose from the confluence of three domestic political tremors in rapid succession: the fragmentation of KANU in 2001, the split within the NARC alliance in 2003 soon after it came to power, and the defeat of President Kibaki's constitutional referendum in 2005. The shock was mediated by a constitutional design that had become marginally more pluralistic but still enabled the president to use his unilateral authority to manipulate ethnic divides and the electoral process. The combined tremors led to the drafting of a new constitution, but also to increased political contestation and fragmentation. The ultimate outcome of this shock was to ignite political polarization, culminating in the disputed election of 2007.

The root of the shock lies in the 1997 elections, after which there was broad recognition among KANU, opposition parties, and the NCEC of the widespread support for comprehensive constitutional reform. But there remained strong differences over process. The NCEC favored a public-driven process, while the government preferred to pursue reform within parliament. Starting in 1998, the NCEC spearheaded new talks among civic actors to forge consensus on a comprehensive constitution-making procedure. At the same time, parliament approved the Constitution of Kenya Review Commission Act, also intended to provide such a road map. Lingering suspicions between NCEC and parliament persisted for almost a year, until December 1999, when parliament approved the appointment of 15 commissioners to the Constitution of Kenya Review Committee (CKRC). The chair of the CKRC, a respected lawyer named Yash Pal Ghai, made frantic efforts in 2001 to include some members of the NCEC on the CRCK, leading to the addition of 12 nonpartisan commissioners.[30] After extensive hearings and consultations across the country, CKRC produced a draft constitutional bill in September 2002, calling for the devolution of authority to district governments, a substantial reduction of presidential authority, and—most controversially—the establishment of a prime ministerial post. But Moi again preempted the movement toward a new constitution, on 25 October 2002, by calling for new elections that would derail the reform process. Notably, this was the same day that delegates to the National Constitutional Conference were meeting at the Kenyan cultural center of Bomas to discuss the draft constitution.[31]

This disruption of the constitution-making process came against the backdrop of debates in KANU about a successor to Moi, who was serving his final term in office. It also exacerbated the scramble for new coalitions and alliances among parties, which altered the political landscape.[32] Following the creation of the New KANU in March 2002, which cemented the partnership between Odinga and Moi, other parties tried to form their own alliances. The National Alliance for Change (NAC), also formed in early 2002, brought together three key leaders and their regionally-based factions: Kibaki's Democratic Party (DP), in Central Kenya; Michael Wamalwa's FORD-Kenya, in Western Kenya; and Charity Ngilu's National Party of Kenya (NPK), in Eastern Kenya.[33] This alliance represented a major step in the efforts that had begun in 1991 to build an ethnic and regional coalition against KANU.

The New KANU presented a public face of unity, but its antagonistic party factions had not resolved the question of who would succeed Moi.[34] Then, without consulting the party, Moi chose Uhuru Kenyatta, a weak candidate who only recently had been co-opted into KANU to boost the party's support among ethnic Kikuyu. But Moi failed to anticipate that his unilateral move would trigger massive defection of key ethnic blocs that he had cultivated in the late 1990s. The leading defector from the New KANU was Odinga, who, in October 2002, created the Liberal Democratic Party (LDP). The fragmentation of KANU also enabled the formation in 2002 of the National Rainbow Coalition (NARC), which combined the LDP with the original NAC opposition alliance. In a unity pact, the NARC signatories agreed to Mwai Kibaki as their presidential candidate and to the terms of a power-sharing arrangement if they won the December 2002 elections.[35] With NARC's creation, Kenya's opposition seemed to have seized the chance to coalesce around a common platform for national renewal. KANU, meanwhile, found limited room in 2002 to repeat its past practices of state-sponsored ethnic violence against opposition supporters, although it still attempted to repeat them. The result was that for the first time the political playing field tilted against KANU despite its formidable use of the state machinery. In the December 2002 elections, Kibaki defeated Kenyatta with 62 percent of the vote. NARC also defeated KANU in parliamentary elections, 132 seats to 67.

KANU's loss of power was the first political tremor, which was celebrated by opposition forces because it seemed to herald a new political era. But it also was perceived more as Moi's personal loss for attempting to impose Kenyatta on the party and country. The outcome of this tremor thus was mainly to inspire hope for opposition unity. In practice, however, NARC unity was short-lived, illustrating the difficulty of building stable alliances in the post-Moi era. Soon after NARC took power, the coalition's stability was tested by the resurgence of ethnic/regional blocs and problems in concluding constitutional reforms. In early 2003, Odinga and his party accused Kibaki of reneging on the pre-election agreement on power-sharing. They also charged that Kibaki had centralized power and become increasingly reliant on a small group of elderly cohorts from the Mount Kenya region, home to the Kikuyu, Embu, and Meru ethnic groups. Thereafter, Odinga led his supporters out of NARC and the cabinet, igniting the disintegration of the NARC coalition.[36]

NARC's internal dissensions were the second political tremor, which hindered the alliance's goal of reviving and codifying the constitutional reforms that had been proposed in the draft bill of October 2002, preempted by Moi. When the National Constitutional Conference reconvened at Bomas in 2003, acrimonious disagreements arose on the issue of presidential powers. The Kibaki government made a *volte face*, opposing the reduction in presidential powers, using the same arguments that Moi had invoked in previous years. Odinga and his allies, by contrast, advocated for a substantial reduction of executive power and devolution to regional districts. Subsequently, the Bomas delegates adopted a revised draft constitution that reflected the popular views captured in the initial CKRC deliberations and recommendations. But the Kibaki government, through draconian tactics, made fundamental changes to the Bomas draft. Kibaki's revision of the draft constitution, which he later would put to a referendum, watered down the provisions on limiting presidential powers, creating a prime minister, and devolving power. This set the stage for an incendiary and violent referendum in November 2005—which the opposition won by 57 percent, handily defeating Kibaki's proposed constitutional reform.[37]

Kibaki lost the referendum because he tried to use state power to override the popular demand for weakening central authority. This defeat was the third political tremor that, combined with the preceding two, constituted a shock to the political system that led to major political realignments. An emboldened opposition under Odinga formed the Orange Democratic Movement (ODM), while Kibaki's allies created the Party of National Unity (PNU), in preparation for the 2007 elections. Kibaki responded to this humiliating defeat by dissolving the cabinet and governing the country for a fortnight with only a small team of advisers.[38] Following the failed referendum and the stalemate on constitution-making, Kenya faced one of the most polarized periods of its history. Ethnic mobilization—particularly along the Kikuyu-Luo divide, which had intensified during the referendum campaign—escalated farther as Kenya approached the 2007 elections.

Shock Four: The Disputed Election of December 2007

The fourth shock was the disputed election of December 2007. Although only time will tell, this shock may turn out to represent the culmination of a cyclical pattern of violent contestation, which since the 1990s has generated the impetus for constitutional reform. The shock was mediated by a constitutional design that now had eroded the president's power somewhat, so that he was less able unilaterally to manipulate electoral and ethnic politics, but had not yet created a new dispensation to reduce the intensity of ethnic politics or address other popular concerns. The outcome of this shock was initially widespread violence, followed by the forging of a government of national unity that appeared to symbolize a national coalescence in favor of a new constitutional design.

The root of this shock was the Kibaki government's failure to appreciate the enormity of its loss in the constitutional referendum. This was probably because of the widespread perception that Kibaki had made tremendous achievements in reversing the economic decline of the Moi era. The economic regeneration during the first few years of the Kibaki government blinded it to the popular yearning for constitutional reforms to reverse the culture of despotic, insular, and unresponsive executive institutions.

The campaign for the December 2007 elections was characterized by ethnic polarization and disenchantment with the Kibaki administration. Odinga's ODM touted a reform agenda of expeditious constitutional change, clean government, and equitable resource distribution. Fairly or not, ODM painted the Kibaki administration throughout the campaign as the major impediment to constitutional reform to decentralize power away from the imperial presidency. Kibaki's PNU and its allies also campaigned vigorously, appealing to constituencies that had benefited from Kibaki's economic reforms.[39]
The results of the elections for parliament were announced first and pointed to an ODM victory, considering that the PNU had lost many seats, including half the members of President Kibaki's cabinet, and there was high turnout. In the parliamentary contest, the ODM won 99 of 210 seats against the PNU's 43. But the ODM's triumphant mood dissipated, as there were inordinate delays in the announcement of the results of the presidential vote in many constituencies. Between 28 and 30 December, the final tabulation of presidential votes descended into chaos, even as the ECK sought to allay fears of massive rigging in favour of Kibaki. The ECK's credibility was dented when its chairman, Samuel Kivuitu, admitted in the course of the counting that some key constituencies had doctored the presidential results. At the end of a politically charged waiting period, and behind closed doors, the ECK hastily announced that Kibaki had won reelection. Kivuitu declared that Kibaki had received 4,584,721 votes and Odinga only 4,352,993, a victory margin of more than 230,000 votes. On the evening of 30 December 2007, Kibaki was sworn in at a private ceremony at State House. Subsequently, Kivuitu stated that the PNU and ODM-K (a party that split from Odinga's) had forced him to announce the results, despite irregularities in the tallying.[40]

The shock of the allegedly stolen election, including opposition complaints of massive rigging, triggered post-election violence that left 1,333 dead and 350,000 internally displaced. Violence took three forms: countrywide spontaneous protests at the initial announcement of the results; organized militia activity, starting in the Rift Valley and gradually spreading to the Central Province; and excessive use of force by government security forces in attempts to contain the spontaneous protests.[41] In early 2008, both the PNU and the ODM were locked in zero-sum mentalities, lacking concrete ideas about how to end the violence. Deepening the stalemate was the attempt by both parties to lay claims to legitimacy: the PNU claimed from the outset that it had won the election, while the ODM claimed the PNU had robbed it of its rightful victory. Into this combustible environment, the international community intervened to pull the country from the brink of disaster by negotiating a compromise.

The shock's ultimate outcome was the internationally brokered power-sharing agreement, embodied in the National Accord and Reconciliation Act, signed on 28 February 2008. The Accord established the parameters and principles for a Government of National Unity (GNU) and for restarting negotiations toward a new constitution. Agenda Four of the National Accord was a prescription to prevent or buffer future shocks. It enjoined the parties to address long-term issues: constitutional, legal, and institutional reforms; land reforms; youth unemployment, poverty, inequity, and regional development imbalances; impunity, transparency, and accountability; and the consolidation of national unity and cohesion. Although there were deep divisions in the GNU about constitutional reform, the specter of the return to civil conflict led to overwhelming approval of a new constitution in a referendum in August 2010. The new constitution incorporates some of the key demands that had driven the reform initiatives since the mid-1990s, including a diminished power of the presidency, and a decentralized system of government, with equitable regional distribution of budgetary resources.

Summary and Conclusions

Three broad lessons arise from this chapter's analysis of shocks in Kenya. First, the country's highly centralized constitutional design, built around a strong presidency, helped trigger—but was unable to buffer against—the economic and political shocks since the 1990s. Moreover, largely because of this centralization, the constitutional design was slow to adapt to the shocks stemming from the decline of the Kenyan economy and the domestic demand for political pluralism. Second, under both presidents Moi and Kibaki, the constitutional design reinforced ethnic dominance, contributing to the national stalemate over a new constitutional order. Although popular pressures for reform signified widespread dissatisfaction with the prevailing constitutional design, the Moi and Kibaki governments were adept at ethnic manipulation, militarism, and political violence, which actually reinforced the ethnic aspect of constitutional design. The government's role in creating the conditions for ethnic violence and instability underlines the failure of the constitution to neutrally arbitrate societal conflicts, which could have mitigated them. Third, endogenous and exogenous shocks have spurred gradual constitutional reforms, but the robustness of these arrangements will be tested as Kenya struggles to implement its latest constitution in the face of additional internal and external challenges.

While shocks may trigger political transformations, they do not always yield sturdy institutions that fortify society against future shocks. Until recently, Kenya's cyclical pattern of shocks compelled only incremental and marginal reform, which actually fostered future shocks that it could not buffer against. The question is whether Kenya's more substantial change of constitutional design, in 2010, will prove sufficient to stabilize elite competition, alleviate the socioeconomic grievances that propel political instability, and diminish the perennial resurgence of violence. Constitutions should, ideally, anticipate and provide routine preventative mechanisms for future convulsions. But it is too early to tell whether the 2010 Kenyan constitution has both the firmness and the flexibility to undo the legacies of elite fragmentation and ethnic mobilization that have weakened national identity and institutions and triggered strife. It also is uncertain whether the constitutional framework can adequately buffer against other potential shocks, including those from changes in climate, environment, and demography.

Kenya is not unique in the slow evolution of its constitutional arrangements to manage diversity and provide a framework for political order and economic prosperity. Throughout the postcolonial period in Africa of the 1960s and 1970s, hastily crafted constitutions perished in the triumphalism of developmental nationalisms and the search for strong leaders. The economic collapse of African economies in the 1980s foreshadowed the shocks of the 1990s, which culminated in the quest for accountable and representative governments. But constitutional shifts to pluralism, in the 1990s and 2000s, fostered premature hopes, and then growing disappointments, which now are creating additional pressures from diverse groups, including especially the marginalized youth. In societies such as Kenya's, which remain highly fragmented and impoverished, there is growing demand for constitutional design that prevents violent conflict, stabilizes political competition, and promotes economic growth. Kenya's experience offers a model of where other African countries may wish to end up in their own constitutional designs, although perhaps not the ideal way to get there.

CHAPTER 4

Nigeria: Devolution to Mitigate Conflict in the Niger Delta

Eghosa E. Osaghae

This chapter examines how shocks in Nigeria related to its oil industry have been inadequately mediated by constitutional design, leading to persistent violence in the country's Niger Delta region. The period under examination is from 1960, when Nigeria became independent, until 2010, when violent conflict peaked in the Niger Delta despite the government's granting amnesty to militants in a desperate effort to salvage oil production. The chapter focuses on the extent to which Nigeria's constitutional design was able to cope with these shocks, and the reforms introduced when it was not. To control for geographic variation within Nigeria, all of the shocks under examination originated in its Niger Delta region. But the consequences of those shocks—including resulting demands for decentralization and revenue sharing—affected the entire country and thus implicate national constitutional design.

Three related but distinct shocks are examined. First was the rise of oil as the country's major revenue earner, an important trigger of the regional and fiscal disputes that led to both civil war in 1967–1970 and the emergence of hyper-centralized military governments. This period also witnessed the agitation for separate states within Nigeria's federal system by ethnic minorities in the oil-producing regions of the Niger Delta.[1] Such dissent was a reaction to perceived domination by Nigeria's major ethnic groups, whose elites controlled the three regions into which the federation was structured at the time. Paradoxically, the minorities also favored a strengthening of the federal government, to counteract the enormous powers enjoyed by the regions in which they were oppressed and marginalized.

The second shock was the oil-related environmental degradation that became a point of political contention, mobilization, and agitation starting in the 1990s, following years of neglect by the federal government and oil companies.[2] The federal government's failure to protect the rights of the oil-bearing communities and its adoption of a "stabilization" approach, which suppressed social and nationalist movements, led to increasingly violent conflicts in the 1990s and 2000s. The third shock was a series of oil price spikes and resulting revenue windfalls, starting in 2003. The increase in crude oil prices, especially in 2004–2005, triggered more violent conflicts, even though the country had transited from military governance to civilian democracy.[3]

To what extent can the violent conflicts induced by the shocks be attributed to problems, inadequacies, or ineffectiveness of constitutional design? To what extent did constitutional changes and reforms—Nigeria had six constitutions during the period covered by this chapter—respond to the demands and challenges of the Niger Delta conflicts? The major finding of this chapter is that the violent conflicts in the Niger Delta were not inevitable, but rather resulted from several shortcomings in constitutional design: (1) hyper-centralization of the federal system, which limited the fiscal and conflict management responsibilities of the constituent states; (2) the absence until 1999 of open bargaining in the design of constitutions, which generally were imposed by military fiat; and (3) the emphasis on protecting the oil and gas industry to ensure the steady flow of petro-dollars, rather than on addressing the problems of environmental security, resource control, fiscal devolution, self-determination, and local political autonomy, which have agitated the Niger Delta minorities.

The shocks associated with the Niger Delta conflicts did trigger some constitutional reform by military governments,[4] especially regarding ethnic minority problems and oil revenue allocation to the different tiers of government and to oil-producing states. But the ability of the constitutions to mediate shocks was constrained by prolonged military rule, during which the emphasis was more on palliative and expedient solutions, including coercion. This was a major factor in the outbreak and escalation of violent conflicts in the region. The return to civilian democratic rule in 1999, however, has provided the opportunity for judicial review and open negotiations, potentially enabling more responsive changes in constitutional design.

The remainder of this chapter is organized as follows. The next section presents an overview of Nigeria's history, constitutional developments, and the relevant academic literature. This is followed by a profile of the Niger Delta region and its environmental challenges. The chapter then examines the three shocks, their outcomes, and the mediating role of constitutional design. The final section summarizes the major findings and offers conclusions.

History and Literature Review

Africa's most populous country, with over 160 million people, Nigeria is also a leading producer of oil and natural gas. It is Africa's largest, and the world's eighth largest, producer of crude oil. All of Nigeria's known oil is located in or offshore of the Niger Delta region of the country, which has been described as Nigeria's "oil and gas Republic."[5] Crude oil is the mainstay of the country's economy, accounting for over 40 percent of GDP, 95 percent of export receipts, and 80 percent of total government revenue. Oil has brought tremendous wealth to the country, but that wealth is concentrated in the hands of the country's elite who have access to state coffers. The vast majority of the populace remains poor and deprived, and the Niger Delta region—the source of the wealth—remains one of the poorest and most underdeveloped areas of the country.

Since 1956, when oil was first produced in Oloibiri, the Niger Delta has been the site of massive exploration and production operations by major oil multinationals, which have joint venture and production sharing agreements with the federal government. The largest joint venture is operated by Shell Petroleum and Development Company (SPDC), which produces nearly 50 percent of the country's crude. These operations have produced devastating effects on local communities. Flaring, spillages, and carbon dioxide emissions have polluted the environment, destroyed marine life and forests, provoked population displacements and conflicts over land rights, created endemic health problems, endangered lives and property, and decimated fishing and farming—the major local occupations. A 2011 study conducted by the UN Environment Program (UNEP) in Ogoniland, the heart of the region, reported that oil spills occurred with alarming regularity, exposing residents to hazardous levels of pollution and contamination in air, soil, and water. One of the most alarming findings was that drinking water from wells in some communities contained over 900 times the safe level of benzene established by the World Health Organization. The study also found that soil was contaminated as deep as five meters at some spill sites, which would necessitate up to thirty years of remediation to decontaminate drinking water and restore land, creeks, and ecosystems to full health.[6]

At least three schools of academic literature have examined the political mobilization in the Niger Delta that seeks redress from the federal government and oil multinationals. The first is what is now known as the "resource curse" school. According to two pioneering proponents of this perspective, dependence on one or a few commodities substantially increases the risk of conflict, unless the commodity is "extremely plentiful" or the country's government is open, democratic, and stable—or has developed a strong sense of national identity.[7] Maass writes that "Countries dependent on resource exports—especially oil but also natural gas, diamonds and other minerals—are susceptible to lower growth, higher corruption, less freedom and more warfare."[8] Nigeria illustrates how this risk of conflict may be increased when the commodity is localized in one part of the country. The second school explores the environment-conflict nexus, including the roles of environmental injustice and climate change. Nigerian minority rights activist Ken Saro-Wiwa notably brought the plight of the Niger Delta's peoples to global attention, prior to his being executed by the military regime in 1995.[9]

The third strand of literature focuses on conflict management in the context of identity crisis, minority rights, and resource disputes.[10] The main emphases of this school are the state and its mostly short- to medium-term palliative measures, and the roles of civil society and the international community. This approach, however, may underplay the need for enduring structural solutions to the issues of self-determination, autonomy, resource control, fiscal relations, and true federalism that are fundamental to the Niger Delta crisis. As Human Rights Watch aptly notes, "there can be no solution to the simmering conflict in the oil-producing areas of the Delta until the people gain the rights to participate in their own governance and until the protection of the rule of law is extended to their communities."[11] I previously have explored Nigeria as an example of "runaway" conflicts, which tend to defy conventional policy prescriptions.[12] The Niger Delta's violent conflicts intensified during the period 1993–2010, despite the conflict-management interventions of the federal government. Such resource-based and environment-related conflicts may pose challenges that scholars of constitutionalism, federalism, and minority problems have yet to fully grapple with.

Constitutional Evolution

Nigeria is a widely acclaimed example of constitutional design to manage diversity. This is largely on account of the country's federal system of government that, from its inception in 1954, has offered a flexible framework of political accommodation. Since independence, the country has had a total of six constitutions—1960, 1963, 1979, 1989, 1995, and 1999—two of which (1989 and 1995) were never really used. This is a large number over such a short time, but it is an indicator of how much faith Nigeria's political elite reposes in the efficacy of federal creativity and constitutional solutions. This is especially true of Nigeria's military governments, which authored four of the constitutions: 1979, 1989, 1995, and 1999. Indeed, military governments supervised virtually all of the innovative instrumentalities that distinguish Nigerian federalism—executive power sharing, fiscal arrangements, electoral reform, and the creation of states and localities to address minority problems and demands for autonomy.

Nigeria's constitutions, especially those passed by military governments, illustrate key aspects of constitutional design for conflict management. The first is federalism, involving the distribution of power between the federal government and its constituent units: states and localities. Originally, there was relative balance between the federal government and the regions, which enjoyed a great deal of political and fiscal autonomy under the 1960 and 1963 constitutions. The 1979 constitution, however, bore the imprint of prolonged military rule and set the path for all subsequent constitutions, enhancing the dominance of the federal government.

Critical changes in fiscal arrangements included the diminution of the principle of "derivation"—by which oil revenue had been returned to Niger Delta areas of production. Now, the lion's share of oil revenue was allocated to the federal government, empowering the center at the expense of the periphery. Another momentous reform, following a panel recommendation in 1976, was to create many new states (and localities). The new entities, however, proved unable to function as autonomous financial entities, leaving them dependent on resources pooled and controlled by the federal government.

Paradoxically, therefore, this decentralization reform actually strengthened the power of the center. The hyper-centralizing inclinations of military rule have been a source of contention and conflict among the country's constituent units, notably in the Niger Delta. To date, however, scholars have paid inadequate attention to the problems and challenges of the Niger Delta from the perspective of federalism and constitutionalism.

As a backdrop to the analysis of this interface between constitutional design and the Niger Delta's conflicts, we shall first consider the major elements of the various constitutions (Table 4.1). Over time, centralization expanded in its extent and scope—in regards to fiscal matters, the distribution of powers between the federal and state governments (skewed in favor of the former), and the introduction of the presidential system of government (from 1979 onwards) in place of the parliamentary system (1960 and 1963). This heightened the stakes over access to, and control of, executive power at the federal level. The country has long suffered allegations of ethnic, regional, and religious discrimination—which were major triggers of civil war in 1967 and the adoption in the 1960s and 1970s of the quota system (for the military, public service, and federal educational institutions). Accordingly, "federal character" was enshrined in the 1979 constitution among the "directive principles," which provide the criteria to be followed in implementing policy.

The federal character principle, which guarantees ministerial and other top executive slots to all states, is a form of accommodation to diverse groups. This principle also has been employed in other creative ways that include the division of the country into six geopolitical zones for the purpose of regulating access to power and distributing national resources. Another step was the 1995 constitution, which included multiple vice presidents from different zones. The application of the federal character principle and zoning formulas has been of great benefit to minority groups throughout the country in guaranteeing access, which their small populations otherwise would have inhibited. Top appointments in important institutions such as the National Assembly, the electoral commission, anti-corruption bodies, and military and security agencies are made to reflect and balance the geopolitical zones.

The constitutional federal character principle also has produced virtuous spillover effects. For example, Goodluck Jonathan, an ethnic Ijaw from Bayelsa state, emerged as president in 2009 not because the rest of the country wanted to placate the Niger Delta (as some local youth leaders believe). Rather, it was largely because the zoning formula used by the People's Democratic Party requires rotation of candidates between the north and south of the country. Zoning was a choice of the party, rather than being a constitutional requirement. But this demonstrates how the federal character principle has been incorporated voluntarily as a domestic norm for regional distribution of political benefits.

The main structural approach to dealing with issues of political autonomy, group rights, and self-determination has been the creation of new states and localities from existing ones. The focus of dissent by minority groups from the 1940s to the 1960s was the agitation for separate states to free them from the stranglehold of the ethnic majority groups in the extant regions. One major obstacle was the stringent procedure for creating new states, which required the concurrence of two-thirds of the existing states, including the one from which a new state was to be created. These provisions have remained basically the same in all constitutions since 1960, which explains why it has been difficult for civilian regimes to accommodate groups by creating new states. Military governments, however, faced no such difficulties and repeatedly created new states as a strategy of political accommodation via constitutional design. In this way, they attempted to address challenges of ethnic nationalism and separatism, political balance among the big ethnic groups, and equitable development.

For example, the establishment of the Mid-West region in 1963, and then twelve states in 1967, were each expected to "solve" the problem of minorities—including in the Niger Delta, where new states created some measure of autonomy. I have argued elsewhere that this failed, however, not only because state creation produced new minority problems, but because the process was hijacked by the elite of the big ethnic groups in the competition to control the federation. The number of states "belonging" to an ethnic group became a major determinant of the political influence of that group's elite.[13]

As the principle of derivation was eroded in the 1970s, a major source of contention has been the huge share of oil revenue enjoyed by the federal government, even though the 1979, 1989, 1995, and 1999 constitutions nominally empower the National Assembly to determine the revenue allocation between the federal government and the constituent units.[14] A major goal of political agitation in the Niger Delta has been the restructuring of fiscal arrangements to restore to states the fiscal powers enjoyed by the regions under the 1960 and 1963 constitutions. The partial restoration of derivation to a minimum of 13 percent in the 1995 and 1999 constitutions was a significant response, but the oil-producing states want a much higher share (50 to 100 percent), as well as greater control of the industry. The 1979 and subsequent constitutions

Table 4.1. Evolution of Nigeria's Constitutional Design

Year	Origins	Key provisions	Major changes from predecessor
1960	Independence constitution. Product of 1954 and 1958 constitutional conferences.	Parliamentary system, bicameral legislature, 3 regions, entrenched regional autonomy, separate regional constitutions, 100% derivation, regional marketing boards, Niger Delta Development Board.	
1963		Establishment of Republic and creation of Mid-West region as 4th region.	Republican constitution. Number of regions increased from 3 to 4.
1979	Product of consultative Constituent Assembly, but passed by military fiat.	Presidential, bicameral, separation of powers, 19 states, electoral reforms, revenue allocation formula determined by National Assembly. Increased central control of legislative matters at the expense of state governments. Exclusive federal control and management of oil and gas sector and revenues. Electoral reforms and guaranteed local autonomy. Provisions for impeachment of president and governor.	Presidential system. Federal government strengthened at expense of states. 19 states in place of 4 former regions. National Assembly determines revenue allocation formula. Single constitution for federal and state governments. Federal character principle for sharing executive positions. Local government autonomy.

1989	Passed by military fiat.	Federal dominance. 21 states. Principle of recall of elected representatives. Presidential system and separation of powers in local government administration.	Presidential system for local government administration. 19 → 21 states.
1995	Product of National Constitutional Conference but passed by military fiat. Constitution was never used.	Federal dominance. Presidential, but with multiple vice presidents from the six geopolitical zones into which the country was divided for the purpose of power sharing. Restoration of derivation principle—minimum of 13 percent.	Introduced zoning and power rotation of top federal executive positions to complement the federal character principle, including multiple vice presidents. Partially restored principle of derivation.
1999	Passed by military fiat.	36 states and 774 local government areas. Derivation minimum of 13 percent. Extended federal legislative dominance (exclusive control over 68 items, including oil and gas, and dominant control over 30 concurrent items).	36 states and 774 localities. Expanded federal executive and legislative powers.

also give the central government control over the following functions: the electoral process (through the regulation of political parties, which by law have to be national), the police and security agencies, and several executive intergovernmental bodies.

Over time, diverse regions and minority groups came to view the establishment of new states (and then localities, after these became a third tier of government with allotted powers in the 1979 constitution) as essential to gaining some measure of political autonomy and access to the enormous resources concentrated at the federal level. This gave rise to frenzied agitations for more states in the 1980s and 1990s, until in 1996 the number of states was raised to 36, boosting the number of local governments to 774. After that, however, the frenzy reduced drastically. A possible explanation is that many of the new political entities proved to be nonviable economically and therefore dependent on statutory allocations from the federal government.

Roots of Conflict in the Niger Delta

Covering an estimated 14,000 to 43,000 square miles (by comparison, these are the areas of the U.S. states of Maryland and Virginia), the Niger Delta is one of the world's largest wetlands and the largest in Africa (see Figures 4.1 and 4.2).[15] The tortuous terrain and environmental challenges of the region—including the seasonal flooding and erosion of freshwater swamps, and the brackish water of mangrove swamps—have been exacerbated over the years by the oil and gas industry. The region is also home to nearly 80 minority ethnic groups and subgroups, which have faced off in long-standing or recent disputes over the environment and access to resources.[16]

Officially, the Niger Delta includes the nine oil-producing states of Abia, Akwa Ibom, Bayelsa, Cross River, Delta, Edo, Imo, Ondo, and Rivers,[17] although sometimes the term is used more narrowly.[18] The ethnic Ijaws, concentrated in these areas, claim to be the fourth largest ethnic group in the country and to represent the Niger Delta.[19] The region is unevenly developed, and its problems vary between states, localities, and even communities. Oil is produced in all of its states, but only in some parts of those states. The oil-producing areas of these states have been in the forefront of political and violent agitations, protesting the use of their resources to develop other parts of their own states, just as the Niger Delta states as a whole have accused the federal government of redistributing their wealth to other parts of the coun-

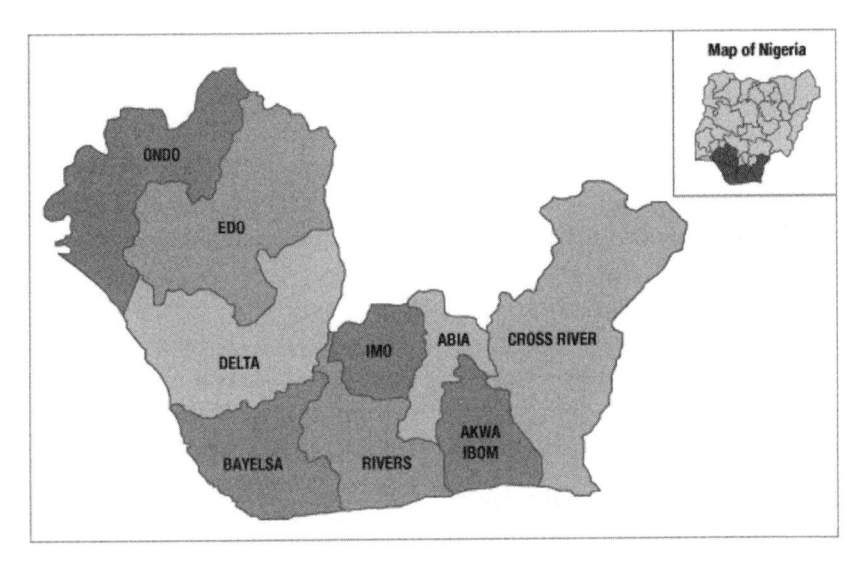

Figure 4.1. Niger Delta of Nigeria. Source: http://ndpifoundation.org/.

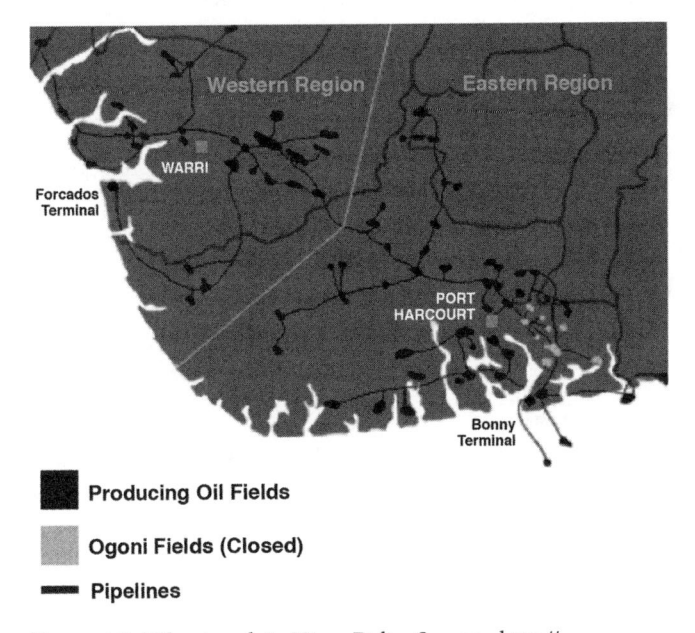

Figure 4.2. Oil network in Niger Delta. Source: http://geographicalconcepts.wikispaces.com.

try. Indeed, intra-Delta disputes are as much a challenge as the conflict between the Delta and the rest of Nigeria.

Years of exploitation, neglect, and deprivation eventually ignited war in the Niger Delta—especially in the core states of Bayelsa, Delta, and Rivers—starting in the late 1990s. The main actors have been various ethno-nationalist organizations, militant groups, warlords, and youth gangs. Guerrilla warfare against the federal government and oil companies has included abductions, robberies, sabotage (destruction and seizure of oil flow stations and oil pipelines), and illegal bunkering (theft of stored crude oil for export).[20]

Shock One: Emergence of Oil

The first of Nigeria's oil shocks was the emergence of this commodity as the country's main export. Crude oil became Nigeria's main revenue earner in the late 1960s, even before the spike in global oil prices of the early 1970s. Previously, the country's major exports had been agricultural.

Under military rule at the time, the constitutional design could not prevent the federal government from issuing a series of decrees to consolidate oil and gas as national resources under its control. Fiscal centralization came at the expense of the oil-producing areas, which, through the steady diminution of the derivation principle, lost the huge revenues and other benefits that were expected to accompany the ascendancy of Nigeria to the status of an oil-rich economy. The major legal instrument was the Petroleum (Drilling and Production) Regulations Act (formerly Decree no. 51) of 1969, which gave the federal government active ownership and control of all petroleum under the country's land and waters, and is still the main regulatory framework for the country's oil and gas industry. The government also established the Nigerian National Petroleum Corporation to be the main agent of control and revenue collection, via joint ventures (with oil majors) in which it held 55 percent equity.

The federal fiscal takeover entailed the massive reduction—and, at one point, elimination—of the derivation principle of redistributing revenue to states and localities that produced oil. In 1971, the federal government introduced a distinction between onshore and offshore rents and royalties, and gave 100 percent of offshore revenue to the federal government. In 1975, the share of onshore revenue redistributed to oil-producing states was reduced from 50 to 20 percent. In 1979, derivation was eliminated altogether, although

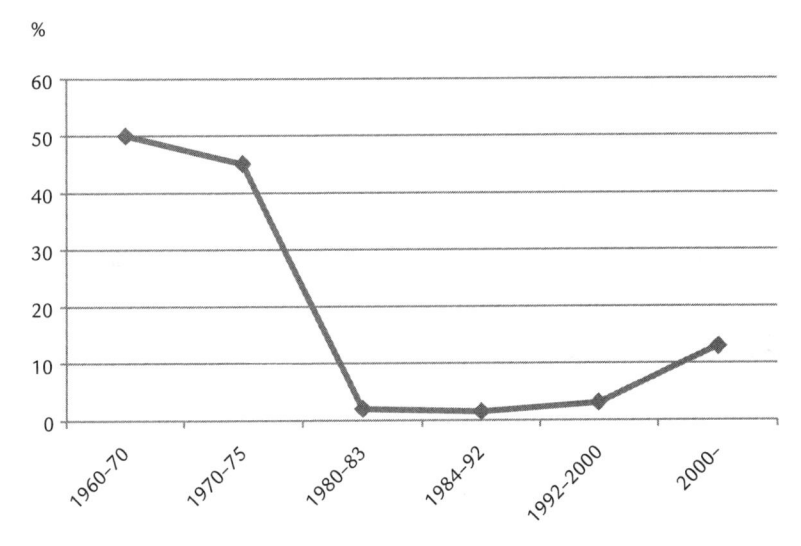

Figure 4.3. Mining revenue allocated to states based on "derivation."

it was subsequently partially restored after sustained protests by oil-producing areas. The rapid diminution and only marginal restoration of the derivation principle is illustrated in Figure 4.3.

The initial outcome of the oil windfall, as mediated by the hyper-centralized constitutional design, was the civil war of 1967–1970, triggered by the secession of Biafra in the country's southeast (see Figure 4.4). This protracted and deadly conflict also informed subsequent disputes over resource control in the Niger Delta. The federal government's immediate response was to institute constitutional reform in hopes of marginalizing the secessionists. It created Rivers state to empower ethnic minorities in the region, so that they would oppose the locally dominant ethnic Igbo leading the secession. This sharpened ethnic distinctions, including by leading to the redefinition of the ethnic Ikwerre as non-Igbo.

Biafra collapsed soon after it lost control of the Niger Delta oilfields, and the federal government took steps in the immediate postwar period to consolidate its control of the war "booty." Indeed, Okonta and Douglas argue that the civil war was all about the "quest by the federal government to win back the oilfields of the Niger Delta from Biafra." They also assert that oil was a major consideration in the decision of northern officers to refrain from *araba* (secession) and of Britain to support the federal government.[21]

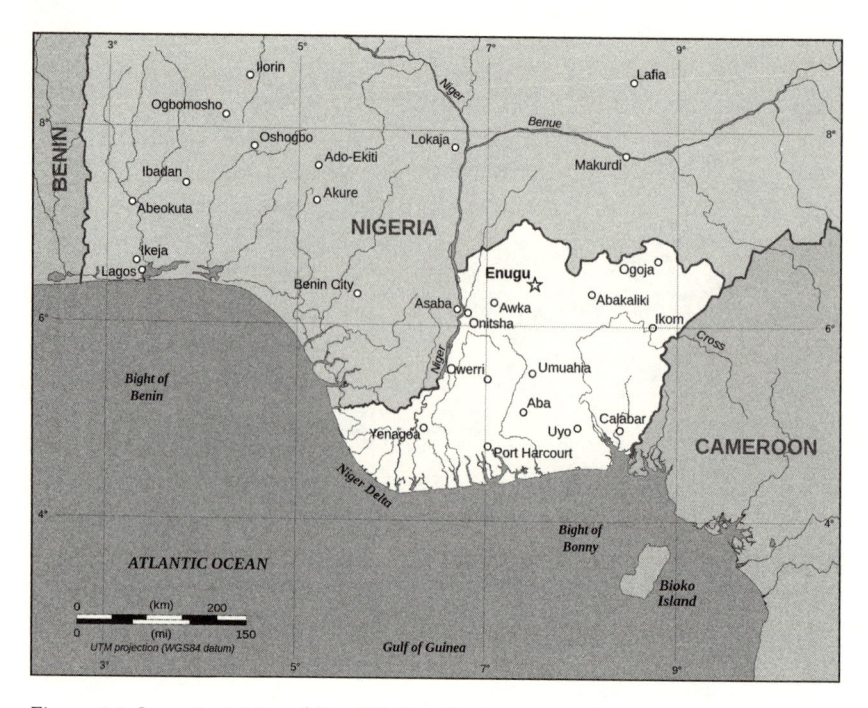

Figure 4.4. Secessionist Republic of Biafra, 1967–1970. Source: Wikipedia Commons.

After the war, the government's ambitious, capital-intensive program of rehabilitation, reconstruction, and reintegration—facilitated by the oil boom of the early 1970s—provided a justification for fiscal centralization. The government reduced derivation as the basis for distributing revenue in favor of other criteria such as population, territory, and equitable development, thereby advantaging the non-oil-producing states, especially those of the larger and more populous major ethnic groups. This heightened the feeling of exclusion and injustice among Niger Delta minorities and strengthened their determination to defend their rights. They demanded resource control, political autonomy, and reform of the revenue sharing formula to assign more weight to derivation.[22] They did not, however, immediately resort to further violence.

This lack of violence in the Niger Delta in the 1970s and 1980s in part represents a success of the constitutional reform agenda of the military governments of the time. The regime sought to reduce the divisive effects of the pre-war constitutional order, which had been characterized by powerful regions, political domination of elites from the major ethnic groups, and marginalization of minorities. The military regime replaced the three regions with a greater number of states in 1967 and 1976, and emphasized more equitable distribution of resources and political representation via the quota system and federal character principle. Political space opened further during the country's return to democratic rule in the short-lived Second Republic (1979–1983). For two decades, such partial accommodation helped assuage the concerns of ethnic minorities in the Niger Delta and other parts of the country. Further violence also was deterred by memory of the harrowing civil war, which no one wanted to repeat.

Shock Two: Environmental Degradation

The second shock to be examined was the widespread environmental degradation of the Niger Delta that came to global attention in the 1990s. The rapid expansion of oil operations had magnified the problems of gas flaring, pollution, spillages, and other environmental hazards, leading to greater demands for compensation and restoration of derivation. Constitutional design at the time—comprising ultra-authoritarian military governments that took fiscal centralization and corruption to the zenith—only exacerbated the region's discontent, making violence more likely. Other factors besides constitutional design also emboldened the Niger Delta protest movements. For example, emerging global norms demanded environmental protection and justice, minority rights, and democratization. The 1990s also were marked by austerity and structural adjustment programs, exacerbating the economic plight of the Niger Delta.[23] The failure of the state—and of the oil companies that were now a major target of complaints—to respond adequately to the legitimate demands for redress is what triggered violent conflicts over the environment and resources, starting in the 1990s.

The Delta states demanded increased derivation as the minimum compensation for years of environmental devastation and under-investment that had kept them less economically developed than the non-oil-producing parts of the country.[24] Many Niger Delta leaders attributed this neglect to the domination of the state since inception by major ethnic and religious groups. They also blamed oil companies for refusing to pay adequate compensation for land acquisition and environmental pollution, for failing to hire local residents preferentially, and for not extending to local communities the First World infrastructure and services provided to their expatriate staff—including electricity, roads, potable water, and health centers. Ultimately, however, regional officials held the state responsible for failing to protect them from the excesses of the oil companies.

Oil spills and gas flaring account for most of the environmental problems in the Niger Delta. The NNPC estimates that, based only on cases reported by oil companies, a total of about 600,000 gallons of oil are spilled in 300 separate incidents yearly.[25] In 2006, the National Oil Spill Detection and Response Agency reported that there were more than 1,150 abandoned spill sites in the region. From 2001 to 2010, in Nigeria, Shell reported that it experienced over 500 spills from operations and 1,200 from sabotage.[26] Operational spills typically are caused by old and poorly maintained equipment and pipelines, most of which have not been replaced or upgraded since they were constructed in the 1960s and 1980s.

Regarding gas flaring, Nigeria is reportedly responsible for 20 percent of the global total.[27] By one account, nearly 70 percent of total gas produced in the Niger Delta is flared.[28] All efforts to stop flaring, including legislation and deadlines, have failed so far. The oil operators consider the necessary means, namely replacements of pipelines and reinjection, to be too costly. The year 1984 was the initial deadline to halt flaring, but this has been postponed repeatedly, most recently until 2012. That latest deadline also has been missed, due to both the recalcitrance of the oil majors and Nigeria's failure to enact a pending comprehensive Petroleum Industry Bill (PIB), which addresses environmental protection, resource control, and financial compensation to oil-bearing communities. The legislation has been stalled by protracted disagreements between the oil companies, various regional groups, and other vested interests.

The de jure constitutional design during these years was somewhat accommodative, which enabled fairly strong environmental laws. In practice, however, the federal government ignored the laws in favor of the oil companies. The Petroleum Act (1969) requires oil companies to take all necessary precautions, including acquisition of up-to-date equipment, to prevent spillage, and failing that to take prompt action to control and clean up any spills. The Act also provides for "fair and adequate" compensation, fees, and royalties where extraction affects protected and productive trees and felling rights, and it forbids destruction of venerated objects except with permission of the state. The Mineral Oils (Safety) Regulations Act of 1963 goes further by authorizing revocation of oil licenses where operators fail to comply with "good oil field practices."[29] The Act further obliges operators to maintain equipment to prevent pollution and spills, to comply with local planning laws, and to grant local inhabitants access to the roads they build. The Oil Pipelines Act provides for compensation in respect of value of land affected by pipeline construction and passage. The Environmental Impact Assessment Act (Decree 86 of 1992) makes EIA compulsory for oil and gas fields as well as construction of refineries.

These regulations appear far reaching but generally have not been enforced, and oil companies enjoy a great deal of latitude and discretion in the determination of compensation.[30] The rules also hinge greatly on the chastity of oil companies, which are expected to make honest declarations, including with regard to environmental impact assessments, land claims and valuation, spillage, and compensation. In the absence of independent data and verification by government agencies, the communities are left at the mercy of the oil companies.

A main outcome of the shock of environmental degradation—as mediated by the centralized constitutional design that in practice gave short shrift to the concerns of the Niger Delta—is that local actors escalated their illegal bunkering and sabotage activities, which ironically exacerbated the environmental shock. Almost every notable warlord or militant is involved in illegal production and refining of crude oil, as are security agents and politicians. As a result, oil companies now attribute the vast majority of spills to sabotage, although this may be deliberately exaggerated because sabotage-related spillage is not eligible for compensation under the Petroleum Products and Distribution (Anti-Sabotage) Act of 1975.

Starting in the 1990s, local communities also became more aggressive in pursuing compensation from the government and oil companies.[31] Typically, they employed three strategies: (1) political mobilization and propaganda by new ethno-nationalist organizations, aiming to garner domestic and international support; (2) presenting the federal government with a bill of rights that articulated the problems and demands of the oil-producing communities; and (3) direct confrontation with the oil companies, entailing the issuance of deadlines for expulsion of oil companies operating in their areas, as well as various acts of sabotage, notably seizure and blowout of oil flow stations and pipelines.[32] The Ogoni case, especially the Ogoni Bill of Rights, established a model for subsequent movements.[33] At least five major points were common to these petitions: (1) reaffirmation of being part of Nigeria but based on guaranteed rights as autonomous political units, resource control, and fiscal federalism; (2) repeal of laws considered inimical to the justiciable right to the resources in the land, including the Petroleum Act of 1969 and the Land Use Act; (3) provision of infrastructure and social services and payment of adequate rents, royalties, and compensation directly to communities, localities, and states; (4) decentralization of security organizations, and demilitarization and withdrawal of military forces from the region; and (5) environmental protection and review of contracts with oil companies.

The failure of the state to respond to these bills and other peaceful demands eventually led to violence.[34] The state was perceived as failing to protect the rights of its people in the face of the oil companies' excesses. A critical part of this failure had to do with limitations on access to justice and the perceived ineffectiveness of judicial institutions. Human Rights Watch argues that "the lack of a properly functioning legal system [that] could promptly and fairly rule in cases involving compensation, pollution or contracts" was a major factor in the Niger Delta conflicts.[35] This shortcoming underlies the resort to extralegal and nonsystemic options for seeking redress. Warlords, underground militant groups, and criminal gangs all claimed to be fighting for the liberation of the Niger Delta from "internal colonialism" and environmental destruction by the oil companies, in the absence of legal redress.[36]

Constitutional design did include separation of powers, however, which permitted some adjudication that may have averted even greater violence. For example, in 2002, the federal government attempted to restrict the scope of derivation to only onshore territory in order to increase its share of pooled revenues, in the so-called "offshore-onshore" case. The federal government contended that the seaward boundary of a littoral state is the low water mark of the land surface of such state (or, for archipelagos, the seaward limit of inland waters within the state). Eight littoral states disagreed with the federal position. They contended that their boundaries extended into the water and onto the continental shelf, so that natural resources derived from offshore exploration were subject to the minimum 13 percent derivation principle in the Constitution. The case had deep political connotations, especially because the federal government's position was supported by the northern states, which persistently have opposed the derivation principle.[37]

The Supreme Court ruling, which affirmed the position of the federal government, was greeted with protests in the Niger Delta, and became an issue in the failed impeachment of President Obasanjo at the National Assembly in 2002. The protests and threat of impeachment compelled the president and federal government to seek a political compromise. The outcome was an agreement to abolish the onshore-offshore dichotomy—later codified by an executive bill—and to redefine the littoral states to include the continental shelf for the purpose of revenue allocation. Although the new law was temporarily challenged in the Supreme Court by 22 states (including all 19 northern ones), it was a major example of Nigeria's use of informal and expedient intergovernmental negotiations, understandings, and pacts to resolve differences and conflicts—especially between the federal and state governments. These mechanisms—elements of "informal" constitutional design, but facilitated by provisions of the 1999 constitution for intergovernmental cooperation and collaboration[38]—have emerged as key features of Nigerian federalism since the restoration of civilian democracy in 1999, helping to avert violent conflicts.[39]

Another partial accommodation by the federal government, in response to sustained agitations in the Niger Delta, has been the enhancement of federal institutions to promote the region's development. In 1992, the government established the Oil Minerals Producing and Development Commission (OMPADEC) to manage derivation revenues. In November 1994, the Petroleum Special Trust Fund was set up to channel revenue from higher petroleum prices for infrastructural development nationwide. In 2000, the Niger Delta Development Commission (NDDC) was established under the direct supervision of the presidency, and in 2004 published a master plan for comprehensive development of the region. This form of accommodation culminated in creation of a federal Ministry of Niger Delta in 2007. However, all of these initiatives faced funding shortfalls, as actual receipts from the federal government and other sources, including oil companies, have fallen far short of budget allocations, as illustrated in Table 4.2.

The federal government was not alone in promoting development in the Niger Delta, as several of the region's state governments established similar agencies. Portions of derivation funds received by the states were set aside for these agencies, in hopes that at least some oil revenue would flow back to the communities where production had wreaked environmental havoc. But such partial devolution and accommodation have been insufficient to fully address the grievances of oil-producing communities, which continue to accuse their governments of diverting derivation funds to develop non-oil-producing

Table 4.2. Underfunding to OMPADEC and NDDC (millions of Naira)

OMPADEC			NDDC		
Year	Allocation	Receipt	Year	Allocation	Receipt
1992	6,042	1,614	2001	10,000	7,500
1993	6,414	2,619	2002	12,650	11,385
1994	6,621	2,629	2003	10,064	10,064
1995	27,827	3,215	2004	14,000	7,000
1996	38,596	3,077	2005	60,150	17,357
Total	85,500	13,154	2006	96,250	26,130
			2007	26,565	24,000
			2008	79,200	19,050
			Total	308,879	122,486

Source: Augustine Ikelegbe, *Oil, Resource Conflicts and the Post Conflict Transition in the Niger Delta Region: Beyond the Amnesty*, Centre for Population and Environmental Development (Benin City: Ambik Press, 2010), 53–54.

areas of their states, just as the oil-producing states accuse the federal government of diverting funds to non-oil-producing parts of the country.

Shock Three: Oil Price Spikes

The third shock was the oil price spikes of the period 2003–2010, which swelled the government's so-called "excess crude" accounts. This inspired the Niger Delta claimants—state and local governments, warlords, militia groups, and criminal gangs—to seek their share of the increased revenue. Adding impetus to these demands were repeated scandals over corruption and waste, stemming from the initial absence of laws or guidelines for spending the excess funds.[40] Starting in 2007, however, excess crude revenues were shared among the tiers of government as part of the Federation Account, thus providing windfalls to states and localities. For example, Bayelsa state received up to $200 million in some months in 2008. But rather than satisfying local claimants, the effect was to exacerbate conflict, because there was now more money to fight over.[41] Constitutional design—namely, the political and fiscal dominance of the federal government—thus fostered grievance and violence in reaction to the revenue windfall.

The Movement for the Emancipation of the Niger Delta (MEND) emerged as the most important of the militant groups, predominantly composed of youths. The militants' tactics included sabotage, abduction of oil workers (especially expatriates), attacks on and seizures of oil installations, increased bunkering, and bombings and armed attacks (which later spread to other parts of the country, notably Lagos and Abuja). Bunkering entailed the diversion and processing of crude oil using so-called "bush refineries." Although illegal and criminal,[42] bunkering is a popular and widespread instrument of "self-determined resource control."[43] The desperation of the militants is captured in the slogan adopted by the Ijaw Youth Council, led by Asari Dokubo: "Resource control and self-determination by every means necessary." The criminal aspects of the struggle extended to piracy on the high seas, thus threatening the peace and stability of the entire Gulf of Guinea. The greatest casualty, of course, was the oil industry and its revenues. Losses were huge and costly, as oil production dropped to less than one million barrels per day by 2007, down from previous daily averages above 2 million barrels. The Technical Committee on the Niger Delta set up by the federal government reported that in 2007 and 2008 there were over 50 attacks on oil installations, leading to shutdowns and spillages that reduced revenue by an estimated $20 billion, with another $3 billion lost to illegal bunkering.[44]

The federal government responded by deploying special military units that the militants described derisively as "occupation forces." The overriding federal objective was the protection of the industry to ensure a steady supply of crude oil, the country's economic lifeline. But pushback continued from state governments—and from ethnic and civil society organizations, some connected to transnational coalitions—demanding local resource control, fiscal restructuring, true federalism, and social and environmental justice for the oppressed minorities.

While the war against the federal government and the oil companies was the most notable violent conflict in the Niger Delta, there also were horizontal violent conflicts among various groups and communities, exacerbating insecurity and instability.[45] Derivation and compensation politics provoked fierce contests and conflicts among states regarding jurisdiction over oil fields, the major criterion for derivation allocations. For example, great controversy was stirred by the decision of the federal government to allocate Bayelsa state (the home of President Goodluck Jonathan) derivation revenue based on nine additional oil wells located beyond the 200-meter isobath depth of the state's seaward boundary, on grounds that the environmental impact of exploration had devastated the state.[46] Although this particular recommendation was said to have been made by the National Boundary Commission and the

Revenue Mobilization, Allocation and Fiscal Commission (RMAFC), such irregular actions provoked tension and conflict among the Niger Delta states.

The two most notable disputes were those that Akwa Ibom state had with the states of Cross River and Rivers over oil wells in a triangular portion of the sea between them. In 2006, at the intervention of the federal government, a "political solution" (i.e., not based on history, law, or science) was agreed by the governors of the three states. The deal gave Cross River 74 wells, and Akwa Ibom 14 wells, of the 88 that lay between them. It also divided equally the 172 wells that lay between Rivers and Akwa Ibom states, providing 86 to each. However, by the end of 2007, Akwa Ibom state (which now had a new governor) repudiated the latter provision to claim all 172 wells between it and Rivers state, on historical grounds. The RMAFC accepted this claim and in April 2009 starting paying derivation to Akwa Ibom state as owner of all 172 wells. Rivers state then appealed to the Supreme Court on grounds that the RMAFC had violated section 162(2) of the 1999 constitution by acting without approval of the National Assembly. The court ruled in favor of Rivers state, restoring its control of 86 wells and ordering a refund with interest of all derivation funds wrongly paid to Akwa Ibom state.[47]

This dispute well illustrates how one aspect of Nigeria's constitutional design (fiscal hyper-centralization) exacerbated conflict from the shock of the oil windfall, while another aspect (separation of powers) helped manage that conflict relatively peacefully. The independent judiciary rejected a decision by an executive agency because it did not respect the authority of the legislative branch, and the decision was observed by both the federal government and the adversely affected state (Akwa Ibom). This underscores how one element of constitutional design—ensuring access to legal recourse—is vital to the peaceful management of disputes.

Major Findings and Conclusions

The violent conflicts in the Niger Delta were not inevitable. Rather, they demonstrate how a constitutional design of only limited accommodation may exacerbate grievance in the periphery—from neglect, violation of rights, bad governance, and inappropriate responses to demands for redress—among peoples affected by oil shocks. These institutional shortcomings stem partly from the fact that Nigeria's post-independence constitutions typically were imposed by military regimes without consensual bargaining. Indeed, in one of the great ironies of Nigeria's political history, there has been less public input to the design of the country's constitutions since independence than there had been during the latter years of colonialism. In the 1950s, constitutional conferences were held in which representatives of regional governments, political parties, and other political stakeholders bargained to reach agreement on a constitution that could pave the way to independence. In the late 1990s, at the height of the agitation for true federalism, advocates urged the convening of a similar Sovereign National Conference where various interest groups could negotiate a new constitution. Such a conference never materialized, however, and instead the Obasanjo administration in 2006 convened a National Constitutional Conference that failed to satisfy opposition demands for a true renegotiation of the national charter.

Nigeria's centralized constitutional design, especially the concentration of fiscal and legislative powers at the federal level, has prevented states and localities from functioning as devolved and autonomous levels of government. With regard to the Niger Delta in particular, the federal government has dominated policymaking ever since the independence constitution of 1960 enshrined a special development commission for the region. Subsequent constitutional reforms failed to devise structures to respond directly to the demands of aggrieved oil-bearing communities, for which extant states and local government entities did not suffice. These weaknesses constrained the efficacy of the federal solution to the Niger Delta conflicts.

Another institutional shortcoming was the state's failure to protect the rights of individuals and groups by enforcing the laws and regulations governing operations of the oil and gas industry. Prolonged military rule also engendered a culture of impunity that the famous Nigerian legal scholar B. O. Nwabueze has described as "lawless autocracy, that is to say, a government not limited by law."[48] Military regimes overreached in many ways: issuing suspension and modification decrees that made laws enacted by military governments superior to the constitution; suspending legislatures, political parties, and nongovernmental organizations; and eviscerating the judiciary. The absence of effective constitutional restraint enabled the military regimes to treat the Niger Delta as a security problem and to suppress politically mobilized groups—rather than pursuing negotiation and peaceful compromise—which only led to festering grievance.

Subsequent reform of constitutional design to address the grievances of the Niger Delta has comprised mainly two elements: marginal increases in derivation funds to oil-producing states, and greater access to opportunities by applying the federal character principle. But these have not addressed other fundamental demands from the region: environmental protection; resource control; greater derivation to states and localities; guaranteed minority rights, including self-determination; political autonomy; devolution of greater authority to states in the realms of police, security, and elections; repeal of laws such as the Petroleum Act and Land Use Act; and review of agreements with oil companies. In particular, the constitution fails to assign to any specific level of government the responsibility for protecting the environment, which is so crucial to the Niger Delta conflicts. In practice, however, the federal government's authority over environmental protection and emergency agencies, as well as ecological funds, gives it the means to protect the environment, which the Delta region feels it has failed to do.[49]

Another structural problem is that the oil revenue redistributed to the Niger Delta via derivation often does not reach the communities most devastated by oil production. Although states have established special development agencies to address this problem, it may be necessary to create a fourth tier of government—beneath federal, state, and local authorities—comprising village governance committees, as recommended by the Technical Committee on the Niger Delta. This committee also recommended the creation of a National Minorities Commission, whose mission would include the following:

> to protect and advance the rights of minorities and micro minorities; ensure full compliance with affirmative action policies and programs; engage in public education/awareness campaigns on minority issues; work with international organizations and relevant bodies to ensure the domestication of global declarations and actions affecting minorities; assist government with research and policy development on minority issues.[50]

The committee justified its focus on short- to medium-term development initiatives on the grounds of the region's long history of dashed hopes. To restore faith, it argued, the first step must be "a dramatic intervention that has tangible short-term results." But the failure of previous, federally dominated development initiatives suggests that more fundamental shortcomings of constitutional design need to be addressed. Why, for example, have state and local governments in the Niger Delta, which are closer to the people, not made more progress despite the huge revenue they have received from derivation funds in recent years? Given this past performance, does the solution really lie in allocating an even greater share of the country's pooled revenue to the states of the Niger Delta, as demanded by the region's nationalists and state governors?

Questions such as these have not been adequately posed and addressed because the Niger Delta conflicts rarely have been analyzed through the prism of constitutional design and federalism. That is true despite the supposed, and much acclaimed, diversity management capacity of Nigeria's federal system to address issues of ethnic pluralism, minority politics, and national cohesion.[51] It is hoped that this chapter's focus on constitutional design, and specifically Nigeria's inadequate devolution of authority, can helpfully direct attention to these under-explored causal elements of the Niger Delta crisis. Indeed, this analytical prism may offer the key to addressing the region's persistent and increasingly violent demands for self-determination, political and fiscal autonomy, resource control, human rights, and true federalism—which arise in large part from the environmental degradation and other oil-related shocks in the Niger Delta.

CHAPTER 5

Sudan: "Successful" Constitutional Reform Spurs Localized Violence

Karly Kupferberg and Stefan Wolff

Constitutional design—a country's major political institutions—can play an important role in both preventing violent escalation and restoring peace after a period of violent confrontation.[1] At the same time, such institutions can have the opposite effect: rather than mitigating violence, they can create new grievances or exacerbate preexisting ones. But this dual effect does not occur in a vacuum. Constitutional design's effect on conflict management is context dependent. To be effective in maintaining political stability, political institutions must fit the specific circumstances of the domestic situation and the international environment, so that the necessary compromises are attractive and sustainable. Otherwise, even well-intended institutions can have perverse effects. Thus, lessons about how institutions impact on violence need to be case-specific. They can draw on broader insights about institutional design and contribute to understanding general patterns of how institutions can mitigate the risk of violent conflict, but there is no one-size-fits-all blueprint of "successful" institutional design for managing conflict.

This caveat clearly applies to the case we explore in this chapter. The largest country in Africa prior to its split in 2011, Sudan had an area of nearly one million square miles (approximately one-third that of the continental United States) and a population of about 45 million. The country is rich in natural resources—fertile land, mineral deposits, and oil—but levels of development vary significantly, with the Arab-Muslim areas in the north along the Nile significantly better off on most indicators than the South and the rest of the country.

Such uneven development is partly a legacy of the country's colonial history and the way in which Britain administered Sudan until independence. It has been exacerbated since independence by the political dominance of Sudan's North, which has shaped the design and reform of the country's institutions and domestic policies, contributing to the persistence and exacerbation of the colonial legacy. This has been compounded by the discovery and exploitation of oil, and by mismanagement of the consequences of environmental degradation. Unsurprisingly, the violent conflict that has plagued Sudan almost constantly since independence can be defined along these major geographical, social, economic, and cultural fault lines. Individually, none of these underlying factors need have resulted in the intense, widespread, long-term violence afflicting the Sudanese people. But in light of Sudan's underlying structural challenges—especially the uneven development and at times hostile neighbors—its political institutions and government policies have not been up to the task of maintaining stability.

Three major axes of violent internal conflict have confronted Sudan since independence.[2] Among them, the North-South conflict is the most significant because of its duration and outcome. It began in 1963, saw an eleven-year respite after 1972, and resumed in 1983. Over the next twenty years, neither side was able to gain a significant military advantage. Eventually, a settlement—the Comprehensive Peace Agreement (CPA)—was brokered in 2005 by a sub-regional organization in the Horn of Africa, the Inter-Governmental Authority on Development (IGAD).[3] Subsequently, 99 percent of southern voters supported secession in a referendum in January 2011, and South Sudan formally declared independence on 9 July 2011.

The inhabitants of South Sudan are often summarily described as southerners, but this is merely an umbrella term for various predominantly non-Arab tribes and communities—including Dinka and Nuer as the two largest groups.[4] Overall, the South contained about one-quarter of Sudan's territory, and one-fifth of its population, prior to independence in 2011.[5] The Sudan People's Liberation Movement (SPLM) has been the primary political and military representative of the South since the beginning of the second civil war in 1983. However, the party was never able to overcome tribal divisions and construct a truly unified southern identity. The main reason for this was that its political and military support was drawn mainly from one ethnic group, the Dinka,[6] which led to the emergence of various splinter rebel and political groups in the South during the course of the conflict.[7] South Sudan remains a highly heterogeneous territory, composed of ten

Figure 5.1. Sudan with partition line. Source: Nations Online Project.

states (see Figure 5.1). In contrast to the arid North's deserts and mountains, South Sudan has a tropical climate. Its economy is heavily dependent on agriculture, and it exports some timber. But the combined region's resource wealth is dominated by oil, including in areas still contested between North and South.

This chapter examines two shocks: first, the government's decision to make peace and share power with southern rebels in 2005, and subsequently the South's vote for secession in January 2011. Both events fit the CDCM project definition of "shock" as a relatively sudden change in the balance of power and resources. These specific shocks are also useful to explore because they produced a variety of outcomes. There was no full-blown resumption of war between North and South, yet localized violence did erupt between the two sides, and within each side. In the North, fighting has occurred in the disputed Abyei area, as well as in Blue Nile and South Kordofan states, leaving hundreds of thousands of refugees and internally displaced persons (IDPs). In the South, violence has broken out in Jonglei, Unity, Upper Nile, and Warrap states, resulting in 350,000 IDPs,[8] even before the escalation of fighting and civilian targeting in late 2013 that followed accusations of an attempted coup. In order to explain these outcomes, the chapter examines to what extent the constitutional design of the CPA and resulting institutions can be credited with constraining renewed North-South war, or may be culpable for the violence that broke out within each region, or both.

Our analysis finds that the CPA's constitutional design of institutions to regulate core North-South issues did successfully foster compromise in that realm, with assistance from international engagement. But the CPA did not similarly succeed at establishing political institutions to regulate intergroup conflicts within each region, so violence did recur beyond the scope of core North-South issues. The one significant outbreak of North-South violence, in Abyei, was contained relatively quickly with international assistance because that dispute did not threaten the core interests of the South.[9]

For the CDCM project as a whole, these findings highlight the role of two contextual factors—local leadership and international diplomacy—to help explain the success or failure of political institutions in mitigating the impact of shocks to reduce violence consequences. In other words, institutions are important, but their effectiveness is conditioned by the behavior of local and international leaders.[10] Ostensibly perfect institutions may fail due to poor stewardship, while even imperfect ones can succeed at preventing violent escalation if local and international political leaders have sufficient political will.

The chapter proceeds in several steps. The next section provides a brief historical background to Sudan's conflicts and their management. The following section contains the heart of the analysis. It traces the implementation process of the CPA from 2005, and establishes the reasons why—and the extent to which—the institutions and processes provided in the CPA were able to secure a relatively peaceful North-South separation, at least in the sense of avoiding renewed all-out North-South war. It also explores why the CPA failed to prevent localized violence—between North and South in Abyei, and within several states of the North and South. The conclusion summarizes the chapter's findings, offers policy prescriptions, and suggests avenues for further—including comparative—research.

Historical Background

Sudan's North-South differences are many and have a long precolonial and colonial history. Over the centuries, what eventually became the northern part of the independent state of Sudan went through a cultural process of Arabization, starting with the arrival of nomadic tribes from Egypt. By the time Britain colonized the region, these Arab communities were firmly established and favored by the British. Their elites developed a new understanding of Sudanese-Arab identity,[11] and the North became the center of Sudanese nationalism.[12] Regional disparities in Sudan were exacerbated by the British policy of separately administering the North and South.[13] The binary concepts often used as shorthand for this divide—North-South, Arab-African, Muslim-Christian/Animist—mask a far more complex heterogeneity of the populations and regions of north and south Sudan.[14]

The run-up to independence in the first half of the 1950s was characterized by both violence and dialogue. A brief but intensely violent mutiny in the South was put down by northern troops in August 1955. Northern political parties then promised southern activists a federal constitution in exchange for their support of independence. But the northerners reneged on this promise in the first constitution to come into force upon independence in 1956, which established a highly centralized, unitary state. The South's initial reaction was to eschew violence, despite continuing institutional marginalization and discrimination, in part because of the memory of the brutal crushing of the 1955 mutiny. But educated southerners began to organize politically in the 1950s, foreshadowing southern regional activism and growing militancy.[15] Frustrated in their demands for a federal state structure, southern politicians refused to continue supporting a government coalition of northern parties after the 1958 elections—which were followed by a military coup in November 1958, and two unsuccessful counter coups in March and May 1959. Military rule brought a degree of development and prosperity to the North, but the South remained poor, politically marginalized, and culturally repressed. As a consequence, by 1964, initially localized southern rebel movements converged to form the Anya-Nya rebellion.

The military regime fell in October 1964, but the new constitution, being almost identical to the 1956 version except for the switch to a unicameral legislature, failed to address southern demands. An additional three years of North-South negotiations also led nowhere, because the committee charged with drafting a new national constitution in 1967 affirmed the role of Shari'a law, in clear opposition to the express wishes of southern representatives.[16] This lack of northern concessions can be explained in part by the relative ineffectiveness of the Anya-Nya, who had been weakened temporarily by two factors. First, they suffered in-fighting among armed factions and between the rebels and southern politicians in Khartoum. Second, the Khartoum regime successfully armed and trained tribal militias to contain them.[17]

In May 1969, a carefully planned military coup in Khartoum brought to power Ja'afar Numayri, who would remain there until spring 1985. In part to help consolidate his rule, Numayri in 1971 turned his attention to the South, only to realize quickly that the conflict there had reached a stalemate and could not be resolved militarily. The southerners by this time had coordinated their military and political efforts with the founding of the South Sudan Liberation Movement (SSLM) in January 1971, were receiving military equipment and training from Israel, and enjoyed the openly expressed sympathies of Ethiopian Emperor Haile Selassie.[18] This encouraged Numayri to seek an agreement to end the civil war. Through the mediation of Haile Selassie and because of both sides' willingness to make concessions and reach compromises, the Addis Ababa Agreement was concluded in 1972, ending the first phase of the North-South civil war.[19] The Agreement established a southern region with its own legislature, significant political and economic autonomy, control of its own security forces, and representation in the central government by three cabinet ministers.[20] The combination of self-governance and at least some central power-sharing offered a modus vivendi between North and South that marginalized, for the time being, those in the South who demanded independence and those in the North who argued for more central control.

Over time, however, the "hegemonic preferences" of the government undermined the Agreement.[21] A growing conflict over the control of valuable oil resources also threatened the self-governance arrangements.[22] By 1983, the gradual chipping-away at the Agreement had undermined relations to such an extent that another southern rebellion emerged, igniting the second phase of the civil war between North and South that was to last until 2005.

Constitutional Design of the CPA

The North-South conflict, to a significant degree, is a center-periphery dispute over power and resources.[23] There also has been an important religious dimension,[24] especially the rejection by the South of the imposition of Shari'a law.[25] These two aspects of the conflict gave rise to a significant secessionist current, which grew in importance during the second phase of the North-South war. The institutions provided by the 2005 CPA addressed these issues in a variety of ways. The CPA established a South Sudan region of ten states, with its own legislative assembly and executive, and separate southern security forces. It also ensured representation of the SPLM not only in the legislatures of South Sudan and its constituent states, but also in the national parliament and civil service. These power-sharing provisions were further enhanced through qualified voting procedures that offered an additional level of safeguards against unilateral changes by the North to the CPA.

To address one of the main conflict issues—the exploitation of South Sudan's natural wealth by the North—a detailed wealth-sharing agreement was the first to be concluded during negotiation of the CPA. This created an important source of revenue for the newly autonomous government of South Sudan (GoSS)—namely, half the net revenue from oil produced in the South—and also for its states, which were to receive at least an additional 2 percent of the revenue from oil produced in their territory. In addition, the CPA provided that the GoSS was entitled to half of all non-oil revenue collected by national authorities in the South.

The CPA and its associated Interim National Constitution (INC) acknowledged the importance of respecting cultural, religious, and linguistic diversity, although few concrete commitments followed.[26] In addition, the Agreement mandated that "the legislature of any sub-national level of government may adopt any other national language(s) as additional official working language(s) at its level." The CPA also limited the mandatory application of Shari'a law in the South and provided for the protection of the rights of non-Muslims in the North, including in Khartoum.

Crucially, the CPA also provided for a vote on independence in the South within six years. A parallel referendum was to be conducted in the Abyei area, and popular consultations were to be held in South Kordofan and Blue Nile states. Combined, the CPA referenced these as the "three areas." The referendum in the South took place in January 2011, resulting in an overwhelming majority in favor of secession. Abyei, South Kordofan, and Blue Nile remain unresolved issues between North and South. Abyei was to hold a referendum in 2011 to determine its status, but the vote was suspended because the sides could not agree on the terms of the referendum. Popular consultations in South Kordofan and Blue Nile never fully got underway, and since 2011 both states have experienced fighting between the Khartoum government and the SPLM-North, the northern counterpart of the former southern rebel party that now governs South Sudan, as discussed below.

The CPA thus had two crucial objectives. One was to make it attractive for the South to remain in Sudan, by providing for a six-year interim period in which the Agreement's power-sharing institutions could prove their value.[27] Failing that, the CPA aimed to ensure a peaceful separation of North and South, by building a referendum clause into the Agreement and committing the parties to respecting the results of the popular vote. In contrast to this substantial accommodation of the South, Sudan's other regions and groups received much less accommodation in the CPA's text, and even less in its implementation. This was at least partly because the international community focused its pressure on persuading Khartoum to accommodate the South with the secession referendum.

The First Shock: Power-Sharing with the Former Enemy

In dealing with the initial shock of power-sharing between mortal enemies, the CPA's implementation was sporadic and halting.[28] The complexity and comprehensiveness of the Agreement's provisions, as well as the "constructive ambiguity" with which many of them were phrased, in part explain the considerable delays that occurred. These were exacerbated by the intransigence of Sudan's two dominant political parties that were ostensible partners in the CPA—the National Congress Party (NCP) and the Sudan People's Liberation Movement (SPLM)—as well as by the lack of political experience and expertise on the part of the latter. A final perturbing factor was the international community's fluctuating attention to the CPA, due partly to the distraction from other Sudanese conflicts in Darfur and, to a lesser extent, the east of Sudan.[29]

Another hindrance to implementation of the CPA was the divisions within each region.[30] The SPLM remained internally divided on the most important question—secession—while the NCP faced a power struggle among its leaders.[31] At the same time, each party faced political and violent challenges to its dominance in its own region.[32] These internal challenges no doubt distracted from efforts to implement the CPA.

Accordingly, the CPA's implementation was uneven at best. On the positive side, its power-sharing institutions and security arrangements worked relatively well, albeit with occasional delays. But arrangements for the three disputed areas were deeply problematic. Likewise, vital democratic processes—such as elections and censuses—were often delayed (or still await completion), or were disputed in their conduct or results.[33] For example, although the national census was conducted, it was widely criticized as manipulated by the regime in Khartoum.[34] National elections—which occurred in April 2010 after being postponed twice—were also regarded as rigged in favor of the ruling NCP.[35] State elections in South Kordofan were delayed by over a year, until May 2011. The suspension of the Abyei referendum, and the consequent inability to resolve this territory's future, brought both sides again to the brink of war.

What is remarkable, however, is that despite at times very tense relations between North and South since 2005, the two sides rarely have crossed the threshold of violence directly against each other. That holds true from the moment of the CPA's signing, through the secession, to the time of this writing (in early 2014). Moreover, where violence has occurred during that time, it generally has been locally contained, and the SPLM and NCP have proved relatively effective at crisis management and de-escalation, especially compared to the preceding two decades. A key question that remains to be answered, however, is the extent to which this absence of renewed North-South war can be explained by the institutions established in the CPA.

Another facilitating factor was the generally conducive international environment. External spoilers were almost completely absent. Although tensions between Sudan and Chad in and over Darfur—and the occasional spill-over of violence from Uganda's conflict with its rebel Lord's Resistance Army—were destabilizing factors, they were not of a scale to derail the CPA. The international community, after longstanding international engagement in the negotiations to achieve the CPA, also provided funding for its implementation, as well as for emergency humanitarian relief.[36]

It was only when the international community shunned Sudan over the Darfur conflict—for example, the United States applied sanctions and the International Criminal Court (ICC) issued two indictments of President Bashir—that there were serious problems implementing the CPA, such as the 2007 crisis that led the SPLM temporarily to leave the Government of National Unity. The return of international engagement in 2009 and 2010, notably a substantial and prolonged U.S.-led international mediation effort, helped overcome the hurdles to conducting the secession referendum. Similarly, the de-escalation of violence in Abyei in spring 2011 became possible, in part, through the swift deployment of Ethiopian peacekeepers, followed by a new United Nations Interim Security Force for Abyei (UNISFA).[37]

The most perilous moment of the implementation occurred in October 2007, when the SPLM withdrew from the Government of National Unity. The southerners threatened not to return unless progress was made within three months on a series of demands. These included the Abyei Roadmap, distribution of oil revenue, North-South border demarcation, and withdrawal of Sudanese Armed Forces (SAF) units from the South. Despite some further, low-level clashes between the SPLA and the SAF (or its allies) in South Kordofan and Northern Bahr el-Ghazal, the SPLM rejoined the government after winning a series of concessions. SPLM officials were named as ministers of foreign affairs and cabinet affairs, and SAF units departed the South. On oil revenue, a report from the Wealth Sharing Group—part of the CPA's Assessment and Evaluation Commission that included international participation—declared that the GoSS was owed $55 million from the years 2005–2007. By 2010, all arrears had been settled.

Such institutions under the CPA—including the NCP-SPLM Joint Leadership Committee, and the NCP-SPLM Joint High Political Committee—also proved crucial for resolving many other disputes peacefully, facilitated by the swift appointment of the Government of National Unity. Via these institutions, the parties maintained effective channels of communication that enabled them to overcome impasses in the implementation process. For example, the deadlock over the report of the Abyei Boundaries Commission, charged with defining and demarcating the Abyei area, was resolved after prolonged discussions in the NCP-SPLM Joint Leadership Committee and its political subcommittee between 2006 and 2008. Eventually, the issue was resolved as part of a broader package, the so-called "Roadmap for Return of IDPs and Implementation of Abyei Protocol," which the parties negotiated and agreed after the one major outbreak of North-South violence during implementation of the CPA. That outbreak occurred in Abyei, in March 2008, between SPLA units and northern-allied Misseriya tribesmen, who compete for scarce land and water resources along their grazing routes through Northern and Western Bahr el-Ghazal states. In the Roadmap, the NCP and SPLM agreed on submitting the boundaries issue to the Permanent Court of Arbitration in The Hague, one of four options for resolving the dispute specifically identified at a Joint Leadership meeting of NCP and SPLM in May 2006. The Roadmap also provided for the appointment of an SPLM Administrator and an NCP Deputy Administrator for Abyei, redeployment of SAF and SPLA units from Abyei, and subsequent return of IDPs, while also reaffirming the sharing of oil revenues according to the CPA's Abyei Protocol.

The drawn-out crisis of 2007–2008 and its incremental resolution illustrate the ability and grudging willingness of the NCP and SPLM to compromise as necessary in order to avoid a collapse of the CPA and a return to full-blown war. While the SPLM walked out of the power-sharing government in 2007, it returned just over a month later, even though only some of its demands had been fulfilled. A subsequent escalation, including military confrontation between the parties over Abyei in March 2008, prompted them to agree to the Abyei Roadmap, an indication again that neither side was prepared to risk full-scale return to war. Both sides apparently viewed implementing and preserving the institutions that the CPA had created as more worthwhile than renewed violent confrontation with an uncertain outcome.

Most other disputes during CPA implementation also were resolved by mutual agreement between North and South. The census of April 2008 proved to be particularly controversial and potentially destabilizing. The SPLM rejected the results, when they were officially released more than a year later in June 2009, and objected to them being used for delimiting constituency boundaries or for changes in the CPA-mandated allocation formulas for power- and wealth-sharing. After months of negotiations, a partial deal was reached in February 2010, adding 40 seats for southern parties in the national assembly (for a total of 26 percent), and agreeing to recount census data in South Kordofan.

At a CPA review conference in Washington in June 2009, the NCP committed to accept as final the impending arbitration decision on Abyei, which subsequently was delivered in July 2009. In August, the parties agreed to another action plan to move forward on CPA implementation, but remained stuck on the census dispute and the CPA-mandated independence referendum. The stalemate continued for three months, exacerbated by violence in Jonglei and Darfur, as well as by an SPLM boycott of the national parliament. The crisis on the referendum was only resolved by a last-minute deal between the NCP and SPLM in December 2009, which addressed three major points of contention, as follows: the secession referendum would require only a simple majority vote and a minimum 60 percent turnout; in Abyei, voter eligibility criteria were defined for its referendum; and regulations were set out for the popular consultations in the other two disputed areas: South Kordofan and Blue Nile.

The timetable for national elections also slipped significantly, partly because of delays in releasing the census data necessary for drawing voting districts. In April 2009, national and regional elections were initially postponed, by mutual agreement, for seven months, until February 2010. Additional problems with voter registration, restrictions on campaign activities, and widespread campaign-related violence prompted the SPLM—and a number of other Northern opposition parties—to pull out of the nationwide parliamentary poll of April 2010 in most northern states. The NCP also pressured the SPLM to withdraw its candidate for the national presidency, which the southern party eventually did in March 2010, in return for the census deal. The elections, held in April 2010, were far from perfect by international standards, but suited both parties' core interests in confirming the dominance of the SPLM in the South and, albeit less decisively, the NCP in the North.

Again, the parties had walked to the brink and pulled back to achieve a compromise that assured their core interests: for both sides, dominance in their respective areas; and for the South, the conduct of the referendum. In addition, the SPLM received 9 out of 36 government ministerial posts in the coalition cabinet formed in June 2010 after the elections. In August 2010, the two sides also agreed on the composition of the South Sudan Referendum Commission, with a northerner as secretary-general and a southerner as his deputy.

The Second Shock: Secession

With all the pieces now in place for the referendum, the vote on southern independence was conducted during 9–15 January 2011, with almost 99 percent of voters favoring independence. President Bashir officially accepted the outcome on 8 February. South Sudan then formally declared independence on 9 July, joining the United Nations as its 194th member state shortly afterward.

In stark contrast to the referendum on southern independence, however, the referendum in Abyei, mandated by the CPA to take place in parallel, was canceled because the parties could not agree on criteria for voter eligibility, despite intense international mediation and pressure. Ever since, Abyei has been plagued by violence, predominantly between local communities. But in May 2011, direct clashes broke out between SPLA and SAF units, prompting an SAF invasion of the disputed territory. Violence subsequently continued in Abyei between the SAF and SPLM-North. Despite subsequent commitments by North and South to seek a solution, little progress had been made by early 2014, other than an agreement to allow the deployment of UNISFA peacekeepers in Abyei.

Similar clashes also erupted in Blue Nile and South Kordofan states. An agreement between the contending sides on political and security arrangements in these two states, reached in June 2011, was torn up shortly afterwards by the government. Khartoum then declared a state of emergency in Blue Nile state, removed the elected SPLM-North government, and banned the SPLM-North as a political party. Thus, although there was no full-blown resumption of North-South war in the wake of southern independence, violence did erupt in the three disputed areas.

The crises in South Kordofan and Blue Nile have taken on a broader national dimension following the alliance between the SPLM-N and the main insurgent movements in Darfur, under the combined banner of the Sudan Revolutionary Front (SRF).[38] In January 2013, this alliance also concluded an arrangement with the National Consensus Forces, consisting of political parties and civil society organizations in Sudan opposed to the current regime in Khartoum. The resulting agenda for change, captured in the so-called New Dawn Convention of 5 January 2013, emphasizes a "political vision that shifts Sudan from [its] totalitarian system towards democracy, integrity, peace and . . . equal citizenship."[39] Significantly, Arabs from the Misseriya and Hawazama tribes, formerly major government supporters in Darfur and Kordofan, have begun to join SPLM-N and SRF insurgent groups. While the government in Khartoum seems willing at most to negotiate local agreements, the opposition presents an increasingly united front pressing for more comprehensive change.

The relative failure of the CPA's institutions to keep peace in the disputed areas is due not to poor design but to a shortage of political will and perceived strategic necessity on both sides. The procedures for the referendum in Abyei were no more or less codified in the CPA than those for the southern independence referendum. But the incentives for both sides to compromise on the main secession referendum were more compelling, because neither side had an interest in renewal of all-out war. For the SPLM, avoiding war and holding the referendum were essential to achieving independence. For the NCP's Bashir, avoiding renewed war was important for consolidating political control in the North, escaping international sanctions, and possibly achieving a temporary suspension by the UN Security Council of the ICC indictments against him.

By contrast, the South's core interests were not affected by the popular consultations to be held in South Kordofan and Blue Nile, which were only about their internal arrangements and their relationships with Khartoum. For the SPLM, these external issues were hardly worth endangering their main goal of peaceful independence. Abyei did offer the possibility of another oil-rich area joining the South, but for the SPLM the "big prize" was independence, and derailing that process for the sake of an uncertain referendum outcome in Abyei was not compelling.

The SPLM, in any case, faced significant security challenges of its own in the South. Perceived ethnic Dinka domination of southern Sudan's politics and military alienated and radicalized other communities.[40] Encouraged by Khartoum, various southern militia groups emerged as rivals to the SPLM during the civil war. These militias, and the issues underlying their emergence, have persisted during the CPA interim period and beyond. Indeed, in late 2013, accusations of an attempted coup ignited intercommunal killing of hundreds of civilians, followed by the outbreak of a new civil war between the army and one of its formerly allied militias.[41] The new state of South Sudan thus inherited both an anti-SPLM insurgency and high levels of intercommunal conflict.[42]

The escalation of violence in South Sudan in late 2013 had all the superficial signs of an interethnic civil war between the Dinka and Nuer. However, it arose from a political power struggle between Salva Kiir, a Dinka and the president of South Sudan, and Riek Machar, a Nuer and formerly vice president of South Sudan until fired by Kiir in July 2013. Machar, although a Nuer, enjoyed the backing of several high-profile Dinka members

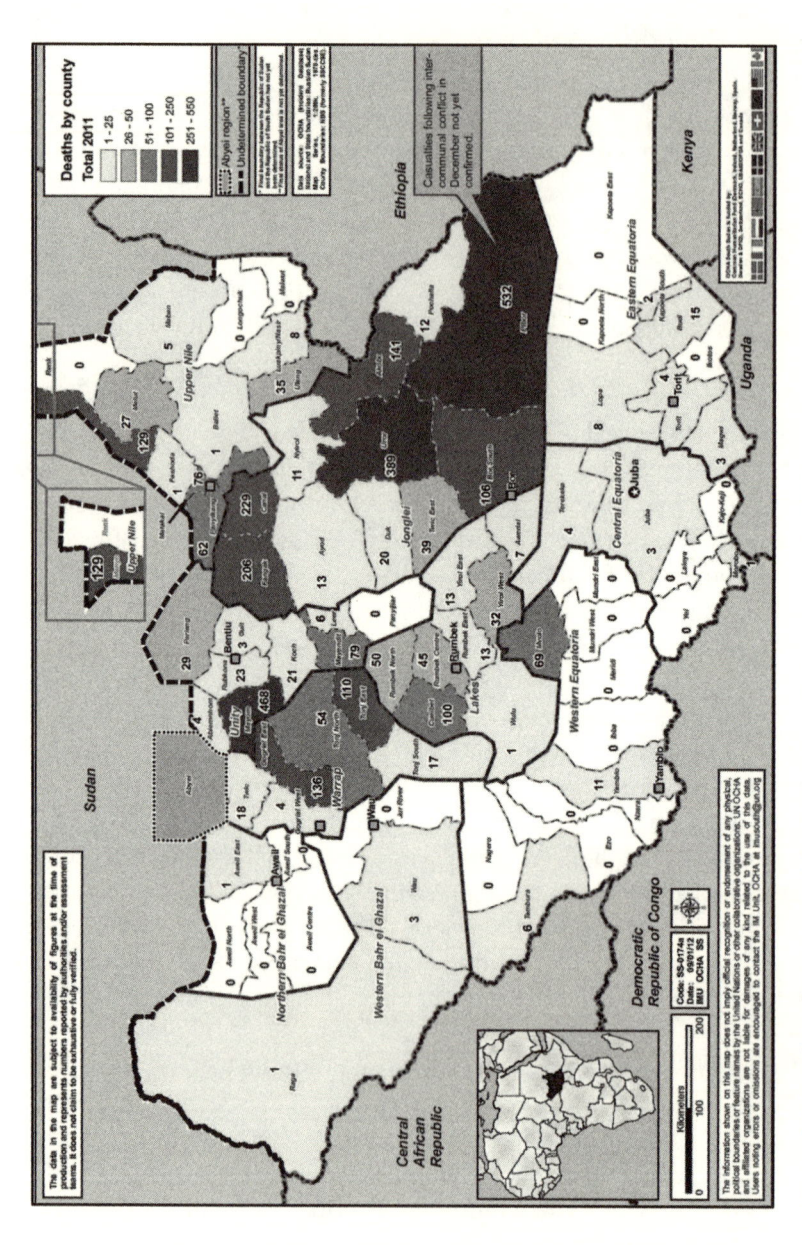

Figure 5.2. South Sudan: reported deaths from conflict per county in 2011.
Source: UN Office for the Coordination of Humanitarian Affairs.

of the SPLM, including the widow of long-time SPLM leader John Garang. Violence was fueled by several factors: demands for more democracy in the SPLM and South Sudan; frustration at the government's inability to deliver improved quality of life that the populace expected from independence; and pre-existing inter-communal and anti-SPLM grievances that the CPA failed to address.

This persistent, mid-level violence in southern states, and in the northern states of Blue Nile and South Kordofan, before and after the January 2011 referendum, fits into an established pattern of the two sides' leaders seeking to consolidate power in their respective areas, and grudgingly accepting the other's control of his own region, despite some continued meddling. Although each side most likely supported proxies across the border, they limited their involvement because they each prioritized the core objective of maintaining political control in their own region. This helped contain violence and prevent renewal of all-out war. Once each side's core objectives were achieved, when Bashir officially recognized the outcome of the southern referendum in early February 2011, the two were no longer locked into a power-sharing deal that required cooperation to achieve their principal objectives. Their dependency on each other decreased, limiting the attractiveness of—and necessity for—compromise that had been essential throughout the 2005–2011 period of CPA implementation.

This prioritization by each leader of his own interests also helps explain the subsequent, nonviolent resolution of North-South disputes in the aftermath of the referendum, especially on citizenship and the sharing of oil revenue. Four days after southern independence, Khartoum amended its citizenship law, rendering stateless about one million southerners who were living in the North. The South had little to no influence on this decision, but essentially accepted it. The protracted stalemate over the future of sharing oil revenues was not resolved until March 2013,[43] more than two years after the secession referendum, but it too was resolved peacefully. In the absence of a viable alternative route for its exports, South Sudan must depend on northern transit routes, while the North benefits from relevant transit fees. This mutual dependency and benefit eventually facilitated a resolution of the dispute, despite resentment on both sides. It also explains why Bashir vocally supported Kiir, when the latter was confronted by an escalation of armed challenges in South Sudan starting in late 2013. Bashir was concerned that the fighting in the oil-rich South Sudan states of Jonglei and Unity, where Kiir's opponents have strong power bases, had created fuel shortages in Sudan and would threaten a vital source of Sudanese government revenues from the oil transit fees charged to South Sudan.[44]

Conclusion

This case study of Sudan illustrates the sometimes pivotal impact of political institutions on violent conflict. The CPA of 2005, based on institutions of regional self-government and central power-sharing, ended the second phase of the North-South war. While failing to hold together Sudan as a single country, the CPA provided the framework in which the South's independence could be achieved without triggering renewed war between North and South. Yet, the Agreement's framework and implementation—which focused more on the primary North-South dispute than other conflicts within the country— failed to resolve the ongoing dispute over Abyei, or the internal power struggles within the North and South.

This makes clear that political institutions are not the only decisive factor. Equally important are two other elements—leadership and diplomacy. Institutions do not just come into being or disappear on their own. The CPA of 2005, at its heart a North-South compromise, was facilitated by broad international support, which continued during the implementation phase, including by helping overcome major implementation crises in 2007–2008 and 2009–2010.

It is this trinity of factors—leadership, diplomacy, and institutional design—that accounts for the success and failure of conflict management in Sudan. Without unduly generalizing this finding, it is important to bear in mind that "peace requires not just a balanced constitutional order but a disposition on the part of all sizable communities to accept compromise,"[45] as well as appropriate external support. The CPA did facilitate a largely peaceful outcome in the face of two major shocks: power-sharing with the former enemy; and subsequent secession of the country's main oil-producing region. This highlights that well-designed institutions, while not sufficient in themselves, can play an important role in ending and preventing violent conflict.

The lesson is that careful negotiation of institutions in which all sides have a sustained interest, and in which they depend on each other to achieve their respective core objectives, is vital to buffering shocks. Institutional resilience depends on widely shared interests of the conflict parties to "reproduce" constantly the institutions they negotiated. Such interests can be honed by external actors offering additional incentives and using, as necessary, pressure to get parties to stick to their agreements. But such resilience also depends on a lock-in mechanism that creates mutual dependency for achieving respective core objectives, even in the face of compromises.

The case of Sudan also highlights the importance of committing the parties to a Plan B—a second-best outcome for at least one of the parties. The referendum option built into the CPA, and the parties' commitment to accepting the popular vote, were consistent with such a Plan B. But its success was conditional upon the fact that this Plan B still allowed the parties to secure their core objectives: political and territorial control in their respective areas.

Given the particular case examined here of a separatist conflict, it should be possible to refine these results by a broader comparative study. Within this book, the cases of Senegal and Nigeria are obvious points of comparison, and beyond that the case of Western Sahara. Outside Africa, secessionist conflicts in the Balkans, the former Soviet Union, Cyprus, Northern Ireland, Aceh, West Papua, Tibet, Mindanao, Bougainville, southern Thailand, and Kashmir all would offer potentially suitable cases for comparison. Indeed, such a collection of cases could form the basis of a broad study of the effect of institutions on the propensity towards violent conflict resulting from shocks in societies particularly vulnerable to separatist tendencies.

INTEGRATION CAN WORK

CHAPTER 6

Ghana: The Complements of Successful Centralization: Checks, Balances, and Informal Accommodation

Justin Orlando Frosini

Ghana has been referred to as "the shining star of democracy on the African continent," due to its past two decades of elections that have been judged "free and fair," including those in 2000 and 2008 that produced peaceful alternation of power between political parties.[1] Indeed, Ghana's electoral results have not been questioned since 1992, when opposition parties rejected the reelection of Jerry Rawlings and then boycotted the subsequent parliamentary elections. Since then, the country's stability has been notable, especially in light of Africa's overall shaky record of democracy and Ghana's recent discovery of offshore oil that could have increased the incentive for an extraconstitutional seizure of power.

As one commentator noted after Ghana's successful 2008 elections, "the recent trend of botched elections on the continent, with stalemated outcomes in Kenya and Zimbabwe, and ongoing electoral challenges in Côte d'Ivoire, Nigeria, and Senegal, had cast a pall over Africa's democratic progress. Thus the polls in Ghana tested the prospects of sustaining multiparty democracy at precisely the moment when its success on the continent appeared most tenuous."[2] Some scholars attribute Ghana's successful democracy to the country's history of chieftaincy. For example, Maxwell Owusu argues that the traditional values of this culture were incorporated into the 1992 Constitution, which helped promote the "orderly evolution, domestication, and consolidation of constitutional democracy" by "promoting the values of consultation and popular participation in political decisions, power-sharing, compromise, conciliation, peaceful settlements of disputes, and respect for the ancestral cultural heritage."[3]

Yet, it is important not to romanticize Ghana's postcolonial history. In the aftermath of independence in 1957, Ghana suffered four coups d'état. These were accompanied by varying degrees and durations of military rule, abuse of human rights, and violence—even if, in some cases, the coups may have averted more serious fighting. Additional violence has flared in northern, resource-scarce communities, pitting land-owners against pastoral and farming communities. Conflicts also have occurred between multinational corporations (MNCs) and artisanal miners, aggrieved at the lack of revenue sharing with their local communities.

Still, Ghana remains one of the few African countries to emerge from authoritarian rule and carry out repeated multiparty elections that have produced alternation of power—without suspension of democracy or widespread violence. This success requires an explanation, especially because it occurred in the face of multiple "shocks"—political, economic, and demographic—of the type that have triggered the suspension of democracy and widespread violence in other African countries. To investigate Ghana's resilience, this chapter examines four shocks and their outcomes in the country over the last six decades. It mainly investigates whether constitutional design played any role in buffering these shocks, but also explores other explanations.

In light of the protracted time-span under analysis—from Ghana's independence in 1957 to the present—the shocks to be analyzed were selected to provide variation in the type of shock and underlying constitutional design. Chronologically, the first shock is the construction of the Volta Dam. This occurred during three different regimes (colonial, parliamentary monarchy, and presidential republic) in the 1950s and 1960s, but all under the leadership of Kwame Nkrumah, often referred to as Osagyefo, the "Redeemer." The other three shocks are the elections of 1992, 2000, and 2008, under the democratic constitution of 1992.

The next section of this chapter summarizes the evolution of Ghana's constitutional design since independence. This is followed by an explanation of the methodology utilized to conduct the case study, including the selection of shocks to be examined. The core of the chapter then discusses how constitutional design mediated the impact of the four shocks. Finally, the conclusion suggests possible amendments to Ghana's current constitution of 1992, bearing in mind the work that already has been carried out by the country's Constitutional Review Commission.[4]

Evolution of Ghana's Constitutional Design

On declaring independence in 1957, Ghana enacted the so-called Monarchical Constitution, which basically followed the British model, combining constitutional monarchy and parliamentary democracy.[5] The Monarchical Constitution was amended several times in the following years, including the Constitutional Repeal of Restrictions Act 1958, which changed amendment procedures, and the Constitutional Amendment Act 1959, which dissolved the Regional Assemblies and halted elections.

In 1960, under a new constitution, Ghana became a sovereign unitary republic. The president was allowed to act without advice from any other person (Art. 8), and therefore was not subject to the ministers. This autonomy was similar to that of the president of the United States, who is responsible to the people rather than the Congress. Unlike the U.S. example, however, there initially was no system by which the legislature could check or balance the executive. The legislature could not unseat the president, but he could dissolve the National Assembly (although he then would have to run for reelection, or retire). The president also had veto power over legislation. Ministers were selected from among members of parliament (in contrast to the U.S. cabinet), but they were not collectively responsible to parliament. Rather, they assisted the president in exercising executive power. Thus, despite a superficial division of powers, the institutional design overwhelmingly empowered the president. Indeed, Trevor Jones characterizes the constitution as "a painted backdrop against which the political game was played with only an occasional nod in its direction."[6] The constitution did, however, attempt to provide for intermingling of indigenous customary law with English common law.

Authoritarian accretion was enabled by a series of controversial laws adopted in the first years after independence. In 1957, a law was passed banning tribally based political associations, which provoked an alliance among opposition groups, culminating in the formation of the United Party in 1958. The Preventative Detention Act 1958 was criticized by the opposition as a transparent attempt to establish the supremacy of the ruling Convention People's Party (CPP) through physical intimidation of its critics.[7] When the law was sustained in court, domestic critics complained that civil liberties in Ghana had become less protected than under colonial rule.

In 1961, the Emergency Powers Act granted the president the authority to declare a state of emergency without approval by parliament. That same year the Criminal Code Amending Act made it an offense to show disrespect toward the head of state. It also enabled the government to take action against "citizens of Ghana who make false reports injuring the reputation ... of the government."[8] One of the most controversial aspects of this law was that it was applied retroactively—to March 1957—violating a fundamental principle of democratic pluralistic legal systems. In 1960, the Criminal Procedures Act authorized the president to appoint special courts, which could issue the death penalty to "political offenders." The 1962 State Lands Act (and subsequent amendments) introduced compulsory acquisition, under which the president unilaterally may seize land for the public interest, paying compensation based on market or replacement value.[9]

A major power struggle during the early independence period pitted on one side the political parties, mainly the CPP, against the senior civil service, which was responsible for running the administration. The civil service was based on the British model—which afforded career security and professional anonymity—and Ghanaian civil servants worked closely with their British counterparts during colonial times. Indeed, many British civil servants stayed behind after independence to ensure a smooth transition.

Although the civil service generally admired Nkrumah and his CPP for forging the path to independence, "direct experience of working with the CPP after 1951 convinced many civil servants that the party was riddled with corrupt and untrustworthy men, unfit to hold public office."[10] Conversely, government ministers were frustrated with the civil service, because it was largely autonomous. Consequently, after independence, the government made moves to control the civil service. Under the Republican Constitution of 1960, the government passed the Civil Service Act that, although recognizing the importance of anonymity in the civil service, ultimately granted the president the power to appoint and dismiss officers "of paramount importance," thus diminishing the authority of the Civil Services Commission.

In February 1966, while Nkrumah was on a state visit to North Vietnam and China, his government was overthrown in a military coup led by Emmanuel Kwasi Kotoka and the National Liberation Council (NLC). As John Kraus points out:

The NLC immediately authorized a large number of judicial commissions of enquiry into the old regime.... The extent of the corruption and arbitrary rule disclosed by the commission proceedings and reports astounded even the more jaundiced, thoroughly discredited the old regime, and undoubtedly cooled the public's desire for a rapid return to party politics.... The NLC immediately justified its assumption of power by its promise to restore democratic, civilian rule under a new constitution which would provide a separation of powers and thus prevent another such concentration of power in the hands of a single man.[11]

David Apter says this rhetoric was sincere: "Despite their method of coming to power, the military and police officers who ruled Ghana believed deeply in the principles of law and order regulated by the legislative process. They were anxious to get the country 'back on the right track.'"[12] An electoral commission was established, and a new electoral register was prepared. As Apter underscores, "the constitution itself reflected both the desire to correct the excessive unitarism of the previous constitution and to prevent the revival of domestic dictatorship while still enabling a government of the day to govern effectively."[13]

In 1969, power was indeed transferred to a civilian government led by Prime Minister Kofi Busia. But three years later Busia was overthrown in another coup. The resulting military regime itself was toppled in 1979, in yet another coup led by Flight Lieutenant Jerry John Rawlings, who initially took control of Ghana for only a brief period in 1979, and then transferred power to newly elected president Hilla Limann of the People's National Party. In 1981, however, Rawlings deposed Limann in yet another coup, on 31 December. Naming himself chairman of the Provisional National Defense Council (PNDC), he went on to govern Ghana by military rule until 1992, when a democratic constitution was approved.

The main organization coordinating democratic political pressure on the military government of Jerry Rawlings, according to John Wiseman, was the Movement for Freedom and Justice (MFJ), launched in Accra in August 1990.[14] But it is not clear what ultimately compelled Rawlings to support the restoration of democracy. As Jeffries and Thomas write, "once most of the demands were conceded, [the MFJ] liked to present the transition to constitutional government and multiparty elections as the result of their own pressure on a reluctant PNDC. Rawlings, on the other hand, argued that he was merely implementing his own, long-planned, democratizing political agenda."[15]

In 1991, Rawlings announced that "our eyes are now firmly set on the final phase of our journey as a provisional government and on the road towards establishing for Ghana a new constitutional order."[16] Indeed, both strong internal and external pressures led to the movement away from Jerry Rawlings's no-party electoral regime towards a multiparty democracy. On 10 May 1991, the government released a White Paper that provided for the establishment of a Committee of Experts to draft constitutional proposals.[17] The Constitutional Commission took more than a year to deliberate, eventually seeking to create a hybrid parliamentarian/presidential system to avert repeating the failures of Ghana's past attempts at democratic rule.[18] The Constitution was put forth via referendum to the Ghanaian people on 28 April 1992, and was accepted with overwhelming endorsement from both Rawlings's party and opposition groups, as 92 percent of the population voted in favor.[19]

One of the most interesting aspects of the 1992 Constitution is that a series of provisions aims to guarantee and preserve the traditional system of chieftaincy in Ghana.[20] Any current chief is prevented from taking part in party politics, but he is able to seek office or election to Parliament by abdicating this traditional office. The Constitution also allows chiefs to be appointed to any public office if they possess the necessary qualifications. Under the 1992 Constitution, chiefs also maintain an important role in Ghanaian culture and politics, due to their role as members of the Regional Houses and a National House of Chiefs, in addition to Traditional Councils that deal with chieftaincy matters. They undoubtedly have played a fundamental role in mediating societal stress. One chief is nominated by the National House of Chiefs to the Judicial Council, allowing him to play an active role in Ghana's judiciary, including by proposing judicial reforms to the government to improve judicial efficiency and administration of justice. Finally, the president of the National House of Chiefs has a direct political impact by holding the position of ex officio member of the Council of State, an independent state institution charged with enforcing the constitution and advising the president on bills passed by parliament.[21]

Under the 1992 Constitution, the Ghanaian government is established as a hybrid presidential and parliamentary system in which general elections are held every four years. The president is elected by popular vote. The leading candidate has to win more than 50 percent of the vote, or else a run-off vote is required between the two leading candidates within 21 days of the first-round vote. Parliamentary elections, by contrast, are first-past-the-post, in 230 single-member constituencies in 10 regions across the country.[22]

Methodology

The methodology used to carry out this chapter's research on Ghana is consistent with this book as a whole. Using a diachronic method, one shock was chosen from the decade surrounding independence. The other three shocks were selected from the past quarter century, in light of the significance of Ghana's successful alternation of democratic power during this period. Shocks also were selected to include at least two types identified by the CDCM project: (1) climate-related, involving construction of the Volta Dam; and (2) politics-related, focusing on the turbulent elections of 1992, 2000, and 2008. The coups that have occurred in Ghana since independence in 1957 were not selected as shocks for examination, because the "project focuses on how constitutional design mediates the impact of" shocks (see introductory chapter of this volume). Although extra-constitutional events such as coups are absolutely essential in setting the context of the Ghanaian case study, it would be paradoxical to search for the "mediating role" of constitutional design when the latter is ignored, put aside, or swept away by a coup. (The field research for this chapter was conducted prior to the 2012 presidential election and the subsequent Supreme Court decision of August 2013, rejecting an appeal and confirming the narrow election victory of President John Mahama.)

Shock 1: Construction of the Volta Dam

The construction of the Volta River Dam was a shock—of significant magnitude and duration—because it required the permanent resettlement of 80,000 Ghanaians.[23] Exacerbating the shock were several factors, including that the displaced population spoke a wide variety of languages and that there were few large towns for resettlement. In 1953, when the country was still the colonial Gold Coast, Nkrumah publicly declared that no one should be made worse off as a result of creating the lake.[24] How to go about doing that was a contentious issue, so in that year a Preparatory Commission was established under Sir Robert Jackson, which would begin preliminary investigations for the Volta River Project (VRP). It was composed of engineers, sociologists, agronomists, and other experts. The commission regarded it as a legal obligation that the resettled receive compensation, including by paying displaced property owners an additional 20 percent of the assessed value of private buildings as a "disturbance element."

The commission considered different models but ultimately recommended resettlement through self-help, guided by incentives, to promote communal initiative. Accordingly, the displaced were entitled to money not for new homes, but rather for building materials. The commission aimed to keep the cost of such subsidies to no more than 4 million British pounds sterling, with any additional costs covered by the Gold Coast government rather than the VRP.

The commission submitted its report at the end of 1955, but the project was delayed for the next five years. During this time there were two other resettlement schemes in other areas of Ghana (Frafra and Tema), both of which had difficulties. The government learned from these efforts, and the Department of Social Welfare and Community gained enhanced standing in resettlement matters. The key finding from the Tema resettlement experience was that failure to provide adequate housing could raise serious political difficulties for the government.[25]

Constitutional design played a key, if contingent, role in the ultimate success of the resettlement plan. By 1959, after independence, the VRP secretariat was losing momentum due to significant staff shortages. Other departments would not give up quality personnel to the new office. But the secretariat enjoyed high status because the now Prime Minister Nkrumah associated himself closely with the project and took personal responsibility for it. Because of the country's highly centralized constitutional design, this one person—the prime minister—could ensure that the project received the resources and attention to succeed. Of course, this was not a robust, institutionalized way of buffering against shocks more broadly, but rather depended on the personal interest and involvement of Nkrumah in this specific shock.

In 1961, the Volta River Development Act created the Volta River Authority (VRA), which succeeded the VRP. The VRA enjoyed insulation from political interference, but was in the limelight because of the prestige of the work. Civil servants were well aware that the VRA and Ghana would be judged internationally by the success or failure of the resettlement operation.[26] Extensive surveys were commissioned, including a census, topographical survey, and social survey, which aimed to determine how best to group villages into new settlements with minimal conflict.[27]

Different agencies began to establish priorities for the resettlement project. The VRA and the Social Welfare Department wanted to create higher standards of living for the resettled population, namely by providing better building materials for new homes. The Ministry of Agriculture (MoA) saw the resettlement as an opportunity to fund and promote more modern farming methods for the displaced populations, especially since they would have less land after the flooding. The government established a Working Party (a special committee of investigation), which accepted the ministry's recommendations to put resettled populations to work on permanent farms, run cooperatively—by sharing large equipment—and using modern techniques.

The resettlement scheme considered different housing options for different populations—for example, traditional round houses for communities in the north—but this became a political issue when communities worried that they would receive what amounted to second-class housing. Eventually, the VRA decided that uniformity in construction would be simpler, since organized labor was difficult to come by. In 1962, the VRA/Working Party established a permanent team of social workers in the field to educate the population about resettlement and the dam.

With heavy floods in 1963, local populations such as Tongu fishermen were convinced that a larger flood was indeed coming and agreed to be officially resettled. VRA realized that the resettlement population was 80,000, significantly more than their previous estimate of 62,500. The expenditure ceiling was subsequently raised from 4 million to 8.5 million pounds, and the Volta Basin Area Development Plan was revised to envision consolidating small villages into large towns. Ultimately, over 700 abandoned settlements became 52 new townships (see Figure 6.1).[28] All this was accomplished without provoking significant political instability, a feat that must be attributed significantly to early, sustained, and sufficient commitment of resources to resettling the displaced in a manner learned from past experience. This successful government effort to buffer the shock of displacement resulted largely from the fortuitous combination of Ghana's highly centralized constitutional design at the time and the personal interest and involvement of the man at the center of that design.

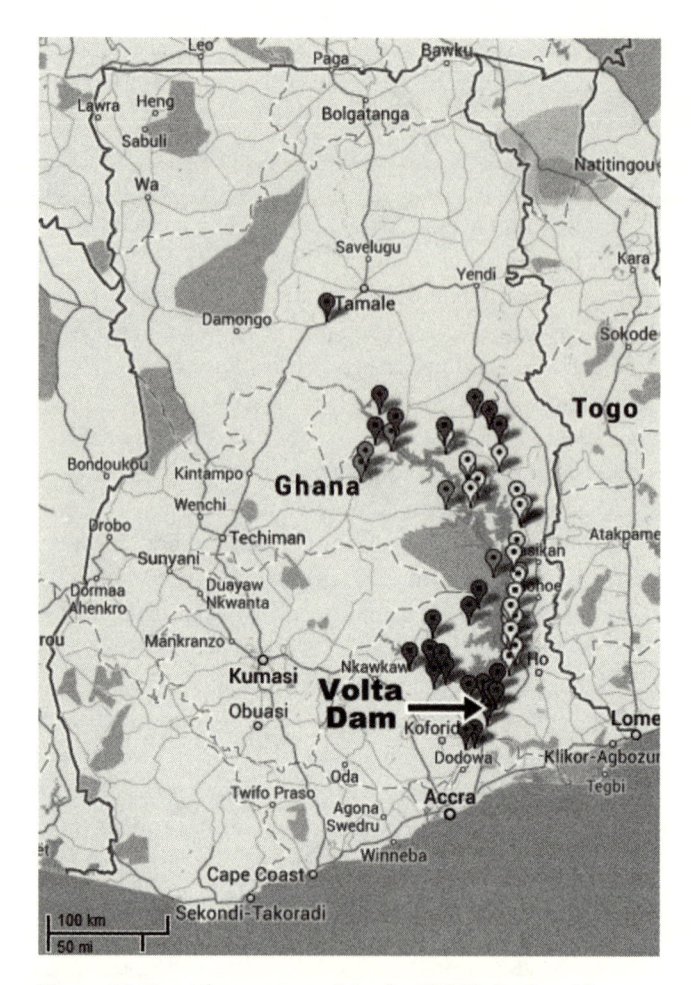

Figure 6.1. Resettlement townships for 80,000 displaced by Volta dam. Source: https://sites.google.com/site/ghanaplacenames/places-in-perspective/lake-volta.

Shock 2: The 1992 Elections

Following approval of the new democratic constitution, Flight Lieutenant Jerry Rawlings ran as presidential candidate for the party alliance of the National Democratic Congress (NDC) and National Convention Party (NCP), as well as for the Egle Party, while his main opponent was the New Patriotic Party

(NPP) candidate, Prof. Adu Boahen. The shock arose from the opposition parties' rejecting the results of the 1992 presidential elections. They did so on three main grounds. First, the democratization process and electoral timetable were dictated by Rawlings's party at the time, the NDC. Second, the electoral playing field was tilted toward Rawlings because he effectively was able to campaign before anyone officially was able to declare candidacy, and also because he was able to use official resources to assist his party's campaign. Third, although the ban on party politics was lifted on 1 May 1992, the opposition parties had to wait another two months before they could register, leaving them with only three months to campaign before the presidential election.[29] In addition, with the complicity or at least negligence of the Interim National Electoral Commission (INEC), massive rigging of election-day balloting and vote counting was alleged. Despite this, the 1992 elections were found to be "free and fair" by the majority of election observers and the international community.[30]

The official results declared that Rawlings had won the election with 58.3 percent of the vote, negating the need for a runoff election. (Notably, the tally reported that he won an improbably high 93.3 percent of the vote in the Volta Region.) Adu Boahen, the next closest candidate, received 30.4 percent of the vote. Soon after the results were announced, the opposition parties called for their suspension until complaints of irregularities could be investigated.[31]

The disputed elections were a clear shock to the country. Demonstrations and riots broke out, and three bombs exploded in Accra. But the violence did not become widespread. On 13 November 1992, the opposition parties announced that they were withdrawing from the subsequent parliamentary elections unless they were supervised by a "genuinely independent electoral commission employing a new voters' register and voters' identity cards." Despite this boycott, the legislative elections were held on 29 December and were contested by the three pro-Rawlings parties. The NDC won 189 seats of 200, the NCP won 8, and the Egle Party won 1, with two independents also winning a seat each. Turnout was extremely low, at 29 percent.[32] It has been estimated that if the opposition parties had contested the parliamentary elections, then based on their performance in the presidential election they would have won around 70 seats, and thus could have played a significant role in the government, instead of being excluded.[33]

The constitutional design, it could be argued, had partially failed to buffer the shock. In response to the stolen presidential election, the opposition rejected the outcome, boycotted the parliamentary elections, and engaged in sporadic violence. Relatively quickly, however, the violence died down and the public accepted the electoral outcome, and this too may be attributable to another aspect of constitutional design. Specifically, Ghana has an independent court system with functioning judicial review, which provides opposition parties an alternative forum to challenge the government. From 1993 to 1996, because of the opposition's boycott of the 1992 elections, Ghana de facto had a one-party system in the executive and legislature. But during this time, the opposition was still able to challenge the government and maintain an influence in national politics through successful attempts at constitutional review. This reduced the opposition's incentive for violence and laid the groundwork for its re-entering electoral politics in 1996 and then triumphing four years later.

Shock 3: The 2000 Elections

The shock of the 2000 elections was the defeat of the NDC political party of John Rawlings, who had held power in Ghana continuously for 18 years, first in military uniform and then as a civilian.[34] Rawlings himself was barred by term limits of the 1992 constitution from running again, but he campaigned intensively for his heir apparent, John Evans Atta Mills. Indeed, relying on his strong base of support in the military command, Rawlings had warned voters that rejecting his party could jeopardize the peace of the country.[35] Such defeat of an entrenched incumbent party is the type of shock that often has led to violence elsewhere in Africa.

But in this case, the outcome was Ghana's first peaceful, democratic alternation of power. The first pleasant surprise was that Rawlings did not attempt to amend the constitution to waive term limits to permit him to run again, as has occurred in many other developing countries.[36] The second benign outcome was that the incumbent party did not attempt to steal either round of elections. In the first round, the opposition candidate, John Agyekum Kufour of NPP, led by only a small margin of 48 to 45 percent over Mills. Yet, in the run-off, Kufour triumphed with 56.9 percent.

The parliamentary elections also produced a peaceful transfer of power. The NPP won 100 of the 200 seats, while NDC's seats decreased from 133 in the previous parliament to 92. The remaining seats were won by independents and smaller party candidates who had backed Kufour during the presidential runoff, providing the new president an effective majority in parliament.[37]

Aspects of constitutional design may partially explain the successful, peaceful alternation of power after the shock of the 2000 elections. First, the relatively short-term limits (eight years) in the constitution meant Kufour did not have to run against the entrenched Rawlings, whose aura and machine probably would have propelled him to reelection. But the term limits also reassured Rawlings's NDC stalwarts that, if they accepted the loss of the presidency, Kufour would hold office for at most eight years, when they could try to return their party to power without facing an incumbent.

A second helpful factor was the Ghanaian tradition—an element of "informal" constitutional design—under which the president ensures broad ethnoregional representation in the cabinet and executive, regardless of the ruling party's ethnoregional basis of support. This helps compensate for the distortions that typically arise in first-past-the-post parliamentary electoral systems, such as Ghana's. It also reassures voters that even if their favored candidate loses the election, their interests still will be represented in government, reducing their incentive to resort to violence.

A third constitutional provision that proved helpful in this case was media freedom, which permitted the aggrieved to express and debate their complaints peacefully. In some other countries, however, free media has turned into hate media, exacerbating conflict and violence. In Ghana, this aspect of constitutional design proved beneficial only because it interacted with the other moderating factors indicated.

A fourth institution that fostered the peaceful acceptance by the NDC of its defeat was Ghana's independent electoral commission, whose credibility had been reinforced by reforms following the disputed and boycotted elections of 1992. In 1994, the commission instituted the Inter-Party Advisory Committee (IPAC), to improve the trust, confidence, and working relationships between the commission and registered political parties and to enhance transparency in its operations. As the official website of the Electoral Commission states:

> IPAC provided an innovative mechanism for the Electoral Commission to meet representatives of political parties as well as donors that supported the electoral process. They also discussed issues concerning election preparations. Furthermore, IPAC discussed confidence building measures like the issue of photo identity cards, provision of transparent ballot boxes, and holding of presidential and parliamentary elections on the same day to avoid the Band-wagon Syndrome.

IPAC also advocated the need to involve the political parties in many stages of the political process.[38]

As a result, the commission is now considered a model in West Africa and beyond, and its independence is recognized despite the fact that the president appoints its members.[39] The transparency of the commission, and the trust it had built with the parties by that time, surely helped convince the NDC to accept that it had lost at the ballot box, reducing any incentive for violence.

Shock 4: The 2008 Elections

The presidential election of 2008 was also a shock, not merely because the candidate of the incumbent party lost, but because he nearly won outright in the first round, only to be defeated in a run-off by less than one-half of a percent. The incumbent NPP's candidate, Nana Akufo-Addo, received 49.1 percent of votes in the first round, to 47.9 percent for John Evans Atta Mills of the NDC. But Mills then prevailed in the run-off, by 50.23 to 49.77 percent, Ghana's closest election ever. In other African countries, either such a switch in the winner between the first and second rounds—or such a close outcome—has by itself triggered post-electoral violence.

In Ghana, however, despite the confluence of these factors, the country peacefully implemented the election results. The former opposition also defeated the incumbents in parliament. The NDC captured 114 of the 230 seats, just shy of a majority 116, while NPP won only 107 seats, and the rest were divided among smaller-party candidates and independents.

Rather than resort to violence, NPP leaders pursued constitutional means to contest the outcome. Surprised at the run-off results, they filed a motion with the Accra Fast Track High Court to prevent the Electoral Commission from declaring the results final until the allegations of NDC electoral malpractices in the Volta region could be investigated. When this motion failed, the NPP initially continued to dispute the results despite public calls for them to accept them. But then the incumbent President Kufour, of the NPP, released a statement calling for everyone to accept the Electoral Commission results, indicating that he would hand over power to Mills on 7 January 2009, as required by the Constitution.[40]

The elements of constitutional design already discussed in the 2000 elections were again important in persuading the NPP to accept its loss peacefully. But additional factors helped avert a widespread violent response to this shock. In particular, the sitting president's decision to ask his party's candidate, Akufo-Addo, to concede defeat, rather than persist in contesting the validity of the elections, contributed enormously to managing the situation peacefully. Another helpful factor was that Mills's party simultaneously prevailed in the parliamentary elections, reinforcing the perceived legitimacy of his presidential victory. It is impossible to know if the outcome would have been quite so peaceful if the elections had resulted in different parties controlling the presidency and parliament (known as "cohabitation").[41]

Summary: Why Does Peace Generally Reign?

Why was the outcome of the shocks examined herein *not* widespread violence? Was it due to the constitutional design? By traditional metrics, Ghana's constitutional design is highly centralized, which many academics believe is suboptimal for cushioning shocks, because it can exclude large segments of society from representation. But many elements of Ghana's post-1992 constitutional design, discussed above, do help ensure the opposition that it has constitutional means to pursue its interests. These include the following: (1) term limits; (2) a tradition of ethno-regional representation in the cabinet and executive; (3) free media that amplify other moderating factors; (4) an independent court system where the opposition can pursue judicial review; and (5) an independent electoral commission that has built trust through transparency.[42]

Even some of the centralizing aspects of Ghana's constitutional design—as they interact with other factors—appear to have contributed to the country's successful absorption of shocks. For example, Ghana's first-past-the-post parliamentary elections have fostered the emergence of a two-party system, which interacts positively with Ghana's lack of an ethnic majority. (The Akans are no doubt the most dominant group culturally and linguistically, but they are not politically monolithic.) Under a two-party system without an ethnic majority, candidates must make cross-group appeals. For example, the last few presidential elections have been characterized by north/south ticket pairings of Muslims and Christians. This contributes to fluid rather than static winning ethnic coalitions and a sense among all groups that they may attain political power through constitutional means. The same is true for the parties themselves. Whichever major party loses an election knows that it has a fairly good chance of returning to political power in the foreseeable future, so it need not resort to violence. By contrast, a proportional representation system might relegate certain parties or sectors of society to permanent exclusion from ruling authority, thereby generating grievances that could foster violence. In Ghana, unlike some other countries in Africa, there are no permanent winners and losers.

The growth of lower-level political institutions, and their ability to incorporate lessons learned, also has helped cushion shocks. For example, in the wake of its longstanding experience with refugee and disaster management, Ghana has built new specialized bodies, such as the Ghana Refugee Board,[43] and the National Disaster Management Organisation (NADMO),[44] which institutionalize lessons from past crises and failures. Another helpful aspect of informal constitutional design is astute use of disinterested, or "outsider," Chiefs to mediate protracted local conflicts outside their own jurisdictions.[45]

But other factors beyond constitutional design also have played a role in buffering shocks. As Ghana experts note, the country's politicians perceive there is "life outside politics," thus reducing the problem of "life-long political professionalism" that characterizes many other countries, and incentivizing them not to react violently to controversial electoral losses. [46] Another cultural aspect is that Ghanaians, especially the Akans, have a tradition of choosing what the scholar H. Kwasi Prempeh has termed "flight" over "fight." In other words, when times get tough, such as in the 1970s and 1980s, there has been a "brain drain" emigration of the middle and lower-middle classes, who might otherwise have opted for militant opposition. Ghanaian political culture also prides itself on having moved beyond military regimes to set an exceptional example of stable democracy in Africa, and the military accepts this civilian control. Such norms can be self-perpetuating, helping foster stability in the face of shocks.[47]

Durable Peace?

So what does the future hold for Ghana, and can this country be considered a model for others in Africa? With regard to the second part of the question there is no easy answer. Much ink has been spilled debating the pros and cons of legal transplanting.[48] But regardless whether Ghana can or ought to be considered a model for other countries in Africa, it is reasonable to explore whether peace is durable in Ghana itself and whether the country's constitutional design will continue to play an important mediating role.

On the twentieth anniversary of the 1992 constitution there were calls from several quarters in Ghana for amendments. Indeed, Constitutional Instrument 2010 (C.I.) 64 established a Constitution Review Commission (CRC) as a Commission of Inquiry to conduct a consultative review. Several levels of consultations and activities had been undertaken to fulfill the first prong of the three-prong mandate. These activities included consultations with Ghanaians at the individual, Community, District, Regional, Special Category, and Diasporan levels to elicit their opinions and concerns on the operation of the 1992 Constitution.[49]

Then, in March 2011, there was a landmark event. For the first time in Ghana's history, a conference to review an operational Constitution took place. Nearly three thousand Ghanaians from all strata of society met in Accra and deliberated on the various submissions made during the Constitution Review exercise.[50]

In addition to the findings from that Ghanaian review, this case study identifies certain aspects of Ghana's constitutional design that might be ameliorated. First and foremost, the overwhelming power of the president, resulting from a centralized constitutional design, could be reduced by enhancing the existing system of checks and balances. As noted, the two-party system and majoritarian elections are not destabilizing per se, especially in light of Ghana's demographics and fluid electoral coalitions. But the system could benefit from greater separation of powers both horizontally and vertically.

Regarding horizontal separation of powers, a potential reform would be for an all-party parliamentary committee, rather than the president, to appoint the members of the Election Commission. The same procedure could be used for many other important institutional appointments, thereby diluting the concentration of power at the center. Regarding vertical separation of powers, Ghana is also quite centralized, as the president appoints all local mayors and a third of the members of local councils. Decentralization and local government reform—for example, the introduction of elected mayors—would further reduce this concentration of power in the presidency. Under such devolution, the party in opposition to the central government in the capital could still be the ruling party in other areas of the country. This would enable the "opposition" to participate in governance rather than anxiously awaiting the next national elections as its only hope of returning to office.

Finally, Ghana's constitution might benefit from two administrative reforms. The first arises from the uneven population size of electoral districts, which has begun to fuel grievance. In this regard, Ghana could take inspiration from its former colonial ruler, the United Kingdom, which recently enacted the Parliamentary Voting System and Constituencies Act 2011 (PVSCA). This statute requires the redrawing of constituency boundaries of the House of Commons, so that the number of electors is spread more evenly across parliamentary seats.[51] The second reform would be preventive, establishing procedures for the eventuality of divided government. So far under Ghanaian democracy, since 1992, the president's party also has controlled parliament. But at some point in the future, a Ghanaian president will face an opposition-controlled parliament, creating a shock that intensifies competition over the separation of powers. Ghana's constitution would be better equipped to buffer such a shock if it were amended preventively to provide explicit procedures for managing such divided government.

For more than half a century, including the last two decades under democratic rule, Ghana has proved resilient against an array of shocks, despite a highly centralized constitutional design that many scholars argue is suboptimal for buffering shocks. This resilience may be partly due to Ghanaian culture, as discussed. But it also is partly attributable to complementary aspects of Ghana's constitutional design, which promote fluid electoral coalitions, alternation of power, and checks and balances against the executive. In this regard, Ghana demonstrates that a highly centralized constitutional design, including a strong presidency and first-past-the-post elections, is not inconsistent with stable democracy, so long as it is complemented by other robust liberal institutions in a country with a diverse ethnic demography.

CHAPTER 7

Senegal: The Limits of Hyper-Centralization

I. William Zartman, Hillary Thomas-Lake, and Arame Tall

This chapter explores how, if at all, constitutional design affected the handling and thus the outcome of specific "shocks" in Senegal.[1] Two types of shocks are considered here: a rebellion that sought secession in the southern part of the country, and widespread flooding in the capital area. The first was endogenous, coming from within the political system, when longstanding demands and hopes for autonomy suddenly faced the prospect of nonrealization and so escalated into violence, challenging the power of the state. The second was exogenous, as floods swamped the capital area, displacing hundreds of thousands. The constitutional design of the state—including its decision-making structures for state-building and governance—prevented the government from producing effective conflict resolution responses. In Senegal, the constitutional design—defined by the introductory chapter of this book as "the formal and informal structures of countrywide governance"—overly concentrated power in the capital city to the neglect of the periphery.[2] (This is sometimes likened to the biological pathology of an enlarged head termed "hypercephalism.") The capital was seen as the country, and all resources were concentrated on it. It was this constitutional design that helped both to cause—but especially to determine the outcome of—these two extraordinarily different shocks.[3]

When a distant and detached peripheral region demanded recognition of its separate identity, the cause was domination and neglect from the center. The outcome was violence, punctuated by ceasefires instead of solutions—that is, conflict management without conflict resolution.[4] When the poor peripheral suburbs of the capital faced a crisis from flooding, it was again because of inattention and neglect from the center (itself under water, although less so). The central government did not know how to handle either prevention of, or response to, the flooding. The outcome was a popular rejection of the ruling party, which prompted the government, contradictorily, to disengage and create new but inoperative agencies. Again, this was management without solutions. In each crisis, the chronology was similar: policy delay and institutional inattention, pressure buildup, a shock affecting the distribution of power, a gradual satisficing response by the state institutions, and then nonimplementation until the pressure again exploded.

Relatively little academic attention has been paid to the Senegalese constitutional design of the state. There is more written on the building blocks of Senegal's domestic policy—clan, clienteles, communities[5]—but little on the state that these dynamics have built. There are only rare studies of the structures of governance,[6] and a few publications in France mainly comprising reprints of official documents.[7] Lately, much has been written on Senegalese democracy. But this is analogous to discussing the contents of a box in Senegal, rather than the "optimal" shape of the box for Senegal.

There is also a small literature on the Casamance secessionist rebellion. Several such analyses identify the roots of the secession as a coincidental combination of elements: expansion of Diola cultural awareness and mounting resentment against carpetbaggers from the North following the 1972 land reform; the opening of national political competition after 1974; and the anniversary of a political promise of independence. This pushed a cultural association first into political activism, and then further into violence, because of severe repression.[8] All agree that the shock was endogenous, triggered by an internal evolution. Less has been written on the flooding shock, since it is relatively recent. But a few Senegalese technical analyses, as noted below, underscore that three decades of drought—considered at the time to be normal—were in fact an interlude to the baseline characteristic of heavy rains before and afterward.

The chapter will next lay out the dominant notion of state design underlying the constitutional structure of Senegalese decision-making. Following that, it will in turn examine the shocks of the secessionist rebellion and the flooding, and the way each was handled. The chapter ends with conclusions on constitutional design, the impact this has had on Senegal's handling of shocks, and an outline of necessary correctives in institutional design and policy.

Constitutional Design in Senegal

The central government installed in Dakar in the transition to independence in 1960, and restructured once the duality of power between the prime minister and the president was resolved in favor of the latter in December 1962, was a highly centralized system reminiscent of French bureaucracies. It was based on the inherited colonial government structures—even more so than in other Francophone countries, because of Dakar's status as the capital of French West Africa.[9] As Collin writes:

> We inherited highly concentrated administrative structures from the colonizers. During the territorial administration reorganization attempts in 1960 and 1964, we kept those concentrated structures.... The goal was to encourage a better level of rural production to support economic and social development in the rural areas, but we were still in a Napoleonic system, where the majority of the orders and decisions came from the central administration while the powers of the local authorities were diminished.[10]

Administratively, Senegal is divided into regions, each headed by a governor and consisting of three *départements*, *communes*, or districts (4 in the Dakar region), each headed by a prefect and further subdivided into *arrondissements*, each under a sub-prefect and composed of a number of villages that constitute the bottom of the administrative ladder. But these divisions are merely local administrative structures of the central state, holding no independent political power. The governors and prefects, who are appointed by the president, oversee and regulate the functioning of the lower-level elected officials in each geographic unit.

The state established by the constitution of 7 March 1963 was an apparatus designed and run by President Léopold Sédar Senghor, a master social entrepreneur, diplomat, negotiator, unifier, poet, and conflict manager. He followed the political model termed "integration" in this book (see introductory chapter). The constitutional structure was totally centralized as a presidential regime, in which the Gaullist inspiration wiped out the vestiges of the Fourth Republic evident in the preceding constitution.[11] The president explicitly has been the "guardian of the constitution" ever since the 1960 version.

Senghor perceived the enormous task of successful nation-building as one that could only be accomplished through deliberate centralization. As Ismaila Fall explains:

> The dominant traits of the Senegalese political regime bear indelibly the mark of the first president.... One can say, without exaggeration, that the political institutions of Senegal owe to President Senghor what the French institutions owe to General de Gaulle.... Leopold Sedar Senghor was inspired by the Gaullist doctrine because he was constantly preoccupied by the demands of stability, order, and continuity that guided the pragmatism of his constitutional reforms.[12]

Maintenance of Senegal's territorial integrity has always figured high on the government's list of priorities and is specified in the oath of office of the president, who also "incarnates the national unity."[13] Senghor strongly held to the sanctity of colonially inherited borders throughout the continent and was opposed to the "Balkanization of Africa" by the creation of mini-states, as he wrote in the 1960s, during the Biafran crisis in Nigeria.[14]

Another element of constitutional design, the fundamental legal code, invests the state with responsibility to safeguard social welfare. Law 64-53, of 10 July 1964, on the general organization of civil protection in Senegal, states that "at all times the State is obliged to look after the protection of goods and physical persons and resources of the country." The current constitution makes it a responsibility of the state to provide relief to victims in times of national disasters and posits disaster management as a public good.[15] However, the institutional structure to implement these provisions has been slow in coming. The first mention of environmental conditions in the constitution was in the revision of 20 January 2006, which proposed to finance relocation measures for flood victims by reducing decentralization activities and by postponing parliamentary elections to coincide with the presidential elections the following year.

As a complement to Senegal's highly integrative constitutional design, the state effectively has subcontracted authority to elite allies in rural areas. The state-building model that Senegal inherited from France was based on vertical power relationships with the countryside, which also was not too different from the precolonial domination strategies of large over smaller entities.[16]

Since 1960, the pattern of governance has been for the highly centralized state to "trade power" with rural elites. In other words, the system of social organization has been based on small fiefdoms, in which the rural elites hold great power in their relationships with local peasantries but still are economically dependent upon the modern state.[17] This system has involved some give and take, including an obligation for Dakar to invest in the rural areas whose chiefs have agreed to political alliances with the president and his ruling party. Thus, the central government has been capable of power-trading (but not power-sharing), and has done so relatively successfully with the central Wolof groundnut basin, which is also the center of Senegalese politics. The fact that Wolof culture was based on hierarchical aristocracies—where kings, chiefs, lords, ladies, and the rank they held were relatively easily discernible—has made it easier for the Dakar authorities to identify and co-opt rural leaders and communities.

Devolution has been nominally codified at various times, including through the introduction of rural communities in 1972,[18] and the institutionalization of local collectivities in Title XI of the Constitution of 15 June 1994. But the extent of autonomy actually granted to the "fingers" of local government had been very much dependent on the "arm" of the central administration—namely one of the regional governors, each known colloquially as *le roi de la brousse* ("The King of the Bush") or *le détenteur du coffre-fort* ("The Guardian of the Safe").[19] As Cruise O'Brien explains, "The control which the central government now effectively maintains over local expenditure makes it possible to manipulate this administrative patronage very effectively in building political support."[20] Waterbury also nicely sums this up as a "dialectic. The urban and public sector bourgeoisie wants to appropriate privately generated rural surplus for collective ends. The peasant wants to appropriate collective, state-generated goods for private ends."[21] But this is not some sort of Engels-esque, bourgeois-peasant class struggle.[22] Rather, the system is sanctioned, contained, orchestrated, and accepted under a constitutional tent called the state, with a centralized, personalized structure. Thus, it is somewhat analogous to a feudal people's monarchy—a political system combining aspects of monarchy (the powerful and autonomous Senegalese presidency) with feudal relations (toward local barons), all wrapped in a populist spirit.

By the time the shocks hit, Senghor was no longer in power, having ceded his post at the beginning of 1981 to Abdou Diouf, his prime minister during the preceding decade. In the 1983 elections, the first to test the popularity of

Diouf, his Socialist Party (PS) increased its legislative majority, and Diouf received 82 percent approval, against Abdoulaye Wade of the Senegalese Democratic Party (PDS), who received only 15 percent. The election was followed a month later by a constitutional reform that further strengthened the presidential system, removed the position of prime minister, and made the government directly responsible to the president (although one minor check on the president was that he no longer could dissolve the National Assembly, whose leader was designated the presidential successor).[23] Twelve more constitutional revisions followed during Diouf's two decades in power, generally reaffirming or strengthening the presidential design of the system. Diouf was reelected in 1988 with 73 percent of the vote—defeating Wade, who received 26 percent, and then was arrested—and in 1993 with 58 percent of the vote, over Wade's 32 percent.

But in the 2000 elections, it was Wade who prevailed, and he lost no time in instituting a new constitution, not just a revision. The document, created somewhat unconstitutionally by the president rather than by the National Assembly, was as "presidentialist" as ever. Indeed, Wade considered it his creation, making statements at various times such as "I put in the constitution," or "I wrote the statutes governing the opposition."[24] Wade's domination was the only constant thing about the government, as during his first decade, he had five prime ministers, four presidents of the National Assembly, three chairmen of the Joint Chiefs of Staff, and more than one hundred cabinet ministers, some of whom lasted in office barely a few months.

As the above review illustrates, Senegal's constitutional design has remained highly centralized since independence, although three very different presidents, in three very different ways, drove it in this same direction. The Senegalese constitution itself was not without changes over time: bicameralism in and out, four different lengths of the presidential term of office, off and on again term limits, and dis- and reestablishment of the office of prime minister. But the overarching presidential nature of the constitutional design remained constant. It was on the basis of this constitutional design that Senegal found itself faced with the two major shocks examined in this chapter.

The Endogenous Shock: Casamance Secession

In the Casamance, the system of indigenous local government (and governance) was very different from that in the rest of the country, and was unchanged by either colonization or independence. Traditional rural Casamance society did not have an institutionalized hierarchy. From the days of the weak paramount chief (Mansa) of Kasa preceding French colonialism, through the colonial period and independence, political authority has been dispersed throughout society. (This is somewhat analogous to the biological pathology of "acephaly," or absence of a head to centrally coordinate the body.) Physically distant, geographically "other," humid, tropical, openly animist Casamance—with its quiet pride, and its Sacred Forest reputed to be a source of spiritual protection and oracular wisdom for all (and revered as such by Catholic, Muslim, and animist Casamançais)—did not fit neatly into Senghor's state design for the rest of the country. The northerners hold ethno-class-based stereotypes of the Casamançais as "animists, palm-wine drinkers, and house servants."[25] Casamançais, for their part, speak of "going to Senegal" when they travel to Dakar. Separated by Gambia from the main part of Senegal to the north (see Figure 7.1), Casamance enjoyed close socioeconomic ties with the countries to the south. Cross-border ethnic and family connections with the ethnic Diola (and Balante, Mandinka, Mancagne, and Manjak) of Gambia and Guinea-Bissau explain the fluidity with which combatants

Figure 7.1. Casamance in Senegal. Sources: CIA, Wikimedia Commons.

from Attika—the Casamance secessionists' armed wing—crossed the borders to seek refuge among friendly villages.

Even before independence, Senghor sensed a strong current of Casamançais resistance to the center, and he understood that the egalitarian and politically fragmented society might become a problem that the central government would not be able to control.[26] Following his usual strategy of co-optation and power-trading, he appointed as minister of education in 1964 the ethnic Diola intellectual Emile Badiane, who in 1947 had founded the Movement of Democratic Forces of the Casamance (MFDC) as a peaceful cultural organization. According to a rumor among the Casamançais, Senghor at the time promised the local leaders that they would be granted independence a generation later, assuming that the pledge would be forgotten.[27] But the MFDC did not forget or abandon its goal of independence. Father Diamacoune Senghor (no relation), the symbolic leader of the movement from 1981 until his death in 2007, declared repeatedly that Casamance had wrongly been incorporated into Senegal by French colonial rule. As he wrote to Diouf on 12 May 1982: "I want no other solution for Casamance but independence, nothing but independence, always independence for Casamance."[28]

Accordingly, Senghor was wary of any alliances that would send political or financial resources into the region and directly or indirectly support the development of a separatist movement. But Dakar needed Casamance to produce more of the national staple, rice, and to yield other bounties from its arable and well-irrigated lands.[29] So Dakar imposed a version of its system of direct rule that enriched and empowered the central government while effectively stifling any local political life, through the creation of a strong regional governor directed by the central authority, untouched by local politics. Thus, the political distance between Dakar and Ziguinchor, the capital of Casamance, was reduced and replaced by a distance between the local governor and his constituents.[30] The regional governance structure offered few options for local participation or for airing local grievances, and it offered no political space for indigenous political leaders within the state structures.[31] Central authorities demanded increased rice production (ignoring traditional rites of land treatment and usage that were deeply ingrained in the animist religious traditions), new tax requirements, and arbitrary appropriation of Casamançais lands for gifts to northern religious leaders. These impositions—coupled with the central government's refusal to invest in education, health, and transportation infrastructure in

Cultural Awareness → Cultural Movement → **Shock:** Militant Separatism → **Outcome:** Ceasefires without Solutions

✖ ✖ ✖

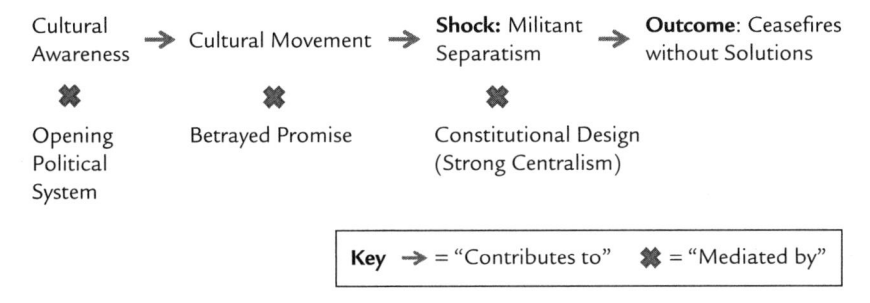

Opening Political System   Betrayed Promise   Constitutional Design (Strong Centralism)

Key → = "Contributes to"   ✖ = "Mediated by"

Figure 7.2. Casamance shock: integrative design manages but does not resolve conflict.

the "backward" region—provoked a mutual relationship of pained tolerance and seething frustration.

Diouf's Conflict Management: Motivations and Results

Senghor, Diouf, and Wade employed different styles of dealing with the Casamance conflict. When Senghor handed over the presidency to Abdou Diouf, at the beginning of 1981, Senegal's political stability was under serious threat from economic stagnation, and the Casamance was increasingly marginalized. Senegal's rising urban unemployment and inflation, falling groundnut prices, drought in the north, and a burdensome structural adjustment program imposed by the International Monetary Fund resulted in a serious economic downturn. A competent and well-respected technocrat, Diouf began to institute a series of political and economic reforms as soon as he took office. At the end of his first year, a fortuitous opportunity to remove the geostructural cause of the Casamance rebellion arose in the form of an attempted coup in Gambia.[32] Diouf intervened militarily in August 1981, and then in December formed a Senegambian Confederation that integrated the military, foreign policy, economic, and monetary institutions. This also reduced the geographic isolation of the Casamance from the rest of the country. At the same time, it became apparent that Diouf was not going to honor Senghor's rumored promise of independence. Rather, he viewed the demands and attempts by Casamance to define itself as a separate political and cultural space as direct threats to the constituted law and order of Senegal.

The initial Casamance shock started with a peaceful demonstration by the MFDC on 23 December 1982, which the Senegalese security forces turned into a bloodbath, leaving four dead and many more seriously injured.[33] The Movement was severely repressed and its leaders, including Abbé Diamacoune, were jailed. A manager above all, Diouf saw the handling of the Casamance situation—with its negative implications for groundnut and rice production—as critical to the stabilization of the economy and the prevention of a major political crisis. Part of his response was definitive—dividing the Casamance into two administrative regions. But in general he was less decisive, wavering between concessions—such as releasing prisoners and engaging in ceasefire negotiations—and military repression.

Diouf appointed a hard-fisted military governor to rule the region for a year in 1990–1991. But the MFDC merely responded in kind, igniting a persistent, low-level violent conflict that persisted for more than a decade, as temporary ceasefires typically were undermined by schisms within the MFDC. The first ceasefire was the Cacheu agreement in May 1991. But splinters of the Movement returned to violence in late 1991. Further ceasefires were negotiated with the MFDC at Ziguinchor in July 1993—broken in June 1995—and again in January 1996. Each violation of a ceasefire was followed by increasingly serious confrontations with the Senegalese army.

Ultimately, Diouf's strategy failed. The Senegambian Confederation was dissolved in 1989, and the MFDC factions continued to fracture, inhibiting prospects for a settlement.[34] The penultimate ceasefire with Diouf was Banjul II in November 1999, which enabled the creation of a Mission for the Observation and Consolidation of the Peace Accord (MOCAP) in December 1999. His last ceasefire was Banjul III, in February 2000, which was intended to create breathing room for negotiations.

Diouf's vision of Casamance—like Senghor's before him—was of a nuisance that needed to be contained in order to free him to go about the business of managing the country and growing the economy. It appears that Diouf had not expected to lose the presidential elections of 2000, and so was just then catching his stride in figuring out how to engage with the MFDC. The Banjul agreements and the MOCAP were likely in preparation for more serious dialogue with the MFDC. But none of the ceasefires was ever followed by substantive talks, and Diouf's initial insistence on focusing on the crisis as a question of law and order rather than as one of peace and justice merely raised the vehemence of separatist activism to the level of armed struggle. On the positive side, the eventual evolution of Diouf's strategy after 1992—from strictly conflict management, law, order, and containment, towards dialogue with the hope of establishing a peace-building framework—did establish the beginnings of a peace process Wade could pick up.

Wade's Conflict Resolution Strategy: Motivations and Results

In March 2000, one month after the Banjul III talks, long-time opposition leader Abdoulaye Wade of the PDS was elected president of Senegal, ending forty years of PS political domination. During his campaign, Wade had promised to seek a resolution of the Casamance crisis in 100 days, if elected. His reputation as a man of dialogue and persistent opposition leader won him the attention of the MFDC and the votes of Casamançais and all Senegalese ready for *sopi* (change), the slogan of his campaign.

Wade was a respected, well-educated lawyer and economist, and his notoriously strong personality, energy, and charisma were welcomed as a breath of fresh political air. His pronouncements on the campaign trail regarding the Casamance crisis sounded ambitious, but beneath the ambition, and a well-recognized tendency toward braggadocio, was a sense that when it came to Casamance, Wade was serious about resolution. He immediately abolished the MOCAP, associated with his predecessor, and cleansed the government of all members who had been involved in the Casamance dossier under Diouf. Building nonetheless on the ground laid by Diouf (whether or not Wade intended or admitted it), he pursued negotiations with the MFDC and Casamance civil society groups during the first three years of his administration, culminating in the Ziguinchor Accord with the MFDC in December 2004, officially ending the twenty-two-year-old war. This achievement had taken Wade some four and a half years—not his promised 100 days—since taking office. The initial Accord was followed by two others—Foundiougne I in February 2005, and Foundiougne II in January 2006—that highlighted substantive challenges for peace and resolution. Despite such apparent progress, combat continued between the Senegalese army and the militant Attika, and factional politics revived within the MFDC. The government soon lost interest in the conflict resolution process, having achieved Wade's personal triumph of a nominal peace accord.

Wade failed to change the essential nature of Senegal's political system that has trapped Casamance in a political no-man's land, so that the only national attention the region gets is through its nuisance power to the president. The Ziguinchor Accord did not resolve the underlying conflict, but only set up bodies to discuss how to resolve the conflict—bodies that have never met. Wade's initially declared intent of conflict resolution may have been sincere, but once the 2004–2006 agreements were signed—and he realized how tough it would be to negotiate and agree on the details, timing and implementation—he lost interest in the process.[35] Moreover, he insisted on controlling the entire process himself, resisting sharing the stage with any of the regional leaders—such as presidents Jammeh of Gambia and Vieira of Guinea-Bissau—who tried to help mediate the conflict.

Ultimately, both Diouf and Wade had a somewhat misguided understanding of what "peace" means, different from the way people living in Casamance would describe it.[36] For both presidents, "ceasefire" and "peace accord" seemed to be considered synonymous. But a ceasefire, by its very nature, is temporary, and in no way equivalent to a permanent laying down of arms or settlement of issues. In their haste to regain control—and in Wade's case, to always appear in control—both Diouf and Wade seemed to believe that they had resolved the conflict, when in fact they had only managed or mitigated it temporarily.

Casamance Outcomes

Senghor's conflict prevention, Diouf's conflict management, and Wade's conflict mitigation were all inadequate responses to the Casamance shock. Senghor's centralized constitutional design and conflict prevention strategy established the framework for Senegal's political system. It marginalized Casamance as a distant region under direct control from Dakar and thereby left a hotbed of social, economic, and political neglect and discontent for Diouf to manage. Senghor's strategy had exactly the opposite of the desired effect. With the change of administration in 1980, Casamançais expectations were once again high, but Diouf quickly showed that he was not going to honor Senghor's "promise" of independence. The resulting frustration, after two decades of political and economic marginalization under Senghor, put the MFDC in a good position to manipulate anger and to press for support of a separatist movement.

Diouf's focus on continued management—rather than resolution—of the Casamance conflict further aggravated the MFDC and alienated many Casamançais. They wanted respectful dialogue at the local government and community group levels, in keeping with the "flat" social order of the Casamance, not the top-down containment strategies imposed on them. Diouf's dialogue efforts in his second decade, from 1992 to 1999, certainly helped prepare the ground for his successor's brand of engagement, but by the time Diouf came to that strategy, the MFDC had suffered several splits over personal ambitions and tactics that inhibited negotiation. Hope sprang again in the bombastic appearance of Wade in the presidency, and he used this opportunity to reach a ceasefire and an agreement to talk about real problems, at Ziguinchor in late 2004. But then he let it drop, confusing conflict management with resolution. In late 2009, violent encounters between the army and the MFDC again emerged in the region, culminating after March 2010 in casualties on both sides. Senegal's hypercentralized constitutional design once again showed itself capable of containing the conflict, but not resolving it.

The Exogenous Shock: Floods

Flooding is a more common shock, usually considered exogenous.[37] Just as it is often said that droughts are natural but famine is man-made, so heavy rains are natural but flooding is man-made, in the sense that preventive societal actions can mitigate significantly the human consequences of heavy rain. The rains starting in the mid-1990s that led to Senegal's flooding were unusual only from a short-term perspective; they actually marked a return toward the annual level of rain of 500–600 mm that had held rather steadily from 1920 to 1970.[38] But from the 1970s to the 1990s, Senegal was subject to a Sahelian drought level of 350mm that drove people out of the countryside to the cities. Population movements during the first two decades of independence had been seasonal, but the persistent drought turned them into permanent in-migrations from the periphery to urban areas. A growing majority of the Senegalese population moved to unplanned shantytowns on flood plains outside Dakar and St. Louis (see Figure 7.1), yet maintained the high birth rate typical of rural areas. This literally compressed the land, so that it could not absorb rain, and obstructed natural passageways for water, which soon sought alternative paths when heavy rains returned in the mid-1990s.[39]

The region is marked by long dunes separated by depressions 15 to 25 meters deep, in an area called Niayes, where the heavy rain can raise the water table with saline seawater above the surface for as long as half the year, flooding the land (and those who live on it), and blocking natural drainage.[40] Since the depressions were dry during the decades of drought, the squatters thought they had a firm base for their flimsy constructions. When the rain came, they were surprised, and the government was caught with its plans down, having failed to make adequate preparations for this predictable contingency.

The sewage system of Dakar itself dates from 1912, with no general system extending into the peri-urban region.[41] In 1999, 2009, and 2010, floods brought the city itself to a standstill.[42] Over the past twenty years, flooding has affected nearly a million people, causing 45 deaths and displacing hundreds of thousands, with damage estimated at over $142 million.[43] Malaria, the leading cause of death in the country, quadrupled in the region during the rainy season of 1996.[44]

Although constitutional over-centralization might suggest special attention to areas near the capital, the state neglected these newly arrived residents in favor of prestige projects in Dakar itself. The neglected population protested the government's inattention in many ways, and in 2005, a local election provided them an occasion to successfully vote out the government party from regional power structures. Despite threats of wildcat violence, however, this sector of the population was too vulnerable and busy with subsistence, so its response remained nonviolently political. The government's reaction to the electoral rebuke was to set up new agencies ostensibly to deal with the problem, but this smacked of tactical conflict management, because the agencies subsequently did little to seek solutions. As the flooding continued, the public outcry reinforced other protests against the Wade regime and its attempt to perpetuate its mandate, and these demonstrations led to sporadic outbursts of violence.

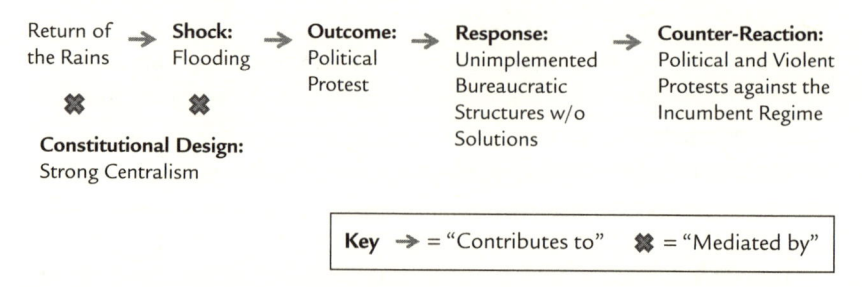

Return of the Rains → Shock: Flooding → Outcome: Political Protest → Response: Unimplemented Bureaucratic Structures w/o Solutions → Counter-Reaction: Political and Violent Protests against the Incumbent Regime

Constitutional Design: Strong Centralism

Key → = "Contributes to"   ✖ = "Mediated by"

Figure 7.3. Flooding shock: centralization hampers reaction, spurring protests.

The government was not prepared to handle weather crises. During the dry years, this neglect led mainly to overcrowding in the capital due to the influx of drought-stricken migrants from rural areas. Nothing organized was done to deal with the wildcat housing during the three decades of drought. A High Commission for Civil Protection was established in 1993 to coordinate disaster prevention. A review of its minutes, however, shows that its interventions were limited to visits of public buildings for conformity with fire and safety regulations, issuance of construction authorizations, and production of televised advisories on road safety measures and dangerous beaches.[45] Nor did this government office do much to prepare for the return of rains. As Sene and Ozer later observed: "What is lacking to contain this dynamic situation is less the administrative framework than its application.... But considering these floods which pile up on each other, one might well ask whether these plans too were not the victims of the long pause in rainfall."[46] The first measure to address the overpopulation of squatters was taken only in the last year of Diouf's administration and not implemented until well afterward.[47] It was only in the middle of the first decade of the 2000s that official activity began to take shape, following some earlier international moves to aid the victims.[48]

The Plan d'ORganisation des SECours—Plan ORSEC, the National Emergency Management Plan—was created by presidential decree 99-172 of 4 March 1999, four years after the first floods, to serve as the master plan for disaster response operations, updating and replacing the 1993 decree. Plan ORSEC offers a good disaster preparedness roadmap. It defines the organization of rescue operations at the national, regional, and district/*départemental*/communal levels. Only the prefect, who represents the central state at the district level, can make the decision to trigger the district-level ORSEC Plan. Even in a disaster of exceptional proportions, the mayor, the elected political head of a commune, is required first to mobilize all available communal means before calling on the higher administration. Similarly, the governor triggers the regional level plan, and the president the national level response. (Although the minister of the interior is nominally head of the national ORSEC Plan Command Unit, he dares not trigger the plan without presidential authorization.[49]) Despite the repeated flooding, Plan ORSEC has been triggered at any level only in three years: 2005, 2008, and 2009. The government also created an inter-ministerial National Commission for the Preventive (*prévisionnelle*) Management of Flooding (CONAGPI), in 2002, but little was heard of it thereafter.[50]

Not until July 2007—following prescriptions of the 2005 Hyogo Framework for Action, adopted in Kobe, Japan—did the country adopt a National Platform for Disaster Risk Reduction. This aimed to coordinate reduction of risks for floods and other climate-related disasters—not merely post hoc disaster response—by NGOs, state institutions, civil society, and the private sector. A UN Development Programme (UNDP)-funded project played an important role in launching the National Platform. All statutes for this strategy were in place by the end of the decade, and two climate-informed national contingency plans have been developed since 2007. The Civil Protection Department (CPD), in charge of coordinating the 2007 Platform, addresses disaster response and execution of the ORSEC Plan once it is triggered, although it has limited financial capacities and its personnel are not trained in climate disaster prevention.[51]

In reality, the national strategy and Platform exist only on paper. The Platform member institutions have met only once, and that was during the launch of the Platform in July 2007. In practice, when floods strike, all planned procedures are set aside. Nongovernmental stakeholders (such as Oxfam, Plan International, or the Red Cross) bypass the state institutions and go straight to communities to conduct their isolated but effective disaster-prevention initiatives.[52]

Some of the heaviest flooding came in August–September 2005. Two hundred thousand people (of the 1.4 million in the peri-urban region) were affected, leaving more than 20,000 houses collapsed or flooded, 30 victims dead, and the others temporarily lodged in tents, schools, and military barracks. Exemplifying the inadequate response, one site for displaced persons had only three portable toilets for 96 families, so garbage and fecal waste were put in pits dug into the soggy sand—"a lethal combination."[53] Rising political pressure from the annual flooding eventually compelled Wade to address the problem. In a landmark declaration on 28 August 2005, he spoke of radical measures needed to ensure that people do not live in savage slums anywhere any more. In their stead, modern cities would rise, and populations would be relocated to safer, dry grounds in a new modern city called Jaxaay (aka Diakhaye), which would overlook the old slums like an eagle (*jaxaay*). The government also began construction of water retention basins in the flooded neighborhoods of Dakar (although the rising water table filled them by the next year).[54] Wade ordered his prime minister to return from a visit to South Africa, declaring "that the Government will no longer be taking vacations

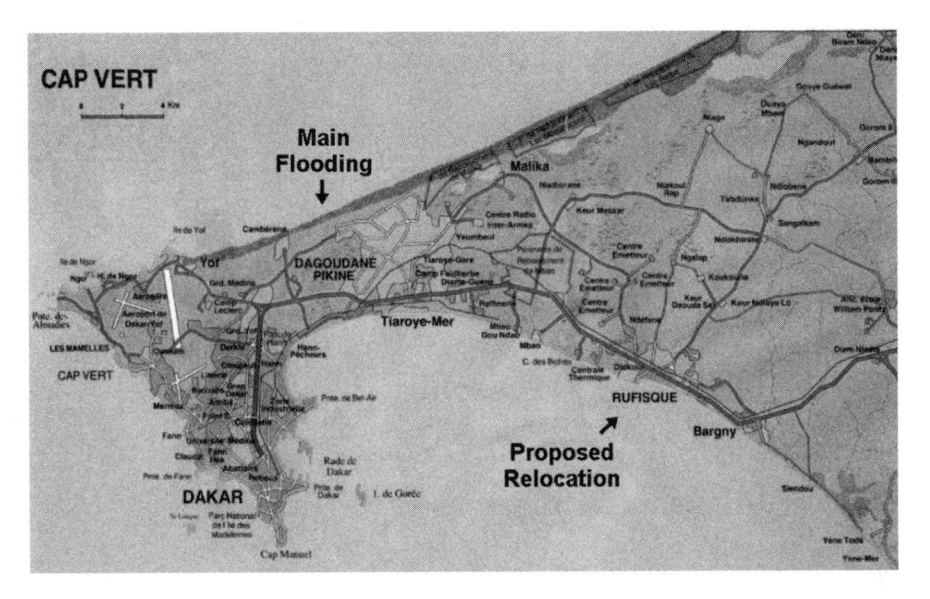

Figure 7.4. Flooding in Dakar suburbs. Source: Adapted by editor.

in August because that is the critical time of the rainy season, when populations need us most."[55]

The Jaxaay relocation plan was to allocate $75 million to move Dakar suburban flood victims into 3,000 new houses to be built farther south and away from the city, in Rufisque district. Of this cost, $65 million would come from using three-quarters of the decentralization budget for 2006, and the rest from the savings from postponing legislative elections to coincide with presidential elections in 2007. The Senegalese African Rally for the Defense of Human Rights (RADDHO) immediately attacked the Jaxaay proposal for using election funds to provide flood relief: "These two problems are completely distinct. They must not be combined."[56] A protest movie on "Plan Jaxaay!" was screened in 2007 to discredit the regime and mobilize domestic opposition to demand "financial accountability."

But these 2007 protests again remained peaceful, due to several factors. First, Senegal's constitutional design provides for the creation of ostensibly responsive agencies under centralized administration—provisions that were implemented and so gave the impression initially that the government was doing its job. Second, the affected population was vulnerable, off guard, and busy seeking dry ground, with little time or energy for taking to the streets, where it had much to lose. Third, in Senegal, peaceful demonstrations are a more typical reaction to government inefficiencies than violence, in a country that prides itself on never having had a military coup or takeover. Lastly, in 2007, the rains were not heavy, so the opposition halted efforts to seek solutions for local communities, even though disaster prevention activities had come to a standstill.

After this brief interlude of lower precipitation, 2008 was another year of heavy flooding. Plan ORSEC was actually triggered, and a law revising the yearly budget provided $15 million to fight the flooding.[57] Some 2,882 households were affected, including about 23,593 people; many stayed in their flooded homes, requiring emergency assistance. Some houses were completely inaccessible, and their inhabitants were contaminated by the use of tap water or by persistent contact with stagnant waters, sewage, solid waste, and worms. Waterborne diseases—including cholera and malaria—exploded.[58]

A popular outcry again rose, spilling over into the March 2009 local elections. Officials from Wade's party were swept away, undermining centralized control. The opposition political alliance, known as Benno Siggil Senegal (Together to Uplift Senegal), won a landslide victory. For the first time, local elected officials in Dakar were not of the same party as the national regime. In the reaction to the flooding, Dakar lost its mayor, and only one pro-Wade mayor was elected in the suburbs.[59] Dakar's new regional council president (the elected counterpart of the governor) launched a National Solidarity Fund initiative, to establish synergies between local communities, and to "implement prevention measures to replace ORSEC responses" with private contributions and partner support.[60]

The government was not slow in responding, albeit to the politics rather than to the flooding, taking action that effectively revised the constitutional design. Prime Minister Souleymane Ndiaye announced that management of floods would devolve to local collectivities, thus thrusting national responsibility onto the local authorities and shedding the national role—a new interpretation of articles 92 and 125 of the 1996 Code of Local Collectivities.[61] Spokesman Ndour Seck affirmed, however, that the central state would be available to help: "Back in the days when local officials were from the same camp as Government, then it was an easy negotiation. Today we'll have to see. But the government will stand available to support the local communities that request assistance." He insisted that this was not political retaliation against the newly elected officials of the Benno opposition.[62]

Confusion seized local populations in Dakar, still literally knee-deep in the preceding year's waters and only a few months ahead of another rainy season that they were dreading. The reaction of constitutional specialists in Senegal and the political opposition was furious. One opposition party, PIT, called for resistance against the executive's attempts to shed its flood management responsibilities. "Flood management has always been the responsibility of the state. . . . Why suddenly change? And why, above all, right after defeats in local elections?"[63] Likewise, former minister Abdoulaye Mattar Diop criticized the central government's dereliction of duty:

> We don't need a dictionary to fathom that flood management is a responsibility of the state. The 1996 decentralization laws are very clear. . . . Furthermore by tradition, the government has addressed floods. . . . When local collectivities were in the hands of the liberal regime, this issue of decentralized flood management responsibilities was never raised.[64]

Just before the beginning of the rainy season, a community-based organization, ADDAD, marched to demand that the state take action, yelling: "We are not frogs! . . . We demand water evacuation equipment and water pumps." The minister of decentralization and local collectivities, Aliou Sow, reassured them the state would be by their side, but he later returned to corroborate the prime minister's announcement that flood management was now a local responsibility.[65] After permitting the polemics for a month, Wade announced during the weekly council of ministers meeting that he "instructed the prime minister to support the action of local collectivities in the capital in favor of the populations."[66]

But the flooding came again in 2009, inflicting substantial damages. The forecast had been for "rainfall less abundant than last year."[67] So the region was unprepared when, at the end of August, severe floods hit Dakar itself, inflicting seven deaths by drowning. The floods directly affected some 360,000 people in the peri-urban areas of Dakar, and 125,000 in the rest of the country,[68] at an estimated cost of $103 million.[69]

Plan ORSEC was triggered at the end of August 2009, and $30 million was disbursed. For the first time, meaningful long-term actions and not just showpiece construction works were proposed. A study was launched by the Direction de la Protection Civile to map out the hydrographic network of the 52 neighborhoods of the Dakar suburbs. The goal was to reinstate natural drainage by digging canals to link the five former natural lakes and to pump water from the largest lake (Wouye) to the ocean. Yet feelings of neglect rose among flood victims in Dakar's peri-urban region. The state administration was invisible in the field, despite the sums people heard were disbursed. Affected residents were convinced the perceived neglect was in retribution for having voted for the opposition.[70] Rumors of corruption and fraud involving ORSEC funds were rife.[71] The prime minister was advised to cancel his sympathy visit to these suburbs for risk of being welcomed by stoning and protests.[72]

At the beginning of 2010, Wade belatedly announced preventive measures. In the council of ministers, he declared that flood zones posed a real danger for populations who had chosen to erect houses there and announced a draft law that would determine—after the fact—areas that would not be authorized for construction of houses.[73] He instructed his government in March to make the fight against floods a national priority. The following month the National Committee for the Fight against Floods and Slums met in the Saly seaside resort to elaborate a program for the definitive eradication of floods. The interministerial flooding commission, CONAGPI, met in May and set aside $1.25 million toward the new initiative's total estimated cost of $225 million.[74] The media began to focus on the need for definitive "eradication" of floods in the Dakar region,[75] blaming in part the poor urban planning to date. The state finally was realizing that floods could endanger its regime.[76]

In mid-August 2010, massive rains hit Dakar and its suburbs. "Dakar under siege!" headlined *Sud Quotidien*.[77] The rains even flooded "Karim's tunnel," built by Wade's son for the 2008 Organization of the Islamic Conference summit meeting in Dakar, at a cost of $30 million. About 3,000 families were displaced.[78] Four months after the end of the rainy season, the population of Dakar's suburbs still was at risk.[79] Pumping into retention basins was halted, because they were filled, and the water table continued to rise, causing septic pits and defecation pots to leak into houses, again bringing cholera.[80]

As this chronology shows, the Senegalese government's response to flood crises has been inefficient, disorganized, and delayed. There were few preventive measures, and instead a series of reactions to flood shocks, from 1995 to 2010. Political maneuvering against the opposition seems to have provided the main motivation for the government response, which has focused more on public relations than on effective action. The detailed narrative of the 2000–2010 decade has been elaborated to illustrate this routinized pattern of shock and inadequate response. By 2011, annual protests against the flooding merged into mounting demonstrations against the Wade regime itself and its attempts to prolong the president's mandate and bring his son into power.[81]

In closing the analysis of this shock, it is useful to note one particular incident during the floods of 2009 that typifies the drawbacks of Senegal's hypercentralized constitutional design. Wade was absent on annual vacation in Switzerland in August, which as noted is the height of the flood season. Minister of Interior Becaye Diop remained in Senegal, but did not dare trigger the ORSEC Plan in Wade's absence. "You want me to get fired?" he retorted to one request to make the decision.[82] Nor could he even contact the president immediately, because only Wade's chief of staff was permitted to call him in Switzerland. When the president returned, the Plan was activated, but too late. Such an episode, though anecdotal, demonstrates how the extent of centralization around one person undermines the efficient functioning of Senegal's institutions and thereby hinders the state's ability to buffer society from shocks.

Flooding Outcomes

The government of Senegal has managed flooding shocks in an ad hoc, ex post fashion, addressing crises only when political pressure explodes, with weak foresight ahead and poor implementation afterward. It is a system of inattention followed by crisis management, even for problems that have become regular events and are exacerbated by such routine inattention.[83] Senegal's constitutional design lacks the organizations and practices to routinize prevention and resolution of recurrent problems. Instead, at times of crisis, the state adopts a series of ad hoc measures that are difficult to implement and unlikely to survive after the immediate pressure of the crisis alleviates.

Ostensibly, Senegal has a constitutional design to enable the state to buffer shocks. The central government has supplied itself with institutions—response and relief plans—to meet its obligations to avert crises. A democratic, multiparty system is supposed to bring public demands to the government's attention prior to the outbreak of disasters. But the design has failed in implementation. This is largely because its operation is tied to the centralized political structure of the state and depends on a button-push by the head of state alone. When the state failed repeatedly to respond adequately to the flooding shock, the result was a popular challenge to the ruling political party.

In turn, the government's response was twofold: punish the opposition voters (despite claiming not to) and devolve responsibility from the central government to the local (opposition) level. The government reacted to protect its reputation by scapegoating, and thus enhanced its reputation for irresponsibility.

Such an inadequate response to the flooding shock reflects several structural shortcomings in Senegal's constitutional design. Perhaps most obviously, the mere existence of institutions does not guarantee that they will take timely action of prevention or warning. Long-term planning needs to be, but is not, part of the country's political ethos or state design. Fundamentally, Senegal's hypercentralized constitutional design lacks an institutionalized, upward channel for bringing needs from demand-bearing groups to the attention of the government before or even during a crisis. Only after the population took their grievances to the streets and the polls was the government obliged to act. The government's defeat in the 2009 elections showed the power of the people to reclaim their destiny when the government was unresponsive to their needs. But when the political crisis passed, so did the urgency of the government's response. Civil society in Senegal is rich and active, but it remains unable routinely to compel government response.

Shock Treatment

The common pattern in the handling of the two shocks examined in this chapter was initial delay and then, when pressure built to a sharp climax, government proposal of a satisficing measure that took the edge off the pressure—but ultimately was not implemented. This pattern was unpreparedness and reaction, rather than preparedness and proactivity. In both cases, the government's eventual response after prolonged inattention was to stop at the level of conflict management, which carries with it the promise of conflict resolution but removes the pressure for it. When that promise remained unfulfilled, the problems festered, leaving the society potentially even more vulnerable to the next shock. Instead of taking advantage of the momentary popular welcome of the government's initial conflict management responses, the government lost interest and attention, thereby exacerbating resentment.

The delayed and ultimately inadequate nature of the government's responses was not due to a lack of state resources, because at times the state did respond appropriately. Rather, it was a matter of constitutional design, and how that design was implemented in policy. This led to government failures not only to understand conditions and consequences ahead of time, but even to implement the government's own proposed solutions. It need not have been so.

Senegal is only fifty years old. Despite that youth, it is a regional leader in elections that are usually free and fair, in multiparty competition, in scheduled and nonviolent transfers of power, and in free press and judiciary. It has benefited from an established notion of itself and its state, based on an enduring constitutional design. That is actually an advantage over many other young states, especially in Africa, that have few or inconsistent notions of their constitutional nature and institutional structure. But this advantage also means that sudden, unforeseen events—or even foreseeable events that outrun established ways—are shocks that can overwhelm the state's buffering capacity. Despite repeated bouts of such turmoil, Senegal's constitutional design has not been adjusted, and the government instead has relied on inefficient but established routines to maintain stability.

This has been the story of three presidents—Senghor, Diouf, and Wade. They were not of the same temperament by any means, but they all fit into and perpetuated the same constitutional design. Senegal is now in the regime of a fourth—Macky Sall—who is not of the same temperament either. History will tell whether he can change the system and its results.

The next step in sociopolitical growth is to develop some flexibility, so that new problems—or accumulated old problems—can be handled effectively within a revised constitutional design and do not overwhelm the state. That will require a more responsive democracy and better functioning institutions. As one environmental analyst, Madeleine Diouf Sarr, has concluded: "That means an adjustment of behaviors, of means of subsistence, of infrastructure, of laws and policies, and of institutions." [84] Ultimately, what is needed is better governance in the form of sustained flexibility, so that the state can be more attentive and responsive to large challenges—that is, shocks.

CHAPTER 8

Zimbabwe: The Unintended Consequences of Authoritarian Institutions

Andrew Reynolds

This chapter focuses on two dimensions of the evolution of the Zimbabwean state: constitutional design and the effect such political institutions have had on inter-ethnic relations. At times the institutional set-up of the state has lessened the polarization among communal groups, while at other moments constitutional changes have, by design, exacerbated social divisions. This analysis focuses on shocks to the body politic, the mediating role of constitutional design, and the resulting consequences for Zimbabwe's populace, especially regarding welfare and ethnic divides. In this study, I examine three main shocks and their consequences: (1) in the early 1980s, a breakdown between Shona and Ndebele political alliances characterized by increasing Ndebele paramilitary mobilization against the state, which provoked the Gukurahundi massacres in the Matabeleland region; (2) in 2000, the shocking defeat of the government's constitutional referendum, which sparked the Third Chimurenga land occupations and seizures, white flight, and breakdown of law and order; and (3) the 2008 electoral victory by the opposition Movement for Democratic Change (MDC), which led to a violent aftermath (Operation Ngatipedzenavo) that reversed the democratic will. These moments were situated in a changing constitutional landscape in which power has moved from being illegitimately centralized (under the colonial/settler state), to dispersed and democratized (in the early days of Zimbabwe), to again illegitimately re-centralized (with gathering force over the last decade).

Zimbabwe is unusual in that the majority of shocks visited on the country have not been spurred by natural disasters, global economic downturns, or foreign interventions. Rather, the shocks have been caused by the state itself, as the result of its persistent efforts to eliminate dissent. The country's evolving constitutional design has enabled the regime to survive each shock, but only by further constraining political participation, including through violence, thereby fostering the next shock. Thus, constitutional design has not only mediated shocks, but in some cases has helped trigger them.

Despite this sad record, there may be an unexpected and unintended "silver lining." The most remarkable characteristic of Zimbabwe today is that, after three decades of rule, Robert Gabriel Mugabe—through extremely violent, psychological, and at times pathological repression of all foes, regardless of race or ideology—has created the closest approximation that Africa has seen to a truly nonracial nation. His equal opportunity perpetration of state violence has forged a nation in reply. Black and white, Shona and Ndebele, now march hand in hand, not as a multi-ethnic rainbow nation but rather as Africans whose common suffering has rendered their divergent ancestry irrelevant. In essence, Mugabe has brought to life Robert Sobukwe's dream of a nonracial Pan-African. There is a danger in romanticizing such inter-ethnic and inter-racial alliances during times of stress, only to see them crumble when the threat is gone. Indeed, ethnic and racial divisions still characterize much of the Zimbabwean narrative. But in Zimbabwe the fire of state repression has, in deep and transforming ways, molded a new sociopolitical reality.

A Moving Constitutional Target

The growth of authoritarianism in Zimbabwe has been characterized by constitutional and institutional reforms that have made the government ever more majoritarian, centralized, exclusionary, and detached from the populace. As President Mugabe's paranoia and intolerance of dissent has grown, he has drawn power more tightly around himself, and his office, through both a de jure redesign of the institutions of governance and a de facto manipulation of how even supposedly "democratic" institutions—especially elections, the legislature, and the judiciary—function in practice.

At a de jure level, Zimbabwe's constitution has traveled virtually full circle over the last forty years, from an exclusionary, settler, authoritarian state—which disenfranchised the majority of the population—to an elite-driven, authoritarian state that allows the veneer of democracy but pursues disenfranchisement through extrajudicial means. The governments of both Southern Rhodesia (henceforth "Rhodesia") of the 1970s and subsequently Zimbabwe, controlled since independence by the Zimbabwean African National Union (ZANU), have been characterized by state violence and repression, cronyism, and contempt for human rights.

The country's evolving constitutional landscape can be separated into four relatively distinct eras: (1) the Rhodesian settler state before Zimbabwean independence in 1980; (2) the Lancaster House transition constitution that remained largely in force from 1980 to 1985; (3) the gathering majoritarian concentration of power from 1985 to 2008; and (4) the "power-sharing" executive in place after the disputed elections of 2008. (A fifth era, starting from Mugabe's overwhelming electoral victory in summer 2013 that precluded the need for power-sharing, is too recent for empirical analysis.)

Before the Lancaster House agreement that created Zimbabwe, Rhodesia was a race-based oligarchy in which 50 of the 66 seats (76 percent) in parliament were reserved for the small white and Asian minority, comprising less than 5 percent of the population. While Ian Smith's white-led government cut the strings to mother Britain's apron in 1965, the Rhodesians held tight to a Westminster majoritarian form of government. The executive was parliamentary, centralized, and exclusionary—based on winner-take-all, first-past-the-post (FPTP) elections and weak regional and local government. Only a small proportion of all the people were recognized as valid citizens. The majoritarian system suited the tone of the exclusionary settler state but also served the function of stifling any opposition parties within the white and Asian communities.

The Lancaster House agreement, which came into force with the first nonracial elections of 1980, arguably had deep flaws. Not least, it precluded space for rapid socioeconomic transformation and land redistribution by perpetuating existing minority landownership in the absence of funds for compensation. But the agreement did offer some hope for democratic transformation, based on a much more inclusive constitutional design. The executive remained parliamentary, but elections were altered to proportional representation with a common roll—that is, no separate ethnic or racial constituencies—to elect 80 MPs in ten districts, using a 10 percent threshold for representation. Another 20 seats were reserved for whites and Asians, elected by FPTP.

In those first democratic elections, four parties won seats. Mugabe's ZANU, dominated by the majority Shona ethnic group (about 80 percent of the population), took the majority of the PR seats (57 of 80) with 1.7 million votes. By contrast, Smith's Rhodesian Front (RF) won all 20 of the reserved white/Asian seats with a mere 14,000 votes. Joshua Nkomo's Zimbabwe African People's Union (ZAPU), dominated by the minority black Ndebele ethnic group (about 10 percent of the population), won 20 seats with 600,000 votes. Meanwhile, Abel Muzorewa's African National Council (ANC) won just three seats with 200,000 votes. The parliament was bicameral, including a weak senate with a membership based on ethnic and racial quotas. Constitutional amendments required a two-thirds majority.

In the mid-1980s, Mugabe's suppression of dissent included constitutional reforms. In 1985, for example, the electoral system reverted from PR to FPTP. In 1987, the white/Asian seats were eliminated. By 1990 the Senate had been abolished to enlarge the lower house.

But perhaps most significant was the Unity Accord of 1987, which absorbed Nkomo's ZAPU into ZANU and thereby facilitated Mugabe's election to the newly powerful position of president. As Godwin notes, the "switch from a British-style prime ministership to an executive presidency sealed Mugabe's dictatorial metamorphosis."[1] Elections in Zimbabwe in 1990 and 1995 were models of a one-party state. ZANU won 117 of 120 seats in both elections, with only a splinter Shona-Ndau party and a couple of independents able to break Mugabe's monopoly on the National Assembly.

As the space for opposition in parliament became increasingly curtailed and constrained, labor unions, civil society, and religious organizations stepped into the vacuum. These groups coalesced around union organizer Morgan Tsvangirai and his Movement for Democratic Change (MDC) for the elections of 2000. In its first time at bat, the MDC came within 1.6 percent of ZANU's national vote, winning 57 parliamentary seats, compared to 62 for Mugabe's party. However, Mugabe was able to appoint another 20 MPs and 10 tribal chiefs, ensuring a comfortable majority in the House. In 2002's deeply rigged presidential elections, Mugabe won by 56 to 42 percent over Tsvangirai. The 2005 parliamentary elections were characterized by massive fraud—before, during, and after polling—as the MDC fell to 41 seats and ZANU increased to 78. In the aftermath, Mugabe sought to manipulate the constitutional design once more by expanding the house of assembly from 150 to 210 members. He also reestablished a relatively weak senate, comprising

93 seats, only 60 directly elected (six from each province). This enabled Mugabe to control both houses, based on ZANU's electoral dominance and his authority to fill many of the seats with appointments.

The violent and destabilizing 2008 presidential elections are described in more detail below, but in the legislative elections preceding them the MDC was finally able to end Mugabe's majority control. The opposition party won 100 seats in the House of Assembly, against 99 for ZANU and 10 for an offshoot of the MDC led by Arthur Mutambara. In the chaos that followed the subsequent presidential election, a power-sharing deal was brokered between Mugabe and Tsvangirai, leaving the former as president and the latter as prime minister. Of the 31 cabinet ministers, 15 were appointed by ZANU, 13 by MDC, and 3 by Mutambara's MDC faction. The president and prime minister were mandated to work hand-in-hand to salvage the state, but during the following five years power-sharing was a façade. Mugabe and ZANU still ruled the roost, and Zimbabwe returned to a type of authoritarian state not wholly dissimilar from Rhodesia of more than three decades earlier.

Underlying Demography

Ethnic fragmentation and segmentation have been triggers of conflict throughout sub-Saharan Africa, but Zimbabwe is a somewhat idiosyncratic case. The country has been characterized by shifting political fault lines and ethnic alliances that initially were reinforced by class, elite power, and urban-rural cleavages. What is most interesting about Zimbabwe is that the patchwork of alliances and animosities has changed dramatically over time, often in concert with the differing constitutional eras described above. In essence, constitutional design—by affecting how the state wields power—has played a large role in determining the extent and nature of inter-ethnic conflict.

When analyzing the trajectory of ethnic conflict in any country, it is common to focus on violence and the degree to which party politics are defined ethnically. The narrative of Rhodesia and Zimbabwe has been framed by race—black versus white, indigenous versus interloper—but the real story is far more complex. *Intra*-communal divisions have been key in defining political competition. Zimbabwe is not merely black and white, but also Asian. Its main languages have been—and continue to be—English, Shona, and Ndebele. But deeper layers exist: in addition to whites who speak English and

Afrikaans, there are various Shona subgroups—Karanga, Zezuru, Manyika, Korekore, Rozvi, Ndau—and the ethnicities of Ndebele, Kalanga, Tonga, Venda, and Shangaan. But Terence Ranger argues persuasively that while modern intra-Shona divisions are politically salient, and at times mold political behavior, they are at best weakly rooted in demography or anthropology. In reality, they are colonial and postcolonial constructions used to explain (and sometimes promote) division.[2]

In precolonial times, Shona civilizations dominated much of the region. But in the early nineteenth century, an offshoot of the Zulu tribe of South Africa, the Ndebele, was driven northward by Afrikaners and came into conflict with the Shona in what is modern-day Zimbabwe. Thus, a Shona-Ndebele cleavage has long been present in the region. The influx of Europeans in the nineteenth century further complicated matters, as there was massive conflict during colonialism between European settlers and indigenous Africans. To some degree, colonialism forged common cause among the various indigenous groups, but not entirely. Until the early 1960s, opposition to the Rhodesian government was led by ZAPU, dominated by ethnic Ndebele and led by Nkomo. But in 1963, Mugabe and other leading Shona broke away to form ZANU. Each militia was deeply mistrustful of the other's intentions—a distrust that carried over into the electoral sphere after independence. The 1980 and 1985 general elections were largely ethnic censuses: ZANU's vote was Shona, ZAPU was Ndebele, and the Rhodesian Front was white. There was virtually no crossover vote. Even after the merger of ZANU and ZAPU into the catch-all ZANU-PF party (hereafter abbreviated as ZANU) in 1987, ethnic tensions persisted. In the 1990s, Joshua Malinga, mayor of Bulawayo, warned that there would be bloody ethnic conflict similar to what had occurred in Rwanda in 1994 "if discrimination against the Ndebele did not cease."[3] Despite this tension, in 1990 and 1995 the new ZANU received virtually all the black votes, including both Shona and Ndebele, with only the tiny minority Ndau ethnic group supporting the breakaway ZANU-Sithole party. Whites no longer played a significant role in the electoral sphere.

Prior to the 1990s, however, white settlers and then white Zimbabweans were a significant part of the political landscape, regardless of their fluctuating and relatively small proportion of the population. In 1891, there were around 1,500 Europeans in the Rhodesian territory, but they quickly monopolized resources and governance. As their numbers grew to 75,000 in 1945 and doubled over the next decade to 150,000, they had a lock on every aspect of the state. At its peak in the 1960s, Rhodesia's white population reached 270,000, still only 5 percent of the country's total population. The advent of black majority rule in 1980 led to massive white flight. In the ten-year period from 1980 to 1990, approximately two-thirds of the white population left Zimbabwe. But much land stayed in white hands, and Mugabe saw it as useful to maintain the whites as scapegoats in his demagoguery. By the mid-1990s, around 70,000 white people remained in Zimbabwe. In 2002, the census recorded just 46,743 whites, of whom more than 10,000 were elderly and fewer than 9,000 were under age fifteen. By 2013, the number of whites has probably dropped below 20,000 (less than 0.2 percent), but their political importance has reemerged with the growth of the multi-racial MDC.

Shocking Moments

This chapter explores the three greatest shocks to confront Zimbabwe so far during its post-independence history. In each case, the Mugabe regime's reaction was influenced heavily by the country's exclusionary constitutional design, prompting violent outcomes (see Table 8.1). First, when facing nascent intra-black ethnic tensions between the majority Shona and minority Ndebele in 1980, Mugabe responded by repressing ZAPU and former Rhodesian officials, escalating to the Gukurahundi massacres by 1983. Second, after the failure of Mugabe's constitutional referendum in 2000, his regime launched land occupations and seizures, resulting in white flight and the breakdown of law and order. Third, following the MDC nominal election "victory" of 2008, Mugabe again resorted to repression, effectively reversing the electoral outcome. In the latter two instances, the shock arose from a dispute over political institutions, so the analysis below must contend with the challenging

Table 8.1. Three Shocks and Outcomes

Era	Shock	Outcome
1980s	Shona-Ndebele tensions	Gukurahundi massacres
2000s	Failed constitutional referendum	Seizure of white-owned farms
2008	MDC electoral victory	Repression and reversal of electoral outcome

questions of whether and how a country's constitutional design can mediate a conflict about constitutional design itself.

Gukurahundi: The Matabeleland Massacres of the 1980s

"Robert Mugabe's government in Zimbabwe has launched a new campaign of extraordinary brutality in Matabeleland," read the first line of the 8 April 1984 article in the *Sunday Times*, breaking news to the world of mass atrocities occurring in Zimbabwe. Peter Godwin, and later other journalists, entered the restricted area and conducted interviews undercover, collecting haunting first-hand narratives from individuals who survived the nightmare. They described not merely forced participation in rallies for the ZANU party, but beatings, torching of entire villages, and mass murders. They also reported many detailed accounts of individuals being raped or tortured at the hands of the infamous Fifth Brigade of Zimbabwe's military.

The background structural precursors of ethnic and regional tension between the Shona and Ndebele had been in place for centuries. The competition between Mugabe and Nkomo—and between ZANU and ZAPU, and thus between Shona and Ndebele—had been escalating since the elections of 1980. Sabelo Ndlovu-Gatsheni notes that the very name *Zimbabwe*, seized on by some nationalists during the struggle, was fraught with ethnic exclusion. "Great Zimbabwe," he observes, was a site and civilization associated with the Karanga-Shona, while the Ndebele preferred the postcolonial state to be named Matopos. After the Shona-ZANU breakaway from ZAPU in 1963, the liberation struggle and ultimately independence became "a product of deeply tribalized nationalism."[4] Eldred Masunungure notes that while Zimbabwe as a state came into being in 1980, Zimbabwe as a nation did not.[5] ZANU celebrated its triumph in the 1980 elections "not only as a victory of a liberation movement over settler colonialism but also as a victory of Shona political elite over Ndebele political elites."[6]

While the background causes of Mugabe's purge of the Ndebele are relatively transparent, the actual trigger for the Gukurahundi massacres is murkier. It is unclear to what extent former Ndebele officers from ZAPU (and white "Rhodesians") were actually mobilizing by 1983 to challenge the ZANU-dominated government, or whether Mugabe exaggerated this ostensible insurrection. The seeds lay in the troubled integration into the Zimbabwean National Army (ZNA) of three former armed factions: the Zimbabwe

African National Liberation Army (ZANLA, the armed wing of ZANU), the Zimbabwe People's Revolutionary Army (ZIPRA, the armed wing of ZAPU), and the Rhodesian Front forces. Shona combatants of ZANLA were favored in the new army, while the Ndebele leadership of ZIPRA was sidelined. Despite their role in the liberation struggle, those from Matabeleland were excluded from the highest levels of government and military leadership. During the integration, clashes at assembly points broke out between ZANLA and ZIPRA fighters. ZANU leaders—including Enos Nkala, Edgar Tekere, and Mugabe himself—then poured oil on the smoldering flames.

Violence briefly broke out in the wake of Nkala's incendiary anti-Ndebele speech in Bulawayo in November 1980, and then resurged with greater loss of life the following February. A number of ZIPRA soldiers defected from the ZNA and took up arms against what they perceived to be an exclusionary Shona-led state, perhaps in the belief that they could win a battle of secession. The ZANU government accused ZIPRA (and by association ZAPU and Nkomo) of stockpiling weapons in secret caches, and this gave Mugabe an excuse to fire Nkomo from the cabinet. ZIPRA leaders were accused of planning a coup d'état, prompting 4,000 former ZIPRA members to desert the ZNA.[7] Mugabe's campaign of repression was given a fillip when former ZIPRA guerrillas attacked the prime minister's house with gunfire and reportedly launched random attacks in Matabeleland.[8] In addition, 13 military planes were destroyed by South African agents, supposedly aided by ex-ZIPRA forces within Zimbabwe.[9] Although a treason trial in 1982 failed to convict former ZIPRA and RF officers, it drove more ZIPRA soldiers underground and heightened the sense of trepidation.

As the newly independent Zimbabwe faced this shock of nascent interethnic violence, constitutional design played a key mediating role in determining the state's response and the ultimate outcome. If the state's political institutions had been set up to accommodate minorities—notably, the Ndebele ethnic group and ZAPU party—Mugabe would have had greater incentive and means to de-escalate the conflict and resolve it peacefully. But in light of the state's exclusionary and centralized constitutional design, Mugabe preferred and was able instead to resort to brute force.

Mugabe early on had laid the groundwork for such action against domestic enemies. Soon after ascending to prime minister in 1980, he signed an agreement with the president of North Korea to train the Zimbabwean army's Fifth Brigade. This elite subgroup of the security forces was tasked with targeting dissidents: Ndebele, white, and some Shona. The brigade was col-

Figure 8.1. Ethnic regions of Zimbabwe. Source: Wikimedia Commons.

loquially known as Gukurahundi, meaning in Shona "the early rain that washes away the chaff before the spring rains." Aptly named, Gukurahundi's havoc in Matabeleland was only the beginning of Mugabe's decades-long cleansing of Zimbabwe's political opposition. In July 1982, Mugabe reinstated a Rhodesian law, the Indemnity and Compensation Bill, which gave immunity from prosecution to government agents so long as their actions fell under the broad and vague category of preserving the state's security. This gave the Fifth Brigade's future work a stamp of approval before it even began. A subsequent amnesty was also granted in 1988 for actions taken in the name of "unity."

Operationally, the Fifth Brigade was unique in the way it reported directly to the prime minister, not to the military top brass. Indeed, its radio and other equipment operated independently from other military factions.[10] The brutality of the Fifth Brigade was manifested in eerie, systematic patterns that— within weeks of its initial deployment in January of 1983—had destroyed hundreds of homes, inflicted beatings on thousands, and murdered more than 2,000.[11] The Fifth Brigade often arrived at a destination with lists of individuals to arrest, usually ZAPU officials and men of military age.[12] These pre-prepared lists reflected an organized operation rather than a few soldiers gone off the deep end, as did the brigade's actions such as marching thousands of individuals to school yards for forced ZANU rallies in various districts. At these rallies, the Ndebele-speaking people of Matabeleland were forced to sing Shona-language songs supporting the ZANU party—and to shout pro-ZANU and even pro-Fifth Brigade slogans—while many of them were also beaten with sticks. The rallies concluded with executions of individuals, often at random.[13]

Many Ndebele targets were forced to dig their own graves before being executed and buried in them, while others were made to dig the graves of family members or friends after witnessing their execution. Many Ndebele disappeared, and it is still unknown how they met their demise. While the Fifth Brigade was notorious for its operation in the region, the Central Intelligence Organisation (CIO) also played a role in this abuse, and later ZANU's Youth Brigade joined the fray.[14] A strict curfew was imposed in Matabeleland, giving the Fifth Brigade free rein to shoot anyone who moved more than 50 yards from home during the long curfew hours from six at night to six in the morning. The curfew was lifted in April 1983 only to be reinstated with new food restrictions in 1984. The latter were an especially blunt instrument of counter-insurgency. In its attempt to "starve dissidents"—who numbered only about 200—the Fifth Brigade closed all stores and would not permit relief for some 40,000 Matebeleland civilians, despite the ongoing three-year drought.[15] The year 1984 also ushered in yet another system of abuse. The Fifth Brigade began rounding up civilians and torturing them in bases rather than in public, making it more difficult to count the number of victims as truckloads of bodies departed the camps at night.[16]

The Gukurahundi killings were a state-sponsored reaction to political fragility, born from paranoia and a desire to remove potential sources of threat before they could position themselves to injure the ruling party and ethnic group. Ultimately, the Fifth Brigade slaughtered an estimated 20,000 individuals in Matabeleland from 1982 to 1987. The Gukurahundi instilled fear in a group of people not traditionally aligned with Mugabe's ZANU party through an ethnically-focused, partial extermination.

Constitutional design enabled Mugabe's actions because the Ndebele of Matabeleland were not represented in the central government and had no other power to protect their people in their own region, as there was no decentralized government to check the majoritarianism at the center. If the institutions of immediate post-independence Zimbabwe had empowered black minorities—as these institutions initially protected the white minority economically and politically—then the Gukurahundi massacres would have been less likely. Accommodations between Shona and Ndebele could have been made within the government, and Ndebele representatives could have been given more oversight of the actions of security forces. In 1987, after the bloodshed in Matabeleland, Joshua Nkomo and Robert Mugabe joined their parties together, and the targeted violence ceased. At the same time, to avoid conceding any real authority, Mugabe changed the Zimbabwean constitution to enable him to become the executive president soon after.

Gukurahundi leaves a legacy of fear and suspicion even to this day, on both sides. Matabeleland is far from healed, and no state apology or state investigation has ever taken place. Godwin suggests that Mugabe's continuing reticence to leave office is based in part on fear of being held accountable for these crimes, whether formally or informally:

> Even though the Matabeleland massacres were perpetrated 25 years ago, they still loom large to the people here—an unrequited tragedy that shattered their society, and festers at the heart of everything. Roy Bennett [a white opposition politician] reckons that what happened in Matabeleland remains Mugabe's biggest motive for holding on to power: he fears that if he leaves office he will become victim to what the Shona call *kudzorera pamavambo*—retributive justice, the real blood revenge, the kind that doesn't need the Hague to happen.[17]

Third Chimurenga: Land Seizures Starting in 2000

Rural areas have always been home to most of Zimbabwe's workers. Jacob Chikuhwa notes that in 1980, two-thirds of the labor force was involved in agriculture, although that sector comprised only 14 percent of GDP. In 1990, a similar 68 percent of the labor force was in agriculture, contributing 13 percent of the GDP. By 1998, 64 percent of the labor force still was in agriculture, which now represented 28 percent of GDP.[18] Not surprisingly, land reform and redistribution was an area of great concern after independence. But Mugabe's government spent nearly two decades avoiding the issue. Eventually, in 2000, land did become a focus of violence and instability. Ironically, this was due not to any economic crisis, such as a spike in food prices. Rather, it was because the ZANU government lost a national referendum in February that year—by a vote of 55 to 45 percent, despite its large parliamentary majority—on whether to pursue a new draft constitution in parliament. The proposed amendments would have empowered the government to acquire land compulsorily, without compensation, for Mugabe to redistribute to assuage the growing unpopularity he faced due to creeping economic and social breakdown. The shock of defeat at the ballot box—mediated again by Zimbabwe's constitutional design, which had become even more centralized after the 1990 expiration of accommodative guarantees to the white minority (see below)—prompted the state to unleash the paramilitary style War Veterans Association to occupy and "re-possess" white-owned farms.

The root of the problem, of course, was inequitable distribution of land. Zimbabwe had inherited from Rhodesia a racially divided system that gave land rights and the most productive territory to whites, while blacks were permitted to inhabit only the less arable, communal territory, where they had a right to use the land and the potential to buy some.[19] Even after the 1979 repeal of some of Rhodesia's former land laws, the distribution of land was grossly unequal. 6,700 white farmers—less than 1 percent of all farmers—owned 40 percent of the land, while another 80 percent of the population shared the communal lands, which comprised just 41 percent of the territory.[20]

The Lancaster House agreement constrained the Zimbabwean government's ability to appease land-hungry masses. The British-drafted constitution required Zimbabwe's government to pay compensation for any land that it acquired, and the UK offered to pay only 50 percent of this compensation.[21] Moreover, the government could not acquire land unless the owners were willing to sell or had abandoned it, because nationalization was strictly prohibited.[22] These provisions of the constitution, among others, were entrenched for ten years and then could be amended only by a two-thirds vote of parliament.[23] (Other constitutional amendments required approval by two-thirds of the Senate and at least 70 members of the House.)[24] Not surprisingly, after this ten-year waiting period, numerous amendments were tacked on to the constitution, including one in April 2000 that authorized the government to redistribute land.[25] However, due to international pressures from donors to slow the pace of land reform, and internal pressures to maintain farm production, redistribution of the land proceeded at a gradual pace that failed to appease many black Zimbabweans. The opposition MDC accused Mugabe's regime of corruption and incompetence for having resettled only 70,000 families by the year 2000, two decades after independence.[26] Starting in 2000, however, Mugabe turned the tables—using the issue of land reform to beat a populist drum and distract Zimbabweans from the declining economy. Indeed, he tarred any opponent who dared criticize this new method or rapid pace of reform as a colonial sympathizer.

The magnitude of the land-reform challenge was daunting, and droughts in the 1980s compounded the already complicated task. But there was also growing distrust among many Zimbabweans, who saw a small group of political elites capturing land for themselves. Even prior to 2000, tracts of land went to Mugabe's favorites rather than to the landless peasants who desperately needed them. This prompted some peasants to start invading farms that government insiders had settled, including in the late 1990s the Coburn Estate, which comprised some 35,000 acres and a work force of 300. Elite recipients of land would later include the deputy speaker of the parliament, an assistant commissioner of police, a director of the Ministry of Environment and Tourism, and other governmental officials.[27] A 2009 news report indicated that Mugabe even had 10,000 acres of his own that he had obtained through seizing land.[28] While elites taking land may not have been the most significant barrier to land reform, it contributed to a growing lack of trust in Mugabe's ability to rule Zimbabwe and address this problem, which no doubt contributed to the vote against his constitutional referendum in 2000.

The new constitution would have expanded Mugabe's powers, and he put the referendum on it before the public in February 2000. Legally, this was purely for consultative purposes, because the constitutional amendments required only a two-thirds majority in parliament, which ZANU already enjoyed. The real purpose of the referendum was political. Mugabe hoped the exercise would earn him greater public support in upcoming elections.[29] Aiming to attract rural votes, a last-minute addition to the referendum would have permitted the government to seize any land, while also requiring Britain to pay the entire compensation (which was unrealistic, because it grossly exceeded British financial commitments under the Lancaster House agreement).[30] Two days after the referendum was defeated, war "veterans" began occupying farms, although many of the occupiers were too young to have participated in the independence war that had ended two decades earlier.[31] The ostensible veterans publicly blamed whites for the failure of the referendum, which they attributed to opposition to land redistribution.[32] Chikuhwa concludes that the government then supported the land invasions to gain political support prior to upcoming parliamentary elections.[33] When ZANU subsequently garnered only 63 of 120 seats in the June 2000 election, the party dropped the push for constitutional reform, because it had lost the two-thirds parliamentary majority necessary for constitutional amendments.[34]

In March 2000, the Supreme Court ruled that the occupiers of the land had to leave by court order. But the police failed to evict them, and Mugabe began to refer to the white farmers who refused to give up their land as "enemies of the state."[35] If this threat wasn't enough, he clarified in mid-March: "Those who try to cause disunity among our people must watch out because death will befall them."[36] After twenty years of independence, Mugabe was reigniting black-white racial tensions to help him retain uncontested power. On 6 April 2000, Mugabe again sought to avoid paying compensation and instead to compel Britain to pay white farmers for any land Zimbabwe seized for redistribution. This time it was done through a constitutional amendment that parliament approved immediately before being dismissed later that month.[37] The absurdity was that Zimbabwe still had a 1992 law on the books, the Land Acquisition Act, which required government compensation for land takings. Thus, the victims of the land seizures could challenge the acquisitions in court within 30 days.[38] Failure to amend that law, despite passing the constitutional amendment, was seen by many as an indication of the government's incompetence and its prioritization of political showmanship over substantial reforms in the lead-up to the June elections.[39]

Less than 25 days before the elections, on 2 June 2000, a gazette published a list of 804 mostly white-owned farms to be acquired by the government.[40] Later that year, in November 2000, white farmers sought a ruling from the High Court that the new constitutional amendment was invalid.[41] The High Court did eventually find the takings under the new amendment to be unlawful, but Mugabe replied that he would not permit court orders to hinder his land reform process.[42] Indeed, the chief justice retired the following March, amid pressure from the government.[43] Land owners continued to file numerous suits against the government until 2006, when yet another constitutional amendment prohibited this avenue of relief.[44] Many had expected the land seizures to subside after the elections, but Mugabe encouraged war veterans to stay on the occupied farms until "the government comes with the law and the necessary mechanisms to deliver land to them."[45]

The invasion of farmland was accompanied by violence and threats of violence against land owners, including threats by the government itself. Jocelyn Alexander notes that land reform in 2000 was largely characterized by *jambanja*, or lawlessness.[46] Unlike occupations of land in the 1980s, these takings no longer were accompanied by discussion of democracy, unity, or reconciliation with white farmers. Rather, the rhetoric had been turned on its head, and Mugabe—now sporting military attire—transformed the land issue into an internal war against whites and political opponents of ZANU. At the start of the invasions, seven white farmers were killed. Black farm workers, particularly those working under white farmers on commercial lands, endured threats, violence, and forced "re-education."[47] Ever since the 1980s, ZANU often had scapegoated black farm workers for failed land reforms, labeling them mindless laborers for whites.[48] Now, those who refused to attend ZANU meetings to be re-educated were beaten in front of others.[49] By June 2000, according to the National Employment Council for the agricultural industry, "3,000 [black] farm workers had been displaced from their homes, 26 killed, 1,600 assaulted, and 11 raped."[50]

This partial suspension of the rule of law had a clear political agenda. The police stood idly by as ZANU supporters violently occupied land, but the authorities arrested and punished MDC-affiliated individuals for their alleged crimes. In 2002, Human Rights Watch reported an increase of beatings and torture by the police. The military and police were also suspected of assisting in the land takeovers, as witnesses described both groups assisting in the transport of looted items. Furthermore, the police did nothing—unless ordered specifically by ZANU—when occupiers remained on territory that was not initially listed in, or had been removed from, a gazette of land to be acquired.[51]

At the close of 2001, some 9 million hectares (22 million acres, equivalent to nearly 35,000 square miles) had been listed for seizure. "ZANU land acquisition committees" were tasked with doling out the land through a "Fast Track" program. In Matabeleland, the appointed governor announced that only ZANU members and veterans would receive land through the program. Debates over title to lands ensued as those already resettled on land contested its reallocation, and veterans fought among themselves for particular properties.[52] Elite takeover of land also continued. In 2003, for example, 1,000 settlers had to vacate a farm in Zvimba to allow the widow of Mugabe's nephew to move in. Near Masvingo City, police burned 1,000 homes on Windcrest Farm to forcibly evict the already resettled peasants, in order that a political crony could have a new home.[53]

Some battles over land have dragged on for years. In one instance, in 2000, a few dozen war veterans occupied the farm of Mike Campbell. Seven years later, he took his case to the Southern African Development Community Tribunal in Namibia, spurring 77 other white farmers to join the case. In November 2008, the tribunal condemned such seizures as racist theft and found that the land reform program was lawless. Shamelessly, Mugabe labeled the ruling "nonsense," even though he had signed a treaty establishing the tribunal.[54] Campbell was unable to attend the ruling because he and his wife both had been tortured for nine hours in June 2008, following Mugabe's controversial reelection.

The chaos that ensued with the land invasions made farming nearly impossible, thereby triggering a humanitarian crisis in which more than half the population needed food aid. The Fast Track program redistributed land quickly but was unable to provide the additional services and resources needed for productive farms, such as fertilizer. This had the additional effect of collapsing many schools, which often were connected to these farms. In short order, only 600 white commercial farmers remained of approximately 4,500 prior to the invasions. Many of the whites fled with their mobile assets to border countries, including Zambia, where they brought an estimated US$100 million.[55]

Zimbabwe's land reform and farm occupations demonstrate the devastating consequences when a state suspends the rule of law in order to assuage a militant constituency. In this case, the legacy was astronomical inflation, a deep crisis of poverty, homelessness, malnutrition, and burgeoning environmental degradation. Since 2001, Zimbabwe has had no access to IMF funds or World Bank loans, has been subject to U.S. sanctions, and has watched agricultural productivity plummet.[56] Many Zimbabweans, unable to make a living by farming, have resorted to other sources of sustenance, including poaching endangered species. A nongovernmental organization, Wildlife and Environment Zimbabwe, reported a loss of 362 black rhinos in one conservancy alone.[57] The director of the Zimbabwe Environmental Law Association cites land reform as the biggest contributor to deforestation, because there is no accompanying oversight to ensure that timber harvesting is sustainable.[58]

A key question is why, after twenty years of cooperation between a black majority government and the economically successful but tiny white minority, did the government break this arrangement and unleash chaos? Evidence suggests that the declining popularity of the ZANU government by 2000 compelled Mugabe to make a populist gesture to the impoverished and increasingly alienated black population.

Constitutional design, in this case the fragility of the accommodative political institutions in the Lancaster House agreement, was a key factor. After the expiration of the ten-year guaranteed entrenchment of these power-sharing provisions, they were too easy to rescind when Mugabe was confronted by the shock of the unexpected and unpredicted defeat of his constitutional referendum in 2000. At that point, Mugabe decided that he needed black votes more than white businessmen—and the constitutional design provided no constraint on this power grab, paving the way for the violent land invasions that triggered Zimbabwe's downward economic spiral.

Operation Ngatipedzenavo: Political Violence in the 2008 Elections

On 29 March 2008, Zimbabweans voted in presidential elections whose run-up had been tainted by corruption, violence, and manipulation. The Election Commission was packed with Mugabe stalwarts, the economy had deteriorated to make election logistics and access to the polls extremely difficult, and state violence against opposition candidates and activists was pervasive. However, votes in the first round still broke in favor of Mugabe's nemesis, Morgan Tsvangirai. Here was the shock—looming defeat for the long-term autocrat—that unleashed a third wave of crisis in Zimbabwe.

By 2008, Zimbabwe's inflation rate had skyrocketed, rendering its currency almost worthless and unusable. Less than a year after the elections, Zimbabwe would produce the world's first trillion-dollar note. Eighty percent of the population were below both the poverty and food datum lines, defined respectively as the minimum income required to survive in reasonable health and to buy sufficient food for survival. A combination of inflation, lack of international donors, and inability to maintain infrastructure meant that Zimbabwe experienced chronic shortages of fuel, electricity, and water.[59] Life expectancy was forty-nine in 2008, a sharp drop from sixty-one a mere two decades earlier.[60] In light of these rapidly declining living conditions, it would not have been surprising for the twenty-eight-year incumbent party to expect less than a landslide at the ballot box.

After votes were cast, MDC secretary-general Tendai Biti reported that a survey of one-third of the polling stations showed that Tsvangirai had captured 67 percent of the vote. But the final results were not officially announced until 2 May, some five weeks later. During this period, Biti reported to CNN that his party had used all legal avenues to press for the release of the election results.[61] Throughout the delay, Mugabe engineered a campaign of manipulation and fear to ensure that there would be a second-round, run-off election that he would win to sustain him in office. The campaign of violent intimidation was known as Operation Ngatipedzenavo ("Let us finish them off").

A leaked overview of the elections, by Zimbabwe's Central Intelligence Organisation (CIO), acknowledged that "President Mugabe will lose the election as the people . . . now have the confidence to come out and express their feelings without fear." However, it finished with a section titled "Covert Operations to Decompose the Opposition," which recommended "harassing MDC activists and driving MDC supporters out of ZANU-PF strongholds, and massive rigging by any means possible, e.g., manipulation of postal votes in ZANU-PFs favor and reduction of polling stations in MDC strongholds."[62] As early as mid-April 2008, there were emerging reports of torture camps set up throughout the country.[63] In May, the first-round result of the presidential election was reported to be 47.9 percent for the MDC's Tsvangirai and 43.2 percent for Mugabe, leaving the opposition candidate without a majority to take office and the prospect of a bloody run-off.

In April, witnesses had reported to Human Rights Watch that individuals were rounded up at night and taken to torture camps, and that many were interrogated for days about information regarding the MDC.[64] Additional accounts of beatings and torture were documented by Godwin, who interviewed individuals in hospitals seeking treatment for their wounds. In the end, Human Rights Watch estimated that the 2008 elections resulted in the "killing of up to 200 people, the beating and torture of 5,000 more, and the displacement of about 36,000 people," all with impunity.[65]

Despite Tsvangirai's continuing claims to have won a first-round majority, he decided to participate in the second round to be held on 27 June. But on 22 June, Tsvangirai announced that he was withdrawing from the run-off, describing it as a "violent sham" and saying that his supporters risked being killed if they voted for him. The second round of elections went ahead with Mugabe as the only actively participating candidate, although Tsvangirai's name remained on the ballot.

After the vote, a power-sharing agreement between the two presidential candidates was forged with the assistance of South African President Thabo Mbeki, and was finalized in September 2008. Despite domestic and international hopes, however, the implementation fell short of expectations. On the positive side, some of the worst aspects of economic and social collapse were alleviated—for example, in the realms of education and currency—but

ZANU's state-sponsored violence actually increased in anticipation of the next elections. By 2011, the unity accord had become essentially a dead letter, compelling Tsvangirai to declare that "the next election must produce a legitimate government so that we don't have the losers trying to negotiate their way back into power through some form of an arrangement or some form of a coalition like the government of national unity."[66]

As with the preceding two shocks, constitutional design also exacerbated the consequences of this third shock from the looming electoral defeat of the longtime incumbent. Rather than constraining or encouraging Mugabe to accept the electoral outcome, the state's extreme centralization of power enabled and motivated him to steal the election and then to violate the power-sharing agreement. An alternative constitutional design might have mitigated this negative outcome. For example, an independent and robust election commission could have delivered a fairer election. Another constitutional flaw was that the winner-take-all nature of the election system—at both executive and legislative levels—provided a strong disincentive for the ruling party to accept a loss. However, there is inevitably a limit on the ability of constitutional design to constrain powerful political interests. Mugabe's actions within the "power-sharing" government since 2008 show how—in Zimbabwe, at least—the agency of elites can overwhelm the nominal constraints of political institutions.

The Silver Lining?

The evidence that a new, nonracial Zimbabwe now exists in embryo emanates from the blurring of ethnic lines within opposition movements over the last twenty years. Through a brutal but equal opportunity disregard for humanity, Mugabe has bred a steely common purpose among black and white, Shona and Ndebele. His core support base has been reduced to a dwindling, compliant elite of business and security-force members and a residue of rural Shona voters who have been marginally insulated from some of the worst of the economic collapse. MDC treasurer Roy Bennett, who is white, is emblematic of the opposition's unity across skin color. Elected as MDC MP for his home constituency of Chimanimani, Bennett is a farmer who speaks chiNdau (Shona) like the local he is. After enduring harassment, prison, and beatings alongside his fellow MDC members, Bennett was nominated as deputy minister of agriculture in the 2008 Unity government, but he was forced to flee the country while on the way to his swearing in, after being tipped off that he was about to be arrested by Mugabe's henchmen. Bennett's story warrants telling in much greater detail, but as Godwin notes, "despite appearances, the Roy Bennett story is no longer about race, it has moved beyond that."[67] Godwin also quotes Tsvangirai in the midst of the presidential election of 2008: "In the last eight years there has been such anti-white rhetoric from Mugabe, but we Zimbabweans are non-racial now. It's unlike South Africa—here the racial barriers have been broken down. There is really no desire to settle old scores."[68]

The evidence of a new dawn of post-ethnic, post-racial politics is reinforced by the shifting landscape of competitive party politics in Zimbabwe. As noted, elections between 1980 and 1995 were effectively ethnic censuses, but by 2000 the fight had become between a ZANU that was overwhelmingly based on rural Shona votes and an MDC that was visibly inclusive of Shona, Ndebele, and whites in both its leadership and popular support. Arthur Mutambara's breakaway MDC in 2008 was more Ndebele than Shona, but it was significantly led by both black and white Zimbabweans. Civil society groups also are overwhelmingly multi-ethnic, multi-racial, and opposed to the state's policies and behavior.

The evolution of President Robert Mugabe's public pronouncements also reflects the shift from ethnic polarization to reconciliation—but in a mirror image. Upon first coming to power, he began with a surprisingly conciliatory tone. But over time, as the opposition integrated, he has become more and more of an ethnic and racial chauvinist. In 1980, Mugabe appealed to whites: "Stay with us, please remain in this country and constitute a nation based on national unity."[69] But by 2000 the rhetoric had changed dramatically: "Our party must continue to strike fear in the heart of the white man, our real enemy!" By 2008, he based his survival on tarring all of his political opposition as fronting for Britain's intervention in Zimbabwean affairs, saying: "I will never, never, never, never surrender. Zimbabwe is mine. I am a Zimbabwean. Zimbabwe for Zimbabweans. Zimbabwe never for the British. Britain for the British."[70]

Conclusion: Zimbabwe's Trajectory

Figure 8.2 illustrates the connections over time between constitutional design, ethnic divisions, democracy, and stability since the late 1970s in Zim-

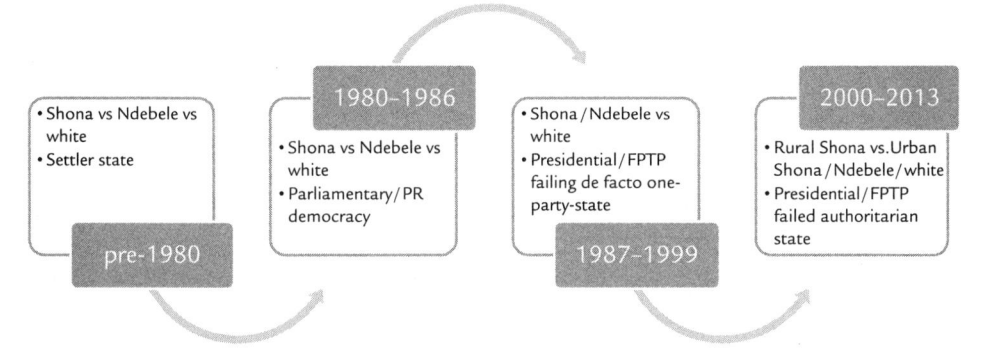

```
┌─────────────────────┐      ┌─ 1980-1986 ─┐      ┌─────────────────────┐      ┌─ 2000-2013 ─┐
│• Shona vs Ndebele vs│      │             │      │• Shona/Ndebele vs   │      │             │
│  white              │      │• Shona vs Ndebele vs│   white             │      │• Rural Shona vs.Urban│
│• Settler state      │      │  white      │      │• Presidential/FPTP  │      │  Shona/Ndebele/white│
│                     │      │• Parliamentary/PR│  │  failing de facto one-│    │• Presidential/FPTP  │
│                     │      │  democracy  │      │  party-state        │      │  failed authoritarian│
│                     │      │             │      │                     │      │  state              │
└──── pre-1980 ───────┘      └─────────────┘      └──── 1987-1999 ──────┘      └─────────────┘
```

Figure 8.2. Constitutional design, ethnic coalitions, and conflict over time.

babwe. The constitutional nature of the state has gone from extreme (settler) majoritarianism, to more inclusive accommodation, and then back to extreme majoritarianism, which was not effectively mitigated by the temporary power-sharing government after 2008. Patterns of ethnic conflict and alliances have tracked, and been affected by, these changing political institutions. During colonialism, majoritarianism was a framework that reflected the power dynamics and polarization between black and white. Upon independence, Zimbabwe's democracy demonstrated more inclusion, accommodation, and unity among the different language groups, and between whites and blacks. But that was quickly destroyed by Operation Gukurahundi.

Starting in the 1990s, increasing majoritarianism—including a presidential system, greater centralization, FPTP elections, and a loss of judicial independence—ironically contributed to the lessening of the ethnic dimension of Zimbabwean political conflict. Although ZANU has become a rump Shona party, primarily of rural voters, the opposition MDC—which in the mid-2000s had majority support—is the closest thing to a nonracial party in Africa. Elections before 2000 were basically ethnic censuses, but today the MDC's base includes Shona, Ndebele, white, and Asian. Crucially, civil society and religious groups are also multi-ethnic and multi-racial. Robert Mugabe's Zimbabwean state was able to unleash violent operations—Gukurahundi, the Third Chimurenga, and Ngatipedzenavo—on the population precisely because the constitutional design failed to provide sufficient political inclusion or institutional constraint. But in the wake of the government fostering such sociopolitical violence, the consequences are confounding, beyond central control, and still to be fully determined.

APPLYING THE LESSONS

CHAPTER 9

Africa's Domestic Institutions of Integration and Accommodation: A New Database

Eli Poupko

In contemporary conflict management scholarship, it has become generally accepted that institutions matter.[1] This principle implies that constitutional design—broadly defined as the overall institutional structure framing the political order—has significant effects on the extent and specific manifestations of social conflict. These effects of constitutional design are particularly relevant for the deeply divided societies of most African states. The predominant institutionalist approach assumes that constitutional design mediates a variety of historical and environmental sources of conflict, as well as sociological sources, such as demographic patterns of ethnic divisions.[2] Constitutional design is thus somewhat analogous to a semiconductor of social currents, capable of either amplifying or resisting the flows of shocks and stresses that make up the circuitry of conflict. Although there is general agreement on the importance of constitutional design as a mediating variable of conflict, there is wide-ranging debate on how particular institutions might serve to either magnify or pacify societal tensions. Consequently, scholars disagree about which institutions should work best for resolving conflict in general, or in any particular case.

Much of the literature on constitutional design for conflict management consists of either targeted case studies focused on one or a few countries, or broad deductive claims about how different institutional structures should mediate various types of conflict. This chapter aims to provide a base for wider empirical study of these dynamics across Africa by surveying and categorizing the constitutional design of all African countries from a conflict management perspective. In order to make these classifications, I construct an index that assesses the extent to which domestic political institutions promote *integration* or *accommodation* across three dimensions of constitutional design. The roots and meaning of the integration versus accommodation typology are explored in the next section, which provides the theoretical background and analytical framework. The subsequent section explains the methodology used to operationalize the constitutional design index on a five-point scale. The final section provides a brief analysis of the findings and makes suggestions for further research. Summary explanations for the coding of constitutional design in each country are provided in Appendix 1. This chapter does not aim to resolve the substantive debates in the literature regarding the connection between constitutional design and conflict management. But the new database does provide a basis for future research into these questions.

Theoretical and Analytical Framework

Building on literatures that examine ethnicity, nation-building, and state-building,[3] the more specific debate about constitutional design for conflict management in Africa may be traced back to competing proposals for the South African transition from the Apartheid regime to democracy. In his 1985 work, *Power-Sharing in South Africa*, Arend Lijphart warned against imposing democratic institutions based on principles of majority rule in a deeply divided society such as South Africa. According to Lijphart, majority rule can work only in societies that enjoy some level of fundamental consensus about the common good. In such cases, there may be a realistic possibility of alternation in government as a result of shifting political opinion among individuals and groups, and the underlying consensus can keep the society relatively unified as political power shifts between different groups. But in deeply divided societies, that fundamental consensus is lacking, and political preferences are more rigidly attached to group identities. Under such circumstances, according to Lijphart, a purely majoritarian system, devoid of assurances for minorities of their participation in government, is likely to lead either to an authoritarian dictatorship or to civil war.[4]

As an alternative, Lijphart outlined his constitutional design for a consociational democratic system, which he argued would offer the best possibility for a peaceful transition from the Apartheid regime in South Africa. As defined in his previous work, Lijphart's consociational design consists of four basic institutional elements: (1) executive power-sharing through a coalitional cabinet; (2) group autonomy through federalism or other decentralization of authority; (3) proportionality in the electoral system, as well as in the civil service and allocation of public spending; and (4) constitutional provision for some form of minority veto.[5] Lijphart concluded (in 1985) that overall conditions in South Africa were favorable for a consociational democracy, although he also considered the possibility of partition as a fallback option.

Another side of the debate may be traced back to the 1991 work of Donald Horowitz, *A Democratic South Africa? Constitutional Engineering in a Divided Society*.[6] Horowitz was more supportive of majoritarian democratic institutions, although he conceded the need to modify their more extreme forms in deeply divided societies. While agreeing that a plurality, first-past-the-post (FPTP) electoral system would be inappropriate for South Africa, Horowitz cautioned against Lijphart's recommendation for proportional representation (PR) in the legislature, due to its tendency to reinforce group identities by facilitating votes along racial and ethnic party lines. Horowitz's basic concern was that electoral systems should provide incentives for transcending boundaries of ascriptive identity, rather than producing in effect an ethnic census, which would risk exacerbating tensions over social divisions. Horowitz also was skeptical about the prospects for formation of a post-electoral, power-sharing coalition among all major groups, as called for by Lijphart's consociational design. Pointing out that consociationalism relies on development of cooperation among elites, rather than at the constituent level, Horowitz predicted that elites in deeply divided societies like South Africa would be unable to form or maintain governing coalitions in the face of extremist pressures from within their own groups.

In place of consociationalist PR elections, Horowitz recommended that South Africa adopt the alternative vote (AV). Also known as "instant runoff" elections, AV requires voters to rank-order ballot choices from a list of candidates running in single-member districts (SMDs). When ballots are counted, votes for losing candidates are assigned to the next preference on the ballot until a majority vote winner is obtained. Horowitz argued that AV represents a middle ground between consociationalist PR and majoritarian FPTP elections. Most important, Horowitz theorized that AV elections would provide incentives for formation of pre-electoral coalitions, because candidates from one group would be motivated to seek support of voters from other groups for second or third preference on their ballots. Such electoral mechanisms that reward cross-group campaigning are known as "vote-pooling" systems, because they encourage groups to pool their votes prior to elections.

Horowitz also believed that democratic accountability demands an electoral system that offers choices between specific candidates, not just their political parties. If AV were rejected, he favored the single transferable vote (STV)—a modified PR system that allows preference voting for candidates—over the traditional PR system. Horowitz also endorsed the majoritarian institution of a directly elected presidency for South Africa, although he recommended that the electoral system be modified with a vote-pooling formula that would require a share of votes to be obtained from subnational units. He also recommended a federal system of government, not so much for purposes of providing group autonomy, but more for conflict management through vote-pooling and administrative separation of powers.[7]

Timothy Sisk offers a potential synthesis in his 1996 book, *Power Sharing and International Mediation in Ethnic Conflicts*. Sisk categorizes power-sharing institutions as either consociational—with PR elections, government quotas, and often ethnically based federalism—or integrative, with vote-pooling electoral systems, identity-blind government policies, and a unitary state or nonethnic federal structure. According to Sisk, a combination of both approaches may be needed for effective conflict management, depending on the specific nature of societal divisions and political conditions.[8] This dual framework has been extended by Milton Esman, who identifies two broad institutional strategies for managing ethnic conflict: (1) curtailing identity-based politics through assimilationist policies, overt or implicit; or (2) recognizing and legitimating identity-based divisions by providing for consociational power-sharing and autonomy. Like Sisk, Esman concludes that various combinations of the two approaches may be necessary in any given context, and that no single institutional design should be regarded as ideal for conflict management in all cases.[9] Similarly, Bernard Grofman and Robert Stockwell offer a framework that distinguishes between communal and integrative institutions, though they further subdivide each category into mass- or elite-based elements. Grofman and Stockwell concur that no single approach should be recommended for managing conflict in all cases, but rather suggest that optimal designs can be reached by combining various elements of the different institutional strategies.[10]

Other scholars, however, have favored one of the two approaches. Andrew Reynolds, in his 1999 work, *Electoral Systems and Democratization in Southern Africa*, also distinguishes two strategies: the inclusionary approach, which features PR elections, parliamentary executives, and other consociational arrangements; and the exclusionary approach, which features plurality or majority electoral systems, presidential executives, and other majoritarian structures. Based on a study of five Southern African countries, Reynolds concludes that inclusionary institutions are more likely to lead to political stability and peaceful consolidation of democracy in divided societies, while exclusionary structures are more likely to perpetuate and inflame social conflict.[11] René Lemarchand reaches similar conclusions in his study of Rwanda, Burundi, and the DRC, although he concedes that in practice it is difficult to implement fully the institutions of consociational design.[12]

Benjamin Reilly's 2001 book, *Democracy in Divided Societies: Electoral Engineering for Conflict Management*, differentiates institutions that are either centripetal—promoting movement toward a moderate political center—or centrifugal, tending toward polarization and reinforcement of societal divisions. Reilly thus sides with Horowitz in criticizing PR electoral systems for yielding a political elite that mirrors, rather than overcomes, ethnic differences. He generally endorses Horowitzian vote-pooling through AV or STV elections to encourage the formation of pre-electoral coalitions among moderates from different groups. However, Reilly concedes that such vote-pooling electoral systems are ineffective where patterns of demographic concentration inhibit the formation of sufficiently heterogeneous electoral districts.[13]

Horowitz and Lijphart themselves have elaborated their debate in more recent scholarship. Horowitz continues to recommend vote-pooling and centripetal designs meant to incentivize pre-electoral coalitions among political moderates, although he acknowledges that local factors may trump such recommendations.[14] Lijphart, meanwhile, has concentrated on expanding his substantive recommendations, translating his original consociationalism into a broader index of "consensual"—as opposed to majoritarian—democracy.[15] He makes specific recommendations on a host of institutional structures for constitutional design in divided societies, including the following: PR legislative elections, a parliamentary executive with a power-sharing cabinet, federalism or decentralized group autonomy, proportional representation in government positions, bicameralism, strong judicial review, a high threshold for constitutional amendments, and a strong central bank.[16] Scholars critical

	Integration			Accommodation				
A S S I M I L A T I O N	**Republicans**	**Socialists**	**Liberals**	**Centripetalists**	**Multiculturalists**	**Consociationalists**	**Territorial pluralists**	S E C E S S I O N
	Common good	Class consciousness	Individual rights	Incentives for moderation; Decentralization	Cultural autonomy; Proportionality	Power-sharing; Proportionality; Some territorial autonomy; Veto rights	Strong territorial autonomy	

Figure 9.1. Spectrum of constitutional design. Source: Adapted from John McGarry, Brendan O'Leary, and Richard Simeon, "Integration or Accommodation? The Enduring Debate in Conflict Regulation," in *Constitutional Design for Divided Societies: Integration or Accommodation?* ed. Sujit Choudhry (London: Oxford University Press, 2008), Table 1, 69.

of Lijphart's recommendations include José Antonio Cheibub, who defends the merits of presidentialism,[17] and David Lake and Donald Rothchild, who question the effectiveness of territorial federalism or autonomy as strategies for conflict management.[18]

John McGarry, Brendan O'Leary, and Richard Simeon have provided the most comprehensive typology to date of constitutional design for conflict management. Integrative and accommodative approaches are situated within a larger spectrum bounded at the extremes by assimilation and secession (see Figure 9.1). The authors do not provide details on the boundary between accommodation and secession, but they are careful to describe the nature of integration and how it differs from both assimilation and accommodation. Integrative institutions attempt to create a unified public identity, although they allow private societal differences to persist. This distinguishes integrationists from assimilationists, who aim to eradicate even private differences, and from accommodationists, who allow for persistence of social divisions in public institutions.

Lijphart's consociationalism is situated near the accommodation end of the spectrum, lacking only territorially autonomous self-government. The multiculturalist approach is described as providing cultural autonomy through diversity in language and education policies, as well as proportional representation in public institutions. The centripetalist approach associated with Horowitz is situated nominally within the accommodationist school, but bordering on the integration side of the scale, directly in the middle of the McGarry et al. spectrum. Finally, the integrative rubric includes civic republicanism that champions the unitary nation-state as a communitarian institution, socialism emphasizing class differences over identity-based dis-

```
┌─────────────┐     ┌─────────────┐
│ Integration │ ──▶ │Unified Civic│
│             │     │  Identity   │
└─────────────┘     └─────────────┘
                                    ↘
┌─────────────┐     ┌─────────────┐   ┌─────────────┐
│ Centripetal │     │Fluid Inter- │   │             │
│Accommodation│ ──▶ │group, Pre-  │──▶│  Peaceful   │
│ (Horowitz)  │     │electoral    │   │  Democracy  │
│             │     │Coalitions   │   │             │
└─────────────┘     └─────────────┘   └─────────────┘
                                    ↗
┌─────────────┐     ┌─────────────┐
│Consociational│    │Fixed Inter- │
│Accommodation │──▶ │group, Post- │
│  (Lijphart) │     │electoral    │
│             │     │Coalitions   │
└─────────────┘     └─────────────┘
```

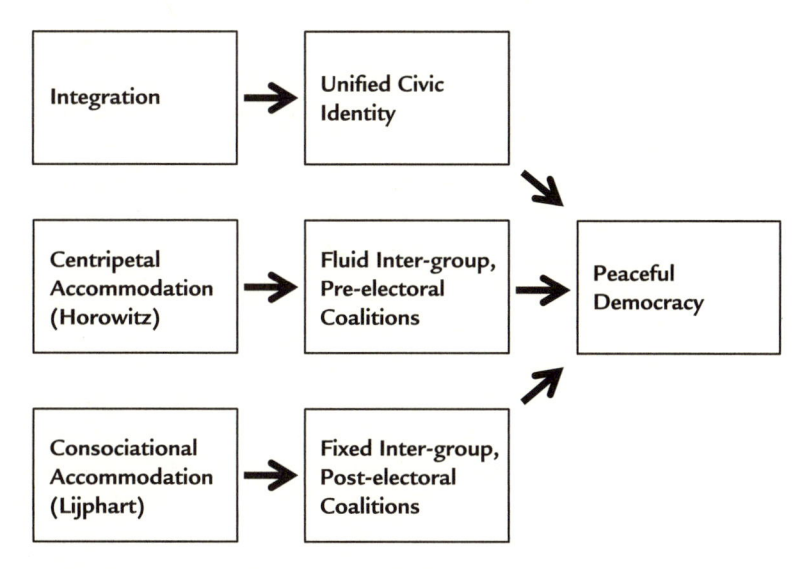

Figure 9.2. Three constitutional strategies, one objective.

tinctions, and classical liberalism advocating egalitarian individual rights over group-based claims.

The ultimate conflict-management objective of integrative and accommodative constitutional design strategies is the same: a peaceful, democratic political system. The differences arise in the mechanisms through which this objective is posited to be achieved, as indicated in Figure 9.2.

Lijphart's consociationalist theory predicts that if political institutions guarantee proportional representation of societal divisions, this will foster fixed and stable coalitions among different groups following elections. Horowitz's centripetal theory suggests that relatively fluid coalitions among different groups, formed through pre-electoral, cross-group appeals, are most likely to prevent conflict. Integrative constitutional design differs from both these approaches in that it is aimed not at building coalitions, but rather at manufacturing a unified civic identity from among disparate groups. There is not much scholarly support for predominantly integrative institutions in deeply divided societies, nor for assimilationist approaches, in part due to normative aversion to the required means.[19]

McGarry et al. provide a list of political institutions and other elements of constitutional design associated with integrative and accommodative approaches.[20] Integrationists generally promote a unified national identity, sometimes declaring one official language, and often prohibiting political parties based on ethnic, religious, or subnational identification. Accommodationists, on the other hand, embrace a pluralist national identity, generally allowing for multiple official languages, and tending to encourage group rights and political institutions based on existing group divisions. Integrative approaches are thus more likely to support centralization of power through a unitary state structure and to avoid decentralization to subnational units along group lines, while accommodative approaches generally support federal systems or decentralization along such group lines.

In constituting the national legislature, integrationists generally advocate for majoritarian electoral systems, while most accommodationists prefer proportional representation and/or seat quotas for specific groups. For the national executive, integrationists generally support a directly elected presidency, while accommodationists favor a parliamentary executive or a rotating presidency. Within accommodationist approaches, consociationalists focus on the need for an inclusive power-sharing cabinet. The centripetal approach, also classified by McGarry et al. as a type of accommodation, may be viewed as overlapping somewhat with integration in advocating a modified majoritarian system for legislative elections, and a presidential executive elected through a vote-pooling majoritarian system. This approach aims to promote cross-cutting, pre-electoral coalitions, diminishing the political salience of group differences without erasing them. As noted, however, geographic demography can inhibit the centripetal approach, if it proves impossible to draw electoral districts of heterogeneous constituencies that enable cross-group appeals by candidates.[21]

Methodology

In classifying African countries along a spectrum from integration to accommodation, this chapter follows the typology of McGarry et al., but simplifies their categories, as explained below. Consistent with its use throughout this book, constitutional design is defined to include not just the constitutional text and legal framework of political activity, but the overall institutional context that frames the state's political order. To operationalize the index, countries are evaluated on three separate but interrelated dimensions: executive, legislative, and administrative. In coding each country, it is necessary to look closely not only at the institutional design on each dimension, but also at how each dimension interacts with the others.

The executive dimension is coded based on whether the system of governance is presidential or parliamentary, as well as how the executive cabinet is formed. All countries having a directly elected president are referred to as presidential, and all other countries (excluding monarchies) as parliamentary.[22] A directly elected president is generally considered a highly integrative institution, although a two-round majority electoral system could be considered slightly more accommodative than a simple plurality system. Presidential term limits are somewhat accommodative, as they increase the possibility of alternation in power, assuming they are observed. A Horowitzian vote-pooling system for presidential elections or a rotating presidency shifts the ranking toward the center of the spectrum. A parliamentary system with a prime minister indirectly elected by the legislature is considered accommodative, unless that legislature is elected by a majoritarian system. Ranking presidential systems that also have a prime minister as head of government depends on the legislative electoral system and how the prime minister is appointed, as well as the distribution of power between the president and the prime minister. Executive cabinets appointed by a directly elected president are generally considered integrative, although some accommodation can be provided by requiring appointees to be confirmed by the legislature or to be drawn from diverse groups within society.

In coding the legislative dimension, the primary consideration is the electoral system for the lower (or only) house of the national legislature. List PR systems with sizeable districts and minimal thresholds for representation are deemed the most accommodative, and systems of plurality voting in SMDs the most integrative. A modified majoritarian vote-pooling system like AV falls in the middle of the scale, while mixed systems are evaluated based on the proportion of seats chosen by integrative or accommodative electoral mechanisms. Legislative quotas guaranteeing seats to minority groups shift the ranking toward accommodation.[23] Bicameralism can sometimes provide accommodation—for example, if it over-represents specific subgroups, such as rural areas in the United States—but an upper legislative house constituted without regard to identity-based divisions could promote integration. The relation of legislative power to the executive must always be considered. Even a highly accommodative legislature has little influence on the overall constitutional design if power is concentrated in a strong presidency and the legislature is denied countervailing authority. In assessing this balance of power, relevant factors include provisions for votes of no confidence (empowering the legislature) or dissolution of parliament (empowering the executive).

The third dimension, labeled administrative, is coded on several factors. First is whether the state is unitary or federal, and whether authority has been devolved to subnational entities. Second is how any devolved authority structures interact with identity-based divisions to determine whether there are significant integrative or accommodative effects. This includes an evaluation of any grants of autonomy—with full territorial autonomy deemed the most accommodative, and cultural or religious autonomy less so. Lack of official recognition for subnational groups shifts the ranking toward integration. Quotas and other affirmative action policies are accommodative. A state religion or a single official language is considered integrative, while separation of religion and state, or recognition of multiple official languages, is more accommodative. Other administrative factors include constitutional provisions that explicitly endorse the goal of either national integration or accommodation of identity groups. Also relevant are any regulations of political parties that may have integrative or accommodative effects, such as prohibiting parties from forming along identity group lines, or requiring parties to declare a group association.

Based on the general principles described above, countries are coded on a five-point scale, with −2 representing a hyper-integrative constitutional design, −1 an integrative design, and +2 and +1 the same on the accommodative side. The 0 category is meant to represent a balance between accommodative and integrative factors associated with centripetal designs. Countries are evaluated based on their constitutional design across the three dimensions as of 1 January 2011. Although the intent is to provide a cross-sectional sample for analysis, it often is necessary to look back several years to establish the current institutional context. Coding based on so many qualitative factors is obviously somewhat subjective, but these raw scores for the three dimensions are then aggregated in the following methodical manner. If all three dimensions are predominantly integrative or accommodative, the score is −2 or +2. If two of the three dimensions point in the same direction, the score is a −1 or +1. The 0 category is especially heterogeneous because it includes both distinctive centripetal designs, such as vote-pooling systems that encourage voluntary cross-group appeals, and other relatively balanced mixes of accommodative and integrative institutions.

In the overall evaluation of constitutional design, this chapter considers de facto or informal rules and practices to be more significant than de jure constitutional provisions. However, the coding starts with de jure provisions, and then proceeds to a de facto assessment. For example, a country might have a constitutionally stipulated PR legislature and an ethnofederal structure, but if a centralized presidency wields all practical power, the country would ultimately be coded not as +1, but more likely as −1, or even −2, depending on the extent of presidential dominance. Similarly, the lack of free and fair elections, or of guarantees for basic civil rights, may easily undermine the effects of de jure accommodative electoral systems or administrative structures. Conversely, de jure integrative institutions may be implemented in an accommodative manner because of de facto agreements to guarantee minority representation in government institutions such as the cabinet.

The main coding, as provided in Table 9.1, reflects a country's de facto political structure, measured on the integration/accommodation scale, at the start of 2011. A separate de jure coding is provided parenthetically if it differs from the de facto coding. (The de jure codings are also listed in Appendix 2.) While specific coding decisions in some cases require judgment calls that may be subject to debate, the aggregate results for all countries provide at least an approximation of the current distribution of constitutional design across the African continent.

One potential objection to the foregoing methodology is that it draws on a literature that is explicitly focused on democratic or democratizing states with deeply divided polities.[24] But, in reality, most African countries embody these attributes, and all have constitutional designs that can be classified using this methodology.[25] Even current autocracies have identifiable constitutional designs, generally including both written constitutions and observable political orders. De facto coding of autocratic institutions is admittedly more difficult, requiring deeper investigation into how these institutions function in practice. For example, rigged elections or violations of minority rights contribute toward a coding of de facto integration, because their effect is to concentrate power in central authorities. Similarly, a presidential dictatorship, which is the norm in African autocracies, is usually highly integrative. As a result, the category of hyper-integrative is also heterogeneous in that it includes both fully democratic countries with highly integrative institutions and some autocracies. Yet, even presidential dictatorships may have accommodative aspects, such as informal clientelist or patrimonialist arrangements, through which groups are provided with resources or autonomy in return

Table 9.1. De Facto Coding of Constitutional Design of African Countries as of 1 January 2011

Hyper-integrative: −2	Integrative: −1	Balanced: 0	Accommodative: +1	Hyper-accommodative: +2
Algeria (−1)	Benin	Comoros	Botswana	Mauritius
Angola (−1)	DRC (+1)	Kenya	Burundi	(Somalia)*
Burkina Faso (−1)	Djibouti (−2)	Nigeria	Cape Verde	South Africa
Cameroon	Ethiopia (+1)		Lesotho	
Central African Republic	Ghana (−2)		São Tomé & Príncipe	
Chad (−1)	Guinea-Bissau			
Congo	Mali (−2)			
Côte d'Ivoire	Namibia			
Egypt	Sudan			
Equatorial Guinea (−1)	Tanzania			
Eritrea (−1)	Uganda (−2)			
Gabon				
The Gambia				
Guinea (−1)				
Liberia				
Libya				
Madagascar (−1)				
Malawi				
Mauritania				
Morocco (−1)				
Mozambique (−1)				
Niger (−1)				
Rwanda (−1)				
Senegal				
Seychelles				
Sierra Leone				
Swaziland				
Togo (−1)				
Tunisia				
Zambia				
Zimbabwe (−1)				

Notes: De jure codings in parentheses, if different. *Somalia, effectively in a state of anarchy as of 1 January 2011, is coded as having a de jure, but not a de facto constitutional design.

for political support.[26] This underscores that the spectrum reflects not the level of democracy but rather the centralization or dispersion of political power and national identity among societal groups.

Unlike the rest of this book, the current chapter does not seek to explain the observed consequences of constitutional design, in part because the codings are only for one recent snapshot in time. Nevertheless, in order to facilitate future research on the correlates of constitutional design, scores are provided (where available) for each country on the 2010 Polity IV democracy variable, measured on a scale of 0–10 (see Table 9.2).[27] A metric for coding states as deeply divided societies, or not, would also be useful for testing conflict management theories, but these data do not appear to be available at the present time.[28]

Analysis

Looking at the codings of constitutional design across Africa as of early January 2011 (Table 9.1), the pattern of integration is readily apparent. Approximately 80 percent of countries are coded either −1 or −2 in the de facto assessment, and even the de jure codings (Appendix 2) fall more than three-quarters within these two categories. Most countries that have a different de facto coding—20 of 53—are more integrative in practice than de jure. The four exceptions are Djibouti, where an informal power-sharing agreement modifies an otherwise highly integrative constitution; Ghana, where a tradition of informal accommodation provides broad representation in the executive branch; Mali, where coalitional politics performed a similar function (prior to armed conflict in 2012); and Uganda, where an informal system of political patronage has accommodative effects. No countries were coded as having de facto adjustments that made their overall constitutional design accommodative in practice, although this could be an artifact of the overall de jure trend toward integration.

The primary contributor to the integrationist trend is the widespread institution of a directly elected presidency, as shown in Table 9.2. Excluding the monarchies of Lesotho, Morocco, and Swaziland, and two states that were totalitarian/anarchic (as of January 2011), Libya and Somalia, only five African countries lack directly elected presidents: Botswana, Eritrea, Ethiopia, Mauritius, and South Africa. In practice, most African presidents exert strong control over all executive functions through cabinet appointments and other means, even in countries with a separate titular head of government. Accommodative cabinets are rare, and agreements for intergroup power-sharing in

Table 9.2. Elements of Constitutional Design in African Countries

Country	Executive	Legislative (lower house)	Administrative	Polity IV (democ)
Algeria −2 (−1)	presidential	PR	unitary	3
Angola −2 (−1)	presidential	PR	unitary	2
Benin −1	presidential	PR	unitary	7
Botswana +1	parliamentary	plurality SMD	unitary; some autonomy	8
Burkina Faso −2 (−1)	presidential	PR	unitary	2
Burundi +1	presidential; power-sharing cabinet	PR	unitary	7
Cameroon −2	presidential	mixed (majority SMD and modified block vote/PR)	unitary	1
Cape Verde +1	presidential	PR	unitary; some autonomy	10
Central African Republic −2	presidential	majority SMD	unitary	1
Chad −2 (−1)	presidential	mixed (modified block vote/PR and majority SMD)	unitary	1
Comoros 0	presidential (rotating); power-sharing cabinet	mixed (majority SMD and indirect election)	federal	9
Congo −2	presidential	majority SMD	unitary	0
Côte d'Ivoire −2	presidential	plurality SMD & MMD	unitary	—
Djibouti −1 (−2)	presidential; informal power-sharing	plurality MMD	unitary	3
DRC −1 (+1)	presidential	mixed (PR and plurality SMD)	unitary; some autonomy	6
Egypt −2	presidential	mixed (majority MMD)	unitary	1

(continued)

Table 9.2. *continued*

Country	Executive	Legislative (lower house)	Administrative	Polity IV (democ)
Equatorial Guinea −2 (−1)	presidential	PR	unitary	0
Eritrea −2 (−1)	parliamentary	plurality SMD	unitary	0
Ethiopia −1 (+1)	parliamentary	plurality SMD; minority quotas	federal	3
Gabon −2	presidential	majority SMD	unitary	4
The Gambia −2	presidential	mixed (plurality SMD)	unitary	0
Ghana −1 (−2)	presidential	plurality SMD	unitary	8
Guinea −2 (−1)	presidential	mixed (PR & plurality SMD)	unitary	6
Guinea-Bissau −1	presidential	PR	unitary	7
Kenya 0	presidential; vote-pooling formula	plurality SMD	unitary; some autonomy	8
Lesotho +1	parliamentary (nonpolitical monarchy)	mixed-member proportional	unitary	8
Liberia −2	presidential	majority SMD	unitary	7
Libya −2	n/a	indirect election	unitary	0
Madagascar −2 (−1)	presidential	mixed (plurality SMD & PR)	unitary; some autonomy	3
Malawi −2	presidential	plurality SMD	unitary	6
Mali −1 (−2)	presidential	majority SMD & MMD (party lists)	unitary	7
Mauritania −2	presidential	mixed (majority SMD/MMD & PR)	unitary	0
Mauritius +2	parliamentary	plurality MMD; minority quotas	unitary; full autonomy	10
Morocco −2 (−1)	monarchy	PR	unitary	0
Mozambique −2 (−1)	presidential	PR	unitary	5
Namibia −1	presidential	PR	unitary	6

(*continued*)

Table 9.2. *continued*

Country	Executive	Legislative (lower house)	Administrative	Polity IV (democ)
Niger −2 (−1)	presidential	mixed (PR and plurality SMD)	unitary	4
Nigeria 0	presidential; vote-pooling formula	plurality SMD	federal	4
Rwanda −2 (−1)	presidential	PR	unitary	0
Sao Tome & Principe +1	presidential	PR	unitary; full autonomy	*
Senegal −2	presidential	mixed (plurality SMD & PR)	unitary	7
Seychelles −2	presidential	mixed (plurality SMD & PR)	unitary	*
Sierra Leone −2	presidential	plurality SMD	unitary	8
Somalia n/a (+2)	parliamentary	appointment quotas	federal	—
South Africa +2	parliamentary	PR	federal	9
Sudan −1	presidential	mixed (plurality SMD & PR)	federal	1
Swaziland −2	monarchy	mixed (plurality SMD & executive appointment)	unitary	0
Tanzania −1	presidential	plurality SMD; minority quotas	federal	2
Togo −2 (−1)	presidential	PR	unitary	1
Tunisia −2	presidential	mixed (plurality party-list MMD & minority quotas)	unitary	1
Uganda −1 (−2)	presidential	plurality SMD	unitary	1
Zambia −2	presidential	plurality SMD	unitary	7
Zimbabwe −2 (−1)	presidential	plurality SMD	unitary	3

Note: codings are de facto (and de jure in parentheses, if different). See Appendix 1 for full summaries of constitutional design by country, and for coding sources. The Polity IV democracy (democ) score ranges from 0 to 10 (with 10 denoting the most complete democracy) and is given for 2010. Cells in this column with a dash (—) denote cases not scored due to interregnum or anarchy; * denotes cases missing from the Polity IV database.

government institutions are rarely sustained. Many African presidents also remain in office for extended periods of time due to lack of formal term limits—in 13 of the 43 presidential systems—or manipulation of elections.

African legislatures also lean toward integration, based typically on majoritarian elections in single- or multimember districts. Proportional representation characterizes a significant minority of legislative bodies—in 18 countries, including three that have mixed systems with at least two-thirds PR seats—but in most of these cases the legislature is institutionally weak or even effectively powerless compared to the executive. Federal structures are found in only six countries (excluding the anarchic state of Somalia), although an additional seven grant at least some governing autonomy to subnational territorial entities. Furthermore, a majority of African constitutions expressly endorse principles of integration over accommodation by placing restrictions on formation of identity-based political parties and by declaring explicit goals for establishment of a unified national identity.

The advice from scholars of constitutional design in divided societies, such as Lijphart and Horowitz, appears not to have had much impact. Horowitz's AV proposal for legislative elections has not been adopted anywhere in Africa, and only Nigeria and Kenya utilize a vote-pooling system for presidential elections, as he recommends. Lijphart's prescriptions for consociational or consensual democracy also seem largely to have been ignored. Only South Africa comes close to implementing Lijphart's full institutional suite, and even there political power is in practice fairly centralized, and the federal structure provides only limited regional autonomy. The only other hyper-accommodative design (again excluding Somalia) is in Mauritius, which despite its mainly majoritarian legislative electoral system is coded as +2 because of other accommodative elements, including a parliamentary executive, full governing autonomy for a sub-state territorial unit, and a quota of seats reserved for "best losers" (which ensures representation of all major ethnic groups).

The demonstrated tendency toward integration over accommodation in African constitutional design, contrary to the typical recommendation of outside experts, should perhaps come as no surprise. Horowitz has detailed the many impediments to constitutional reform that emerge in practice.[29] Furthermore, as noted by McGarry et al., states are by nature integrative; they only implement accommodative design elements reluctantly and under pressure from a mobilized opposition.[30]

Options for constitutional reform may be limited. Constraining executive authority and better enforcing institutional separation of powers could provide accommodative effects in many countries, especially where legislatures already incorporate proportional representation. Such marginal shifts in the institutional balance of power may be more feasible than broad overhaul of constitutional design. However, even small changes may be exceedingly difficult to achieve because of entrenched interests, and reforms that appear major on paper may turn out to be insignificant in practice.

Deficiencies in basic liberal institutions—including free and fair elections, political rights and civil liberties, unbiased public administration, and a strong judiciary and civil society—can undermine implementation of even an optimal constitution. When such fundamental institutions become better entrenched across Africa, opportunities may improve for managing conflict through constitutional innovation. Electoral administration is especially important, as it provides a cornerstone for the functioning of any democracy. When an election lacks legitimacy, as often in Africa, it creates a potential source of conflict beyond the reach of any prescription for constitutional design. Studies of independent electoral commissions and mechanisms for resolving election disputes, as well as techniques for increasing political participation, could provide lessons for addressing this foundational challenge.

To test the effects of constitutional design on conflict outcomes, it would be useful to expand this chapter's cross-sectional analysis into a panel dataset documenting changes in constitutional design over time. Better metrics are also needed to code the social distance between groups, so that any distinctive effects in deeply divided societies can be differentiated. Such metrics should account for the spatial distribution of identity groups and the drawing of electoral districts in both majoritarian and proportional systems. The analysis presented here is primarily an exploratory survey of current trends in African constitutional design, but it could serve as a foundation for future quantitative research.

Conclusion

This chapter provides a coding of constitutional design in all African countries on a spectrum from integration to accommodation. It finds that African countries tend to have integrative political institutions, and that scholarly advice for constitutional design in divided societies has generally not been heeded. Whether there are causal connections between the data presented here and conflict management outcomes in specific cases, or across the continent, is beyond the scope of this chapter.

The strong tendency toward integration in African political systems, even in countries that de jure have more accommodative institutions, may constrain fundamental changes in constitutional design. If governments have decided a priori to pursue integrative institutions, it may be more effective to look for conflict management opportunities within majoritarian systems rather than insisting on a paradigmatic switch to accommodative institutions. Indeed, it could prove difficult to modify institutions even marginally in an accommodative direction, given existing political arrangements and demographics. Although constitutional design is almost universally agreed to be an important factor in conflict management outcomes, the lack of consensus on the optimal institutions in theory, and the challenge of implementing reforms in practice, both underscore the need for further research on the best strategies going forward. Such research should be facilitated by this chapter's new database of constitutional design across Africa.

Appendix 1: Summaries of Constitutional Design in African Countries as of 1 January 2011
(de jure codings in parentheses, if different)[31]

ALGERIA: −2 (−1)

The 1963 constitution of Algeria, as amended through 2008, provides for direct election of a president through an absolute majority (two-round) electoral system. Presidential term limits were abolished in 2008. The president appoints the cabinet, as well as one-third of the upper legislative house, the remainder of which is indirectly elected by provincial authorities. The lower house is elected by proportional representation (PR), but it has little independent power. The government has ruled under a declared state of emergency since 1992. Algeria is a unitary state with a stated constitutional objective of "consolidation of national identity and unity." Identity-based political parties are constitutionally prohibited.

ANGOLA: −2 (−1)

The Angolan constitution of 1992 provides for a president directly elected by absolute majority; however, presidential elections have not been held since

1992. A new constitution promulgated in 2010 abolishes direct election of the presidency in favor of indirect parliamentary election. The unicameral legislature is elected by PR, but it is effectively under presidential control. In 2008 legislative elections—the first since 1992—the president's party won over 80 percent of seats. Angola is a unitary state, and political parties are constitutionally required to contribute to national unity. PR elections and a parliamentary executive could provide a basis for more accommodation in the future, but the continued concentration of power in the president of over thirty years provides for a de facto highly integrative structure.

BENIN: −1

The 1990 constitution of Benin provides for a president elected by absolute majority. The president has plenary power to appoint a cabinet. In 2005, the president stepped down rather than attempting to amend the constitution to allow him to run again. The unicameral legislature is elected by PR and has some institutional authority, although it retains only limited influence over the executive. Benin is a unitary state, and constitutional restrictions on political parties mandate respect for the territorial integrity and secularism of the state. There have been efforts at decentralization, but local elections in 2008 were subject to numerous irregularities and allegations of fraud.

BOTSWANA: +1

The 1966 Botswana constitution provides for a parliamentary system with a president indirectly elected by the lower house of the legislature. Calls by some for direct election of the president were rejected in 2008. The president appoints a cabinet from among members of the legislature. The lower house of the legislature is elected by plurality voting in single-member districts. The upper house—a mostly advisory body without significant power—consists of permanent tribal representatives and other indirectly elected members. Botswana is a unitary state, with local administrators appointed by the central government. However, rights of cultural and educational autonomy are guaranteed by the constitution, and considerations of identity group divisions are expressly permitted in allocation of public funds and positions.

BURKINA FASO: −2 (−1)

The 1991 constitution of Burkina Faso, as amended through 2002, provides for a presidential head of state elected by absolute majority vote. The president appoints a prime minister and other cabinet members. A two-term limit has not been applied retroactively to the current president, who has served since 1987, and was reelected in 2010 with 80 percent of the vote. The advisory upper house of the legislature was dissolved in 2002, leaving a unicameral national assembly elected by PR. The legislature has some institutional authority, including the ability to vote no confidence in the government, but the president retains power to dissolve the legislature. In practice, the president's party has largely dominated the legislature, and elections have been strongly influenced by the ruling party's control of state resources. Burkina Faso is declared a unitary state, and identity-based parties are expressly prohibited by the constitution.

BURUNDI: +1

The 2005 constitution of Burundi provides for a president directly elected by absolute majority vote. The president appoints two vice presidents, who are required to be from different ethnic groups and political parties. Any party holding more than 5 percent of seats in the national assembly is entitled to a cabinet position. The national assembly is elected by a PR system, with diversity requirements for party lists and extra seats reserved to meet ethnic quotas. A senate is indirectly elected by provincial councils and is also subject to quotas. Burundi is a unitary state, with recognition of ethnic and religious diversity; however, the stated function of the regime is to "unite, reassure, and reconcile all Burundians." Political parties are required to reflect a national character, and formation of identity-based parties is prohibited. The current president was indirectly elected in 2005, and then ran unopposed in 2010 after opposition parties withdrew among accusations of electoral fraud.

CAMEROON: −2

The 1972 constitution of Cameroon, as amended through 2008, provides for a president elected by plurality vote for a seven-year term. A 2008 amendment removed presidential term limits. The president appoints a prime minister and members of the cabinet. The constitution calls for a bicameral legislature, but in practice only a national assembly has been established. The legislative electoral system is split evenly between plurality SMD seats and a modified majoritarian (party block vote) / list PR system (with PR being used only if there is no majority winner). In practice, however, the authority of the legislature is minimal. Cameroon is a unitary state, nominally decentralized, but with the president and central government retaining most actual authority. The proliferation of nearly 200 political parties has inhibited vigorous competition and contributed to continuing one-party dominance.

CAPE VERDE: +1

The 1992 constitution of Cape Verde, as amended through 2010, provides for a presidential head of state elected by absolute majority vote. A prime minister and cabinet ministers are appointed in accordance with the balance of power in the legislature. The unicameral legislature is elected by list PR, and it has significant authority, including a no confidence vote. Representation in the national assembly has generally been split between two large parties, and there has been peaceful transfer of power to the opposition. The state has a unitary structure, with prohibitions on formation of regional or religious political parties; however, the constitution emphasizes pluralism and provides some rights of cultural autonomy.

CENTRAL AFRICAN REPUBLIC: −2

The 2004 constitution of the Central African Republic, as amended in 2010, provides for a presidential head of state elected by absolute majority vote. The president appoints a prime minister and members of the cabinet. Although opposition leaders hold cabinet positions pursuant to a 2009 peace agreement, the president's party retains most power, with key positions held by members of the president's ethnic group. The unicameral legislature—which has little institutional power—is elected by absolute majority in SMDs. 2005 elections were subject to claims of irregularities and fraud, and elections scheduled for 2010 were postponed for 2011. The state has a unitary structure, with the president appointing heads of regional and local councils. Associations deemed contrary to national unity are prohibited, and political parties are forbidden from advocating identity-based interests.

CHAD: −2 (−1)

The 1996 constitution of Chad, as amended in 2005, provides for a presidential head of state elected by absolute majority vote. The president appoints a prime minister and cabinet. A 2005 amendment abolished presidential term limits, and in 2006 the current president won a third term in elections boycotted by opposition groups. Although the constitution calls for a senate, only a national assembly has been established. The legislative electoral system is mixed, with over 80 percent of seats elected through a modified party block vote/list PR system, and the remaining seats elected by absolute majority in SMDs. The last legislative elections, held in 2002, provoked widespread allegations of fraud after the president's party was awarded over two-thirds of legislative seats. In practice the legislature is ineffectual, although it does have formal power to vote no confidence in the government. A 2007 peace agreement called for electoral reforms but did not provide for power-sharing among opposition groups. Chad is a unitary state with the president appointing all regional and local authorities. The constitution expressly prohibits identity-based propaganda deemed to undermine national unity or secularism.

COMOROS: 0

The 2001 constitution of Comoros provides for a president elected by plurality vote, but the office of the presidency rotates between three autonomous islands. The president appoints a cabinet whose membership is also required to equitably represent the islands. Just over half the unicameral legislature is elected by absolute majority in SMDs, with the remaining members indirectly elected by the legislative assemblies of the islands. However, the legislature has relatively little power, with the president and cabinet initiating legislation, and the legislature denied any institutional check on the executive. Comoros is a federal union of autonomous island-states, with each island having independently elected executives and legislative bodies. The islands have financial autonomy, while religion and nationality issues are reserved to the central government. The preamble to the constitution invokes Islam as the source of principles for the regime.

CONGO (BRAZZAVILLE): –2

The 2002 constitution of the Republic of Congo provides for direct election of a president by absolute majority vote for a maximum of two seven-year terms. The president unilaterally appoints a cabinet; the position of prime minister was abolished in 2009. The president has exclusive authority to initiate legislation. The bicameral legislature consists of a national assembly elected by absolute majority in SMDs, and a senate indirectly elected by provincial councils. The legislature is relatively weak, with the 2002 constitution having reduced its authority; however, it is protected from executive dissolution.

The current president has been in office since 1979, excluding a five-year period in the 1990s. The 2009 presidential elections were boycotted by the opposition and attracted low voter turnout. The state has a unitary structure, and parties are required to maintain a national character without identity-based distinctions. Cultural autonomy is guaranteed only to the extent that it does not prejudice national unity.

CÔTE D'IVOIRE: −2

The 2000 constitution of Côte d'Ivoire provides for a presidential head of state elected by absolute majority vote. The president has authority to appoint a prime minister and members of the cabinet. A 2003 power-sharing agreement included opposition members in the government, but continuing conflict has impeded its implementation. The unicameral legislature is elected by plurality vote in single- and multimember districts, but it has little institutional power. The state has a unitary structure, with local authorities appointed by the central government. Identity-based political parties and propaganda are constitutionally prohibited. Presidential elections in 2000 were marred by violence and fraud, and subsequent elections were repeatedly postponed until late 2010. The result of that election was in dispute as of January 2011.

DEMOCRATIC REPUBLIC OF CONGO (DRC): −1 (+1)

The 2006 constitution of the DRC provides for a presidential head of state elected by absolute majority vote, subject to a two-term limit. The president appoints a prime minister from the majority party in the legislature, and the cabinet is generally required to be nationally representative. The legislature is bicameral, with a senate indirectly elected by provincial legislative bodies. The national assembly is elected through a mixed system, with almost 90 percent of seats elected by list PR in small multimember constituencies, and just over 10 percent of members elected by plurality vote in SMDs. The institutional authority of the legislature is weak vis-à-vis the president, with a no-confidence provision of uncertain application, but clear presidential power of dissolution. Elections in 2006 were the first since independence in 1960, and they were deemed mostly credible, although marred by some intimidation and irregularities. The DRC is a unitary state with nominally decentralized autonomous provinces. The provinces are constitutionally guaranteed a 40 percent share of central government revenues, but provincial elections have been dubious, and provincial governments are still institutionally fragile. Due to limited capacity and inadequate infrastructure, the central government exerts only limited authority outside the capital area, especially where rebel groups or warlords are powerful. Local elections had been repeatedly postponed as of January 2011.

DJIBOUTI: –1 (–2)

The 1992 constitution of Djibouti calls for a presidential head of state elected by absolute majority for a six-year term, with power to appoint a prime minister and cabinet. Under current implementation of an informal power-sharing agreement in place since 1994, the prime minister and roughly half the cabinet members are appointed from an opposition ethnic group. The unicameral legislature is elected through a block voting system (plurality vote in multimember districts), but only parties loyal to the president are represented, as the opposition has boycotted all recent elections. A 2010 constitutional amendment revoked presidential term limits and also called for creation of a senate. Djibouti is declared a unitary state, and political parties are prohibited from having any identity-based character. Regional elections held in 2006 were meant to initiate a decentralization process to appease ethnic tensions, but there has been only minimal devolution of power from the central government.

EGYPT: –2

The Egyptian constitution of 1971, as amended through 2007, provides for a presidential head of state with a six-year term of office and no term limits. A 2005 amendment changed the presidential electoral system from a single candidate referendum to a multicandidate contest by absolute majority. The president appoints a prime minister and cabinet, and may appoint one or more vice presidents. The bicameral legislature consists of an upper house, with two-thirds of its members elected by absolute majority and one-third appointed by the president, and a lower house elected by absolute majority in two-member districts, with each district represented by at least one "worker or farmer." In 2005, opposition parties for the first time gained a significant number of legislative seats, winning over 25 percent of seats in the lower house. But constitutional amendments in 2007 limited opposition political rights, leading to a boycott of 2010 elections. The amendments also gave the president authority to unilaterally dissolve the legislature, although a legislative no-confidence vote in the government was instituted as well. As of

January 2011, prior to the Arab Spring, the Egyptian state had a unitary structure, with Islam declared as the state religion, but the formation of religious political parties was strictly prohibited.

EQUATORIAL GUINEA: –2 (–1)

The 1991 constitution of Equatorial Guinea, as amended through 1995, provides for a presidential head of state elected by plurality vote for a seven-year term with no limits. The president appoints a prime minister from the majority party in the legislature, but in practice this has always been the president's own party. Members of the opposition have occasionally been included in the cabinet, but presidential influence dominates the government. The unicameral legislature is elected by list PR, but it has very limited institutional authority. Elections have generally been considered fraudulent, with overwhelming majorities for the president's party; the current president has held power since 1979. The state has a unitary structure, with provincial governors appointed by the president. Identity-based political parties are constitutionally prohibited.

ERITREA: –2 (–1)

The 1997 constitution of Eritrea provides for a parliamentary system with a president indirectly elected by the legislature. The unicameral national assembly is elected by plurality vote in SMDs. However, the Eritrean constitution has yet to be implemented, and elections have been indefinitely postponed since 2001. A transitional government has been in power since independence in 1993; the current president was appointed by the transitional legislature at that time. Although the transitional legislature retains the primary de jure authority of the state, de facto power has been highly concentrated in the presidency. The state structure is unitary, although nominally decentralized, and political parties are required to adhere to principles of national unity. In practice Eritrea remains a one-party state, as several opposition movements have been disqualified.

ETHIOPIA: –1 (+1)

The 1995 constitution of Ethiopia instituted a parliamentary system of government, with a head of state indirectly elected by two-thirds vote of the bicameral legislature. The lower legislative house is elected by plurality vote in SMDs, with a small quota reserved for minority ethnic groups. A majority of the lower house elects the prime minister, who is head of government with chief executive authority. The upper house is indirectly elected by substate legislative councils. As of 2011, the current prime minister had held office since 1991, and national power was highly centralized in his party. In 2005 elections, opposition parties made some gains, but claims of fraud led to violence and increased political repression. In 2010 elections, which were judged not free and fair, the ruling party won only about 70 percent of votes nationally, but was awarded over 99 percent of legislative seats. Ethiopia has a federal structure of ethnic sub-states that are granted extensive autonomy, including even the right to secession. The constitution calls for strict separation between religion and state and equal recognition of all national languages.

GABON: −2

The 1991 constitution of Gabon, as amended through 2003, provides for a presidential head of state elected by plurality vote for a seven-year term with no limits. The president appoints a prime minister and cabinet, and is authorized to dissolve the legislature. The bicameral legislature consists of a lower house elected by majority vote in SMDs, and an upper house indirectly elected by municipal councils and other local authorities. In practice, the president's party has dominated national politics, with repeated accusations by opposition parties of undue influence and fraud in elections. The current president is the son of the previous president, who remained in power from 1975 until his death in 2009. The state has a unitary structure, with the president appointing all provincial authorities. The constitution authorizes regulation of political parties to prevent ethnic identification.

THE GAMBIA: −2

The 1996 constitution of the Gambia, as amended through 2009, provides for a president elected by absolute majority with no term limits. The president appoints a vice president and cabinet, in practice always from the president's own party. The current president has been in office since a 1994 coup. The unicameral legislature is elected mainly through a plurality SMD system, with about 10 percent of seats reserved for presidential appointment. The legislature has a nominal no-confidence vote by which it can call for a referendum on presidential removal, but in practice the president exerts control over the legislature. The Gambia is an effective one-party state, with opposition parties claiming fraud and undue influence in recent elections. The state has a unitary structure, with presidential appointment of most local officials.

National integration and unity are constitutionally mandated principles of state policy, and political parties are prohibited from having any identity-based character. Cultural autonomy rights are subject to regulation in the interests of national unity, although tribal chiefs retain traditional authority in limited areas.

GHANA: −1 (−2)

The 1992 constitution of Ghana, as amended in 1996, provides for a president elected by absolute majority, subject to a two-term limit, which has been observed. The president appoints a cabinet with legislative approval. An informal aspect of accommodation is that by tradition the cabinet and the executive branch are selected to be broadly representative of the country's ethno-regional diversity. The unicameral legislature is elected by plurality vote in SMDs. Ghana is a multiparty democracy, which has had generally free and fair elections and two transfers of presidential power since 1992. The state is unitary in structure, and the constitution explicitly calls for active integration of all ethnic groups under a national character that transcends identity-based loyalties. There has been only limited decentralization to local authorities, but the traditional institution of chieftaincy is protected under the constitution.

GUINEA: −2 (−1)

The 1990 fundamental law of Guinea, as amended in 2001, provides for a presidential head of state elected by absolute majority for a seven-year term with no limits. The president appoints a prime minister and cabinet without restriction. The unicameral legislature is made up of two-thirds members elected by PR in a national constituency, and one-third by plurality vote in SMDs. However, the legislature has little institutional authority, and has in fact been dissolved since a military coup in 2008 in which the constitution was suspended. The previous president held office for 24 years before the coup. The constitution was reinstated in 2010 with a new president taking office after the first freely contested elections in the country's history. Guinea is declared a unitary state, with constitutional prohibitions on identity-based political parties and punishment authorized for acts undermining national unity.

GUINEA-BISSAU: −1

The 1984 constitution of Guinea-Bissau, as amended through 1996, provides for a presidential head of state elected by absolute majority for a limit of two consecutive terms. The president appoints a prime minister and cabinet in consultation with the legislative majority. The unicameral legislature is elected by list PR; it has a no-confidence vote in the government, but the president has power of dissolution. A new constitution approved by the legislature in 2001 was never implemented, and efforts in 2007 to form a coalitional government were obstructed by the president. Legislative elections in 2008, however, were judged free and fair. In 2009, the president—who had been in office for 23 years—was assassinated, but a new president was seated through peaceful and credible elections that same year. Guinea-Bissau is a unitary state with nominally decentralized regions. Political parties are required to respect national unity, and identity-based political activity is prohibited.

KENYA: 0

The 2010 constitution of Kenya provides for a president elected for a limit of two terms through a modified, vote-pooling majoritarian system: to win in the first round, a candidate must gain a majority that includes more than a quarter of the vote in more than half the regional counties. The president appoints a deputy president and cabinet with legislative approval, and the entire executive is mandated to reflect regional and ethnic diversity. The bicameral legislature consists of a national assembly elected primarily by plurality vote in SMDs, and a senate providing regional representation. The provisions of the new constitution, which include increasing legislative power vis-à-vis the presidency and devolution of authority to subnational units, had not yet been fully implemented in January 2011. Prior to drafting of the new constitution, conflict had broken out in 2007 over disputed presidential elections, resulting in a negotiated power-sharing coalition with appointment of an opposition prime minister and evenly split cabinet posts. The new constitution calls for devolution of power "to foster national unity by recognizing diversity," and to provide for autonomous self-governance. The state is mandated to protect cultural and language diversity and to provide affirmative action for marginalized minority groups; however, political parties are required to support national unity and avoid identity-based distinctions.

LESOTHO: +1

The 1993 constitution of Lesotho, as amended through 2004, prescribes a hereditary monarchy, although in practice the position of the king is largely nonpolitical. The king appoints the leader of the majority party in the legislature as prime minister, and the king can dissolve the legislature generally only on advice of the prime minister or after a legislative vote of no confidence. The bicameral legislature consists of a senate of hereditary chiefs and appointees, and a national assembly elected through a mixed-member proportional system (MMP), in which PR seats are allocated to compensate for disproportionality in the SMD seats. The MMP system was instituted in 2001 to provide better opposition representation after violent conflict following the 1998 elections. Opposition parties gained seats in subsequent elections as a result of the change, but disputes continue over the proportionality of seat allocation. The state structure is unitary, with local elections first held in 2005. The constitution makes no mention of identity-based divisions.

LIBERIA: –2

The 1986 constitution of Liberia provides for a president elected by absolute majority for six years with a two-term limit. The president appoints cabinet members with consent of the upper legislative house. The constitution calls for both houses of the bicameral legislature to be elected by absolute majority vote in SMDs, but the most recent elections in 2005 were conducted by one-round plurality. Prior elections in 1997 were conducted using a PR system to implement a peace agreement following civil war. The 2005 elections were declared relatively free and fair, and the president's party failed to gain a legislative majority. Liberia is a unitary state, with nominal decentralization for administrative purposes; the president retains authority to appoint local officials. The preservation of national unity and elimination of identity-based distinctions are constitutionally declared policy principles. Formation of ethnic or regional political parties is strictly prohibited.

LIBYA: –2

As of 2011, Libya did not have a permanent constitution, although a temporary constitutional proclamation was issued after the military coup in 1969 that brought the Mu'ammar Qaddafi regime to power. The political structure is generally established in accordance with the 1975 "Green Book" of Qaddafi, the de facto head of state and government, and a 1977 declaration establishing a legislative forum. Members of the legislative forum are indirectly elected by local councils. The forum has formal authority to confirm executive cabinet members, but practical power is centralized around Qaddafi. The state has a unitary structure, with Islam as the formal state religion and Arabic the official language. Political parties are banned entirely.

MADAGASCAR: –2 (–1)

The 2010 constitution of Madagascar calls for a presidential head of state directly elected by absolute majority for five years with a two-term limit. The president appoints a prime minister from the majority party in the lower house, but the president retains power to dissolve the legislature. The constitution calls for a bicameral legislature, with a lower house elected by a mixed system of plurality vote in SMDs and PR seats; however, in recent elections the PR seats have been limited to less than 10 percent of the total. Two-thirds of the upper house, which provides regional representation, is indirectly elected by provincial bodies, with one-third appointed by the president. The new constitution, approved following a de facto coup and dissolution of the legislature in 2009, has yet to be implemented. The current legislature is comprised exclusively of appointees, and the current president is also unelected. A governmental power-sharing agreement was abandoned in late 2009, and elections have been postponed to 2011. The new constitution also restores provincial autonomy, which had been eliminated in a previous reform. The state is declared unitary and secular, with a constitutional principle of maintaining ethnically neutral policies to preserve national unity. Political parties based on identity-based distinctions are prohibited.

MALAWI: –2

The 1994 constitution of Malawi, as amended through 2003, provides for a president elected by plurality vote for a maximum of two terms. The president unilaterally appoints the executive cabinet. The de facto unicameral legislature is elected by plurality vote in SMDs. The constitution also calls for a senate to provide representation for tribal chiefs and other groups, but it has not yet been established. Multiparty elections since 1994 have been judged relatively free and fair, although irregularities and claims of fraud by losing candidates have persisted. Presidential term limits have been upheld against attempts at elimination, but there has yet to be a transfer of power to an opposition party. Malawi has a unitary state structure, and there are no constitutional provisions regarding national unity or identity-based politics. Power is effectively concentrated in the central government, with local elections postponed indefinitely since 2005.

MALI: −1 (−2)

The 1992 constitution of Mali provides for a presidential head of state elected by absolute majority, limited to two terms in office. The president appoints a prime minister, who in turn appoints cabinet ministers. The unicameral legislature is elected by a two-round majority in SMDs and party-list multimember districts. Although the legislature can exercise a no confidence vote, power has been concentrated in the presidency since 2007, when parties aligned with the president gained the legislative majority. Presidential term limits have been respected, and broad electoral and governing coalitions have provided some de facto accommodation in recent years. The state has a unitary structure with limited administrative decentralization. Political parties are constitutionally required to respect national unity, with prohibitions on identity-based distinctions.

MAURITANIA: −2

The 1991 constitution of Mauritania provides for a presidential head of state directly elected by absolute majority. A 2006 amendment reduced the presidential term from six to five years and instituted a two-term limit. The president appoints a prime minister and cabinet and has power to dissolve the legislature. The lower house is elected through a mixed system, using primarily two-round majority voting in single or two-member districts, with less than 15 percent of seats elected by PR. An upper house representing local authorities is indirectly elected by municipal councils. The legislature has limited institutional authority relative to the president, although it does have a nominal vote of no confidence. Mauritania has been subject to numerous military coups since independence, although two such events in the last decade were both followed by competitive elections judged credible by international observers. The state has a unitary structure with strongly centralized administration, despite some nominal efforts to devolve through local elections. Mauritania is declared an Islamic republic, and the formation of political parties deemed to undermine national unity is prohibited.

MAURITIUS: +2

The 1968 constitution of Mauritius, as amended through 2010, provides for a parliamentary system, with a presidential head of state indirectly elected by the legislature. The president appoints a prime minister from the legislative majority, and cabinet officers at the prime minister's recommendation. The unicameral legislature is elected primarily by plurality (block) vote in multimember districts, but over 10 percent of seats are reserved for appointment under a "best losers" system intended to ensure representation for all ethnic groups. Governing coalitions are the norm in Mauritius, with most institutional authority residing in the legislature; however, a 2003 amendment gave the president power to dissolve the legislature on advice of the prime minister. The state has a unitary structure, but full governing autonomy is granted to the island of Rodrigues. Educational autonomy is also constitutionally guaranteed. Political candidates are required to declare a community affiliation when running for office.

MOROCCO: –2 (–1)

The 1972 constitution of Morocco, as amended through 2005, provides for a hereditary monarchy. The king appoints a prime minister and cabinet members on advice of the prime minister. The bicameral legislature consists of a lower house elected by list PR, and an upper house indirectly elected by local councils. The legislature has gained increased influence over the years, but the authority of the king still dominates. The king is authorized to dissolve the legislature, and although the lower house has a no confidence vote, it has not been exercised in practice. An official policy of "alternance" permitted opposition parties to participate in government beginning in 1998, but while there have been governing coalitions, the power of opposition parties has not been consolidated. The state structure is unitary, with regional administration centralized through governors appointed by the king. Islam is the declared state religion.

MOZAMBIQUE: –2 (–1)

The 1990 constitution of Mozambique, as amended through 2004, provides for a presidential head of state elected by absolute majority for a limit of two consecutive terms. The president appoints a prime minister and cabinet, and retains power to dissolve the legislature. The unicameral national assembly is elected by a PR system with no percentage threshold, although numerous small parties continue to be excluded. Since a 1992 peace agreement ending a civil war, one party has remained in power, and in 2009 it gained the two-thirds majority required to amend the constitution. The legitimacy of recent elections has been questioned, with disputes over party eligibility and issues of election administration. Mozambique is a unitary state with nominal decentralization to local levels. Consolidation of national unity is listed as a fundamental constitutional objective, along with pluralism and tolerance. Political parties are required to respect national unity, and acts deemed to threaten that unity are punishable by law.

NAMIBIA: –1

The Namibian constitution of 1990, as amended through 2010, provides for a presidential head of state elected by absolute majority for a limit of two terms (although a third term was extended exclusively to the first president in a 1998 amendment). The president appoints a prime minister and cabinet from among members of the legislature, and is required generally to act in consultation with the cabinet. The president may dissolve the legislature, but doing so triggers new presidential elections. The bicameral legislature consists of a lower house elected by list PR from a national district, and an upper house—mainly an advisory body—indirectly elected by regional councils. The legislature has moderate institutional authority vis-à-vis the executive, including the power of impeachment. Recent elections have been judged relatively free and fair, but not without irregularities, and opposition parties have contested the results of the last election. The same ruling party has held executive and legislative power since independence. The state has a unitary structure, with regional councils functioning primarily as extensions of the central government. Affirmative action policies are authorized by the constitution.

NIGER: –2 (–1)

The 2010 constitution of Niger provides for a presidential head of state elected by absolute majority for a limit of two terms. As of January 2011, the country was ruled by a military junta that displaced the previous president, who had revised the constitution in order to remain in office beyond the two-term limit. An appointed civilian prime minister has held executive authority, while the legislature has remained dissolved pending elections called for early 2011. The unicameral legislature is elected primarily by PR, with less than 10 percent of seats reserved for election by plurality SMD. The legislature retains moderate institutional authority in the new constitution, although the president still has power of dissolution. The state has a unitary structure with local decentralization, in which opposition parties have made some electoral gains. The new constitution also adds protection for the authority of traditional tribal chiefs. Identity-based political parties are prohibited, and identity-based propaganda is punishable by law.

NIGERIA: 0

The 1999 Nigerian constitution provides for a president elected by a modified, vote-pooling majoritarian system: to win in the first round a candidate must secure a plurality of votes that includes at least one-quarter of votes in two-thirds of subnational states. The president is limited to two terms in office, and an attempt to amend the constitution to allow a third term was defeated in 2006 by the legislature. The president appoints cabinet ministers with confirmation of the senate, and the government is required to reflect regional and ethnic diversity. The lower house is elected by plurality vote in SMDs, and the senate, which represents the states, is elected by plurality vote in mostly multimember districts. Recent elections have been deemed flawed and have occasioned violence, with results contested by opposition parties. Nigeria has a federal structure of 36 states and a capital district, all with governing autonomy. The number of states has expanded over time to accommodate increasing autonomy demands, but de facto centralization of power remains a matter of contention. The constitution calls for active encouragement of integration to a national identity, and political parties founded on identity-based distinctions are prohibited.

RWANDA: −2 (−1)

The 2003 constitution of Rwanda provides for a presidential head of state elected by plurality vote for a seven-year term with a two-term limit. The president appoints a prime minister and members of the cabinet, but if one party holds a majority in parliament, it may not receive more than half of the cabinet seats. The legislature is bicameral, with the lower house elected primarily by list PR in a national district with a 5 percent threshold. The upper house is indirectly elected by local councils and other interest groups, including several seats appointed by the president meant to ensure minority representation. In practice, the current president—a former military leader in power since 1994—holds highly centralized power, and the legislature has only limited authority. Elections in 2010, in which the president and his legislative coalition won overwhelming majorities, were of questionable credibility and occasioned violence and political repression. The Rwandan state has a unitary structure, with a declared constitutional goal of eliminating all identity-based divisions. Political parties are prohibited from having identity-based distinctions or acting to destabilize national unity.

SÃO TOMÉ AND PRINCIPE: +1

The 1990 constitution of São Tomé and Principe, revised through 2003, provides for a presidential head of state elected by absolute majority with a two-term limit. A prime minister and cabinet are appointed in accordance with the distribution of seats in the legislature. The unicameral national assembly—elected by list PR—is declared the highest organ of the state. Its broad authority includes a vote of no confidence, although the president retains dissolution power. Recent elections have been deemed free and fair, and politics have been characterized by peaceful transfers of power and coalitional government, although there has been some political instability. The state has a unitary structure with a declared principle of integration to a national identity. However, the island of Principe is granted full governing autonomy, and there has been significant decentralization of power through local elections.

SENEGAL: −2

The 2001 constitution of Senegal, as amended through 2008, provides for a presidential head of state elected by absolute majority, limited to two terms in office. To win in the first round a candidate must secure the votes of at least one-quarter of all registered voters. The president appoints a prime minister, who appoints other cabinet members in consultation with the president. The lower house of the bicameral legislature utilizes a mixed electoral system, with three-fifths of seats elected by plurality vote in SMDs, and two-fifths by PR. The senate, which was abolished in 2001 but reinstated in 2007, consists mostly of presidential appointees, with 35 percent of its membership indirectly elected by local councils. The legislature's authority is limited relative to the president, who has the power of dissolution, but the national assembly does have a nominal no confidence vote. In 2000, the first transfer of power between parties took place, but recent legislative elections were postponed and then boycotted by the opposition. The Senegalese state has a unitary structure, with decentralization at the local level providing some accommodative representation to opposition parties; however, the president appoints regional governors. Political parties are prohibited from identifying with any identity-based group, and identity-based propaganda is punishable by law.

SEYCHELLES: −2

The 1993 constitution of Seychelles, as amended through 2000, provides for a president elected by absolute majority with a three-term limit. The president, as head of both state and government, unilaterally appoints a cabinet, and may retain principal ministerial portfolios. The unicameral legislature is composed of over 70 percent seats elected by plurality vote in SMDs, with the remainder elected by a PR system with a high (10 percent) threshold. In recent legislative elections, the opposition gained nearly half of the PR seats, but won barely one-quarter of the SMD seats. The legislature has only limited institutional power, with the president holding power of dissolution. There was a short period of a coalition government at independence in 1976, but a coup the following year established one-party governance, which effectively continues today, as the current president was initially appointed by the coup leader. The state has a unitary structure with centralized authority, and the constitution makes no mention of social divisions.

SIERRA LEONE: −2

The 1991 constitution of Sierra Leone, as amended through 2008, provides for a president elected by absolute majority for a limit of two terms. A candidate needs 55 percent of the vote to win in the first round. The president appoints cabinet ministers subject to legislative approval. The unicameral legislature is elected by plurality voting in SMDs, although elections in 1996 and 2002—during and immediately after the civil war—were held under a PR system. In practice, the legislature has only minimal institutional authority. During the civil war there was an unsuccessful attempt at executive power-sharing. In the 2007 elections there was a transfer of both presidential and legislative power to the opposition party. The state has a unitary structure, with a stated constitutional objective of promoting national integration, and a prohibition against identity-based political parties. Tribal chiefs are granted significant local autonomy, but they are not generally viewed as representative, and preservation of the chieftaincy may be seen as conflicting with other efforts at devolution to elected local authorities.

SOMALIA: n/a (+2)

The internationally recognized government of Somalia operates under a 2004 transitional charter that provides for a parliamentary system with a president indirectly elected by the legislature. The president appoints a prime minister, who in turn appoints the cabinet. The unicameral transitional legislature consists of members appointed mainly according to identity-based quotas. In 2009, the legislature was expanded to accommodate the major opposition party, which was also included in the cabinet. The transitional charter provides for a federal structure with two or more self-determined states. In practice, Somalia is a failed state, with the transitional government having limited power given ongoing violent conflict, and transitional institutions remaining mostly symbolic and undeveloped. There are two fully autonomous regions in the north, one of which (Somaliland) has asserted independence since 1991.

SOUTH AFRICA: +2

The 1996 South African constitution, as amended through 2009, provides for a parliamentary executive, with a president indirectly elected by the legislature. The president unilaterally appoints members of the cabinet, who may be subject to a no-confidence vote together with or separately from the president. The lower house of the legislature is elected through a list PR system, divided equally between a national district and nine provincial districts. The upper house, which represents regional and minority interests, is indirectly elected by provincial legislatures. Although opposition parties have recently made some gains, there has been effective one-party rule under the new constitution so far. However, this de facto one-party rule results mainly from demographic factors, not from a failure to implement de jure accommodative institutions. Transitional provisions in the constitution originally mandated power-sharing executives for all levels of government, but these provisions expired in 1999. The state has a federal structure with provincial governments granted considerable de jure autonomy, although in practice much authority has remained centralized at the national level. Cultural and linguistic autonomy rights are guaranteed, and affirmative action policies are mandated for advancement of 11 official languages.

SUDAN: −1

As of January 2011, Sudan was governed under a 2005 interim constitution produced through a post-civil war peace agreement. The interim constitution provides for a president elected by absolute majority vote for a limit of two terms. The president appoints a cabinet led by two vice presidents, the first of whom is required to be a member of the opposition. The current president has been in power since a 1989 coup, and he was first elected under the current constitution in 2010 amid multiparty elections that were deemed highly flawed. Prior to these elections, a power-sharing government awarded a 30 percent quota of ministerial portfolios to the opposition, but the current government is dominated by members of the president's party. The bicameral legislature consists of a lower house elected through a mixed system of mostly plurality voting in SMDs, with a small percentage of seats set aside for PR, and an upper house indirectly elected by subnational state legislatures. The legislature is extremely weak relative to the executive, having only limited institutional authority. Sudan has a federal structure, with 25 states granted governmental autonomy, and constitutional guarantees provided for cultural and legal autonomy rights. Southern Sudan is singled out as a fully autonomous region, and was granted the right to hold a referendum on secession.

SWAZILAND: –2

The 2006 constitution of Swaziland provides for a hereditary monarchy, with the king holding supreme executive and legislative powers. The king appoints a prime minister from the lower house of the legislature, which is elected mainly through a plurality SMD system, with about 15 percent of seats reserved for appointment by the king. The senate consists of two-thirds members appointed by the king, and one-third indirectly elected by the lower house. The legislature has only minimal institutional authority, as power is highly centralized in the monarchy. The state has a unitary structure, with nominal decentralization through regional administrators appointed by the king. The constitution provides for integration through a declared duty of citizens to foster national unity, but traditional authority structures are also protected. Political parties were previously banned completely, and while they are not specifically prohibited by the current constitution, in practice party identification has not been permitted in elections.

TANZANIA: –1

The 1977 Tanzanian constitution, as amended through 2005, provides for a presidential head of state elected by plurality vote for a limit of two terms. Prior to 2000, the president was elected through a two-round majority system. The president appoints a prime minister from the majority party in the legislature, and cabinet members are appointed in consultation with the prime minister. The unicameral legislature is elected primarily through plurality voting in SMDs, with an over-representative share of seats reserved for the autonomous region of Zanzibar. The legislature has moderate institutional authority, including a no-confidence vote and impeachment power, although the president retains power of dissolution. In practice, one party has held power since the return of multiparty elections in 1995, and recent elections have not been deemed credible. Tanzania has a federal structure, with full governmental autonomy granted to Zanzibar since 1964. A 2010 amendment to Zanzibar's constitution instituted a power-sharing government in response to outbreaks of violence that occurred around previous elections. Political parties in Tanzania are legally required to have a national character, and identity-based parties are prohibited.

TOGO: −2 (−1)

The 1992 constitution of Togo, as amended through 2005, provides for a presidential head of state elected by plurality vote, with no term limits since they were abolished in 2002. The president is required to appoint a prime minister from the majority party in the legislature, and a cabinet in consultation with the prime minister; however, in practice this was not followed the one time an opposition party gained the majority in 1994. The national assembly is elected by list PR with no threshold, but the gerrymandering of voting precinct lines appears to greatly limit the proportionality effects, as seen in the results of recent elections. The constitution provides for a Senate to represent local authorities, but it has not been implemented. Power is highly centralized in the presidency, with the current president—son of the previous 36-year president who died in office in 2005—having won two noncredible elections. The Togolese state has a unitary structure, and political parties are required to uphold principles of national unity.

TUNISIA: −2

The 1959 constitution of Tunisia, as amended through 2008, provided for a presidential head of state elected by absolute majority, with no term limits as of a 2002 amendment. The president appoints the prime minister and cabinet and holds highly centralized executive power. The lower house of the legislature is elected primarily by plurality vote from party lists in multimember districts, although nearly one-third of the seats are reserved for appointment of members from losing parties, based proportionally on the election results. The upper house, which was created in 2002, is mainly indirectly elected by regional and local councils, with nearly one-third of the seats appointed by the president. In practice, the legislature has minimal institutional authority and has always been controlled by the president's party. As of January 2011, the current president had been in power for 23 years. Tunisia has a unitary state structure, with regional administrators appointed by the central government. Islam is the declared state religion, and identity-based political parties are strictly prohibited.

UGANDA: −1 (−2)

The 1995 constitution of Uganda, as amended through 2005, provides for a presidential head of state elected by absolute majority, with no term limits since they were abolished in 2005. The president appoints a prime minister and cabinet members with legislative approval. The unicameral legislature is elected by plurality vote in SMDs. In practice, the legislature has minimal institutional authority, although it is immune from dissolution. Political parties were effectively banned prior to 2005, and the president's party has retained control in subsequent elections. The current president has been in power since a 1986 coup. The Ugandan state has a declared unitary structure, although there is decentralization to locally elected authorities, and guarantees for traditional tribal leadership. A highly developed system of informal patronage provides for significant de facto accommodation. The constitution contains a declared objective of fostering national unity and integration along with recognition of ethnic and other diversity. Political parties are required to have a national character without identity-based distinctions.

ZAMBIA: −2

The 1991 constitution of Zambia, as amended through 2009, provides for a president elected by plurality vote. A two-term limit was established by a 1996 amendment, which was observed in 2001. The president appoints a vice president and cabinet from among members of the legislature. The unicameral national assembly is elected by plurality vote in SMDs, with a small number of seats reserved for presidential appointment. The legislature has minimal institutional authority, and it is subject to dissolution by the president. There has been effective one-party rule since the establishment of multiparty democracy in 1991, although opposition parties have made gains in recent elections. After the former president died in office in 2008, an opposition candidate came close to winning a special election that was judged relatively free and fair. The Zambian state has a declared unitary structure, with provincial authorities appointed by the central government. Constitutional provisions grant limited legal autonomy for traditional authorities, including establishment of an advisory body to represent tribal chiefs; however, in practice power remains highly centralized.

ZIMBABWE: −2 (−1)

The 1979 constitution of Zimbabwe, as amended through 2009, provides for a presidential head of state elected by absolute majority for a six-year term with no limits. The president appoints a prime minister and cabinet; pursuant to the 2009 amendment enacted as part of a power-sharing agreement following disputed elections, the prime minister and roughly half the ministers are appointed from the opposition. The amendment also requires the president to consult with the prime minister on major decisions and appointments, but as of January 2011 there were ongoing disputes about enforcement of the power-sharing agreement. The bicameral legislature consists of a lower house elected by plurality vote in SMDs, and a senate elected mostly under the same system with just over one-third appointed seats for regional and tribal representatives. The legislature has a vote of no confidence, but the president holds dissolution authority, and in practice the legislature is institutionally feeble. The current president has held power since 1980, despite close elections in recent years that were deemed fraudulent. The opposition did, however, gain a majority in the lower house in 2008 for the first time since independence. Zimbabwe has a unitary structure, with the central government appointing provincial governors and formally appointing tribal chiefs. There is no constitutional regulation of political parties.

Appendix 2: De Jure Codings of Constitutional Design as of 1 January 2011

Appendix 2: De Jure Constitutional Design Codings

Hyper-integrative: −2	Integrative: −1	Balanced: 0	Accommodative +1	Hyper-accommodative: +2
Cameroon	Algeria	Comoros	Botswana	Mauritius
Central African Republic	Angola	Kenya	Burundi	Somalia
	Benin	Nigeria	Cape Verde	South Africa
Congo	Burkina Faso		DRC	
Côte d'Ivoire	Chad		Ethiopia	
Djibouti	Equatorial Guinea		Lesotho	
Egypt	Eritrea		São Tomé & Príncipe	
Gabon	Guinea			
The Gambia	Guinea-Bissau			
Ghana	Madagascar			
Liberia	Morocco			
Libya	Mozambique			
Malawi	Namibia			
Mali	Niger			
Mauritania	Rwanda			
Senegal	Sudan			
Seychelles	Tanzania			
Sierra Leone	Togo			
Swaziland				
Tunisia				
Uganda				
Zambia				
Zimbabwe				

Note: coding as of 1 January 2011.

CHAPTER 10

Rethinking Constitutional Reform for Democracy and Stability

Alan J. Kuperman

This book's findings call into question the conventional wisdom that espouses radical reform of the constitutional design of African countries that typically have "integrative" political institutions—including a unitary government, strong president, and majoritarian/plurality elections. Experts overwhelmingly advocate the opposing constitutional design of "accommodative" institutions—including federalism, territorial autonomy, parliamentary government, proportional representation, and formal guarantees of ethnic diversity. The case studies in this volume reveal that neither of the two designs—integration or accommodation—guarantees political stability in the face of shocks, whether arising from environmental, political, demographic, or economic change. The good news is that if institutionalized appropriately, either integration or accommodation can provide resilience against such shocks. However, if improperly institutionalized, either design may leave countries highly vulnerable to shocks, thereby magnifying the risks of political instability up to and including civil war and genocide. Thus, a crucial consideration in determining the optimal path for constitutional reform is the relative chance of each design being institutionalized appropriately in practice.

This likelihood of successful implementation, in turn, depends on how radically a proposed reform departs from the political institutions that already exist. As revealed by this book's new database, the vast majority of African countries currently have integrative constitutional designs, albeit ones that are imperfectly institutionalized from the standpoint of good governance and resilience to shocks. Accordingly, these countries would have a much better chance implementing marginal reform—to complement their existing integrative design with liberal institutions to provide greater resilience against shocks—than they would pursuing radical reform to transform into a fully accommodative constitutional design. Attempting the latter would likely result in incomplete or inequitable accommodation, which our case studies demonstrate can have disastrous consequences. For example, Burundi's incomplete accommodation in 1993 triggered genocide and a decade of civil war. Sudan's inequitable accommodation of 2005 led to multiple civil wars in both that country and the secessionist South Sudan. Accordingly, African countries and international aid providers should seriously consider promoting marginal reform of existing integrative constitutional designs, rather than their radical replacement by accommodative designs.

The rest of this chapter starts by documenting the conventional wisdom, which is promoted by both scholars and practitioners, favoring accommodation over integration. It then surveys the small but growing opposition among academics to this dominant position. Next, it explores whether countries emerging from civil war represent a special case requiring accommodation, at least in the short run. The chapter then examines the theory and evidence that radical constitutional reform is difficult to implement. Following that, it details the dangers of incomplete accommodation. Next, it explores whether regime collapse—triggered by revolution or war—improves the prospects for radical constitutional reform. The chapter concludes by discussing the suitability of scholars taking into account the likelihood of successful implementation before making policy recommendations.

Most Experts Favor Accommodation

Academics overwhelmingly assert that ethnically divided societies require accommodative constitutional designs to avert political instability and violent conflict. This stance has variously been characterized as "widely held,"[1] "dominant,"[2] and "a panacea."[3] By contrast, "the scholarly orthodoxy has long rejected majoritarian approaches."[4] Indeed, leading experts have been remarkably unequivocal and even alarmist in urging accommodation over integration. Arend Lijphart, probably the world's most cited expert on comparative constitutional design, declared in 1994 that consociationalism is "the only workable type of democracy in deeply divided societies."[5] Timothy Sisk and Andrew Reynolds, in a 1998 volume for the U.S. Institute of Peace, asserted that "the alternative [to accommodation] is nearly always a catastrophic breakdown of the state and society."[6] Reynolds later elaborated that "parliamentarism, proportional representation, and power-sharing structures provide the foundational level of inclusion needed by precariously divided societies to pull themselves out of the maelstrom of ethnic conflict and democratic instability."[7] By contrast, he insisted, presidential and majoritarian electoral systems lead to "increased ethnic hostility" and "political instability."[8]

Policy-makers offer much the same guidance. Ann Reid of the U.S. State Department intelligence bureau wrote in 1993 that "the key to conflict resolution in a multi-ethnic African state is a political deal that gives a share of power to each of the major ethnic groups."[9] Former U.S. assistant Secretary of State for African Affairs Chester Crocker warned that in deeply divided societies, "If parties appear to be moving toward majoritarian kinds of electoral systems . . . they are playing with fire."[10] International development agencies have a "core prescription" that includes political decentralization, promoting "power-sharing institutions within the state through federalism, constitutional federations, or autonomous regions."[11] Highlighting this foreign role in advocating such reform, the U.S. Agency for International Development (USAID) in 2009 issued a call for proposals that required the contractor to develop "seven laws or amendments promoting decentralization drafted with U.S. Government assistance"—for a single African country.[12]

Growing Voices for Integration

A smaller but gradually growing group of academics is skeptical that accommodative institutions are the only, or even the best, constitutional design to promote political stability in deeply divided societies. Most fundamentally, these scholars argue that accommodating groups on the basis of their differences serves to reify and sharpen these divisions, perpetuating and exacerbating intergroup conflict. They further contend that guaranteeing government posts or other benefits to particular groups is anti-democratic and undermines the political competition necessary to promote good governance via accountability. Fixed quotas also can prove particularly divisive over time if there is a significant change in the underlying dynamics on which they were based.[13]

Veto power, intended to provide minority groups with enhanced security, may instead be wielded by them as a weapon and thereby provoke tension. Territorial autonomy, aimed at averting secessionism, can instead foster it by exacerbating distinct group identities and facilitating mobilization.[14] Thus, accommodative institutions may actually increase the likelihood of political instability and war, contrary to the conventional wisdom.

These skeptics also offer theories and empirical evidence suggesting that integrative institutions promote stability especially well in divided societies like those found in Africa. For example, Benjamin Reilly explains that majoritarian institutions are more likely to promote cross-ethnic appeals if electoral districts are highly diverse ethnically. This is ideal for the continent because the "degree of ethnic heterogeneity is so much higher in Africa than other regions." By the same logic, Africa's preference for presidential executives also should foster cross-ethnic appeals by creating in each country a single voting district containing all domestic ethnic groups.[15] Goran Hyden explains that African leaders long have understood this: "Because these states are generally multiethnic and too culturally fragmented to warrant a federal solution ... the overwhelming tendency has been to favor ... the integrated prefectoral model ... in the name of political stability and national development."[16] At least one statistical study confirms that "the effect of animist diversity [common in Africa] on ethnic civil war is reduced by the establishment of majoritarian systems."[17] Even scholars who promote accommodation, such as Pippa Norris, concede that the alternative design of integration can be significantly enhanced by complementary liberal institutions such as those identified in this volume. As she writes, "Most notably, this includes the vital role of the independent judiciary and constitutional courts, functioning as a classic check on the executive, protecting human rights, and establishing the rule of law as an essential function of the state."[18]

Does Power-Sharing End War?

Most experts, including the skeptics, agree that accommodation may be necessary to achieve the negotiated settlement of civil war. Indeed, some form of power-sharing—political, military, territorial, or economic—was identified by Hartzell and Hoddie in 37 of 38 such agreements reached from 1945 to 1998.[19] Regarding political accommodation specifically, Barbara Walter finds that "warring parties are 38 percent more likely to sign an agreement if it includes guaranteed positions in the future government."[20] Hartzell and Hoddie theorize that power-sharing agreements foster peace in three ways: (1) most obviously, reducing insecurities about who controls power; (2) enabling costly signaling, and opportunities for verification, of good intentions during negotiation, finalization, and implementation; and (3) defining mechanisms for the peaceful management of future disputes.[21] Accordingly, these authors argue that increasing the extent of power-sharing in postwar settlements should improve the prospects of peace.[22] According to them, such accommodation is essential to end violence, because "only proportional systems provide adversaries with sufficient guarantees regarding their access to political power to diminish the appeal of continued warfare or ongoing reliance on self-help mechanisms such as armed militias."[23]

The evidence does suggest that postwar peace is correlated with the extent of power-sharing provisions in peace agreements and their implementation. Negotiated settlements that contain all four types of power-sharing are 18 times as likely to succeed as those without any, accordingly to Hartzell and Hoddie.[24] When military power-sharing provisions are fully implemented, these authors find a 90 percent prospect of peace, compared with 50 percent when such provisions are not fully implemented.[25] During a partially overlapping but more recent period, Jarstad and Nillson find an even higher, 100 percent chance of peace when either military or territorial power-sharing is fully implemented.[26] Although they fail to identify a similar effect for political power-sharing, Mukherjee finds that after civil wars, politically accommodative proportional representation "decreases the hazard rate of peace spells"—in other words, correlates with prolonged peace. By contrast, he reports, "majoritarian institutions do not significantly reduce the hazard rate of peace spells."[27]

As a result of this theory and evidence, accommodative constitutional design has become virtually the default recommendation for negotiated agreements to end civil war. Pippa Norris writes that "reforms which promote and implement power-sharing constitutional arrangements should be more widely recognized as one of the most promising avenues to contribute toward lasting peace-settlements."[28] Ted Robert Gurr identifies "a new international doctrine" that says "accommodation is the optimal strategy for managing conflicts between challenging groups and states."[29]

Yet, a few scholars call into question whether power-sharing agreements actually promote a durable end to fighting. Binningsbø, in a masterful meta-analysis, reveals that prominent published studies employ widely divergent definitions and coding of power-sharing and peace. Considering that the number of cases is relatively small, "these differences most likely influence results from statistical analyses . . . [as] the scores on one variable for one specific case can influence the effect of that variable substantially."[30] Illustrating this problem, Mattes and Savun find that the only form of power-sharing correlated with peace after civil war is political, not military or territorial, which is essentially opposite to the findings of Jarstad and Nillson.[31] Further confounding the results are studies that code some outcomes as "peace" barely four years after the end of fighting, when many experts agree it is premature for such a judgment.[32] It is also possible that the causal relationship between the implementation of power-sharing and the outcome of peace is the reverse of that asserted by most scholars who cite the correlation. In other words, it might be the persistence of peace that provides former adversaries the time and inclination to integrate their forces and to establish regional autonomy, not vice versa.

The statistical correlation between power-sharing agreements and peace could also be spurious. That is because when the parties to a civil war sincerely seek a negotiated settlement, the outcome is more likely to include both peace and power-sharing, thereby producing a high correlation—but no causal relationship—between the latter two. (By contrast, when at least one party negotiates insincerely—due to factors such as insecurity, greed, treachery, or domestic and international audiences—the settlement is more likely neither to produce peace nor to include significant power-sharing, further enforcing the correlation.) To their credit, several academic proponents of power-sharing acknowledge this endogeneity problem, but none overcome it. For example, Mattes and Savun note that they, and scholars such as Page Fortna, concede the possibility that "factors such as the political will of the parties affect both the content of the agreement and the durability of peace."[33] South Africa's Vincent Maphai, who personally lived through a power-sharing settlement, reports that "societies would not adopt consociationalist measures in the first place until levels of hostility had diminished substantially."[34] Thus, Ian Spears quips, "power sharing is most likely to succeed where it is least needed."[35]

Some skeptics go farther, claiming that postwar accommodation actually impedes peace. As Sven Gunnar Simonsen puts it, "the institutionalization of ethnicity has become an important hindrance to peacebuilding."[36] Timothy Sisk, who in the 1990s was a leading proponent of power-sharing to end civil wars, has largely reversed himself, warning that "the war-ending peace agreement itself... may well be counterproductive to long-term peace." He now believes that the essential elements of accommodation—including territorial autonomy, minority vetoes, and proportional representation—"tend to frustrate the pursuit of sustainable peace." Such power-sharing, he says, exacerbates three obstacles to reconciliation: hardening of identity differences, extremist outbidding among ethnic parties, and government paralysis.[37] Indeed, for similar reasons, Anna Jarstad claims that the postwar environment is actually the least appropriate moment for accommodation, complaining that scholars have "underestimated the long-term negative consequences of power-sharing on both democracy and peace... [in] the special conditions of war-torn societies."[38]

Skeptics of accommodation offer a variety of alternative prescriptions to end civil war durably. Philip Roeder proposes a highly integrative constitutional design on grounds that the alternative, accommodation, exacerbates polarization and thereby risks renewed conflict. "For third-party interveners," he explains, "options are frequently limited to fostering polarized or... hegemonic civil society that is more likely to support the peace."[39] Simonsen echoes Horowitz in recommending a centripetal constitutional design, which recognizes but aims to reduce the political salience of multicultural difference by promoting cross-cutting cleavages and incentivizing cross-group appeals by politicians through majoritarian elections.[40] Some of these skeptics concede that power-sharing may be necessary to achieve "a short-term reprieve from violent conflict,"[41] but they call for it quickly to be replaced by a more integrative constitutional design to sustain the peace. For example, Simonsen accepts "proportional ethnic representation in the immediate postconflict setting," but only if other political institutions subsequently "contribute towards a long-term de-ethnicization of politics."[42] Sisk likewise calls for an evolution of constitutional design during the postwar phase "from the rigidities of power-sharing pacts to... more integrated institutions and indeed cross-ethnic or broad-based political parties."[43]

Obstacles to Accommodation

If attempts at radical constitutional reform were likely to succeed, a strong argument might be made for trying. However, scholars have documented how and why past efforts have failed, and why future endeavors are not likely to succeed. Oisin Tansey summarizes the record as follows: "The goals and outcomes of institutional reform rarely coalesce as planned."[44] He identifies three main explanations: the stickiness of old institutions; the complexity of proposed new ones; and the principal-agent dynamic between international bodies that recommend reforms and the domestic politicians who must implement them. This last factor is crucial, he finds: "National elites are often in a position to engage with and constrain international actors, thus limiting their constitutional endeavors and frustrating their efforts at political change."[45] Cheema and Rondinelli likewise observe that "decentralization meets resistance from those whose interests are served by the concentration of power and resources."[46] Accordingly, Horowitz notes, if "new institutions are designed under the auspices of a sitting regime ... the change may be far from complete."[47] Hyden is more blunt: "Sub-Saharan Africa ... is the most obvious graveyard of misconceived development programs carried out under the banner of decentralization."[48]

In theory, radical constitutional reform should be more feasible in the wake of regime collapse, such as after revolution or war.[49] As Horowitz explains, "the slate is far more likely to be blank and the moment ripe for a rethinking."[50] In such cases, previously oppressed groups also acquire some leverage by taking up arms, which puts them "in a position to forswear secession or terrorism in return for guarantees" of accommodation.[51] However, Tansey finds that even where the international community has enjoyed maximum leverage, including during the military occupations of Kosovo and Iraq in the 2000s, it has proved unable to compel full implementation of constitutional reform. This strongly implies that the prospects would be even dimmer in normal circumstances. That does not, of course, mean it is impossible to achieve some constitutional reform in African countries. It does, however, suggest that any attempt to transition from integrative to fully accommodative constitutional design—as many experts recommend—is likely to end up incomplete, inequitable, or both.

Dangers of Attempted Accommodation

Given that such efforts at radical reform are likely to produce incomplete or inequitable power-sharing, it is necessary to examine the consequences of such partial accommodation. Tansey warns: "It is often the case that these new constitutions themselves become a source of tension across the pre-existing divides, and that they lengthen the list of political grievances."[52] In particular, the tendency of peace agreements mainly to accommodate rebels, rather than other elements of society, can backfire terribly. Jarstad explains that "concessions to some warring parties can provide incentives for other parties to use violence in the pursuit of a share of power . . . and give rise to new conflicts."[53] In the same vein, Andreas Mehler concludes that "power-sharing agreements may contribute to the reproduction of insurgent violence."[54]

Even when fighting can be ended momentarily by a power-sharing agreement, Simonsen cautions, the implementation "process of shifting from exclusion to inclusion can also drive a stable society towards instability."[55] That danger is well illustrated not only by this book's chapters on Burundi and Sudan, but also by the cases of Angola in 1992, Rwanda in 1994, and Liberia in 1997, where failed attempts at partial accommodation contributed to more than a million deaths. Even Andrew Reynolds, a leading proponent of accommodative constitutional design, acknowledges that partial accommodation can have terrible consequences: "Events in Liberia, Rwanda, and Angola all illustrate that the structures of inclusion have to be complete and extensive for power-sharing solutions to work."[56] But if radical reform efforts are unlikely to produce structures of inclusion that are "complete and extensive"—and instead more likely to produce partial accommodation that increases the risk of political instability—then it is essential to consider alternative approaches.

Academics as Consequentialists

Some critics view it as inappropriate for scholars to offer policy recommendations based on assessing the feasibility and likely outcomes of various alternatives. From this critical perspective, the academy should stick to recommending ideal-type institutions, regardless of their prospects of actually being implemented or the consequences of failure. This chapter rejects such an approach as irresponsible. Even if a theoretical constitutional design of ideal accommodation could promote better outcomes than one of ideal integration—a contention that is still much debated, as noted—that would be insufficient grounds to formulate a recommendation. From a policy perspective, the relevant metric is the expected outcome of pursuing each path. Assessing that depends crucially on the likelihood of success, as well as the consequences of success or failure for each of the two reform options. This book endeavors to assess all these factors: the relative benefits of accommodation versus integration, the likelihood of achieving either based on the current constitutional design of African countries, and the consequences of success or failure to implement attempted reform.

This chapter, building on the book's introduction, calls for rethinking the conventional wisdom that recommends radical reform of constitutional design, in Africa and elsewhere, from integrative to fully accommodative. The chapter questions this common prescription on two grounds: the dim prospects for full implementation, and the grave risks of partial implementation. Some critics may reject this chapter's logic as overly deferential to path dependence, in that it relegates some African countries to integrative constitutional design merely because such institutions were inherited from colonial masters or post-independence autocrats.[57] On the other hand, it is almost surely wishful thinking to expect that external agents can successfully promote radical constitutional reform. Tansey writes, "one of the lessons of recent state building is that it is important not to overestimate the extent to which international actors can alter domestic politics in any significant way."[58] For that reason, he urges outsiders to "face the reality that these pre-existing structures can retain a level of local legitimacy and resilience that no legal document or international order can remove."[59]

Democracy promotion efforts can, however, play a crucial role. Tansey notes that "international involvement in constitutional design and development is arguably at its peak."[60] Moreover, as Hyden aptly observes, "by virtue of their money, donors remain agenda setters."[61] Accordingly, it would be helpful for international development agencies to rethink the conventional wisdom, which promotes radical constitutional reform to impose an accommodative design, and consider instead enhancing the integrative constitutional design that now prevails in Africa. Such more modest reform efforts could have a better chance of succeeding, while also avoiding the terrible risks of failed accommodation.

NOTES

Chapter 1. Designing Constitutions to Reduce Domestic Conflict

1. For more detail, see Eli Poupko and Alan J. Kuperman, "Selected Annotated Bibliography: Constitutional Design and Conflict Management," CCAPS Program, University of Texas at Austin, 6 March 2011, http://strausscenter.org/ccaps/constitutional-design-publications.html?download=76.

2. Shaheen Mozaffar, "Electoral Systems and Conflict Management in Africa: A Twenty-Eight State Comparison," in *Elections and Conflict Management in Africa*, ed. Timothy D. Sisk and Andrew Reynolds (Washington, D.C.: U.S. Institute of Peace, 1998), 81–98. However, the findings on proportional representation are not as clear in Shaheen Mozaffar, James R. Scarritt, and Glen Galaich, "Electoral Institutions, Ethnopolitical Cleavages, and Party Systems in Africa's Emerging Democracies," *American Political Science Review* 97, 3 (2003): 379–90.

3. Joel D. Barkan, "Rethinking the Applicability of Proportional Representation for Africa," and Andrew Reynolds, "Elections in Southern Africa: The Case for Proportionality, a Rebuttal," in Sisk and Reynolds, *Elections and Conflict Management*, 57–70, 71–80; Andrew Reynolds, *Electoral Systems and Democratization in Southern Africa* (Oxford: Oxford University Press, 1999).

4. Timothy D. Sisk, *Power Sharing and International Mediation in Ethnic Conflicts* (Washington, D.C.: U.S. Institute of Peace Press, 1996); Bernard Grofman and Robert Stockwell, "Institutional Design in Plural Societies: Mitigating Ethnic Conflict and Fostering Stable Democracy," in *Economic Welfare, International Business and Global Institutional Change*, ed. Ram Mudambi, Pietro Navarra, and Guiseppe Sobbrio (New York: Edward Elgar, 2003); Milton Esman, "Ethnic Pluralism: Strategies for Conflict Management," in *Facing Ethnic Conflicts: Toward a New Realism*, ed. Andreas Wimmer et al. (Lanham, Md.: Rowman and Littlefield, 2004): 203–11; John McGarry, Brendan O'Leary, and Richard Simeon, "Integration or Accommodation? The Enduring Debate in Conflict Regulation," in *Constitutional Design for Divided Societies: Integration or Accommodation?* ed. Sujit Choudhry (Oxford: Oxford University Press, 2008), 41–88.

5. These definitions are not universal in the scholarly literature. In particular, there is debate about whether "centripetal" designs should be categorized under

accommodation or integration. Centripetal designs typically employ some of the main political institutions of integration, including a presidential system and majoritarian elections. However, they also employ other political institutions—such as the alternative vote, federalism, or requiring widespread geographic support to get elected—to increase the chance that minority groups and their concerns will be represented in government, which is a goal of accommodation. Yet, centripetal systems in divided societies also often result in the exclusion of at least one substantial minority group from each government, an outcome that is antithetical to accommodation. Accordingly, it is appropriate to locate centripetalism in the middle of the spectrum, in between integration and accommodation.

6. Accordingly, the narrower metric of "centralization" would be a suboptimal proxy to test theories of integration and accommodation. This is demonstrated by comparing the coding of constitutional design, in Poupko's chapter of this book, to the coding of centralization by Stephen N. Ndegwa, "Decentralization in Africa: A Stocktaking Survey," World Bank, Africa Region Working Paper Series 40, November 2002, http://www.worldbank.org/afr/wps/wp40.pdf.

7. For further information on the methodology, see Alan J. Kuperman, "Can Political Institutions Avert Violence from Climate Change?" CCAPS Research Brief 1 (Austin: Robert S. Strauss Center for International Security and Law, 2011), http://ccaps.strausscenter.org/system/research_items/pdfs/48/original.pdf?1312219877.

8. Arend Lijphart, "The Wave of Power-Sharing Democracy," in *The Architecture of Democracy: Constitutional Design, Conflict Management, and Democracy*, ed. Andrew Reynolds (Oxford: Oxford University Press, 2002), 37–54. More specifically, he advocates a power-sharing executive, parliamentarianism, decentralization via grants of autonomy, proportional-representation elections, and proportionality in civil society. See also Arend Lijphart, "Constitutional Design for Divided Societies," *Journal of Democracy* 15, 2 (2004): 96–109.

9. Donald Horowitz, "Constitutional Design: Proposals Versus Processes," in Reynolds, ed., *The Architecture of Democracy*, 15–36. Similar views are expressed by Benjamin Reilly, *Democracy in Divided Societies: Electoral Engineering for Conflict Management* (Oxford: Cambridge University Press, 2001).

10. David A. Lake and Donald Rothchild, "Territorial Decentralization and Civil War Settlements," in *Sustainable Peace: Power and Democracy After Civil Wars*, ed. Philip G. Roeder and Donald Rothchild (Ithaca, N.Y.: Cornell University Press, 2005), 109–32. Similar conclusions are reached by Svante E. Cornell, "Autonomy as a Source of Conflict: Caucasian Conflicts in Theoretical Perspective," *World Politics* 54, 2 (2002): 245–76.

11. Richard H. Pildes, "Ethnic Identity and Democratic Institutions: A Dynamic Perspective," in Choudhry, ed., *Constitutional Design for Divided Societies*, 172–201; Stefan Wolff, "Building Democratic States After Conflict: Institutional Design Revisited," *International Studies Review* 12, 1 (2010): 128–41.

12. See, for example, Daniel N. Posner, *Institutions and Ethnic Politics in Africa* (Oxford: Cambridge University Press, 2005); Jessica Piombo, *Institutions, Ethnicity, and Political Mobilization in South Africa* (New York: Palgrave Macmillan, 2009).

13. A similar definition is used by Annegret Haase, Dieter Rink, and Katrin Grossmann, "Urban Shrinkage as a Shock? Challenges for Modelling Human-Environmental Interaction," 2012 International Congress on Environmental Modelling and Software, Managing Resources of a Limited Planet, Sixth Biennial Meeting, Leipzig, http://www.iemss.org/sites/iemss2012//proceedings/H3_0386_Haase_et_al.pdf, 3, which reviews the literature on shocks related to demographics, economics, and climate. It summarizes as follows: "The use of the term shock in all these debates relates to the following type of events or developments: drastic changes of partly unexpected nature that represent challenges for existing natural and societal regulation systems and mechanisms destabilizing current societal organization principles (e.g., market principles, pension systems, welfare systems). Temporally seen, shocks may relate to sudden events but also to longer-term developments when it comes e.g. to ageing or climate change."

14. Lars-Erik Cederman, Andreas Wimmer, and Brian Min, "Why Do Ethnic Groups Rebel? New Data and Analysis," *World Politics* 62 (2010): 87–119.

15. Paul Collier, Anke Hoeffler, and Dominic Rohner, "Beyond Greed and Grievance: Feasibility and Civil War," *Oxford Economic Papers* 61, 1 (2009): 1–27.

16. James D. Fearon and David D. Laitin. "Ethnicity, Insurgency, and Civil War," *American Political Science Review* 97, 1 (February 2003): 75–90.

17. Barbara F. Walter, "Designing Transitions from Civil War," in *Civil Wars, Insecurity, and Intervention*, ed. Barbara F. Walter and Jack Snyder (New York: Columbia University Press, 1999), 38–69.

18. Because shocks do have such causes, they are not strictly an "independent variable," but this term is commonly used by social scientists to denote a causal variable that is under examination, even if it may be caused by other variables.

19. Examples are found in the following: Sammy Smooha, "Types of Democracy and Modes of Conflict Management in Ethnically Divided Societies," *Nations and Nationalism* 8, 4 (October 2002): 423–31; Ulrich Schneckener, "Making Power-Sharing Work: Lessons from Successes and Failures in Ethnic Conflict Regulation," *Journal of Peace Research* 39, 2 (March 2002): 205; Reynolds, *Electoral Systems and Democratization in Southern Africa*, 106.

20. Robert H. Jackson and Carl Gustav Rosberg, *Personal Rule in Black Africa: Prince, Autocrat, Prophet, Tyrant* (Berkeley: University of California Press, 1982).

21. See, for example, http://www.systemicpeace.org/polity/polity4.htm.

22. Cederman, Wimmer, and Min, "Why Do Ethnic Groups Rebel?"

23. Thanks to Terrence Lyons for this insight.

24. See Shaheen Mozaffar, "Electoral Rules and Post-Civil War Conflict Management: The Limitations of Institutional Design," in *Strengthening Peace in Post-Civil War*

States: Transforming Spoilers into Stakeholders, ed. Matthew Hoddie and Caroline A. Hartzell (Chicago: University of Chicago Press, 2010), 79–104.

25. See Michaela Mattes and Burcu Savun, "Fostering Peace After Civil War: Commitment Problems and Agreement Design," *International Studies Quarterly* 53, 3 (2009): 737–59.

26. For general principles of case selection, see Stephen Van Evera, *Guide to Methods for Students of Political Science* (Ithaca, N.Y..: Cornell University Press, 1997).

27. The cases were selected by consensus at an organizational meeting where the international participants included the prospective authors and expert commentators.

28. Cases were selected prior to the development of this book's database, which rigorously codes the constitutional design of all 53 African countries at the start of 2011. The de facto coding in the database (see Table 9.1) subsequently categorized this book's seven cases as follows: two Hyper-integrative (Senegal and Zimbabwe); two Integrative (Ghana and Sudan); two Balanced (Kenya and Nigeria); and one Accommodative (Burundi). None of the book's seven cases is coded as having a Hyper-accommodative constitutional design in early 2011, but there were only two countries in Africa that were coded as having such a design functioning at the time: Mauritius and South Africa.

29. The liberal institutions that appear most important in this case study are those pertaining to the separation of powers and the integrity of elections. Logically, the liberal guarantee of individual rights—such as property, due process, speech, assembly, religion, and a free press—may also be quite important, because these rights undergird the proper functioning of liberal institutions.

30. The exact figure is 79.2 percent, representing 42 of 53 countries.

31. Horowitz, "Constitutional Design: Proposals Versus Processes."

Chapter 2. Burundi: Institutionalizing Ethnicity to Bridge the Ethnic Divide

1. René Lemarchand and David Martin, *Selective Genocide in Burundi* (London: Minority Rights Group, 1974); René Lemarchand, "Burundi: The Politics of Ethnic Amnesia," in *Genocide Watch*, ed. Helen Fein (New Haven, Conn.: Yale University Press, 1992): 70–86; René Lemarchand, *Burundi: Ethnocide as Discourse and Practice* (Washington, D.C.: Woodrow Wilson Center Press, 1994).

2. Stefaan Vandeginste, "Power-Sharing, Conflict and Transition in Burundi: Twenty Years of Trial and Error," *Africa Spectrum* (2009): 63–86; Stefaan Vandeginste, "Chronique politique du Burundi," in *L'Afrique des grands lacs: Annuaire 2010–2011*, ed. Stefaan Marysse, Filip Reyntjens, and Stefaan Vandeginste (Paris: L'Harmattan, 2011), 1–22; D. P. Sullivan, "The Missing Pillars: A Look at the Failure of Peace in Burundi Through the Lens of Arend Lijphart's Theory of Consociational Democracy," *Journal of Modern African Studies* (2005): 75–95.

3. The other Tutsi group is the Banyaruguru. The Hima were considered "lower class," but they had a strong presence in the army.

4. On this episode, see Lemarchand and Martin, *Selective Genocide in Burundi*; Jean-Pierre Chrétien and Jean-François Dupaquier, *Burundi 1972: Au bord des genocides* (Paris: Karthala, 2007).

5. Term coined in Lemarchand, "Burundi: The Politics of Ethnic Amnesia."

6. Amnesty International, *Burundi: Killings of Children by Government Troops* (London: Amnesty International, 1988); Jean-Pierre Chrétien, André Guichaoua, and Gabriel Le Jeune, *La crise d'août 1988 au Burundi* (Paris: Karthala, 1989); Lemarchand, *Burundi: Ethnocide as Discourse*, 118–30.

7. More information on these provisions and the problems of implementation can be found in Filip Reyntjens, "L'ingénierie de l'unité nationale: Quelques singularités de la constitution burundaise de 1992," *Politique Africaine* (October 1992): 141–46.

8. The 1961 and 1965 multiparty elections were for parliament but not a president. Subsequently, presidential elections were conducted in a single-party context.

9. On the elections, see Filip Reyntjens, "The Proof of the Pudding Is in the Eating: The June 1993 Elections in Burundi," *Journal of Modern African Studies* (1993): 563–83.

10. Filip Reyntjens, *Burundi: Prospects for Peace* (London: Minority Rights Group, 2000), 12.

11. For a discussion of the coup and its immediate aftermath see Filip Reyntjens, *Burundi: Breaking the Cycle of Violence* (London: Minority Rights Group, 1995). Subsequent events are discussed in Reyntjens, *Burundi: Prospects for Peace*.

12. On the difficulties of putting such a system into place in Burundi, see Sullivan, "The Missing Pillars." See also Vandeginste, "Power-Sharing," on the application in Burundi of two typical consociational elements: a grand coalition, and proportionality combined with minority over-representation.

13. Vandeginste, "Power-Sharing," 71–72.

14. An excellent inside story of the transition, and of the role played by the international community and the regional initiative, can be found in Howard Wolpe, *Making Peace After Genocide: Anatomy of the Burundi Process* (Washington, D.C.: U.S. Institute of Peace, 2011).

15. For reasons of political opportunism rather than political conviction, many Tutsi voted for the CNDD-FDD. They anticipated its victory and hoped to capture positions thanks to the ethnic quota. They realized they stood a better chance in a winning "Hutu" party than a losing "Tutsi" party such as UPRONA.

16. Six signatory parties of the Arusha Accord each obtained less than 0.1 percent of the vote, and three others did not even bother to run. These results confirm what was widely suspected—that these parties held the political process for ransom, in order to enjoy the spoils as long they could.

17. On both sides of the ethnic divide, the elections resulted in the "weeding out" of parties without a real base and left only a few in a position to claim a stake in power. This phenomenon has been seen elsewhere in Africa on the occasion of (post-)transition elections.

18. On this and later occasions, the Commission Électorale Nationale Indépendante (CENI) played a crucial role. It was given considerable powers, which it exercised skillfully. Although some of its decisions were far-reaching, they were by and large uncontested. Nevertheless, the vague legal framework forced the CENI to take actions with political consequences, thus exposing it to pressures from many interest groups.

19. "Un plébiscite pour le CNDD-FDD," *Libre Belgique*, 8 June 2005.

20. Twice during the campaign, the army chief of staff intervened in the media to warn politicians against derailing the process. In line with the apolitical stance of the army, he insisted that politicians respect the outcome of the polls and not jeopardize the transition efforts undertaken so far. In addition, he told members of the armed forces to abstain from "militantism" or involvement in political activities. Likewise, the special representative of the UN secretary general, Carolyn McAskie, warned politicians to stop acts of violence, stating that "any use of violence will also affect you and maintain Burundians in poverty." "Burundi: Stop Acts of Violence, UN Envoy Tells Politicians," *IRIN*, 22 June 2005.

21. Union Européenne, Mission d'Observation Électorale, Élections Législatives, Burundi 2005, "Déclaration préliminaire," Bujumbura, 2005.

22. "In case the results of the vote do not reflect the above-mentioned percentages, there shall be a rectification of the imbalances through the co-optation mechanism provided by the electoral code."

23. Twa representation is not taken into account for implementation of Hutu-Tutsi ethnic or gender quotas.

24. "Un ancien président burundais appelle à ne pas avoir 'peur' des FDD," *AFP*, 5 July 2005. Strangely, Buyoya also emphasized the ethnic nature of his party: "UPRONA comes out of the vote as the first party of the Tutsi minority." This is contrary to the party's own official credo, and indeed to Buyoya's previous public statements.

25. This allowed the entry of UPRONA into the upper house, with two senators. After the co-optation exercise, the final numbers for the other parties were 32 CNDD-FDD, 5 FRODEBU, and 3 CNDD.

26. This brought Parena into parliament via former president Jean-Baptiste Bagaza. Of the three other former presidents, two are from FRODEBU and one is from UPRONA.

27. Human Rights Watch, "Pursuit of Power: Political Violence and Repression in Burundi" (New York, May 2009); Human Rights Watch, "Closing Doors? The Narrowing of Democratic Space in Burundi" (New York, November 2010).

28. Wolpe, *Making Peace After Genocide*, 62.

29. The result shows that ADC-Ikibiri made a strategic error by boycotting the parliamentary elections, in which opposition parties otherwise probably would have secured about a third of the vote, making parliament less monolithic and denying the government the ability to amend the constitution.

30. On the 2010 elections, see Vandeginste, "Chronique politique du Burundi."

31. But the consociational mechanisms, including proportional representation, did maintain some political pluralism in parliament, in addition to seats for minorities and women. Without these mechanisms, the CNDD-FDD likely would have captured all elected seats in the National Assembly and the Senate. See Vandeginste, "Chronique politique du Burundi," 11.

32. Matthias Basedau, "Managing Ethnic Conflict: The Menu of Institutional Engineering," Hamburg, GIGA Working Paper 171, June 2011, 22.

33. In 1993, both UPRONA and the Tutsi elites were surprised by the outcome of the elections, while in 2005 they anticipated it and were therefore better prepared to accept it. If someone was taken by surprise in 2005, it was the FRODEBU leadership, but their ability to derail the process was limited.

34. Pippa Norris, *Driving Democracy: Do Power-Sharing Institutions Work?* (London: Cambridge University Press, 2008), 30, draws attention to "how power-sharing arrangements are brokered, and in particular whether they arise from negotiated pacts among all major parties, from one side achieving a decisive victory and seizing control of the state following an armed struggle, or from a peace settlement generated by the international community and external forces."

35. Norris, *Driving Democracy*, 28, notes that "power-sharing regimes based on formal recognition of linguistic or religious groups may magnify the political salience of communal identities, by institutionalizing these cleavages and by providing electoral incentives for politicians and parties to heighten appeals based on distinct ethnic identities." The opposite appears true in Burundi.

36. This explains why vote-pooling arrangements proposed by Donald L. Horowitz, "Constitutional Design: Proposals Versus Processes," in *The Architecture of Democracy: Constitutional Design, Conflict Management, and Democracy*, ed. Andrew Reynolds (London: Oxford University Press, 2002), 23, are more likely to work in multipolar than in bipolar ethnic configurations.

Chapter 3. Kenya: Gradual Pluralization Fails to Buffer Shocks

1. Eliphas Mukonoweshuro, "Authoritarian Reaction to Economic Crises in Kenya," *Race and Class* 31, 4 (1990): 39–59.

2. Benno Ndulu, Stephen O'Connell, and Jean-Paul Azam, *The Political Economy of Economic Growth in Africa, 1960–2000* (London: Cambridge University Press, 2003), 359.

3. Peter Anyan'g Nyong'o, "The Disintegration of the National Coalition and the Rise of Presidential Authoritarianism in Kenya, 1963–1978," *African Affairs* 88 (1989): 229–52.

4. Kate Currie and Larry Ray, "The Pambana of August 1—Kenya's Abortive Coup," *Political Quarterly* 57, 1 (1986): 47–59; Todd Shields, "Kenya: L'état c'est Moi?" *Africa Report* 33, 6 (1988): 49–52; Lindsey Hilsum, "Kenya: The Dynamics of Discontent," *Africa Report* 33, 1 (1988): 22–26.

5. Todd Shields, "Kenya: The Queuing Controversy," *Africa Report* 33, 3 (1988): 47–49; Michael Maren, "Kenya: Hear No Evil," *Africa Report* 31, 6 (1986): 67–71.

6. Makau Mutua, *Kenya's Quest for Democracy: Taming the Leviathan* (Boulder, Colo.: Lynne Rienner, 2008); Jill Cottrell and Yash Ghai, "Constitution Making and Democratization in Kenya (2000–2005)," *Democratization* 14, 1 (2009): 1–25; Susanne Mueller, "Dying to Win: Elections, Political Violence, and Institutional Decay in Kenya," *Journal of Contemporary African Studies* 29, 1 (2011); Edwin Odhiambo Abuya, "Consequences of a Flawed Presidential Election," *Legal Studies* 29, 1 (March 2009); Frank Holmquist, Frank Weaver, and Michael D. Ford, "The Structural Development of Kenya's Political Economy," *African Studies Review* 37, 1 (1994).

7. Mueller, "Dying to Win," 100.

8. Colin H. Kahl, "Population Growth, Environmental Degradation, and State-Sponsored Violence: The Case of Kenya, 1991–1993," *International Security* 23, 2 (Fall 1998): 80–119; Jacqueline M. Klopp, "Ethnic Clashes and the Winning of Elections: The Case of Kenya's Electoral Despotism," *Canadian Journal of African Studies* 35, 3 (2001): 473–517; Peter Mwangi Kagwanja, "Facing Mount Kenya or Facing Mecca? The Mungiki, Ethnic Violence, and the Politics of Moi Succession in Kenya, 1987–2002," *African Affairs* 102 (2003): 25–49. See also Rok Ajulu, "Kenya: One Step Forward, Three Steps Back: The Succession Dilemma," *Review of African Political Economy* 28, 88 (June 2001): 197–212; David Anderson, "Vigilantes, Violence, and the Politics of the Public Order in Kenya," *African Affairs* (2002): 531–55.

9. On Saba Saba riots and government response see Makau Mutua, "The Politics of Doom," *Africa Report* 37, 2 (1992): 14–18; Mutua, "Kenya's Troubled Transition," *Africa Report* 37, 5 (1992): 34–38; Jennifer Widner, "Kenya's Slow Progress Toward Multiparty Politics," *Current History* 565 (May 1992): 214–18.

10. *Weekly Review*, 30 October 1991.

11. François Grignon, Marcel Rutten, and Alamin Mazrui, "Observing and Analyzing the 1997 General Elections: An Introduction," in *Out for the Count: The 1997 General Elections and Prospects for Democracy in Kenya*, ed. Rutten, Mazrui, and Grignon (Kampala: Fountain Publishers, 2001), 2.

12. Smith Hempstone, *Rogue Ambassador: An African Memoir* (Sewanee, Tenn.: University of the South Press, 1997). See also Raymond W. Copson, *Africa's Wars and Prospects for Peace* (New York: M.E. Sharpe, 1994), for a good analysis of Hempstone's role.

13. Holly Burkhalter, "Kenya: Congress Demands More Pressure," *Africa Report* 36, 3 (May–June 1991).

14. "Kenya: U.S. Congress Cautiously Awaits Administration Response," *Inter Press Service*, 23 October 1991; "Kenya: Democracy Could be the Loser," *Africa Confidential* 33, 25 (20 October 1991).

15. "Commonwealth Criticisms Deal Blow to Moi's Credibility," *The Guardian*, 20 June 1992; "Nordic Countries Losing Patience with KANU Government," *Weekly Review*, 23 October 1992.

16. Cited in Joel Barkan, "Kenya: Lessons from a Flawed Election," *Journal of Democracy* 4, 3 (July 1993): 91.

17. The value of the Kenyan shilling fluctuated around $0.03 during this period. Historical exchange rates are available at http://fxtop.com/en/currency-converter-past.php.

18. Government of Kenya, *Kenya Economic Survey, 1991–1992* (Nairobi: Government Printer, 1992).

19. Widner, "Kenya's Slow Progress," 214–18; Mutua, "The Politics of Doom"; Mutua, "The Troubled Transition."

20. Charles Wachira, "Kenya-Politics: Opposition Faces Difficult Times," *Inter Press Service*, 11 October 1994.

21. Mutua, *Kenya's Quest for Democracy*, 105.

22. See the analysis of the model constitution (The Kenya We Want) in Horace Awori, "Kenya-Politics: NGOs Aim at a Fairer Distribution of State Power," *Inter Press Service*, 4 November 1994.

23. Njuguna Nge'the and Musambayi Katumanga, "Transitions and the Politics of Constitution-Making: A Comparative Study of Uganda, South Africa and Kenya," in *The Politics of Transition in Kenya: From KANU to NARC*, ed. Walter Oyugi, Peter Wanyande, and C. Odhiambo Mbai (Nairobi: Heinrich Boll Foundation, 2003), 327–30.

24. Ngethe and Katumanga, "Transitions and the Politics of Constitution-Making," 330. See also Mutua, *Kenya's Quest for Democracy*, 106.

25. Mutua, *Kenya's Quest for Democracy*, 109.

26. Republic of Kenya, National Assembly, The Inter-Parties Parliamentary Group (IPPG), "Reports and Resolution Adopted," 11 September 1997.

27. Maina Kiai, "Commentary: A Last Chance for Peaceful Change in Kenya?" *Africa Today* 45, 2 (April–June 1998): 185–92.

28. Ralph-Michael Peters, "Civil Society and the Election Year 1997," in Rutten, Mazrui, and Grignon, eds., *Out for the Count*, 32.

29. Peter Mwangi Kagwanja, "Politics of Marionettes: Extra-Legal Violence and the 1997 Elections in Kenya," 74, and Alamin Mazrui, "Ethnic Violence and Trans-Ethnic Voting: The 1997 Elections at the Kenyan Coast," 275–96, in Rutten, Mazrui, and Grignon, eds., *Out for the Count*.

30. Mutua, *Kenya's Quest for Democracy*, 117–35. See also Cottrel and Ghai, "Constitution Making and Democratization."

31. Mutua, *Kenya's Quest for Democracy*, 135.

32. Karuti Kanyinga, "Limitations of Political Liberalization: Parties and Electoral Politics in Kenya, 1992–2002," in Oyugi et al., eds., *The Politics of Transition*, 111–12.

33. For a good discussion of electoral alliances prior to the 2002 elections see David Throup, "The Kenya General Elections: December 27, 2002," *CSIS Africa Notes* 14 (January 2003): 1–12; David M. Anderson, "Briefing: Kenya's Elections 2002: The Dawning of a New Era?" *African Affairs* 102 (2003): 331–42.

34. For discussion of KANU factions see Frank Holmquist, and Michael Ford, "Kenyan Politics: Toward a Second Transition?" *Africa Today* 45, 2 (April–June 1998).

35. Joel D. Barkan, "Kenya After Moi," *Foreign Affairs* 83, 1 (January–February 2004); Anderson, "Briefing: Kenya's Elections 2002."

36. See, for instance, Barkan, "Kenya After Moi"; African Development Fund, "Kenya: Country Governance Profile," November 2004; Steven Brown, "Foreign Aid and Democracy Promotion: Lessons from Africa," *European Journal of Development Studies* 17, 2 (2005): 179–98.

37. See, for instance, Barkan, "Kenya After Moi"; Brown, "Foreign Aid and Democracy Promotion."

38. Sebastian Elischer, "Ethnic Coalition of Convenience and Commitment: Political Parties and Party Systems in Kenya," German Institute of Global and Area Studies, Hamburg, Working Paper 68, February 2008, 22–23.

39. For a good analysis of the 2007 campaign platforms, see Fredrick Wanyama, "Voting Without Institutionalized Political Parties: Primaries, Manifestos and the 2007 General Elections in Kenya," in *Tensions and Reversals in Democratic Transitions: The Kenya 2007 General Elections*, ed. Karuti Kanyinga and Duncan Okello (Nairobi: Society for International Development, 2010), 61–100.

40. The Independent Review Commission (IREC), appointed after the conclusion of the mediation and headed by retired South African Constitutional Court judge Johann Kriegler, heaped blame on the ECK and recommended it be disbanded.

41. The inquiry into the electoral violence led by Justice Philip Waki and appointed after the signing of the agreement concurred with this characterization of the violence. See also John O. Oucho, "Undercurrents of Post-Election Violence in Kenya: Issue in the Long-Term Agenda," in Kanyinga and Okello, eds., *Tensions and Reversals*, 491–532; Musambayi Katumanga, "Militarized Spaces and the Post-2007 Electoral Violence," in *Tensions and Reversals*, 533–64; Mueller, "Dying to Win Elections."

Chapter 4. Nigeria: Devolution to Mitigate Conflict in the Niger Delta

1. Billy J. Dudley, *Instability and Political Order: Politics and Crisis in Nigeria* (Ibadan: Ibadan University Press, 1973).

2. Ken Saro-Wiwa, *Genocide in Nigeria: The Ogoni Tragedy* (Port-Harcourt: Saros International Publishers, 1992).

3. Michael Peel, *Swamp Full of Dollars: Pipelines and Paramilitaries at Nigeria's Oil Frontier* (Ibadan: Bookcraft, 2010).

4. The "corrective" constitutions were designed as part of democratic transition programs implemented by military governments but were not observed by the military governments themselves.

5. Tony Tebekaemi, *The Twelve-Day Revolution* (Benin City: Idodo Umeh Publishers, 1982). Oil explorations in the Chad River basin in the northeast of the country, commencing in 1976, have so far not yielded positive results.

6. http://www.unep.org/Nigeria/. See also Jon Gambrell, "Widespread Oil Damage Reported in Nigerian Delta," *Washington Post*, 5 August 2011.

7. Anke Hoeffler and Paul Collier, "Greed and Grievance in Civil Wars," *Oxford Economic Papers* 56, 4 (October 2004): 563–95.

8. Peter Maass, *Crude World: The Violent Twilight of Oil* (London: Allen Lane, 2009), 6. See also Thomas A. Imobighe, "Conflict in the Niger Delta: A unique case or a model for future conflicts in other oil producing countries," in *Oil Policy in the Gulf of Guinea: Security and Conflict, Economic Growth and Social Development*, ed. Rudolf Traub-Mern and Douglas Yates (Bern: Freidrich-Ebert, 2004); Eghosa E. Osaghae, "Fragile States," *Development in Practice* 17, 4–5 (2007); Adekunle Amuwo, "Constructing the Democratic Developmental State in Africa: A Case Study of Nigeria," Institute for Global Dialogue Occasional Paper 59, Pretoria, 2008; C. I. Obi, "The Petroleum Industry: A Paradox or (Sp)oiler of Development?" *Journal of Contemporary African Studies* 28, 4 (2010); John Agbonifo, "The Dynamics of Collective Action: How the Ogoni Mobilized Against the Nigerian State and Shell," *Journal of Modern African Studies*, forthcoming.

9. Maass, *Crude World*; Scott Barrett, *Environment and Statecraft: The Strategy of Environmental Treaty-Making* (Oxford: Oxford University Press, 2003).

10. Celestin O. Bassey and Oshita O. Oshita, eds., *Conflict Resolution, Identity Crisis and Development in Africa* (Abuja: Centre for Peace and Conflict Resolution, Malthouse, 2007); T. A Imobighe, Celestin O. Bassey, and Judith B. Asuni, *Conflict and Instability in the Niger Delta: The Warri Case* (Ibadan: Spectrum, 2001).

11. Human Rights Watch, *The Price of Oil: Corporate Responsibility and Human Rights Violations in Nigeria's Oil Producing Communities* (New York: HRW, 1999), 17.

12. Eghosa E. Osaghae, "Managing Multiple Minority Problems in a Divided Society: The Nigerian Experience," *Journal of Modern African Studies* 36, 1 (1998).

13. Eghosa E. Osaghae, "Do Ethnic Minorities Still Exist in Nigeria?" *Journal of Commonwealth and Comparative Politics* 24, 2 (1986).

14. Following persistent struggles, mostly through litigation, states and localities have managed over the years to increase the proportion of the Federation Account allocated to them. By 2011, 53 percent of the Account went to the federal government, 27 percent to the 36 state governments, and 21 percent to the 774 local government councils (figures do not add to 100 due to rounding). Previously during the Second Republic, the shares were 55 (federal), 33 (states), and 10 (localities). In the period before the Second Republic, the shares were 76 (federal government), 21 (states), and 3 (localities). By contrast, allocations of proceeds from VAT (not based on oil revenue) favor states and localities: 15 percent federal, 50 percent states, and 35 percent localities. See Alhaji Ahmed Iliyasu, "Revenue Allocation Formula in Nigeria: Issues and Challenges," paper presented at Revenue Mobilization, Allocation, and Fiscal Commission Retreat, Uyo, Akwa Ibom, Nigeria, February 2011.

15. The lower end estimate is found in http://www.britannica.com/EBchecked/topic/414800/Niger-Delta (accessed 16 May 2013).

16. Onigu Otite, *Ethnic Pluralism, Ethnicity and Ethnic Conflicts in Nigeria* (Ibadan: Shaneson C.I., 2000); V. A. Isumonah and Jaye Gaskia, *Ethnic Groups and Conflicts in*

Nigeria, vol. 3, *The SouthSouth Zone* (Ibadan: Program on Ethnic and Federal Studies, University of Ibadan, 2001); Institute for Peace and Conflict Resolution, "Strategic Conflict Assessment of Nigeria: Consolidated and Zonal Reports," 2008.

17. NDDC, *Niger Delta Regional Development Masterplan* (Port-Harcourt: NDDC, 2006). These nine states cover 43,000 square miles.

18. The "core" Niger Delta of three states—Bayelsa, Delta, and Rivers—that account for nearly 70 percent of oil production is referred to by Ike Okonta and Oronto Douglas, *Where Vultures Feast: 40 Years of Shell in the Niger Delta* (Benin City: Environmental Rights Action, 2001).

19. Tebekaemi, *The Twelve-Day Revolution*, 57, insists that the Niger Delta is coterminous with the areas occupied by the Ijaws, characterized as the "aboriginal tribe of the Delta." Similarly, Isaac Caution Preboye, *The Core Delta: Iduwini Clan* (Rural Development Nig. Limited, 2005) characterizes Iduwini, the original Ijaw cradle, as the core of the Niger Delta. The definition of the Niger Delta as centered around the interests of the Ijaws, which has been reinforced by the appointments of Ijaws to top government positions from the Niger Delta under the Jonathan administration, has expectedly elicited opposition from the elite of other groups in the region who feel marginalized. For instance, the NDDC and ministry of Niger Delta, created to address developmental challenges of the Niger Delta, were dismissed by an Itsekiri leader as having been established "for the Ijaws and not for the whole of the Niger Delta ethnic groups" (interview with Professor Tony Afejuku).

20. See Dauda S. Garuba, "Trans-Border Economic Crimes, Illegal Oil Bunkering and Economic Reforms in Nigeria," Policy Brief Series 15 (Santiago, Chile: Global Consortium on Security Transformation, 2010).

21. Okonta and Douglas, *Where Vultures Feast*, 36. See also Sarah Ahman Khan, *Nigeria: The Political Economy of Oil* (Oxford: Oxford University Press, 1994).

22. A marginal victory for the region was the 1995 constitutional conference decision to partially restore the derivation rate to 13 percent, which was then codified in the 1999 constitution as a minimum rate. Section 162(2) of the constitution provides that whatever the criteria used for sharing revenue, "the principle of derivation shall be constantly reflected . . . as being not less than thirteen percent of the revenue accruing to the Federation Account directly from any natural resources."

23. Eghosa E. Osaghae, *Structural Adjustment and Ethnicity in Nigeria* (Uppsala: Scandinavian Institute of African Studies, 1995); Eghosa E. Osaghae, "Social Movements and Rights Claims: The Case of Action Groups in the Niger Delta of Nigeria," in *Citizenship and Social Movements: Perspectives from the Global South*, ed. Lisa Thompson and Chris Tapscott (London: Zed, 2010).

24. For example, the Nigerian Economic Support Group reported in March 2011 that Bayelsa state had the highest unemployment rate in the country, at 37 percent, followed by Akwa Ibom state (36 percent) and Rivers state (32 percent)—all in the Niger Delta. By contrast, in the north central zone, the rates in Plateau and Kwara states were 7.1 and 11 percent respectively. See *Guardian*, 31 March 2011, 15.

25. To put this amount in context, it is estimated that the 1989 Exxon Valdez oil spill released 11 million gallons off Alaska, and the 2010 Deepwater Horizon blowout 170 million gallons into the Gulf of Mexico, but both those spills were mainly dispersed at sea.

26. Shell, *Sustainability Report*, 2010, http://reports.shell.com/sustainability-report /2010/servicepages/welcome.html, 32.

27. Maass, *Crude World*, 70.

28. Human Rights Watch, *The Price of Oil*, 72. Shell, *Sustainability Report*, 2010, attributed 20 percent of the company's gas flaring worldwide to operational factors and 80 percent to lack of infrastructure for capturing associated gas. Of the latter, 80 percent was in Nigeria, though the report adds that the security situation and lack of funding by government are critical factors as well.

29. These are defined by the codes of the American Petroleum Institute and American Society of Mechanical Engineering.

30. Evidently, the problem was not the absence of regulations capable of protecting the interests and rights of the people, but the inability—or unwillingness—to enforce them. Rather than apply the rules on safety, environmental protection, and rights of communities, the government and its agencies have instead issued hortatory statements. The NNPC, for instance, merely admonishes oil companies to cooperate with host communities and to extend to them the comfort of First World standards enjoyed at the oil installations and the neighborhoods for foreign workers.

31. Previous movements had been peaceful. The only exception, in 1966, was the twelve-day revolutionary uprising led by Isaac Adaka Boro and his Niger Delta Volunteer Force, which reached its apex by declaring an independent Republic of the Niger Delta—which then was crushed by the federal government.

32. One reason the oil companies were targeted is that they are implicated in the military operations to suppress the Niger Delta insurgents, including funding and providing arms to security forces. For example, they pay for the supernumerary police, whose activities are restricted within the fences of oil operations but whose members are recruited and trained by the Nigerian police. The 1990 invasion by security forces of Shell's facility at Umuechem, east of Port Harcourt, which led to the massacre of about 80 civilians, was said to have followed a request for protection by the Shell station manager. Indeed, it has been argued that Shell had become an "integral part of the Niger Delta conflict system" on account of its deep involvement in highhanded security, alleged complicity in communal conflicts, and environmental excesses. See Maass, *Crude World*, 75.

33. Various groups submitted nine major bills, declarations, and resolutions to the federal government: the Ogoni Bill of Rights (1990); the Charter of Demands of the Ogbia People (1992); the Kaiama Declaration (1998); Resolutions of the First Urhobo Economic Summit (1998); the Akalaka Declaration (1999); the Warri Accord (1999); the Ikwerre Rescue Charter (1999); the Oron Bill of Rights (1999); and the Niger Delta Peoples' Compact (2008).

34. R. Wade, "The Management of Common Property Resources: Finding a Cooperative Solution," *World Bank Research Observer* 2 (1987). The case of the Ugborodo community of Warri is instructive. In 2010, leaders of the community petitioned the federal government, demanding protection of the shoreline and reclamation in the face of turbulent oceanic waves, oil production, environmental degradation, and continued negligence by the state and failure of NDDC to address the problems. When the government did not respond to the petition, the community mobilized to shut down the gas pipeline project located there.

35. Human Rights Watch, *The Price of Oil*, 156.

36. The resort to militancy enjoyed support in the region, even among government officials. A minister of state for environment from the region, Ime Okopido, publicly denounced Shell and other oil companies for their environmental degradation and justified the armed struggles against "oppressors." He was promptly removed from office.

37. Olumide S. Ayodele, Festus O. Egwaikhide, Victor A. Isumonah, and Olugboyega A. Oyeranti, "Supreme Court Judgements and Aftermaths," in *Contemporary Issues in the Management of the Nigerian Economy: Essays in Honour of HMA Onitiri*, ed. Akinola Owosekun, Ode Ojowu, and Festus O. Egwaikhide (Ibadan: Nigerian Institute of Social and Economic Research, 2005).

38. These provisions include establishment of intergovernmental bodies such as the National Security Council, National Economic Council, and National Council of State (which has as members the president, governors, and former heads of state). Although these bodies are mainly advisory, they have provided the platform for cooperation and collaboration on divisive matters, including minimum wage, mitigation of ethnoreligious conflicts, and sharing of excess crude receipts.

39. According to Ayodele et al., "The Supreme Court Judgment," 377, the abrogation "doused tension in the oil-producing states . . . by ensuring that no section is alienated or marginalized."

40. From a high of $30 billion in 2008, the excess crude account fell to $450 million by mid-2010 and $300 million in 2011. While foreign reserves also fell from $42 billion to $32 billion during the same period, domestic and foreign debts in 2010 rose to $29 billion and $4.8 billion respectively.

41. The absence of clear guidelines for sharing the proceeds led to the proposal to establish a Sovereign Wealth Fund to augment budgets, savings for investment, and infrastructure.

42. Several statutes—including the Petroleum Act and Petroleum Products and Distribution (anti-sabotage) decree of 1975—prohibit bunkering and stipulate severe penalties for violation, including death by firing squad. Despite this, the practice has thrived and expanded over the years. Bunkering, not guided by any safety code, has been identified as a major source of spillage and environmental degradation. It is a major preoccupation not only of militant groups, warlords, and criminal gangs, but of prominent elites including security personnel, who also have been implicated. Such theft deprives

oil companies of up to 15 percent of their petroleum output in Nigeria and provides funds for weapons.

43. Maass, *Crude World*, 77.

44. Such large-scale bunkering persists, according to a 2013 report by Chatham House. See Adam Nossiter, "As Oil Thieves Bleed Nigeria, Report Says, Officials Profit," *New York Times*, 20 September 2013.

45. Isumonah and Gaskia, *Ethnic Groups and Conflicts in Nigeria*; Imobighe et al., *Conflict and Instability in the Niger Delta*.

46. While Nigeria enjoys sovereignty over maritime resources down to the 2,500-meter isobath (i.e., sea depth) continental shelf, its littoral states are entitled to a 13 percent derivation of oil resources only down to the 200-meter isobath.

47. See SC.27/2010, *AG Rivers State v. AG Akwa Ibom State and AG of the Federation*.

48. B. O. Nwabueze, *Nigeria '93: The Political Crisis and Solutions* (Ibadan: Spectrum, 1994): 4.

49. Godwin Uyi Ojo and Jaye Gaskia, eds., *Environmental Laws of Nigeria: A Critical Review* (Benin City: Environmental Rights Action, 2003).

50. *Report of the Technical Committee on the Niger Delta*, vol. 1 (2008), 62.

51. Eghosa E. Osaghae, "State, Constitutionalism and the Management of Ethnicity in Africa," *Asian and African Studies* 4, 1–2 (2005); Rotimi T. Suberu, "Nigeria," in *Diversity and Unity in Federal Countries*, ed. John Kincaid, Luis Moreno, and César Colino (Montreal: McGill-Queen's University Press, 2010).

Chapter 5. Sudan: "Successful" Constitutional Reform Spurs Localized Violence

1. We thank Alan Goulty for helpful comments on an earlier draft.

2. Apart from the North-South conflict, Sudan has also seen sustained violence in Darfur, where the Darfur-based Sudan Liberation Movement (SLM) and the Justice and Equality Movement (JEM) began to attack government forces in 2003. Although the Darfur Peace Agreement (DPA) was signed in May 2006, because of the fragmentation of the so-called Western Movements, fighting in Darfur continues with grave humanitarian consequences. The third conflict started in the east in 1996, when the Beja Congress took up arms against Khartoum in the Red Sea, Kassala, and Gedaref states. Given the strategic importance of eastern Sudan, Khartoum began to engage the Beja Congress militarily. For the next ten years, the conflict continued on a low-intensity level, before the Eastern Sudan Peace Agreement (ESPA) was signed in October 2006. Apart from these three violent center-periphery confrontations, there has also been significant violence in the periphery, especially related to power struggles in Darfur and in the South.

3. The CPA was the outcome of a prolonged ten-year IGAD-mediated negotiation process, which resulted in several agreements and protocols, most of them combined

in the CPA. Significantly, as part of the process, the 1998 Constitution was the first to formally establish federal structures in Sudan. However, it reflected strong Islamic tendencies and was promulgated after elections that were boycotted by most major political parties in the North and South. Moreover, it was suspended a year later when President Bashir declared a state of emergency. For details on the IGAD process until 1999, see Michel Hoebink, ed., *Constitutional Perspectives on Sudan* (Durham: University of Durham, Centre for Middle Eastern and Islamic Studies, 1999).

4. Helen Chapin Metz, ed., *Sudan: A Country Study*, 4th ed. (Washington, D.C.: Federal Research Divison, Library of Congress, 1992).

5. M. Paul Lewis, "Ethnologue: Languages of the World. Sixteenth Edition," SIL International, http://www.ethnologue.com, accessed 15 November 2011.

6. John Young, "Sudan: Liberation Movements, Regional Armies, Ethnic Militias & Peace," *Review of African Political Economy* 30, 97 (2003).

7. Young, "Sudan Liberation Movements"; Ali Abdel Gadir Ali, Ibrahim A. Elbadawi, and Atta El-Batahani, "Sudan's Civil War. Why Has It Prevailed for So Long?" in *Understanding Civil War: Evidence and Analysis*, ed. Paul Collier and Nicholas Sambanis (Washington, D.C.: World Bank, 2005); Adam Branch and Zachariah Cherian Mampilly, "Winning the War, But Losing the Peace? The Dilemma of SPLM/A Civil Administration and the Tasks Ahead," *Journal of Modern African Studies* 43 (2004); Robert O. Collins, *A History of Modern Sudan* (Cambridge: Cambridge University Press, 2008); International Crisis Group, "God, Oil and Country: Changing the Logic of War in Sudan," Africa Report 39 (Brussels: ICG, 28 January 2002); John Young, "The Eastern Front and the Struggle Against Marginalization"; "Emerging North-South Tensions and Prospects for a Return to War"; "Armed Groups Along Sudan's Eastern Frontier: An Overview and Analysis," all HSBA Working Papers (Geneva: Small Arms Survey, 2007).

8. http://www.unhcr.org/pages/4e43cb466.html (accessed 13 July 2013).

9. However, the Abyei dispute contributed to ongoing instability in the South, in part because the Sudanese Armed Forces prevented for over six months the return to Abyei of IDPs, most of whom remained in South Sudan's Warrap state during that period.

10. Oli Brown and Alec Crawford, "Climate Change and Security in Africa" (Winnipeg: International Institute for Sustainable Development, 2009); Christalla Yakinthou and Stefan Wolff, "Introduction," in *Conflict Management in Divided Societies: Theories and Practice*, ed. Stefan Wolff and Christalla Yakinthou (London: Routledge, 2011).

11. Heather J. Sharkey, "Arab Identity and Ideology in Sudan: The Politics of Language, Ethnicity, and Race," *African Affairs* 107, 426 (2008).

12. Mohamed Beshir, *The Southern Sudan: Background to Conflict* (London: Hurst, 1968).

13. David Roden, "Regional Inequality and Rebellion in the Sudan," *American Geographical Society* 64 (1974).

14. Christopher R. Mitchell, "Coalition Efforts to Repair Internal Conflict Management in Sudan 1971-72," in *Managing Ethnic Conflict in Africa: Pressures and Incentives for Cooperation*, ed. Donald Rothchild (Washington, D.C.: Brookings Institution, 1997).

15. Beshir, *The Southern Sudan*.

16. Akolda M. Tier, "Freedom of Religion Under the Sudan Constitution and Laws," *Journal of African Law* 26 (1982).

17. On the use of militias in the North-South civil war, see more generally John Prendergast, "The Political Economy of Famine in Sudan and the Horn of Africa," *Issue: A Journal of Opinion* 19, 2 (1991).

18. Collins, *A History of Modern Sudan*, 104–9. On the positive effect the 1972 Agreement had on Sudan's relations with its neighbors, see also Richard P. Stevens, "The 1972 Addis Ababa Agreement and the Sudan's Afro-Arab Policy," *Journal of Modern African Studies* 14, 2 (1976). The abrogation of the agreement in 1983 reversed many of these effects. See Yehudit Ronen, "Ethiopia's Involvement in the Sudanese Civil War: Was It as Significant as Khartoum Claimed?" *Northeast African Studies* 9, 1 (2002): 103–26; and Ioannis Mantzikos, "Why the Islamic Revolution Ended: The Regional Politics of Sudan Since 1989," *Mediterranean Quarterly* 21, 3 (2010): 47–60.

19. Mitchell, "Coalition Efforts."

20. The status of the Southern region was also codified in Article 8 of the 1973 Permanent Constitution, as follows: "Within the Unitary Sudan, there shall be established in the Southern Region a Regional Self-Government in accordance with the Southern Provinces Regional Self-Government Act, 1972, which shall be an organic law, and shall not be amended except in accordance with the provisions thereof." Further reference to the region and its powers can be found in Article 184 on local self-government.

21. Mitchell, "Coalition Efforts."

22. Andrew Mawson, "Bringing What People Want: Shrine Politics Among the Agar Dinka," *Africa: Journal of the International African Institute* 61 (1991): 354–69.

23. Ali, Elbadawi, and El-Batahani, "Sudan's Civil War"; Collins, *A History of Modern Sudan*; Douglas H. Johnson, *The Root Causes of Sudan's Civil Wars* (Oxford: James Currey, 2003); Thomas Schmidinger, "Tyrants and Terrorists: Reflections on the Connection Between Totalitarianism, Neo-Liberalism, Civil War and the Failure of the State in Iraq and Sudan," *Civil Wars* 11, 3 (2009): 359–79; Aleksi Ylonen, "Grievances and the Roots of Insurgencies: Southern Sudan and Darfur," *Peace, Conflict and Development* 7 (2005): 99–134.

24. On the role of religion in Sudan's civil wars, see Monica Duffy Toft, "Getting Religion? The Puzzling Case of Islam and Civil War," *International Security* 31, 4 (2007). On the conflict in and over Nuba, see Alexander De Waal, "Creating Devastation and Calling It Islam: The War for the Nuba, Sudan," *SAIS Review* 21, 2 (2001).

25. ICG, "God, Oil and Country"; Mohammed Zahid and Michael Medley, "Muslim Brotherhood in Egypt & Sudan," *Review of African Political Economy* 110 (2006): 693–708.

26. ICG, "A Strategy for Comprehensive Peace in Sudan," Africa Report 130 (Brussels: ICG, 26 July 2007); Sarah M. H. Nouwen, "Sudan's Divided (and Divisive?) Peace Agreements," *Hague Yearbook of International Law* 20 (2007).

27. This objective was significantly undermined by the death of southern leader John Garang in a helicopter crash in July 2005. Among southern politicians, Garang had been the main advocate of unity (subject to acceptable terms) and was the most trusted by political leaders in the North, including President Bashir. We thank Alan Goulty for this observation.

28. Unless otherwise indicated, the following analysis relies on three principal sources of information: the CPA monitor of the UN Mission in Sudan (UNMIS), http://unmis.unmissions.org/Default.aspx?tabid=2213; the CrisisWatch Database of the International Crisis Group, http://www.crisisgroup.org/en/publication-type/crisiswatch/crisiswatch-database.aspx; and reports by the UN Secretary General on Sudan, http://www.un.org/en/peacekeeping/missions/unmis/reports.shtml, and http://www.un.org/en/peacekeeping/missions/unisfa/reports.shtml.

29. ICG, "Sudan: Preventing Implosion," *Africa Briefing* (2009). Abdelwahab El-Affendi, "Making Peace Gambles Work: The Oslo Accords, the Sudanese Comprehensive Peace Agreement, and Their Spirals of Insecurity," *Journal of Peace, Conflict and Development* 17 (2011).

30. Einas Ahmed, "The Comprehensive Peace Agreement and the Dynamics of Post-Conflict Political Partnership in Sudan," *Africa Spectrum* 44, 3 (2009); Branch and Mampilly, "Winning the War, But Losing the Peace?"; ICG, "Sudan's Comprehensive Peace Agreement: Beyond the Crisis," *Africa Briefing*, 2008; Douglas H. Johnson, "The Sudan People's Liberation Army & the Problem of Factionalism," in *African Guerrillas*, ed. Christopher Clapham (Oxford: James Currey, 1998); Claire McEvoy and Emile LeBrun, "Uncertain Future: Armed Violence in Southern Sudan," *HSBA Working Paper*, Small Arms Survey, Geneva, 2010; Young, "Sudan: Liberation Movements, Regional Armies, Ethnic Militias & Peace"; Young, "Emerging North-South Tensions and Prospects for a Return to War."

31. ICG, "Negotiating Sudan's North-South Future," *Africa Briefing*, 2010; ICG, "Sudan: Preventing Implosion," *Africa Briefing*, 2009.

32. ICG, "Darfur: Revitalising the Peace Process," Africa Report 125 (Brussels: 30 April 2007); ICG, "Sudan: Justice, Peace and the ICC," Africa Report 152 (Brussels: ICG, 17 July 2009); ICG, "Sudan: Saving Peace in the East," Africa Report 102 (Brussels: ICG, 5 January 2006).

33. Johan Brosché, "CPA—New Sudan, Old Sudan or Two Sudans: A Review of the Implementation of the Comprehensive Peace Agreement," *Journal of African Policy Studies* 13, 1 (2007); ICG, "Darfur: Revitalising the Peace Process"; ICG, "Sudan: Justice, Peace and the ICC"; Nouwen, "Sudan's Divided (and Divisive?) Peace Agreements."

34. ICG, "Sudan: Preventing Implosion"; ICG, "Sudan: Regional Perspectives on the Prospect of Southern Independence," Africa Report 159 (Brussels: ICG, 6 May 2010).

35. Human Rights Watch, "Sudan: Flawed Elections Underscore Need for Justice," 26 April 2010, http://www.hrw.org/en/news/2010/04/25/sudan-flawed-elections-underscore-need-justice.

36. Cf. Abdelwahab El-Affendi, "The Impasse in the IGAD Peace Process for Sudan: The Limits of Regional Peacekeeping," *African Affairs* 100 (2001); Sally Healy, "Peacemaking in the Midst of War: An Assessment of IGAD's Contribution to Regional Security," Crisis States Research Centre, London, 2009; ICG, "Sudan's Dual Crises: Refocusing on IGAD," *Africa Briefing* 19 (2004); Ann Kelleher, "A Small State's Multiple-Level Approach to Peace-Making: Norway's Role in Achieving Sudan's Comprehensive Peace Agreement," *Civil Wars* 18, 3–4 (2006).

37. UN Security Council Resolution 1990 (2011).

38. See ICG, "Sudan's Spreading Conflict (I): War in South Kordofan," Africa Report 198 (Brussels: ICG, 14 February 2013); and ICG, "Sudan's Spreading Conflict (II): War in Blue Nile," Africa Report 204 (Brussels: ICG, 18 June 2013).

39. "The New Dawn Convention," unofficial version, *Sudan Tribune*, 5 January 2013, trans. Abdul Izzadine, http://www.sudantribune.com/spip.php?article45151 (accessed 12 January 2014).

40. Ali, Elbadawi, and El-Batahani, "Sudan's Civil War"; Branch and Mampilly, "Winning the War, But Losing the Peace?" Collins, *A History of Modern Sudan*; ICG, "God, Oil and Country"; Young, "Sudan: Liberation Movements, Regional Armies, Ethnic Militias & Peace"; and "Armed Groups Along Sudan's Eastern Frontier."

41. Sudarsan Raghavan, "S. Sudan's Post-Liberation Crisis," *Washington Post*, 28 December 2013.

42. For a more detailed analysis of the insurgencies and intercommunal conflicts that have plagued South Sudan before and since independence in July 2011, see Stefan Wolff, "South Sudan's Year One: Managing the Challenges of Building a New State," *RUSI Journal* 157, 5 (2012).

43. Isma'il Kushkush, "Sudans Sign Agreement to Resume Oil Exports," *New York Times*, 13 March 2013.

44. Adam Mohamed Ahmad, "South Sudan's Crisis Sends Shockwaves through Sudan," *The Niles*, 2 January 2014; Waakhe Simon Wudu, "Sudan's President Pledges Support to South Sudanese Leader as Violence Continues," *The Niles*, 7 January 2014.

45. John McGarry and Brendan O'Leary, "Iraq's Constitution of 2005: Liberal Consociation as Political Prescription," in *Constitutional Design for Divided Societies: Integration or Accommodation?* ed. Sujit Choudhry (Oxford: Oxford University Press, 2008), 368.

Chapter 6. Ghana: The Complements of Successful Centralization:
Checks, Balances, and Informal Accommodation

I would like to thank my project assistants funded by the Constitutional Design and Conflict Management (CDCM) project, Francesco Biagi and Sara Pennicino, as well as CCSDD interns—Jemila Abdulai, David Goodman, Megan Holt, Daniel Lawner, and Irena Peresa—for their precious research assistance. I am also deeply grateful for the critical observations and suggestions I received from Cathy Boone, Carl Le Van, and Henry Kwasi Prempeh at the CDCM case study workshop that took place in Antwerp in May 2011. Finally, special thanks go to H. E. Tullio Guma, former Ambassador of Italy to Ghana; without his intervention it would not have been possible to set up a series of meetings with some of Ghana's most important institutions and research centers during my visit to Accra in September 2011.

1. Lindsay Whitfield, "Change for a Better Ghana: Party Competition, Institutionalization, and Alternation in Ghana's 2008 Elections," *African Affairs* 108 (2009): 621–25. Although not detailed in this chapter, the 2012 presidential election continued this trend. Following an eight-month legal challenge, which transfixed the country, Ghana's Supreme Court ruled in August 2013 to confirm the outcome, but this did not trigger widespread violence.

2. Emmanuel Gyimah Boadi, "Another Step Forward for Ghana," *Journal of Democracy* 20, 2 (April 2009): 137–39.

3. Maxwell Owusu, "Self-Government or Good Government: Traditional Rule and the Challenge of Constitutional Democracy and Development in Africa," paper prepared for Working Conference on Designing Constitutional Arrangements for Democratic Governance in Africa: Challenges and Possibilities, Indiana University, Bloomington, 30–31 March 2006, 38.

4. The author would like to sincerely thank Rowland Atta-Kesson, Baaba Amoah, and Papa Kow Sessah Acquaye from the Constitutional Review Commission for the insightful comments made during a meeting held 13 September 2011. See http://www.crc.gov.gh.

5. For a detailed description of specific changes made, including the role of the Supreme Court, and the relationship between the cabinet and the parliament see Egon Schwelb, "The Republican Constitution of Ghana," *American Journal of Comparative Law* 9, 4 (Autumn 1960): 634–56; and Francis Bennion, *The Constitutional Law of Ghana* (London: Butterworths, 1962).

6. Trevor Jones, *Ghana's First Republic 1960–1966* (London: Methuen, 1976), 28.

7. Ibid., 31.

8. Ibid., 35.

9. Chris de Wet, "The Experience with Dams and Resettlement in Africa," Contributing Paper, World Commission on Dams, 1999, 20.

10. Jones, *Ghana's First Republic*, 48.

11. John Kraus, "Arms and Politics in Ghana," in *Soldier and State in Africa*, ed. Claude E. Welch (Evanston, Ill.: Northwestern University Press, 1970), 188–89.

12. David E. Apter, *Ghana in Transition* (Princeton, N.J.: Princeton University Press, 1972), 394–95.

13. Ibid., 395.

14. John Wiseman, *The New Struggle for Democracy in Africa* (Aldershot: Asgate, 1996), 63.

15. Richard Jeffries and Clare Thomas, "The Ghanaian Elections of 1992," *African Affairs* 92 (1993): 334–35.

16. Emmanuel Gyimah-Boadi, "Notes on Ghana's Current Transition to Constitutional Rule," *Africa Today* 38, 4 (1991): 5–17.

17. Ibid., 5–6.

18. According to Michael Bratton and Nicolas van de Walle, *Democratic Experiments in Africa: Regime Transitions in Comparative Perspective* (Cambridge: Cambridge University Press, 1997), 113, "Jerry Rawlings packed the constitutional commission with his own supporters, stretched out the constitutional drafting deadline, and inserted clauses into the final document favorable to his Peoples National Defense Council." See also Staffan I. Lindbert with Yongmei Zhou, "Co-optation Despite Democratization in Ghana," in *Legislative Power in Emerging African Democracies*, ed. Joel D. Barkan (Boulder, Colo.: Lynne Rienner, 2009).

19. Jeffries and Thomas, "The Ghanaian Elections of 1992," 337.

20. For a detailed account of Ghana's constitutional system and its relatively peaceful transition to democracy, see Justin O. Frosini, "A Constitutional Paradox? Ghana's Peaceful Democratic Transition," *Percorsi Costitutionali* 2–3 (2011): 367–83.

21. Owusu, "Self-Government or Good Government," 34–35.

22. The number of seats was increased from 200 in January 2005.

23. The author would like to thank David Goodman for his research assistance concerning this shock.

24. Robert Chambers, ed., *The Volta Resettlement Experience* (London: Pall Mall, 1970), 13.

25. Ibid., 41.

26. Ibid., 21.

27. Ibid., 48.

28. Philip Gyau-Boakye, "Environmental Impacts of the Akosombo Dam and Effects of Climate Change on the Lake Levels," *Environment, Development and Sustainability* 3, 1 (2001): 26.

29. Jeffries and Thomas, "The Ghanaian Elections of 1992," 339; Frosini, "A Constitutional Paradox? Ghana's Peaceful Democratic Transition," 372–74.

30. Ibid., 338.

31. Ibid., 354–56.

32. Ibid., 363.

33. Ibid., 364.

34. Frosini, "A Constitutional Paradox? Ghana's Peaceful Democratic Transition," 374–75.

35. Daniel Smith, "Ghana's 2000 elections: consolidating multiparty democracy," *Electoral Studies* 21 (2002): 521, reports a "thinly veiled threat that the nation would be engulfed by anarchy if the incumbent party was ousted."

36. For example, reelection has been defined as an "obsession" for many leaders in Latin America. See Justin O. Frosini and Lucio Pegoraro, "Constitutional Courts in

Latin America: A Testing Ground for New Parameters of Classification?" *Journal of Comparative Law* 3, 2 (2008): 61.

37. Emmanuel Gyimah-Boadi, "A Peaceful Turnover in Ghana," *Journal of Democracy* 12, 2 (2001): 103–4.

38. http://ec.gov.gh.cluster.cwcs.co.uk/node/10, accessed 24 February 2013.

39. The credibility of the Electoral Commission subsequently was challenged after the 2012 presidential elections, when the opposition candidate appealed to the Supreme Court to annul John Mahama's election. However, the court dismissed the appeal after eight months without major incident.

40. Whitfield, "Change for a Better Ghana," 624–25.

41. Frosini, "A Constitutional Paradox? Ghana's Peaceful Democratic Transition," 376.

42. In the aftermath of the 2012 presidential elections, this fifth point is now contested.

43. http://mint.gov.gh/index.php?option=com_content&task=view&id=32&Itemid=43, accessed 24 February 2013.

44. http://www.nadmo.gov.gh/, accessed 24 February 2013.

45. On the important role of chieftancy in the "informal constitutional design" of Ghana, see Kwame Boafo-Arthur, "Chieftaincy in Ghana: Challenges and Prospects in the 21st Century," *African and Asian Studies* 2, 2 (2003): 125–53.

46. John Mark Pokoo and Ernest Lartey, interview with author, Kofi Annan International Peacekeeping Training Center, Accra, 13 September 2011.

47. This concept was repeated in several meetings during a field trip to Accra in September 2011, as well as separately by H. Kwasi Prempeh at the CDCM workshop, Antwerp, 27 May 2011.

48. On legal transplanting, see Alan Watson, *Legal Transplants* (Edinburgh: Scottish Academic Press, 1974). Personally, I am somewhat dubious that Ghana should be considered a model of constitutional design for other countries in Africa; see Frosini, "A Constitutional Paradox? Ghana's Peaceful Democratic Transition," 367–83.

49. See http://www.ghana.gov.gh/index.php/information/reports/2573-report-of-the-constitution-review-commission, accessed 4 January 2014.

50. Ibid.

51. Under the new British rules, the average electorate per constituency in the UK has been set at 76,641, and each constituency must be within 5 percent of that quota.

Chapter 7. Senegal: The Limits of Hyper-Centralization

1. We are grateful to Hayat Essakkati for dedicated research assistance.

2. This general design or ethos, and other details, are codified in the constitution itself. Unlike in Charles Call, ed., *Building States to Build Peace* (Boulder, Colo.: Lynne Rienner, 2008), "constitutional" and "state" design are used synonymously here.

3. As used in this book, "shocks" are defined in the introductory chapter. More generally, the term "shock" is used widely in common parlance but often lacks precision. See Claudio Raddatz, "Have External Shocks Become More Important for Output Fluctuations in African Countries?" in *Africa at a Turning Point? Growth, Aid, and External Shocks*, ed. Delfin Go and John Page (Washington, D.C.: World Bank, 2008). Neyla Arnas, ed., *Fighting Chance: Global Trends and Shocks in the National Security Environment* (Washington, D.C.: National Defense University, 2009) defines it as "an event that punctuates the evolution of a trend (a discontinuity that either rapidly accelerates its pace or significantly changes its trajectory) and in doing so undermines the assumptions on which current policies are based." Robert Armstrong, "Postscript—'Swans Happen,'" in *Fighting Chance*, ed. Arnas, 291, defines shocks as major "events that occur outside the realm of normal expectations." Arnas calls the opposite of a shock a trend or normal expectation, defined as "a predictable path along which events are expected to evolve." However, "trend" or equivalent term is not just a normal expectation of external events but also the normal expectation of handling them appropriately—satisfying or satisficing—by established methods. A specific discussion of the floods—S. Wade, S. Faye, M. Dieng, M. Kaba, and N. R. Kane, "Télédétection des catastrophes d'inondation urbaine: Le cas de la région de Dakar" (2009, not published), 1—identified the same characteristics: "The notion of catastrophe [shock] is closely tied to that of major risk which is defined as a dangerous event termed 'chance,' of natural . . . or technical . . . origin and whose foreseeable effects cause numerous victims, important material damages, and a negative impact of the environment." The definition used here hangs on a change in power relations rather than in policies or expectations, although power relations include the expected ability (power) to handle the shock by normal practices. Many of these attempts at definition are conclusionary—that is, it is the impact of the event rather than the nature of the event itself that determines whether the event has been a shock. But in the CDCM project, an event can be a shock regardless whether it leads to a disruptive outcome.

4. For a discussion of the distinction, see I. William Zartman, *Peacemaking in International Conflicts* (Washington, D.C.: U.S. Institute of Peace, 2007).

5. Donal Cruise O'Brien, *Saints & Politicians* (London: Cambridge University Press, 1974); Mark Gersovitz and John Waterbury, eds., *The Political Economy of Risk and Choice in Senegal* (London: Cass, 1987); Catherine Boone, *Political Topographies of the African State: Territorial Authority and Institutional Choice* (London: Cambridge University Press, 2003).

6. Momar Coumba Diop, ed., *Sénégal, trajectoires d'un état* (Dakar: CODESRIA, 1993); Ismaila Madior Fall, *Évolution constitutionnelle du Sénégal* (Dakar: CREDILA, Université Cheikh Anta Diop, 2007); Ismaila Madior Fall, *Textes constitutionnels du Sénégal* (Dakar: CREDILA, Université Cheikh Anta Diop, 2007).

7. Dimitri Georges Lavrroff and Gustave Peiser, *Les constitutions africaines francophones* (Paris: Pedone, 1961); Gerard Conac, *Les institutions constitutionelles et politiques des états d'Afrique francophone et de la République malgache* (Paris: Economica,

1979); Jean du Bois de Gaudusson, Gerard Conac, and Christine Desouches, *Les constitutions africaines publiées en langue française* (Bruxelles: Bruylant, 1998); S. M. Sy, ed., *Mélanges à l'honneur de Dmitri Georges Lavroff: La constitution et ses valeurs* (Paris: Dalloz, 2005).

8. Vincent Foucher, "Senegal: The Resilient Weakness of Casamançais Separatists," in, *African Guerrillas*, ed. Morten Bøås and Kevin Dunn (Boulder, Colo.: Lynne Rienner, 2007), 171–98; Michael Lambert, "Violence and the War of Words: Ethnicity vs. Nationalism in the Casamance," *Africa* 68, 4 (1998); Ferdinand de Jong and Geneviève Casser, "Contested Casamance/Discordante Casamance," *Canadian Journal of African Studies/Revue Canadienne des Études Africaines* 31, 2 (2005): Hillary Thomas-Lake, "Keeping Promises: Building Sustainable Peace After the Peace Accord," Ph.D. dissertation, Johns Hopkins University, 2010; Boucounta Diallo, *La crise casamançaise, problématique et voies de solutions: Origine et fondement de l'irrédentisme casamançais* (Paris: l'Harmattan, 2009); François-Georges Barbier-Wiesser, *Comprendre la casamance* (Paris: Karthala, 1994). Mark Deets, "Bitter Roots: The Obstacles to Peace in the Casamance Conflict," in *African Environmental and Human Security in the 21st Century*, ed. Helen Purkitt (Amherst, N.Y.: Cambria, 2009), 89–110, carries the same message of an identity conflict, although the editor's introduction (xiii) says the chapter highlights desertification. On the evolution from cultural reform groups to nationalist movements to violent resistance, see I. William Zartman, ed., *Elites in the Middle East* (New York: Praeger, 1980).

9. Senegal was born overcentralized, with the Dakar region at independence holding about one-sixth of the 3 million Senegalese. A half-century later, Dakar itself had a population of 3 million, roughly a quarter of the country's 12 million population, with over 4,000 people/sq km. The capital also had 80 percent of the country's industry and 75 percent of its economic and administrative activities. See Wade et al., "Télédétection," 2.

10. Jean Collin, "Déclaration devant l'Assemblée Nationale sur la déconcentration et la décolonisation," Dakar, 19 November 1975, 51, cited in *Le Sénégal sous Abdou Diouf*, ed. Momar Coumba Diop and Mamadou Diouf (Paris: Karthala, 1990).

11. Janet Vaillant, *Black, French, and African: A Life of Léopold Sédar Senghor* (Cambridge, Mass.: Harvard University Press, 1990), 314, 333, 338.

12. Fall, *Évolution constitutionnelle*, 148.

13. Article 30 of the Constitution of 2 March 1998; Article 42 of the 2001 Constitution.

14. "Si l'on veut la paix au Nigeria," *Jeune Afrique*, 1965. He did later write, somewhat revisionistically, "It is because Senegal has always refused to take sides with either party, and has always recommended an immediate cease fire, followed by negotiations with no other pre-condition than the integrity—I do not say unity—of Nigeria, that the manuscript of Raph Uwechue won me over at once." See Raph Uwechue, with forewords by Nnamdi Azikiwe and Léopold Sédar Senghor, *Reflections on the Nigerian Civil War* (New York: Africana, 1971), xiv.

15. According to Article 7, "The State has the obligation to respect and protect [the human person]. Every individual has the right to life, to liberty, *to security* [emphasis added], to free development of his/her personality, to physical integrity including to protection against all physical mutilation. The Senegalese people thus recognize the existence of human rights, inalienable and inviolable, as the basis of any human community, peace and justice in the world."

16. Obiora Chinedu Okafor, *Redefining Legitimate Statehood: International Law and State Fragmentation in Africa* (The Hague: Kluwer, 2000).

17. Boone, *Political Topographies*, 94–102.

18. Law 72-25, of 19 April 1972.

19. Fall, *Évolution constitutionnelle*, 82–83.

20. O'Brien, *Saints & Politicians*, 164, 175.

21. Gersovitz and Waterbury, *The Political Economy of Risk*, 192.

22. Friedrich Engels, *The Peasant War in Germany* (1870; New York: International, 1926).

23. Diop and Diouf, *Le Sénégal sous Abdou Diouf*, 1990.

24. Fall, *Évolution constitutionnelle*, 150. See also Cheikh Yérim Seck, "Wade et ses 'enfants.' Entre les différents héritiers du chef de l'État, la bataille fait rage. En jeu, le contrôle à terme de la famille libérale," *Jeune Afrique*, 30 November 2008.

25. Barbier-Wiesser, *Comprendre la Casamance*, 197.

26. Diallo, *La crise casamançaise*, 35–47.

27. Lambert,"Violence and the War of Words," 591; Thomas-Lake, "Keeping Promises."

28. *Sub-Saharan Africa*, 20 April 1990.

29. Because of desertification in the country's north, the government supported internal migration to Casamance, including the alleged seizure of arable land by wealthy northerners, which exacerbated grievance that increased support for secession. We thank Catherine Boone for highlighting this point.

30. O'Brien, *Saints & Politicians*, 181.

31. Boone, *Political Topographies*, 98.

32. Gambia and Guinea-Bissau were sources of support and refuge for the Casamance secessionists. We thank Hank Cohen for this point.

33. Deets, "Bitter Roots," 91–92; Foucher, "Senegal: The Resilient Weakness," 172.

34. I. William Zartman and Tania Alfredson, "Negotiating with Terrorists and the Tactical Question," in Rafael Reuveny and William Thompson, eds., *Coping with Terrorism* (Albany, N.Y.: SUNY Press, 2010).

35. Abdou Latif Coulibaly, *Wade, un opposant au pouvoir: l'alternance piégée?* (Dakar: Éditions Sentinelles, 2003).

36. There is also question whether the extremists among Casamance secessionists could be satisfied by anything short of independence, which any Senegalese government would be unlikely to grant because of the economic consequences for the rest of the country. The central government would also be concerned that granting devolution to

Casamance could spur similar demands from other regions of the country. We thank Hank Cohen for these observations.

37. Ricardo Fuentes-Nieva and Papa Seck, eds., *Risk, Shocks and Human Development: On the Brink* (Basingstoke: Palgrave, 2010).

38. No unusual flooding was reported in the earlier period because drainage was adequate on the land that had not yet been developed. Sylvestre Dasylva, Claude Cosandey, and Soussou Sambou, "Acuité des problèmes liés à l'eau et nécessité d'une gestion 'integrée' des eaux pluviales dans le domaine des sables dunaires de la région de Dakar," Colloque Développement Durable: leçons et perspectives, Ouagadougou, 2004, 59; Souleymane Sene and Pierre Ozer, "Evolution pluviométrique et relations inondations-événements pluvieux au Sénégal," *Bulletin de la Société Géographique de Liège* 42, 1 (2002): 29, 30.

39. Abdoulaye Diagne, "Analyse de la gestion des inondations dans la region de Dakar," Mémoire de Diplôme d'Études Approfondies, Université Cheikh Anta Diop, Dakar, 2007; Aiguo Dai, "Global Variations in Droughts and Wet Spells: 1900–1995," *Geophysical Research Letters* 25 (1998): 3367–70; A. M. Dia et al., "Apport des données SPOT et Landsat au suivi des inondations dans l'estuaire du fleuve Sénégal," photo-interpretation, 2006/4; Mike Hulme, "Recent Climatic Change in the World's Drylands," *Geophysical Research Letters* 23 (1996): 61–64. This situation can be followed in the *Club du Sahel Bulletin* of the CILSS, OECD.

40. Madeleine Diouf Sarr, "Changement climatique: situation actuelle de vulnérabilité du Sénégal," Direction de l'Environnement et des Établissements Classés, Senegal, 2001, 3.

41. Wade et al., "Télédétection," 2; Sene and Ozer, "Evolution pluviométrique," 32.

42. *Africa News*, 19 August 1999; Dasylva, Consandey, and Sambou, "Acuité des problèmes," 62–63.

43. Wade et al., "Télédétection,"2; CSPLP, "Région de Dakar," Cellule de Suivi du Programme de Lutte contre la Pauvreté, Ministry of Economy and Finance, Paris, undated, 3; *Africa News*, 27 October 2008; World Bank/Government of Senegal 2010.

44. Sylvestre Dasylva, "Les bas-fonds des sables dunaires de la Région de Dakar: Potentialités agricoles et contraintes urbaines," Doctoral thesis, Université de Paris 1-Sorbonne, 2001; "Cholera Hit More Than 25,000 People in 2005," *Africa News*, 27 October 2008.

45. *Activités de la DPC 2001–2010*.

46. Sene and Ozer, "Evolution pluviométrique,"31.

47. PUD, "Plan d'urbanisme de Dakar 2001: Rapport justificatif," Direction de l'Urbanisme et de l'Architecture, Dakar, 2001.

48. CSPLP, "Région de Dakar."

49. Personal communication, 2011.

50. Sene and Ozer, "Evolution pluviométrique."

51. Senegal Hyogo Framework for Action mid-term review report, 2009.

52. Personal communication, 2011.
53. *Africa News*, 27 October 2005.
54. Abdul Aziz Seck, personal communication, January 2011.
55. *Le Soleil*, 26 July 2010.
56. *BBC Monitoring Africa*, 31 August 2005.
57. *Africa News*, 9 September 2008.
58. Senegal Red Cross/IFRC, "Views from the Frontline," Report, Dakar, 2009.
59. *Sud Quotidien*, 3–4 April 2009.
60. Ibid., 3 May 2009.
61. *Walf*, 9 June 2009.
62. *Le Quotidien*, 9 June 2009.
63. *Le Soleil*, 4 June 2009.
64. *Walf*, 22 June 2010.
65. Ibid., 4 June 2009.
66. *Le Quotidien*, 30 June 2009.
67. *Walf*, 12 June 2009.
68. World Bank/Government of Senegal 2010.
69. ISE student report on Dakar floods field trip, September 2009.
70. *Le Quotidien*, 26 August 2009.
71. Personal communication, 2011; *Le Quotidien*, 26 August 2009.
72. *Le Quotidien*, 26 August 2009.
73. *Le Soleil*, 15 January 2010.
74. Ibid., 20 May, 26 July 2010.
75. Ibid., 3 June 2010.
76. Personal communication, 2011.
77. 17 August 2010.
78. *Le Soleil*, 26 July 2010; *Sud Quotidien*, 20 August 2010.
79. *Le Pop*, 6 January 2011.
80. Ibid., 18 January 2011.
81. Rémi Carayol, "Y'en a marre!" *Jeune Afrique* 2622, 31–33 (10 April 2011).
82. Personal communication, 2011.
83. I. William Zartman, ed., *Governance as Conflict Management: Politics and Violence in West Africa* (Washington, D.C.: Brookings Institution, 1997).
84. Sarr, "Changement climatique."

Chapter 8. Zimbabwe: The Unintended Consequences of Authoritarian Institutions

I am indebted to research assistance from Allison Garren and Rebecca Greenberg and the helpful advice of Peter Godwin, Michael Bratton, Alan J. Kuperman, Timothy D. Sisk, and Carl LeVan.

1. Peter Godwin, *The Fear: Robert Mugabe and the Martyrdom of Zimbabwe* (New York: Little, Brown, 2010), 26.

2. Terence Ranger, with Ngwabi Bhebe, eds., *Society in Zimbabwe's Liberation War* (Oxford: James Currey, 1996).

3. As quoted in Andrew Reynolds, *Electoral Systems and Democratization in Southern Africa* (London: Oxford University Press, 1999), 181.

4. Sabelo J. Ndlovu-Gatsheni, "The Changing Politics of Matebeleland Since 1980," http://www.solidaritypeacetrust.org/994/the-changing-politics-of-matebeleland-since-1980/ (accessed 3 February 2013).

5. Eldred Masunungure, "Nation-Building, State-Building and Power Configuration in Zimbabwe," *Conflict Trends Magazine* 1 (2006): 7.

6. Ndlovu-Gatsheni, "The Changing Politics of Matebeleland."

7. Catholic Commission for Justice and Peace and Legal Resources Foundation, "Breaking the Silence, Building True Peace: A Report on the Disturbances in Matabeleland and the Midlands 1980–1988," April 1999, 5, www.sokwanele.com/pdfs/BTS.pdf (accessed 9 May 2011).

8. Peter Godwin, *Mukiwa: A White Boy in Africa* (New York: Grove, 1996), 329.

9. Catholic Commission, "Breaking the Silence," 5, 11, 13.

10. Ibid., 13.

11. Ibid., 14.

12. Godwin, *Mukiwa*, 344.

13. Catholic Commission, "Breaking the Silence," 14; Godwin, *Mukiwa*, 351, 353.

14. Catholic Commission, "Breaking the Silence,"130.

15. Ibid., 14.

16. Ibid., 14–15.

17. Godwin, *The Fear,* 279.

18. Jacob Chikuhwa, *A Crisis of Governance: Zimbabwe* (New York: Algora, 2004), 244–45.

19. Sam Moyo, "Agrarian Reform and Prospects for Recovery," in *Zimbabwe: Picking Up the Pieces,* ed. Hany Besada (New York: Palgrave, 2011), 133.

20. Chikuhwa, *A Crisis of Governance*, 246.

21. Simon Coldham, "The Land Acquisition Act, 1992 Zimbabwe," *Journal of African Law* 37, 1 (Spring 1993): 82; Chikuhwa, *A Crisis of Governance*, 33–34.

22. Chikuhwa, *A Crisis of Governance*, 33; Moyo, "Agrarian Reform,"132.

23. Chikuhwa, *A Crisis of Governance*, 33–34; Jocelyn Alexander, *The Unsettled Land: State-Making and the Politics of Land in Zimbabwe 1893–2003* (Oxford: James Currey, 2006), 105.

24. Chikuhwa, *A Crisis of Governance*, 35.

25. Ibid., 47–48.

26. Ross Herbert, "Whites Fight Land Seizures in Zimbabwe/Whites Mount Legal Effort to Stop Zimbabwe Farm Seizures/Mugabe says Britain Should Pay," *San Francisco Gate*, 10 November 2000.

27. Chikuhwa, *A Crisis of Governance*, 249.

28. "Robert Mugabe Has Built Up 10,000-Acre Farm of Seized Land," *The Telegraph*, 25 September 2009.

29. John Hatchard, "Some Lessons on Constitution-Making from Zimbabwe," *Journal of African Law* 45, 2 (2001): 214.

30. Alexander, *The Unsettled Land*, 184–85; Geoffrey Feltoe, "The Onslaught Against Democracy and Rule of Law in Zimbabwe in 2000," in *Zimbabwe: The Past Is the Future*, ed. David Harold-Barry (Harare: Weaver Press, 2004), 196–97.

31. Chikuhwa, *A Crisis of Governance*, 249.

32. Alexander, *The Unsettled Land*, 185.

33. Chikuhwa, *A Crisis of Governance*.

34. Hatchard, "Some Lessons," 215.

35. Chikuhwa, *A Crisis of Governance*, 250.

36. Feltoe, "The Onslaught," 197.

37. Chikuhwa, *A Crisis of Governance*, 47, 200.

38. Ibid., 48; Andrew Meldrum, "Mugabe Land Seizures Force Hundreds of Farm Owners to Flee," *The Guardian*, 3 June 2000.

39. Chikuhwa, *A Crisis of Governance*, 48.

40. Meldrum, "Mugabe Land Seizures."

41. Herbert, "Whites Fight Land Seizures."

42. Chikuhwa, *A Crisis of Governance*, 250.

43. Ibid., 251.

44. Moyo, "Agrarian Reform," 135.

45. Jonathan Steele, "Mugabe Says Land Seizures Will Continue," *The Guardian*, 3 July 2000.

46. Alexander, *The Unsettled Land*, 185–87.

47. Ibid., 186.

48. Blair Rutherford, *Working on the Margins: Black Workers, White Farmers in Postcolonial Zimbabwe* (Harare: Weaver Press, 2001): 57.

49. Human Rights Watch, "Fast Track Land Reform in Zimbabwe: Human Rights Violations," March 2002.

50. Amnesty International, "Zimbabwe: Constitutional reform—An opportunity to strengthen human rights protection," 2 February 2000.

51. Human Rights Watch, "Fast Track Land Reform."

52. Alexander, *The Unsettled Land*, 188–89.

53. Chikuhwa, *A Crisis of Governance*, 253.

54. "Mike Campbell," *The Telegraph*, 8 April 2011.

55. Alexander, *The Unsettled Land*, 187; Chikuhwa, *A Crisis of Governance*, 258–60.

56. Moyo, "Agrarian Reform," 134.

57. Chikuhwa, *A Crisis of Governance*, 262.

58. Stephen Tsoroti, "Biodiversity in Peril," *The Zimbabwean*, 27 April 2011.

59. Eustinah Tarisayi, "Voting in Despair: The Economic and Social Context," in *Defying the Winds of Change: Zimbabwe's 2008 Elections*, ed. E. V. Masunungure (Harare: Weaver Press and Konrad Adenauer Stiftung, 2009), 11–12.

60. World Bank, "Life Expectancy at Birth: Zimbabwe," 2014, http://data.worldbank.org/indicator/SP.DYN.LE00.IN/countries/ZW?display=graph (accessed 16 August 2014). Life expectancy bottomed out in 2003, at just under forty-three years.

61. Godwin, *The Fear*, 40.

62. Quoted in ibid., 178–79.

63. Human Rights Watch, "Zimbabwe: ZANU-PF Sets Up 'Torture Camps'," 19 April 2008.

64. Ibid.

65. Human Rights Watch, "Zimbabwe: No Justice for Rampant Killings," 8 March 2011.

66. "Morgan Tsvangirai: Zimbabwe Elections Likely in 2012," *BBC*, 6 May 2011.

67. Godwin, *The Fear*, 241.

68. Ibid., 147.

69. "Exiled Mugabe Returns to Rhodesia," *BBC*, 27 January 1980.

70. "'Zimbabwe is mine' Says Robert Mugabe," *The Telegraph*, 19 December 2008.

Chapter 9. Africa's Domestic Institutions of Integration and Accommodation: A New Database

I am deeply grateful to Professor Alan Kuperman for his tireless advice and assistance on both the substance and form of this chapter. Any outstanding errors or omissions are mine alone. Many thanks are also due for helpful comments from the scholars of the Constitutional Design and Conflict Management book project, as well as from discussants at the associated workshop and conference, both held in 2011. I also wish to thank the Robert S. Strauss Center for International Security and Law, at the University of Texas at Austin, for generous financial support during the writing of this chapter.

1. See, e.g., Bernard Grofman and Robert Stockwell, "Institutional Design in Plural Societies: Mitigating Ethnic Conflict and Fostering Stable Democracy," in *Economic Welfare, International Business and Global Institutional Change*, ed. Ram Mudambi, Pietro Navarra, and Guiseppe Sobbrio (New York: Edward Elgar, 2003).

2. See Milton Esman, "Ethnic Pluralism: Strategies for Conflict Management," in *Facing Ethnic Conflicts: Toward a New Realism*, ed. Andreas Wimmer et al. (Lanham, Md.: Rowman and Littlefield, 2004).

3. For some reviews of the literature on alternative paths to establishing political order in multi-ethnic states, see Crawford Young, *The Politics of Cultural Pluralism* (Madison: University of Wisconsin Press, 1976); Ian Lustick, "Stability in Deeply Divided Societies: Consociationalism Versus Control," *World Politics* 31, 3 (April 1979): 325–44; Andreas Wimmer, "Who Owns the State? Understanding Ethnic Conflict in Post-Colonial Societies," *Nations and Nationalism* 3, 4 (1997): 631–65; and Cameron

G. Thies, "The Political Economy of State Building in Sub-Saharan Africa," *Journal of Politics* 69, 3 (August 2007): 716–731.

4. Arend Lijphart, *Power-Sharing in South Africa* (Berkeley: University of California Press, 1985), 5–7.

5. Arend Lijphart, *Democracy in Plural Societies: A Comparative Exploration* (New Haven, Conn.: Yale University Press, 1977).

6. Donald L. Horowitz, *A Democratic South Africa? Constitutional Engineering in a Divided Society* (Berkeley: University of California Press, 1991).

7. Horowitz, *A Democratic South Africa?* 172–89, 205–17.

8. Timothy D. Sisk, *Power Sharing and International Mediation in Ethnic Conflicts* (Washington, D.C.: U.S. Institute of Peace Press, 1996), 47–48.

9. Esman, "Ethnic Pluralism," 209.

10. Grofman and Stockwell, "Institutional Design in Plural Societies," 111, 124.

11. Andrew Reynolds, *Electoral Systems and Democratization in Southern Africa* (Oxford: Oxford University Press, 1999), 268.

12. René Lemarchand, "Consociationalism and Power Sharing in Africa: Rwanda, Burundi, and the Democratic Republic of the Congo," *African Affairs* 106, 422 (January 2007): 1–20.

13. Benjamin Reilly, *Democracy in Divided Societies: Electoral Engineering for Conflict Management* (London: Cambridge University Press, 2001), 21–24, 185–86.

14. See Donald Horowitz, "Constitutional Design: Proposals Versus Processes," in *The Architecture of Democracy: Constitutional Design, Conflict Management, and Democracy*, ed. Andrew Reynolds (Oxford: Oxford University Press, 2002), 15–36; "Conciliatory Institutions and Constitutional Processes in Post-Conflict States," *William and Mary Law Review* 49, 4 (March 2008): 1213–48.

15. See Arend Lijphart, "Democratic Political Systems: Types, Cases, Causes, and Consequences," *Journal of Theoretical Politics* 1 (1989): 33–48.

16. Arend Lijphart, "The Wave of Power-Sharing Democracy," in Reynolds, ed., *The Architecture of Democracy*, 37–54; "Constitutional Design for Divided Societies," *Journal of Democracy* 15, 2 (April 2004): 96–109.

17. José Antonio Cheibub, *Presidentialism, Parliamentarism and Democracy* (New York: Cambridge University Press, 2007).

18. David A. Lake and Donald Rothchild, "Territorial Decentralization and Civil War Settlements," in *Sustainable Peace: Power and Democracy After Civil Wars*, ed. Philip G. Roeder and Donald Rothchild (Ithaca, N.Y.: Cornell University Press, 2005), 109–32; see also Svante E. Cornell, "Autonomy as a Source of Conflict: Caucasian Conflicts in Theoretical Perspective," *World Politics* 54, 2 (January 2002): 245–76.

19. But see Daniel L. Byman, *Keeping the Peace: Lasting Solutions to Ethnic Conflicts* (Baltimore: Johns Hopkins University Press, 2002), 100–124.

20. See John McGarry, Brendan O'Leary, and Richard Simeon, "Integration or Accommodation? The Enduring Debate in Conflict Regulation," in *Constitutional Design*

for Divided Societies: Integration or Accommodation? ed. Sujit Choudhry (Oxford: Oxford University Press, 2008), 41–88; Table 2, 70–71.

21. See Reilly, *Democracy in Divided Societies*, 185–86.

22. No formal distinction is made for semipresidential systems or other systems having a directly elected president as well as a prime minister, although the specific distribution of power in such cases is considered in the index.

23. Quotas for representation of women and other groups with less consistent political preferences, such as young people or the disabled, are not considered to have accommodative effects.

24. Lijphart's wider theoretical framework may apply beyond such cases; see "Democratic Political Systems," 39.

25. Two possible exceptions are Somalia and Libya. As of January 2011, Somalia could be said to have had a de jure constitutional design, but no stable de facto design given its anarchic political order. Libya might be said to have had a de facto design without a de jure constitution, although one could argue that the "Green Book" and a 1977 legislative declaration served as constitutional documents.

26. See Derick W. Brinkerhoff and Arthur A. Goldsmith, "Clientelism, Patrimonialism and Democratic Governance: An Overview and Framework for Assessment and Planning," report to U.S. Agency for International Development (USAID) (Bethesda, Md.: Abt Associates, 2002).

27. Monty G. Marshall, Ted Robert Gurr, and Keith Jaggers, "Polity IV Project: Political Regime Characteristics and Transitions, 1800–2010," Center for Systemic Peace, 2010.

28. The Bogardus social distance scale, which measures the "sympathetic understanding" between different identity groups, would probably provide the best metric for quantifying deeply divided societies. See, for example, Arnold Vedlitz and Sammy Zahran, "Theories of Ethnic Social Distance: Comparative Empirical Tests for Three Distinct Ethnic Groups," *Sociological Spectrum* 27, 5 (2007): 592. Existing measures of ethnopolitical diversity and fractionalization, such as the Cederman et al., Ethnic Power Relations Dataset, do not provide a good proxy for depth of divisions, as they measure the number and size of different groups, and their political relations, but do not address the underlying structures of social divisions. See Lars-Erik Cederman, Brian Min, and Andreas Wimmer, Ethnic Power Relations Dataset, Ethnic Power Relations Dataverse (2009).

29. See Horowitz, "Conciliatory Institutions and Constitutional Processes," 1226–31.

30. McGarry et al., "Integration or Accommodation?" 87–88. Horowitz points out that conflict-prone designs can sometimes actually help leaders in deeply divided societies remain in power by providing opportunities to exploit social divisions for political gain. "Conciliatory Institutions and Constitutional Processes," 1229.

31. Sources used to assemble these summaries include constitutional texts and other sources of law (on file with author); ACE Electoral Knowledge Network (Africa regional

data), http://aceproject.org/regions-en/regions/africa; African Elections Database, http://africanelections.tripod.com/index.html; CIA World Factbook, Country Summaries; Electoral Institute for the Sustainability of Democracy in Africa (EISA), "Democracy Encyclopedia Project," http://www.eisa.org.za/WEP/wepindex.htm; M. Steven Fish and Matthew Kroenig, *The Handbook of National Legislatures* (Cambridge: Cambridge University Press, 2009); International Foundation for Electoral Systems (IFES) Election Guide, Africa region, http://electionguide.org/; Inter-Parliamentary Union (IPU), "PARLINE Database on National Parliaments," http://www.ipu.org/parline-e/parlinesearch.asp; International Institute for Democracy and Electoral Assistance (IDEA), "Table of Electoral Systems Worldwide," http://www.idea.int/esd/world.cfm; U.S. Department of State, Country Profiles. Additional country-specific scholarly and media sources were utilized to assemble information on individual cases (on file).

Chapter 10. Rethinking Constitutional Reform for Democracy and Stability

1. Sven Gunnar Simonsen, "Addressing Ethnic Divisions in Post-Conflict Institution-Building: Lessons from Recent Cases," *Security Dialogue* 36, 3 (September 2005): 310, referring especially to proportional representation in electoral systems.

2. Benjamin Reilly, *Democracy in Divided Societies: Electoral Engineering for Conflict Management* (New York: Cambridge University Press, 2001), 20, referring to consociationalism.

3. Helga Malmin Binningsbø, "Power Sharing, Peace and Democracy: Any Obvious Relationships?" *International Area Studies Review* 16, 1 (March 2013): 89, referring to power-sharing, which the article says is "mostly understood as including political opponents in a joint executive coalition government."

4. Reilly, *Democracy in Divided Societies*, 20, referring to consociationalism.

5. Ibid., 168, citing Arend Lijphart, "Prospects for Power Sharing in the New South Africa," in *Election '94 South Africa: An Analysis of the Results, Campaign and Future Prospects*, ed. Andrew Reynolds (New York: St. Martin's, 1994), 222.

6. Andrew Reynolds and Timothy D. Sisk, "Elections and Electoral Systems: Implications for Conflict Management," in *Elections and Conflict Management in Africa*, ed. Timothy D. Sisk and Andrew Reynolds (Washington, D.C.: U.S. Institute of Peace Press, 1998), 30.

7. Andrew Reynolds, *Electoral Systems and Democratization in Southern Africa* (New York: Oxford University Press, 1999), 268.

8. Ibid., 269.

9. Quoted in ibid., 269, citing Ann Reid, "Conflict Resolution in Africa: Lessons from Angola," INR Foreign Affairs Brief, U.S. Department of State, 1993.

10. Quoted in Timothy D. Sisk, "Elections and Conflict Management in Africa: Conclusions and Recommendations," in *Elections and Conflict Management in Africa*, ed. Sisk and Reynolds, 171.

11. G. Shabbir Cheema and Dennis A. Rondinelli, "From Government Decentralization to Decentralized Governance," in *Decentralizing Governance: Emerging*

Concepts and Practices, ed. G. Shabbir Cheema and Dennis A. Rondinelli (Washington, D.C.: Brookings Institution Press, 2007), 7, 10.

12. Thomas Carothers, *Revitalizing U.S. Democracy Assistance: The Challenge of USAID* (Washington, D.C.: Carnegie Endowment for International Peace, 2009), 26–27, citing "Request for Task Order Proposal (RFTOP) Number 623-EA-09-024 for Encouraging Global Anticorruption and Good Governance Effort (ENGAGE)," USAID East Africa, 29 May 2009.

13. Binningsbø, "Power Sharing, Peace and Democracy," 101.

14. Donald Rothchild and Philip G. Roeder, "Power Sharing as an Impediment to Peace and Democracy," in *Sustainable Peace: Power and Democracy after Civil Wars*, ed. Philip G. Roeder and Donald Rothchild (Ithaca, N.Y.: Cornell University Press), 37.

15. Reilly, *Democracy in Divided Societies*, 184–189.

16. Goran Hyden, "Challenges to Decentralized Governance in Weak States," in *Decentralizing Governance*, ed. Cheema and. Rondinelli, 214.

17. Marta Reynal-Querol, "Ethnicity, Political Systems, and Civil Wars," *Journal of Conflict Resolution* 46, 1 (February 2002): 49.

18. Pippa Norris, *Driving Democracy: Do Power-Sharing Institutions Work?* (New York: Cambridge University Press, 2008), 215.

19. Anna K. Jarstad, "Power Sharing: Former Enemies in Joint Government," in *From War to Democracy: Dilemmas of Peacebuilding*, ed. Anna K. Jarstad and Timothy D. Sisk (New York: Cambridge University Press, 2008), 109, citing Caroline Hartzell and Matthew Hoddie, "Institutionalizing Peace: Power Sharing and Post-Civil War Conflict Management," *American Journal of Political Science* 47, 2 (April 2003): 318–32. For elucidation of these forms of power-sharing, see Caroline A. Hartzell and Matthew Hoddie, *Crafting Peace: Power-Sharing Institutions and the Negotiated Settlement of Civil Wars* (University Park: Pennsylvania State University Press, 2007), 24–25.

20. As cited in Jarstad, "Power Sharing," 109.

21. Hartzell and Hoddie, *Crafting Peace*, 3–4.

22. Ibid., 15.

23. Ibid., 29.

24. Ibid., 49, 78. The ratio of hazard rates is 5.20/0.29 = 18. The findings are based on 49 negotiated agreements from 1945 to 1999.

25. Ibid., 101–3, based on cases from 1980 to 1996.

26. Anna K. Jarstad and Desirée Nilsson, "From Words to Deeds: The Implementation of Power-Sharing Pacts in Peace Accords," *Conflict Management and Peace Science* 25, 3 (2008): 218, declares that "when these pacts are being implemented there is virtually no risk at all that peace will fail." Their findings are based on 83 negotiated settlements of civil war from 1989 to 2004.

27. Bumba Mukherjee, "Does Third-Party Enforcement or Domestic Institutions Promote Enduring Peace After Civil Wars? Policy Lessons From an Empirical Test," *Foreign Policy Analysis* 2 (2006): 428.

28. Norris, *Driving Democracy*, 223.

29. Ted Robert Gurr, "Attaining Peace In Divided Societies: Five Principles Of Emerging Doctrine," *International Journal on World Peace* 19, 2 (June 2002): 35. Gurr says the doctrine embraces this principle, "rather than suppression or forced assimilation of groups that claim separate identities and interests."

30. Binningsbø, "Power Sharing, Peace and Democracy," 106-7. For example, these studies define "power sharing" variously as proportional representation, permitting rebels to form political parties, or guaranteeing government posts to rebels.

31. Michaela Mattes and Burcu Savun, "Fostering Peace After Civil War: Commitment Problems and Agreement Design," *International Studies Quarterly* 53 (2009): 754. This study's causal variable is the existence of power-sharing provisions, whereas for Jarstad and Nillson it is the implementation of those provisions.

32. Jarstad and Nilsson, "From Words to Deeds," 206-23.

33. Mattes and Savun, "Fostering Peace After Civil War," 746.

34. Vincent T. Maphai, "A Season for Power-Sharing," *Journal of Democracy* 7, 1 (1996): 67-81.

35. Ian S. Spears, "Africa: The Limits of Power-Sharing," *Journal of Democracy* 13, 3 (July 2002): 132.

36. Simonsen, "Addressing Ethnic Divisions," 297.

37. Timothy D. Sisk, "Sustaining Peace: Renegotiating Postwar Settlements," in *Strengthening Peace in Post-Civil War States: Transforming Spoilers into Stakeholders*, eds. Matthew Hoddie and Caroline A. Hartzell (Chicago: University of Chicago Press, 2010), 105, 107.

38. Jarstad, "Power Sharing," 106.

39. Philip G. Roeder, "States and Civil Societies following Civil Wars," in *Strengthening Peace in Post-Civil War States: Transforming Spoilers into Stakeholders*, ed. Matthew Hoddie and Caroline A. Hartzell (Chicago: University of Chicago Press, 2010), 55.

40. Simonsen, "Addressing Ethnic Divisions," 306-7, 312.

41. Spears, "Africa: The Limits of Power-Sharing," 123.

42. Simonsen, "Addressing Ethnic Divisions," 298.

43. Sisk, "Sustaining Peace," 112-13.

44. Oisin Tansey, "Statebuilding and the Limits of Constitutional Design," in *The Political Economy of State-building*, ed. Mats Berdal and Dominik Zaum (New York: Routledge, 2013), 72.

45. Ibid., 84.

46. Cheema and Rondinelli, "From Government Decentralization," 9.

47. Donald L. Horowitz, "Some Realism About Constitutional Engineering," in *Facing Ethnic Conflicts: Toward a New Realism*, ed. Andreas Wimmer et al. (Lanham, Md.: Rowman and Littlefield, 2004), 254.

48. Hyden, "Challenges to Decentralized Governance," 213.

49. These are labeled "sovereign moments" by A. Carl LeVan, "Power Sharing and Inclusive Politics in Africa's Uncertain Democracies," *Governance: an International Journal of Policy, Administration, and Institutions* 24, 1 (January 2011), 18.

50. Horowitz, "Some Realism About Constitutional Engineering," 254.
51. Ibid., 252.
52. Tansey, "Statebuilding and the Limits of Constitutional Design," 98.
53. Jarstad, "Power Sharing," 117.
54. Denis M. Tull and Andreas Mehler, "The Hidden Costs of Power-Sharing: Reproducing Insurgent Violence in Africa," *African Affairs* 104, 416 (2005): 375.
55. Simonsen, "Addressing Ethnic Divisions," 302.
56. Reynolds, *Electoral Systems and Democratization*, 270.
57. On the perils of ignoring path dependence, see Paul Pierson, *Politics in Time: History, Institutions, and Social Analysis* (Princeton: Princeton University Press, 2004).
58. Tansey, "Statebuilding and the Limits of Constitutional Design," 98.
59. Ibid., 97.
60. Ibid., 71.
61. Hyden, "Challenges to Decentralized Governance," 217.

CONTRIBUTORS

Justin Orlando Frosini teaches in the Department of Law, Bocconi University, Milan, Italy, and is Director of the Center for Constitutional Studies and Democratic Development (CCSDD) in Bologna, Italy.

Gilbert M. Khadiagala is Chair of the Department of International Relations and Jan Smuts Professor at University of the Witwatersrand, Johannesburg, South Africa.

Alan J. Kuperman is Associate Professor of Public Affairs at the LBJ School of Public Affairs, University of Texas at Austin.

Karly Kupferberg is a Small Arms Light Weapons Technical Adviser at the United Nations Mine Action Service (UNMAS).

Eghosa E. Osaghae is Vice Chancellor and Professor of Comparative Politics at Igbinedion University, Okada, Nigeria.

Eli Poupko, J.D., is a Ph.D. candidate at the LBJ School of Public Affairs, University of Texas at Austin.

Andrew Reynolds is Chair of Global Studies and Associate Professor of Political Science at the University of North Carolina at Chapel Hill.

Filip Reyntjens is Professor of African Law and Politics, Institute of Development Policy and Management, University of Antwerp, Belgium.

Arame Tall is a Climate Risk Management, Adaptation, and Sustainable Development Specialist at the CGIAR Research Program on Climate Change, Agriculture, and Food Security.

Hillary Thomas-Lake is Managing Director and cofounder of LTL Strategies in Washington, D.C.

Stefan Wolff is Professor of International Security, Department of Political Science and International Studies, University of Birmingham, United Kingdom.

I. William Zartman is Jacob Blaustein Distinguished Professor Emeritus, Nitze School of Advanced International Studies (SAIS), Johns Hopkins University.

INDEX

A Democratic South Africa? (Horowitz), 185
Abuja, Nigeria, 91
Abyei, Sudan, 15, 102–9, 112, 252n9;
  Boundaries Commission, 105; roadmap, 105–6; violence in, 99–100, 105–6
accommodation, 18–23, 184, 188–195, 199–201; in Burundi, 13, 27, 34, 240n28; as causal variable, 10–12; centralization and, 238n6; centripetalism and, 237n5; critiques of, 228–29, 231–32; dangers of, 233–34; in Ghana, 16–17; hyper-accommodation, 21–22, 224–25, 240n28; on identity promotion spectrum, 2–3, 6; in Kenya, 14; in Nigeria, 15, 75–77, 85–86, 89, 92; obstacles to, 232–33; in Senegal, 17; in Sudan, 15–16, 103; support of, 226–28, 230; in Zimbabwe, 18, 166, 169–70, 174, 179. *See also* integration
accountability, 19, 186, 228; in Kenya, 55, 68–69; in Senegal, 17, 151; in Zimbabwe, 169. *See also* integration
Accra, Ghana, 121, 127, 133; Fast Track High Court, 130
acephaly, 141
ADDAD (Senegal), 153
Addis Ababa Agreement (1972, Sudan), 101–3
administration, 21–22, 190, 192–93, 196–98; in Burundi, 33; in Ghana, 120, 134; in Senegal, 137–39, 142, 149, 151–52, 154–55; and separation of powers, 186
affirmative action, 33, 94, 192
African National Council (ANC, Zimbabwe), 161
African Union (AU), 38–39
Afrikaans (language), 162–63
Afrikaners (ethnic group), 163

aggrieved groups, 16; in Ghana, 118, 129; in Nigeria, 93; in Senegal, 17; in Sudan, 20. *See also* grievances
Akans (ethnic group), 131–32
Akufo-Addo, Nana (president of Ghana), 130–31
Akwa Ibom, Nigeria, 80, 92, 248n24
Alaska, United States, 249n25
Alexander, Jocelyn, 172–73
Algeria, 194, 196, 201, 224
Alliance des Démocrates pour le Changement (ADC) Ikibiri (Burundi), 48, 242n29
alternative vote (AV), 185–87, 191, 199, 237n5
amendments. *See* constitutional amendments
amnesty, 71, 167
anarchy, 62, 198; in Somalia, 194–95, 199, 268n25
Angola, 194, 196, 201–2, 224, 234
animism, 100, 141–42, 229
Anya-Nya rebellion (Sudan), 101
Apartheid, 184–85
Apter, David, 121
Arabs, 96–97, 100, 108
aristocracy, 139
army. *See* military
Arusha Accord (2000, Burundi), 36–39, 47–48, 241n16
Arusha, Tanzania, 35–39, 41
Asians, 160–62, 179
assassinations, 5, 28, 33
assimilation, 3, 186, 188–89
Attika (Casamance secessionists), 141–42, 145
authoritarianism, 184; in Burundi, 47; in Ghana, 118–19; in Kenya, 54, 60; in Nigeria, 85; in Zimbabwe, 17–18, 159–60, 162, 179

autocracy, 6, 10, 193, 235; in Kenya, 57; in Nigeria, 93; in Zimbabwe, 175
autonomy, 192, 199, 226–29, 232–33; as accommodation, 2–3, 6, 193–94, 238n8; in consociational design, 185–88; in Ghana, 119–20; in Nigeria, 72–75, 77–78, 80, 84, 87–88, 93–95; in Senegal, 135, 139; in South Sudan, 101

Badiane, Emile (minister of education in Senegal), 142
Bagaza, Jean-Baptiste (president of Burundi), 29, 242n26
Baker, James (U.S. secretary of state), 57
Banjul agreements (Senegal), 144–45
Basedau, Matthias, 48–49
Bashir, Omar (president of Sudan), 105, 107–9, 111, 251n3
Bayelsa, Nigeria, 76, 80, 82, 90–91, 248n18; unemployment in, 248n24
Beja Congress (Sudan), 251n2
Belgium, 50
Benin, 194, 196, 202, 224
Bennett, Roy (MDC treasurer), 169, 177–78
Benno Siggil Senegal (political alliance), 152
Biafra (Nigeria), 7, 14–15, 83–84, 138
bicameralism, 21, 140, 161, 187, 191; in Nigeria, 78
Binningsbø, Helga Malmin, 230–31
Biti, Tendai (MDC secretary-general), 175
Blue Nile, Sudan, 10, 15, 99, 102–3, 107–9, 111
Boahen, Adu (NPP presidential candidate), 126–27
Bomas, Nairobi (Kenya), 64–66
Bonaparte, Napoleon, 137
Boro, Isaac Adaka (Nigerian political figure), 249n31
Botswana, 194–96, 202, 224
boundaries: Abyei Boundaries Commission, 105–6; National Boundary Commission (Niger Delta), 91–92; in Nigeria, 88, 91
bourgeoisie, 139
boycotts: in Burundi, 48–49, 242n29; in Ghana, 16, 117, 127–29; in Kenya, 61–62; in Sudan, 107, 251n3
brain drain emigration, 132
Britain, 10–11, 119–20, 134, 161, 258n51; Kenya and, 52; Lancaster House agreement, 160, 170–72, 174; Nigeria and, 83;

Sudan and, 97, 100; Zimbabwe and, 160, 178. *See also* Lancaster House agreement
Bujumbura, Burundi, 32–33, 36, 47–48
Bulawayo, Zimbabwe, 163, 166
bunkering (of oil), 82, 87, 91, 250n42
Burkina Faso, 194, 196, 202–3, 225
Burundi, 7, 10, 13–14, 27–50, 187, 194, 196, 203, 224, 227; accommodation in, 19–20, 23, 227, 234, 240n28; civil war in, 32–35; democratic elections in, 31; elections of 2005, 39–46; elections of 2010, 47–48; ethnic conflicts in, 28–29; peace negotiations in, 35–39; post-2005, 46–50; reforms in, 29–30
Bururi, Burundi, 28–29, 33
Busia, Kofi (prime minister of Ghana), 121
Buyoya, Pierre (president of Burundi), 29–31, 35–36, 42, 44, 242n24

cabinets, 191, 193, 195–96; in Burundi, 30, 32, 35, 37, 45–46, 203; in consociational design, 185, 187, 190; in Ghana, 16, 129, 131; in Kenya, 62–63, 65–67; in Senegal, 140; in Sudan, 101, 105, 107; in United States, 119; in Zimbabwe, 162, 166
Cacheu agreement (1991, Senegal), 144
Cameroon, 194, 196, 203–4, 224
Campbell, Mike (Zimbabwean), 173–74
Canada, 58
Cape Verde, 194, 196, 204, 224
Casamance, Senegal, 10, 140–47, 261nn29, 36; management under Diouf, 143–45; management under Wade, 145–46; outcomes in, 146–47; rebellion in, 17, 136, 140–43
ceasefires: in Burundi, 36; in Senegal, 135–36, 143–47, 260n14
censuses: ethnic, 163, 178–79, 185; in Ghana, 124–25; in Sudan, 104, 106–7; in Zimbabwe, 164
center versus periphery: in Nigeria, 15, 75, 92; in Senegal, 135–36, 147; in Sudan, 102, 251n2
Central African Republic, 194, 196, 204, 224
central bank, 187
Central Bank (Kenya), 61
Central Intelligence Organisation (CIO, Zimbabwe), 168, 176
Central Province (Kenya), 53–54, 68

Index

centralization, 1–3, 193, 195, 238n6; in Ghana, 124–25, 131, 133–34; integration and, 22, 190; in Kenya, 53, 56, 65–66, 68; in Nigeria, 15, 71–72, 76, 82–87, 92–93; in Senegal, 17, 137–40, 146–48, 151–52, 155–56, 260n9; in South Africa, 199; in Sudan, 100–101; in Zimbabwe, 17–18, 158–60, 166, 168–70, 177, 179. *See also* decentralization; hypercentralization
centripetalism, 3, 17, 187–90, 192, 232, 237n5
Chad, 104, 194, 196, 204–5, 225
checks and balances, 17, 191–92, 229: in Ghana, 119, 133–34; in Kenya, 55; in Senegal, 140
Cheema, G. Shabbir, 233
Cheibub, José Antonio, 187–88
chieftaincy, 117, 122, 132
Chikuhwa, Jacob, 169, 171–72
Chimanimani, Zimbabwe, 177
China, 120
chiNdau (language), 177
cholera, 152, 154
Christians, 10, 100, 131, 141
Civil Protection Department (CPD, Senegal), 150
civil rights. *See* human rights
civil service, 185; in Burundi, 33; in Ghana, 120, 124; in Sudan, 102
Civil Service Act (1960, Ghana), 120
Civil Services Commission (Ghana), 120
civil society, 74, 200, 232, 238n8; in Burundi, 33, 38, 46–47, 49; in Kenya, 60, 62; in Nigeria, 74, 91; in Senegal, 145, 150, 156; in Sudan, 108; in Zimbabwe, 161, 178–79
civil war, 9–15, 19–21, 184, 226–32; in Burundi, 20, 32–35, 38–39, 46–47, 227; in Nigeria, 14–15, 71, 76, 83, 85; in Sudan, 7, 97, 101–2, 109, 227
civilian government: in Ghana, 121, 132; in Nigeria, 72, 77, 89
closed-list voting system, 30, 46
CNN (news station), 175
co-optation: in Burundi, 37–38, 43, 45, 48, 242nn22, 25; in Kenya, 59, 63–65; in Senegal, 139, 142
coalitions: electoral, 133–34; ethnic, 64, 131, 179; pre-electoral, 20, 185–87, 189–90
Coburn Estate (Zimbabwe), 171
cohabitation, 131

Cold War, 30, 35
Collin, Jean, 137
colonial era, 10–11, 235: in Ghana, 118–20, 123, 134; in Nigeria, 93; postcolonial era, 55, 69, 118, 163, 165; precolonial era, 100, 138–39, 163; in Senegal, 137–38, 140–42; in Sudan, 97, 100; in Zimbabwe, 158, 163, 165, 179
Commission Électorale Nationale Indépendante (CENI, Burundi), 242n18
commissions. *See* constitutional commissions; electoral commissions
Commonwealth heads of state summit (1991), 57–58
Comoros, 194, 196, 205, 224
compensation: in Ghana, 120, 124; in Nigeria, 85–88, 91; in Zimbabwe, 160, 167, 170–72
Comprehensive Peace Agreement (CPA, Sudan, 2005), 15–16, 97, 99–113, 251n3; constitutional design by, 102–3; North-South separation and, 99–100; power-sharing and, 103–7; secession and, 107–12
compulsory acquisition, 120, 170
Congo, 1, 194, 196, 205–6, 224
Congress: Burundi, 45; United States, 57, 119
Conseil National pour la Défense de la Démocratie (CNDD, Burundi), 35–38, 241n15, 243n31; in 2005 elections, 40–45; after 2005, 46–49
consensual democracy, 187, 199
consensus, 2–3, 47, 64, 184
consociational systems, 3, 11, 184–89, 231; in Burundi, 27–28, 31–32, 36–37, 44, 47–48, 50, 243n31; Lijphart on, 184–85, 187–89, 199, 227–28
consolidation of power: in Burundi, 27–29, 46; in Kenya, 53; in Sudan, 101, 109, 111. *See also* centralization; hypercentralization; power
Constituent Assembly (Nigeria), 78
Constitution of Kenya Review Commission Act (1998), 64
Constitution of Kenya Review Committee (CKRC), 64, 66
constitutional amendments, 6, 187–88; in Burundi, 30–32; in Ghana, 118–20, 133; in Kenya, 53, 55–56, 61; in Zimbabwe, 161, 170–72

constitutional commissions, 30, 122, 257n18
constitutional referenda; in Burundi, 30, 37; in Ghana, 122; in Kenya, 14, 51, 63, 66–68; in Sudan, 15, 20, 97, 102–9, 111, 113; in Zimbabwe, 7, 18, 158, 164, 171, 175
constitutional reforms, 5–7, 13–17, 23, 199, 226–27, 232–35; in Kenya, 20, 51–52, 56, 58–69; in Nigeria, 72, 83–84, 93; in Senegal, 138, 140; in Zimbabwe, 159, 161, 172
Constitutional Repeal of Restrictions Act (1959, Ghana), 119
Constitutional Review Commission (Ghana), 118–19, 133
Convention People's Party (CPP, Ghana), 119–20
Côte d'Ivoire, 117, 194, 196, 206, 225
Council of State (Ghana), 122
coups, 11: in Burundi, 28, 32–33, 35, 38; in Gambia, 143; in Ghana, 118, 120–21, 123; in Kenya, 55; in Senegal, 152; in Sudan, 99–101, 109; in Zimbabwe, 166
courts: Accra Fast Track High Court, 130; constitutional, 229, 246n40; in Ghana, 119–20; High Court, 172; independent, 17, 19, 22, 128, 131; International Criminal Court, 105; Permanent Court of Arbitration, 106; Supreme, 6, 88–89, 92, 123, 172, 256n1
Criminal Code Amendment Act (1961, Ghana), 120
Criminal Procedures Act (1960, Ghana), 120
Crocker, Chester, 228
cronyism, 160
Cross River, Nigeria, 80, 92
cross-group appeals, 186, 189–90, 192, 229, 232; in Burundi, 44; in Ghana, 17, 20, 131
crude oil. *See* oil
Cyprus, 50

Dakar, Senegal, 17, 137, 139, 260n9; Casamance and, 141–42, 146; flooding in, 147–48, 150–54
Darfur Peace Agreement (DPA, 2006), 251n2
Darfur, Sudan, 1, 10, 103–5, 107–8, 251n2
de facto versus de jure coding, 6–7, 10, 21, 193–95
decentralization, 2–3, 6, 228, 233, 238n8; in accommodation, 190; in centripetalism, 188; in consociational design, 185, 187; in Ghana, 133; in Kenya, 67–68; in Nigeria, 71, 76, 88; in Senegal, 138, 151, 153. *See also* centralization; devolution; federalism
Deepwater Horizon, 249n25
Delta, Nigeria, 80, 82
democracy, 10, 193, 195, 200, 232; in Burundi, 13, 20, 30–32, 45, 47, 49–50; consensual, 187, 199; consociational, 3, 184–85, 227–28; foreign aid and, 11, 22–23; in Ghana, 117–22, 127, 132, 134; in Kenya, 54, 57, 60; majoritarian, 185–86; in Nigeria, 72, 74, 85, 89; peace and, 9, 189; promotion of, 1–2, 235; in Senegal, 136, 157; in South Sudan, 108, 111; in Zimbabwe, 158, 160, 173, 178–79
Democracy in Divided Societies (Reilly), 187
Democratic Party (DP, Kenya), 64
Democratic Republic of the Congo (DRC), 29, 187, 194, 196, 206, 225
demographic shocks, 4–5, 11, 55, 226
demonstrations: in Ghana, 127; in Kenya, 54, 61–62; in Senegal, 144, 148, 151–52, 155. *See also* protests; riots
Denmark, 58
Department of Social Welfare and Community (Ghana), 124–25
derivation, 75, 77–79, 92–95; emergence of oil and, 82–84; environmental degradation and, 85–91. *See also* revenue
desertification, 9, 261n29
devolution, 6, 15, 17, 21, 185, 192; in Ghana, 133; in Kenya, 64; in Nigeria, 15, 94–95; in Senegal, 139, 156. *See also* decentralization; federalism
Diamacoune, Abbé (MFDC leader), 144
dictatorship, 9–10, 55, 184, 193; in Ghana, 121; in Kenya, 61; in Zimbabwe, 161
Dinka (ethnic group), 97, 109
Diola (ethnic group), 136, 141–42
Diop, Abdoulaye Mattar (Senegalese political figure), 153
Diop, Becaye (minister of interior in Senegal), 155
Diouf, Abdou (president of Senegal), 139–40, 142–47, 149, 157
diplomacy, 99, 112
direct elections, 21–22, 191; in Burundi, 48; in integration, 190, 195; in majoritarianism, 186; in Zimbabwe, 161–62

Index

Direction de la Protection Civile (Senegal), 153
discrimination, 76, 100, 163
disease, 5
disenfranchisement, 59, 63, 159–60
Djibouti, 194–96, 207, 225
Dokubo, Asari (leader of IYC), 91
dominance: economic, 53; federal, 75, 79, 93–94; fiscal, 90; one-party, 47, 53. *See also* ethnic dominance
donor aid, 11, 23, 235; in Burundi, 33, 38–39; in Kenya, 14, 51, 57–58; policy prescriptions for, 1–2, 22–23; in Sudan, 15–16, 99, 103–5; in Zimbabwe, 170, 175
Douglas, Oronto, 83
DRC. *See* Democratic Republic of the Congo
drought, 5; in Kenya, 53, 58; in Senegal, 136, 143, 147–49; in Zimbabwe, 168, 171

Eastern Sudan Peace Agreement (ESPA), 251n2
economic shocks, 4–5, 11, 226; in Kenya, 14, 52, 55; in Sudan, 118
economy: in Burundi, 33, 44; in Kenya, 52–58, 61–62, 67–70; in Nigeria, 73, 82, 91; in Senegal, 141, 143–46; in Sudan, 98, 137; in Zimbabwe, 18, 170–71, 175–77
egalitarianism, 142, 188–89
Egle Party (Ghana), 126–27
Egypt, 100, 194, 196, 207–8, 225
elections, 5–7, 185–93, 199–200, 240n29. *See also* direct elections; electoral systems; stolen elections
elections in Burundi, 27–28, 30, 37–38; in 1993, 31–32, 35, 243n33; in 2005, 39–46, 243n33; in 2010, 47–49
elections in Ghana, 16, 117–19, 121–23, 132–34; in 1992, 126–28; in 2000, 128–30; in 2008, 130–31; in 2012, 256n1
elections in Kenya, 10, 53, 117; in 1988, 55; in 1992, 56, 59; in 1997, 61–64; in 2002, 64–65; in 2007, 63, 66–68
elections in Senegal, 138–40, 157; in 2000, 144–45; in 2005, 148; in 2007, 151; in 2009, 152–53, 156
elections in Sudan: in 1958, 100; in 2010, 104, 107
elections in Zimbabwe, 117, 158–65, 179; in 2000, 171–72; in 2008, 18, 175–78

Electoral Commission of Kenya (ECK), 63, 67, 246n40
electoral commissions, 2, 22, 200; in Burundi, 37–38, 41–43; in Ghana, 17, 19–20, 121, 127, 129–31, 133; in Kenya, 62–63, 67; in Nigeria, 76; in Zimbabwe, 175
electoral systems, 21, 185–87, 190–92, 199, 237n5. *See also* first-past-the-post (FPTP) elections; majoritarian systems; proportional representation (PR) systems
Electoral Systems and Democratization in Southern Africa (Reynolds), 187
embargos, 35
Embu (ethnic group), 65
Emergency Powers Act (1961, Ghana), 120
emigration, 5, 18, 132
endangered species, 174
endogenous shocks, 9, 11; in Burundi, 27, 49; in Kenya, 14, 51, 53, 57, 69; in Senegal, 135–36
Engels, Friedrich, 139
English (language), 162
Entebbe, Uganda, 39
Environmental Impact Assessment Act (1992, Nigeria), 87
environmental shocks, 4–5, 226, 250nn34, 36; in Kenya, 55; in Nigeria, 7, 15, 72–73, 80, 85–95; in Senegal, 138; in Sudan, 97; in Zimbabwe, 174
Equatorial Guinea, 194, 197, 208, 225
Eritrea, 194, 195, 197, 208, 225
Esman, Milton, 186
Ethiopia, 58, 101, 105, 194, 195, 197, 208–9, 225
ethnic amnesia, 29, 50
ethnic census, 163, 178–79, 185
ethnic coalitions, 64, 131, 179
ethnic conflicts, 14, 186, 228; in Burundi, 20, 27–28, 32, 35, 49–50; intra-ethnic tensions, 49, 162, 164; in Kenya, 52, 55–56, 58–59, 65, 69; in Zimbabwe, 7, 17–18, 158, 162–63, 165–69, 179; *See also* violence
ethnic dominance, 14, 85, 109; in Burundi, 13, 20, 31–33; in Ghana, 131; in Kenya, 14, 68–69; in Nigeria, 71, 83–85; in Sudan, 109
ethnic groups. *See under* specific groups
ethnic identities, in Burundi, 14

ethnic majorities: in Burundi, 13, 20; in Ghana, 131; in Nigeria, 77, 85; in Zimbabwe, 18
ethnic minorities: in Burundi, 13, 20, 29, 32, 37–38; in Nigeria, 15, 71–72, 83, 85; in Zimbabwe, 18
ethnic pacification, 27, 44, 49
ethnic polarization, 11: in Burundi, 35, 49; in Kenya, 7, 51, 66–67; in Zimbabwe, 178–79
Europe, 56–57
Europeans, 163
excess crude. *See* oil price spikes
exclusionary approach, 11, 187; in Zimbabwe, 18, 159–60, 164–66
executive, 6, 190–91, 196–200; in Burundi, 37, 45; in consociational design, 3, 185, 187; in Ghana, 16–17, 119, 128–29, 131, 134, 195; in integration, 19, 21–22; in Kenya, 52, 66–67; in Nigeria, 15, 75–76, 78–80, 92; in Senegal, 17, 153; in South Sudan, 102; in Zimbabwe, 160–61, 177. *See also* checks and balances
exogenous shocks, 11; in Burundi, 27, 49; in Kenya, 14, 53, 57, 69; in Senegal, 135, 147
exports, 5; in Kenya, 53; in Nigeria, 73–74, 82; in Sudan, 98, 111
Exxon Valdez oil spill, 249n25

Fall, Ismaila, 138
famine, 5
Fast Track program (Zimbabwe), 173–74
federal character principle, 76–77, 85
federalism, 2, 21, 185–88, 192, 199, 228–29; accommodation and, 190, 226; in centripetalism, 237n5; in consociational design, 185, 187–88; ethnofederalism, 193; in Nigeria, 15, 71–95; in Sudan, 100, 251n3; support of, 228. *See also* decentralization; devolution; unitarism
Federation Account (Nigeria), 247n14
feudalism, 139
Fifth Brigade (Zimbabwe), 165–68
Finland, 58
first-past-the-post (FPTP) elections, 185; in Ghana, 20, 123, 129, 131, 134; in Zimbabwe, 160–61, 179
fiscal centralization, 82, 85, 92
fiscal federalism, 87–88, 95
fiscal institutions, 15, 75–77, 93

flooding, 5, 9; in Senegal, 7, 17, 135–38, 147–56, 262n38
Forces de Défense Nationale (FDN, Burundi), 38
Forces Nationales de Libération (FNL, Burundi), 35, 45, 47, 49
Forces pour la Défense de la Démocratie (FDD, Burundi), 35–38; in 2005 elections, 40–45; after 2005, 46–50; in 2010 elections, 47–48
foreign aid. *See* donor aid
Fortna, Page, 231
Forum for the Restoration of Democracy (FORD, Kenya), 57, 59, 64
Foundiougne Accord I, II (2005, Senegal), 145
France, 136–38; colonies of, 10–11, 141–42; French embassy, 33
free media, 17, 19, 22, 129, 131
free press, 157
FRODEBU-Nyakuri, 48
Front pour la Démocratie au Burundi (FRODEBU), 31–33, 46, 242n26; in 2005 elections, 40–45, 243n33; Arusha Accord and, 35–36, 38
Front pour la Libération Nationale (FROLINA, Burundi), 35

Gabon, 194, 197, 209, 225
Gambia, 194, 197, 209–10, 225; Casamance and, 141–43, 146, 261n32
Garang, John (Sudanese political figure), 109, 111, 254n27
gas, 73–74, 82, 85–86, 249n28
de Gaulle, Charles, 137–38
gendarmerie (national police in Burundi), 28, 32–33
General Service Unit (GSU, Kenya), 57, 61
genocide, 7, 10, 19, 226; in Burundi, 13, 20, 29, 47, 227. *See also* massacres; violence
Ghai, Yash Pal (chair of CKRC), 64
Ghana, 7, 10, 16–17, 117–34, 194, 195, 197, 210, 225, 240n28; construction of Volta Dam in, 123–26; election of 2000 in, 128–30; election of 2008, 130–31; elections of 1992, 126–28; evolution of constitutional design in, 119–23; liberal institutions in, 19–20; peace in, 131–34
Ghana Refugee Board, 132
Godwin, Peter, 161, 165, 169, 176, 178

Gold Coast, 123–24
Government of National Unity (GNU, Kenya), 68
Government of National Unity (Sudan), 105
government of South Sudan (GoSS), 102, 105
grievances, 4, 19–20, 96, 233; in Ghana, 132, 134; in Kenya, 56, 69; in Nigeria, 15, 89–90, 92–93; in Senegal, 142, 156, 261n29; in Sudan, 16, 96, 111. *See also* aggrieved groups
Grignon, François, 57
Grofman, Bernard, 186
gross domestic product (GDP), 53, 58, 73, 169
group identities, 6, 14, 17, 184–85, 192, 229
guerrilla warfare, 82
Guinea, 194, 197, 210, 225
Guinea-Bissau, 141–42, 146, 194, 197, 210–11, 225, 261n32
Gukurahundi massacres, 18, 158, 164–69, 179
Gulf of Guinea, 91
Gulf of Mexico, 249n25
Gurr, Ted Robert, 230, 271n29
Gusii (ethnic group), 59

The Hague, Netherlands, 106, 169
Harare, Zimbabwe, 57–58
Hartzell, Caroline A., 229–30
Hawazama tribe (Sudan), 108
Hempstone, Smith (U.S. political figure), 57
High Commission for Civil Protection (Senegal), 149
High Court (Zimbabwe), 172
Hoddie, Matthew, 229–30
Horn of Africa (Sudan), 97
Horowitz, Donald, 3, 185–89, 191, 199, 232–33
House of Assembly (Zimbabwe), 161–62, 170
House of Commons (UK), 134
human rights, 95, 193, 229, 261n15
human rights violations; in Burundi, 29, 40, 49; in Ghana, 118; in Kenya, 52, 57–58; in Senegal, 151; in Zimbabwe, 160
Human Rights Watch, 74, 88, 173, 176, 249n28
Hutu (ethnic group), 13, 20; in 1993 elections, 31–32, 38; in 2005 elections, 40–45; after 2005, 46–47, 46–50; Arusha Accord and, 36; in civil war, 32–33, 35; in pre-independence Burundi, 28–29; Pretoria Accord and, 37–38; reforms in Burundi and, 29–30. *See also* Burundi; Tutsi
Hyden, Goran, 229, 233, 235
Hyogo Framework for Action (Japan), 150
hyperaccommodation, 21–22, 194, 199, 224–25, 240n28
hypercentralization: in Nigeria, 71–72, 76, 83, 92; in Senegal, 17, 147, 155–56, 260n9. *See also* centralization
hypercephalism, 135
hyperintegration, 10, 21–22, 193–94, 224–25, 240n28

Iceland, 58
identity, 2–3, 20–22; in Kenya, 69; national, 189–90, 195, 199; in Nigeria, 74; in Senegal, 135; in Sudan, 97, 100
identity groups, 6, 14, 17, 184–85, 192, 229
identity-based politics, 22, 186, 188–89, 191–92, 199
Igbo (ethnic group), 83
Ijaw (ethnic group), 76, 80, 91, 248n19
Ijaw Youth Council, 91
Ikwerre (ethnic group), 83
immigration, 5
inclusionary approach, 18, 187, 234
incumbent parties: in Burundi, 31, 33, 38; defeat of, 7, 11, 130; in Ghana, 16, 128–30; in Kenya, 14; in Zimbabwe, 175–77
Indemnity and Compensation Bill (1982, Zimbabwe), 167
independence: in Burundi, 27–28; in Casamance, 142–43, 146; in Ghana, 118–20; in Kenya, 52–53; in Nigeria, 71, 75, 93; in Senegal, 136–37, 140–42, 147; in South Sudan, 97; in Sudan, 15, 97, 100, 107–9, 111–12; in Zimbabwe, 10, 18, 160, 163, 165, 169, 171
Independent Review Commission (IREC), 246
indictments, 105
indirect elections, 39, 48, 191
inflation, 143, 175
instant run-off elections, 185
institutional reforms, 11, 60, 68, 159, 232–33
institutionalist approach, 183
institutions. *See* liberal institutions

insurgent groups, 108, 234, 249n32
integration, 2–3, 6, 191–95, 226–29; versus accommodation, 13, 18–23, 184, 188–89; centralization and, 238n6; centripetalism and, 237n5; in Ghana, 16, 20; hyperintegration, 10, 21–22, 193–94, 224–25, 240n28; national identity and, 189–90; in Senegal, 137; tendency toward, 199–201. *See also* accommodation
inter-ethnic alliance, 159, 162
inter-ethnic violence. *See* ethnic conflict; violence
Inter-Governmental Authority on Development (IGAD, Sudan), 97, 251n3
Inter-Party Advisory Committee (IPAC, Ghana), 129–30
Inter-Party Parliamentary Group (IPPG, Kenya), 60, 62
Interim National Constitution (INC, Sudan), 102
Interim National Electoral Commission (INEC, Ghana), 127
internal colonialism, 88
internal migration, 5, 147–49
internally displaced persons (IDPs); in Burundi, 33–34; in Ghana, 16, 123–25; in Kenya, 59–60, 67; in Nigeria, 73; in Senegal, 17, 150, 154; in Sudan, 99, 105–6, 252n9; in Zimbabwe, 173, 176
international aid programs. *See* donor aid
International Commission of Jurists, 60
International Criminal Court (ICC), 105, 109
International Monetary Fund (IMF), 143, 174
intra-ethnic tensions, 49, 162, 164
Iraq, 233
Islam, 10, 96, 100, 131, 141
Israel, 101

Jackson, Robert (UN administrator), 123–24
Jammeh, Yahya (president of Gambia), 146
Japan, 150
Jarstad, Anna, 230–32, 234
Jaxaay (Diakhaye) relocation plan (Senegal), 150–51
Jeffries, Richard, 121–22
Joint Chiefs of Staff (Senegal), 140
Jonathan, Goodluck (president of Nigeria), 76, 91, 248n19
Jones, Trevor, 119
Jonglei, Sudan, 15, 99, 107, 111

judiciary, 2, 6, 187, 200, 229 in Burundi, 33; in Ghana, 19, 121–22, 128, 131; in Kenya, 52–53, 55, 59; in Nigeria, 72, 88, 92–93; in Senegal, 17, 157; in Zimbabwe, 159, 179. *See also* checks and balances
Justice and Equality Movement (JEM, Sudan), 251n2

Kagwanja, Peter Mwangi, 62–63
Kalanga (ethnic group), 162–63
Kalenjin (ethnic group), 59
Kamukunji grounds (Nairobi, Kenya), 57, 61
Karanga (ethnic group), 162–63, 165
Kenya, 10, 51–70, 117, 194, 197, 211, 224, 240n28, 245n17; from 1991 to 1992, 56–60; from 1995 to 1997, 60–63; from 2001 to 2005, 63–66; accommodation in, 14, 19–20; elections of 2007 in, 66–68; in independence period, 52–53; under Moi, 53–58; shocks in, 7, 51–52; vote-pooling system in, 199
Kenya African Democratic Union (KADU), 51–52
Kenya African National Union (KANU), 56–65; in elections of 1997, 63–64; in independence period, 51–52; in multi-party elections, 59; Nairobi riots and, 60; NCA reforms and, 61–62; New KANU, 64–65; Saba Saba riots and, 56–57
Kenya African Socialist Alliance (KASA), 54–55
Kenya Air Force, 55
Kenya Economic Survey (1991–1992), 58
Kenya Human Rights Commission, 60
Kenyatta, Jomo (president of Kenya), 53, 64–65
Khartoum, Sudan, 101–4, 108–9, 111, 251n2
Kibaki, Mwai (president of Kenya), 51, 63–69
Kiir, Salva (president of South Sudan), 109, 111–12
Kikuyu (ethnic group), 52, 54, 59, 64–66
Kivuitu, Samuel (chair of ECK), 67
Kobe, Japan, 150
Kosovo, 233
Kotoka, Emmanuel Kwasi (leader of NLC), 120
Kraus, John, 120
Kriegler, Johann (South African judge), 246n40

Kufour, John Agyekum (president of Ghana), 128–30
Kwara, Nigeria, 248n24

labor unions, 161
Lagos, Nigeria, 91
Lake, David A., 3, 187–88
Lancaster House agreement (Zimbabwe), 160, 170–71, 174
Lancaster House constitution (Kenya), 52
Land Acquisition Act (1992, Zimbabwe), 172
land reforms, 5; compulsory acquisition, 120, 170; in Kenya, 68; in Nigeria, 85, 87–88, 94; in Senegal, 136, 142; in Zimbabwe, 158, 160, 164, 169–75
Land Use Act (Nigeria), 88, 94
languages, 38, 123; official, 102, 189–90, 192; in Zimbabwe, 162, 168, 179
Law Society of Kenya, 60
Lebanon, 50
legislatures, 21–22, 190–93, 196–200; in Burundi, 37; in Ghana, 119, 121, 128; in Kenya, 52; in Nigeria, 15, 78–79, 92–93; proportional representation in, 6, 185, 187; in Senegal, 17, 139–40, 151; in South Sudan, 101–2; in Zimbabwe, 18, 159, 162, 177
Lemarchand, René, 28, 187
Lesotho, 194, 195, 197, 211–12, 225
Liberal Democratic Party (LDP, Kenya), 65
liberal institutions, 2, 200, 240n29; in Ghana, 17, 19–20, 134; integration and, 22–23, 227, 229
liberalism, 35, 188–89
Liberia, 194, 197, 212, 225, 234
Libya, 194, 195, 197, 212–13, 225, 268n25
Lijphart, Arend, 3, 184–85, 187–89, 199, 227–28, 238n8
Limann, Hilla (president of Ghana), 121
Luhya (ethnic group), 59
Luo (ethnic group), 52, 54, 59, 63, 66

Maass, Peter, 74
Machar, Riek (vice president of South Sudan), 109, 111
Madagascar, 194, 197, 213, 225
Mahama, John (president of Ghana), 123
majoritarian systems, 6, 184–87, 199–201, 226–30, 232; in Burundi, 37, 50, 203; in

centripetalism, 237n5; in Ghana, 133; integration and, 21, 190–91; in Sudan, 107; in Zimbabwe, 159–60, 162, 164, 169, 179
malaria, 148, 152
Malawi, 194, 197, 213–14, 225
Mali, 194, 195, 197, 214, 225
Malinga, Joshua (Zimbabwean political figure), 163
Mandela, Nelson (president of South Africa), 36, 39
Manyika (ethnic group), 162–63
Maphai, Vincent, 231
Marangara, Ngozi (Burundi), 29
Maryland, United States, 80
massacres: in Burundi, 28–29, 35; in Niger Delta, 249n32; in Zimbabwe, 7, 10, 18, 158, 164–69, 179. See also genocide; violence
Masunungure, Eldred, 165
Masvingo City, Zimbabwe, 173
Matabeleland (Zimbabwe), 18, 158, 165–69
Matiba, Kenneth (Kenyan political figure), 59
Mattes, Michaela, 231
Mauritania, 194, 197, 214, 225
Mauritius, 194–95, 197, 199, 214–15, 224, 240n28
Mazrui, Alamin, 57
Mbeki, Thabo (president of South Africa), 176
McAskie, Carolyn, 240n20
McGarry, John, 188–90, 199
media freedom, 17, 19, 22, 129, 131
Mehler, Andreas, 234
Meru (ethnic group), 65
Micombero, Michel (lieutenant general in Burundi), 28–29
Mid-West region (Nigeria), 77–78
migration, internal, 5, 147–49. See also internally displaced persons
militants: in Burundi, 31, 44, 49, 242n20; in Nigeria, 15, 71, 82, 87–88, 90–91, 250n42; in Senegal, 145; in Sudan, 16, 100; in Zimbabwe, 174
militarism, in Kenya, 52, 59, 69
military, 21, 229–31, 233; in Burundi, 29, 31–42, 46, 49; in Senegal, 143–45, 147; in Sudan, 97, 106, 109; in Zimbabwe, 158, 165–68, 173. See also police; security forces

military governments, 10, 223, 246n4; in Ghana, 118, 120–21, 128, 132; in Nigeria, 71–72, 74–77, 82, 84–85, 92–93; in Sudan, 100–101
Mills, John Evans Atta (political figure in Ghana), 128, 130–31
Minani, Jean (chairman of FRODEBU), 44
Mineral Oils Regulations Act (1963, Nigeria), 86–87
Ministry of Agriculture: in Ghana, 125; in Zimbabwe, 177
Ministry of Education (Senegal), 142
Ministry of Niger Delta (Nigeria), 89
minority groups. *See* ethnic minorities; specific groups
minority protection, 37, 94
minority representation, 37, 193
minority rule, 7, 13, 32
Misseriya tribes (Sudan), 106, 108
Mission for the Observation and Consolidation of the Peace Accord (MOCAP, Senegal), 144–45
mixed voting systems, 21
Moi, Daniel Arap (president of Kenya), 53–59, 62–65, 68–69
Monarchical Constitution (Ghana), 119
monarchies, 118–19, 139, 191, 195
Morocco, 194, 195, 197, 215, 225
Mouvement de Réhabilitation du Citoyen (MRC, Burundi), 40–42, 44
Movement for Democratic Change (MDC, Zimbabwe), 18, 158, 161–62, 164, 177–79; in elections of 2008, 175–76; land seizures and, 170–71, 173
Movement for Freedom and Justice (MFJ, Ghana), 121–22
Movement for the Emancipation of the Niger Delta (MEND), 90–91
Movement of Democratic Forces of the Casamance (MFDC, Senegal), 142, 144–47
Mozambique, 194, 197, 215–16, 225
Mueller, Susanne, 55
Mugabe, Robert Gabriel (president of Zimbabwe), 18, 159–64, 177–79; in elections of 2008, 175–77; in Gukurahundi Massacres, 165–69; land seizures by, 169–75; Mukherjee, Bumba, 230
Mulroney, Brian (Canadian prime minister), 58

multi-party systems, 57; in Burundi, 30, 41, 241n8; in Ghana, 117–18, 121–22; in Kenya, 7, 14, 51–52, 54, 56, 59–61; in Senegal, 155, 157; two-party systems, 17, 31, 131, 133. *See also* one-party systems
multinational corporations (MNCs), 73–74, 118. *See also* specific corporations
Museveni, Yoweri (president of Uganda), 36
Muslims, 10, 96, 100, 131, 141
Mutambara, Arthur (Zimbabwean political figure), 162, 178
mutiny, 100
Mutua, Makau, 62
Muzorewa, Abel (Zimbabwean political figure), 161

Nairobi Stock Exchange (Kenya), 61
Nairobi, Kenya, 57, 60–61
Namibia, 174, 194, 197, 216, 225
National Accord and Reconciliation Act (2008, Kenya), 68
National Alliance for Change (NAC, Kenya), 64
National Assembly: in Burundi, 32, 35, 37–39, 41–42, 44–45, 243n31; in Ghana, 119; in Nigeria, 76–78, 88–89, 92; in Senegal, 140; in Sudan, 106; in Zimbabwe, 161
National Boundary Commission (Nigeria), 91–92
National Commission for the Preventive Management of Flooding (CONAGPI, Senegal), 149, 154
National Commission to Study the Question of National Unity (Burundi), 29–30
National Committee for the Fight against Floods and Slums (Senegal), 154
National Congress Party (NCP, Sudan), 103–7, 109
National Consensus Forces (Sudan), 108
National Constitutional Conference: in Kenya, 64–65; in Nigeria, 93
National Convention Assembly (NCA, Kenya), 61–62
National Convention Executive Council (NCEC, Kenya), 61–64
National Convention Party (NCP, Ghana), 126–27
National Council of State (Nigeria), 250n28
National Democratic Congress (NDC, Ghana), 126–30

National Democratic Party (NDP, Kenya), 63
National Disaster Management Organization (NADMO, Ghana), 132
National Economic Council (Nigeria), 250n38
National Employment Council (Zimbabwe), 173
National House of Chiefs (Ghana), 122
national identity, 189–90, 195, 199; in Kenya, 69; in Nigeria, 74
National Liberation Council (NLC, Ghana), 120–21
National Minorities Commission (Nigeria), 94
National Oil Spills Detection and Response Agency (Nigeria), 86
National Party of Kenya (NPK), 64
National Platform for Disaster Risk Reduction (Senegal), 150
national police. *See* police
National Rainbow Coalition (NARC, Kenya), 51, 63, 65
National Security Council (Nigeria), 250n38
National Solidarity Fund (Senegal), 152
nationalism: in Kenya, 53, 69, 82, 87, 95; in Nigeria, 72, 77; in Sudan, 100; in Zimbabwe, 165
natural gas, 73–74, 82, 85–86, 249n28
natural resources, 88, 96, 102
NCP-SPLM Joint High Political Committee (Sudan), 105
NCP-SPLM Joint Leadership Committee (Sudan), 105–6
Ndadaye, Melchior (president of Burundi), 31–33
Ndau (ethnic group), 161–63
Ndayizeye, Domitien (president of Burundi), 36, 39
Ndebele (ethnic group), 18, 158–59, 161–64, 177–79; massacres of, 10, 165–69
Ndiaye, Souleymane (prime minister of Senegal), 152
Ndlovu-Gatsheni, Sabelo, 165
Ndulu, Benno, 54
Nduwimana, Martin (vice president of Burundi), 45
neo-imperialism, 23
Netherlands, 106
New Dawn Convention (2013, Sudan), 108

New Patriotic Party (NPP, Ghana), 126–28, 130–31
Ngendandumwe, Pierre (prime minister in Burundi), 28
Ngilu, Charity (Kenyan political figure), 64
Niayes, Senegal, 147–48
Niger, 194, 198, 216–217, 225
Niger Delta, 10, 14, 71–72, 248nn19, 24, 32; creation of new states in, 77; derivations and, 94–95; emergence of oil in, 83–85; environmental degradation in, 85–90; history of oil in, 73–74; oil price spike and, 90–92; resource distribution in, 75–76; roots of conflict in, 80–82
Niger Delta Development Board, 78
Niger Delta Development Commission (NDDC), 89–90, 248n19, 250n34
Niger Delta Volunteer Force, 249n31
Nigeria, 7, 10, 14–15, 19, 71–95, 194, 198, 217, 224, 240n28; Bayelsa, 76, 80, 82, 90–91, 248nn18, 24; constitutional evolution in, 75–80; emergence of oil in, 82–85; environmental degradation in, 85–90; gas flaring in, 249n28; history of oil in, 73–74; oil explorations in, 246n5; oil price spike in, 90–92; roots of conflict in, 80–82; Senegal and, 138, 260n14; Sudan and, 113, 117; vote-pooling system in, 199
Nigerian Economic Support Group, 248n24
Nigerian National Petroleum Corporation (NNPC), 82, 86, 249n30
Nile River, 96
Nilsson, Desirée, 230–31
Nkala, Enos (ZANU leader), 166
Nkomo, Joshua (Zimbabwe political figure), 161, 163, 165–66, 169
Nkrumah, Kwame "Osagyefo" (president of Ghana), 118, 120, 123–24
Nkurunziza, Pierre (president of Burundi), 37, 45–46, 48
nongovernmental organizations (NGOs), 150
Norris, Pippa, 229–30, 243n34–35
North Korea, 166
North Vietnam, 120
Northern Bahr el-Ghazal, Sudan, 105–6
Norway, 58
Ntega, Kirundo (Burundi), 29
Nuba Mountains (Sudan), 10
Nuer (ethnic group), 97, 109
Numayri, Ja'afar (president of Sudan), 101

Nwabueze, B. O., 93
Nyangoma, Léonard (CNDD leader), 35, 49
Nyerere, Julius (president of Tanzania), 35–36
Nzomukunda, Alice (vice president of Burundi), 45

O'Brien, Cruise, 139
O'Leary, Brendan, 188
Obasanjo, Olusegun (president of Nigeria), 88–89, 93
Odinga, Raila (Kenyan political figure), 59, 63–67
Ogoni Bill of Rights (Nigeria), 87
oil, 7, 14–15, 71–98, 249n32; environmental degradation from, 85–90; in Ghana, 117; history in Nigeria, 73–75, 82–85; in Kenya, 53; Nigerian conflicts and, 80–82; Nigerian constitution and, 75–80; price spikes for, 15, 72, 90–92, 250nn38, 40; in Sudan, 96–98, 101–6, 109, 111–12, 117
Oil Minerals Producing and Development Commission (OMPADEC, Nigeria), 89–90
Oil Pipelines Act (Nigeria), 87
Okonta, Ike, 83
oligarchy, 160
Oloibiri, Nigeria, 73
one-party systems: in Burundi, 28, 30, 32, 241n8; in Ghana, 128; in Kenya, 51, 53–56; two-party systems, 17, 31, 131, 133; in Zimbabwe, 161, 179. *See also* multiparty systems
Operation Ngatipedzenavo (Zimbabwe), 18, 158, 175–77, 179
Orange Democratic Movement (ODM, Kenya), 66–68
Owusu, Maxwell, 117
Ozer, Pierre, 149

pacification, ethnic, 27, 44, 49
Pan-Africa, 159
Paris Club, 58
parliamentarian systems, 2, 187, 190–92, 226, 228, 238n8; accommodation and, 199; in Burundi, 30–32, 37–48, 241n8, 242nn26, 29, 243n31; in Ghana, 117–20, 122–23, 127–31, 133–34; in Kenya, 53, 55, 59, 60–65, 67; majoritarian, 21; in Nigeria, 76, 78; in Rhodesia, 160; in Senegal, 138; in Sudan, 102, 107; in Zimbabwe, 160–61, 170–72, 179
Parliamentary Voting System and Constituencies Act (2001, UK), 134
Parti pour la Libération du Peuple Hutu (Palipehutu, Burundi), 35
Parti pour le Redressement National (Parena, Burundi), 40–41, 242n26
Party of National Unity (PNU, Kenya), 66–68
patrimonialism, 10
peace agreements, 7, 230–34; power-sharing and, 243n34; in Senegal, 145–46. *See also* Comprehensive Peace Agreement (CPA, Sudan, 2005)
peacekeeping force, in Burundi, 36, 38–39, 46, 49; in Sudan, 105, 108
People's Democratic Party (Nigeria), 76
People's National Defense Council (Ghana), 257n18
People's National Party (Ghana), 121
periphery. *See* center versus periphery
Permanent Court of Arbitration (Netherlands), 106
petroleum. *See* oil
Petroleum Industry Bill (PIB, Nigeria), 86
Petroleum Products and Distribution decree (1975, Nigeria), 87, 250n42
Petroleum Regulation Act (1969, Nigeria), 82, 86, 88, 94, 250n42
Petroleum Special Trust Fund (Nigeria), 89
Plan d'ORganisation des SECours (Plan ORSEC, Senegal), 149–50, 152–55
Plateau, Nigeria, 248n24
pluralism, 187–88, 190; in Burundi, 243n31; in Ghana, 120; in Kenya, 56, 58, 60, 63, 68–69; in Nigeria, 95
plurality voting, 21, 185, 187, 191, 226
polarization. *See* ethnic polarization
police: in Burundi, 28, 30, 33, 37–38, 41, 46; in Ghana, 121; in Kenya, 57, 61; in Nigeria, 80, 94, 249n32; in Zimbabwe, 171–73. *See also* military; security forces
political shocks, 4–5, 14, 226
Polity IV, 195–98
pollution, 85–87. *See also* environmental shocks
population displacement. *See* internally displaced persons
populism, 139, 171

Portuguese colonies, 10–11
postcolonial era, 55, 69, 118, 163, 165
power: concentration of, 93, 121, 133, 160, 193, 233; consolidation of, 27–29, 46, 53, 101, 109, 111; distribution of, 4–5, 75–76, 136–37, 191, 268n22; transfer of, 13, 128, 157. *See also* centralization; decentralization; power, alternation of; powers, separation of
Power Sharing and International Mediation in Ethnic Conflicts (Sisk), 186
Power Sharing in South Africa (Lijphart), 184
power-sharing, 15, 195, 199, 228–34, 271n30; in Burundi, 26–28, 30, 36–38, 50; in consociational design, 185–87, 190; in Ghana, 117–18; in Kenya, 65, 68; Lijphart on, 238n8; Norris on, 243nn34–35; in Sudan, 7, 101–7, 111–12; in Zimbabwe, 18, 160, 162, 174–76, 179
power-trading, 139, 142
power, alternation of, 184, 191; in Ghana, 117–18, 123, 128–29, 134
powers, separation of, 2, 6, 186, 199–200, 240n29; in Ghana, 17, 121, 133–34; in Kenya, 52; in Nigeria, 78–79, 88, 92
pre-electoral coalitions, 20, 185–87, 189–90
precolonial era, 100, 138–39, 163
prefects, 137, 149, 229
Prempeh, H. Kwasi, 132
presidential elections. *See* elections
presidential systems, 21, 187–88, 190–99, 226–29, 237n5; in Ghana, 118, 122–23; in Kenya, 51, 54, 64–66; in Nigeria, 76, 78–79; in Senegal, 137–38, 140; in Zimbabwe, 179
Pretoria Power Sharing Accord (2004), 37
Pretoria, South Africa, 36–37
Preventive Detention Act (Ghana, 1958), 119
prime ministry, 191, 268n22; in Burundi, 32; in Ghana, 124; in Kenya, 64, 66; in Senegal, 137, 140; in Zimbabwe, 161, 167
proportional representation (PR) systems, 2–3, 6, 21, 185–91, 199–200; advocacy of, 226, 228; in Burundi, 42, 46, 203, 243n31; in Ghana, 17, 132; Lijphart on, 238n8; power-sharing and, 230, 232, 271n30; in Zimbabwe, 160
protests: in Kenya, 7, 14, 51, 55–57, 60, 67–68; in Nigeria, 80, 83, 85, 88–89; in Senegal, 7, 10, 148, 151, 155. *See also* demonstrations; riots
Protocol on Political Power-Sharing, Defense and Security (2003, Burundi), 36–37
Provisional National Defense Council (PNDC, Ghana), 121–22

qualified voting procedures, 102
qualified-majority voting, 6
quotas, 2, 6, 21, 228, 241n15, 268n23; accommodation and, 190–92, 199; in Burundi, 29, 33, 37, 43, 46, 48, 203, 242n23; in consociational design, 186; in Ghana, 17; in Nigeria, 76, 85; in Zimbabwe, 161

Ranger, Terence, 163
Rawlings, Jerry (president of Ghana), 117, 121–22, 126, 128–29, 257n18
rebellions: in Burundi, 29, 35–40, 44–47, 49–50; in Nigeria, 7, 15; in Senegal, 17, 135–36, 143; in Sudan, 97, 99, 101–2
redistribution. *See* land reforms
referenda. *See* constitutional referenda
reforms: army, 36, 41; civic, 60; economic, 67, 143; electoral, 75, 78, 205; institutional, 11, 60, 68, 159, 232–33; judicial, 122. *See also* constitutional reforms; land reforms
refugees, 33, 132
Regional Assemblies (Ghana), 119
Reid, Ann, 228
Reilly, Benjamin, 187, 229
religions, 10, 100, 131, 141–42, 190; animism, 229; in Kenya, 61; in Nigeria, 76, 85; state, 192; in Sudan, 102; in Zimbabwe, 161, 179
relocation. *See* internally displaced persons (IDPs)
Republican Constitution (Ghana, 1960), 120
republicanism, 188
resettlement. *See* internally displaced persons (IDPs)
"resource curse," 74
resources: in Kenya, 67; in Nigeria, 74, 80, 82, 85, 91, 94–95; shocks and, 4–5, 15, 55, 99; in Sudan, 102
revenue: in Kenya, 53, 58; in Nigeria, 71–73, 75, 77, 82–84, 88–95; sharing of, 15, 71, 82–84, 118; in South Sudan, 102, 105–6, 111–12; windfalls, 14–15, 72, 90. *See also* derivation

Revenue Mobilization, Allocation and Fiscal Commission (RMAFC, Nigeria), 91–92
Reynolds, Andrew, 187, 228, 234
Rhodesia, 160, 162–63, 170
Rhodesian Front (RF), 161, 163, 165–66
rice production, 142, 144
Rift Valley (Kenya), 54, 59, 63, 68
riots, 9, 127; in Kenya, 7, 10, 14, 51, 56–57, 60–61. *See also* demonstrations; protests
Rivers state, Nigeria, 80, 82–83, 92, 248n24
Roeder, Philip, 232
Rondinelli, Dennis A., 233
Rothchild, Donald, 3, 187–88
Rozvi (ethnic group), 162–63
rule of law, 55, 58, 74, 173–74, 229
rump Sudan, 20–21
Rutten, Marcel, 57
Rwagasore, Louis (prime minister in Burundi), 28
Rwanda, 1, 194, 198, 217–18, 225, 234; Burundi and, 28–29, 50; Lemarchand on, 187; Zimbabwe and, 163
Rwasa, Agathon (FNL leader), 49

Saba Saba riots (1990, Kenya), 56–57, 61
sabotage of oil production, 82, 86–87, 90–91, 250nn34, 42
Sall, Macky (president of Senegal), 157
sanctions, 139, 174; on Kenya, 7, 55, 57; on Sudan, 105, 109
São Tomé and Príncipe, 194, 198, 218, 225
Sarr, Madeleine Diouf, 157
Savun, Burcu, 231
secession, 3, 7, 188, 229, 233; in Nigeria, 14–15, 83; in Senegal, 10, 17, 135–36, 140–45, 261n29; in Sudan, 15, 20, 97–99, 102–9, 112–13, 227; in Zimbabwe, 166
Seck, Ndour (Senegalese political figure), 152
Second Republic (Nigeria), 85
security forces: in Burundi, 36, 49; in Kenya, 68; in Nigeria, 249n32; in Senegal, 144; in South Sudan, 101–2, 105; in Zimbabwe, 166, 169, 177. *See also* military; police
Selassie, Haile (emperor of Ethiopia), 101
self-determination, 72, 74, 77, 91, 94–95
self-governance, 101, 112, 188, 252n20
semipresidential systems, 268n22
senate: in Burundi, 38–39, 45, 243n31: in Zimbabwe, 161–62, 170
Sene, Souleymane, 149

Senegal, 7, 10, 17, 19, 135–57, 194, 198, 218, 225; Casamance Secession in, 140–47; constitutional design in, 137–40; under Diouf, 143–45; flooding in, 147–56; as hyper-integrative, 240n28; Sudan and, 113, 117; under Wade, 145–46. *See also* Casamance
Senegalese African Rally for the Defense of Human Rights (RADDHO), 151
Senegalese Democratic Party (PDS), 139–40, 145
Senegambian Confederation, 143–44
Senghor, Diamacoune, 142
Senghor, Léopold Sédar (president of Senegal), 137–39, 141–43, 146, 157
separation of powers. *See* powers, separation of
separatism, 77, 113, 142–44, 146. *See also* secession
Seychelles, 194, 198, 219, 225
Shangaan (ethnic group), 162–63
Shari'a law, 101–2
Shell Petroleum and Development Company (SPDC), 73, 86, 249n32, 250n36
shocks. *See* economic shocks; endogenous shocks; environmental shocks; exogenous shocks; political shocks
Shona (ethnic group in Zimbabwe), 18, 158–59, 161–63, 177–79; in Gukurahundi massacres, 165–66, 169; intra-ethnic tensions, 162–64
Sibomana, Adrien (prime minister in Burundi), 30
Sierra Leone, 194, 198, 219, 225
Simeon, Richard, 188
Simonsen, Sven Gunnar, 231–32, 234
single transferable vote (STV) system, 186–87, 191
single-member districts (SMDs), 21, 123, 185, 191, 196–98
single-party systems. *See* one-party systems
Sisk, Timothy, 186, 228, 231–32
Smith, Ian (Zimbabwean political figure), 160–61
Sobukwe, Robert, 159
social welfare, 124–25, 138, 158, 239n13
socialism, 188–89
Socialist Party (PS, Senegal), 139–40, 145
Somalia, 58, 194, 195, 198, 199, 219–20, 224, 268n25

South Africa, 36–39, 150, 163, 166, 176, 178, 199, 231, 240n28, 246n40; democracy in, 184–86
South Kordofan, Sudan, 15, 99, 102–9, 111
South Sudan, 10, 97–99, 107–11; civil war in, 20–21, 229
South Sudan Liberation Movement (SSLM), 101
South Sudan Referendum Commission, 107
Southern African Development Community Tribunal (Namibia), 174
Southern Provinces Regional Self-Government Act (1972, Sudan), 253n20
Sovereign National Conference (Nigeria), 93
Sovereign Wealth Fund (Nigeria), 250n41
Sow, Aliou (minister in Senegal), 153
St. Louis, Senegal, 147
State Lands Act (Ghana, 1962), 120
state of emergency, 108, 120, 251n3
Stockwell, Robert, 186
stolen elections, 11, 193; in Ghana, 127–8; in Kenya, 14, 67–68; in Zimbabwe, 177
structural adjustment programs, 85, 143
subnational units, 6, 21, 192; autonomy of, 199; language and, 102, 189–90; vote-pooling and, 186. *See also* devolution
sub-Saharan Africa, 162, 233
Sud Quotidien (newspaper, Senegal), 154
Sudan, 10, 15–6, 58, 96–113, 194, 198, 220–21, 225, 251n2; accommodation in, 19–21, 23, 227; colonial legacy of, 97–98; constitutional design in, 102–3; historical background of, 100–102; as integrative, 240n28; power-sharing in, 103–7, 234; secession in, 107–12; shocks in, 7, 99. *See also* Abyei, Sudan; South Sudan
Sudan Liberation Movement (SLM), 251n2
Sudan People's Liberation Army (SPLA), 105–6, 108
Sudan People's Liberation Movement (SPLM), 97, 102–9, 111
Sudan Revolutionary Front (SRF), 108
Sudanese Armed Forces (SAF), 105–6, 108, 252n9
suffrage, 48
Sullivan, D. P., 28
Sunday Times (newspaper), 165
Supreme Courts, 6; in Ghana, 123, 256n1; in Nigeria, 88–89, 92; in Zimbabwe, 172
Swaziland, 194, 195, 198, 221, 225

Sweden, 58
Switzerland, 155

Tansey, Oisin, 232–33, 235
Tanzania, 29, 35–36, 194, 198, 221–22, 225
Technical Committee on the Niger Delta (Nigeria), 94
Tekere, Edgar (ZANU leader), 166
Tema, Ghana, 124
term limits, 5, 22, 191, 199; in Ghana, 17, 19, 128–29, 131; in Senegal, 140
territorial autonomy. *See* autonomy
territories. *See* subnational units
terrorism, 233
Third Chimurenga (Zimbabwe), 18, 158, 169–75, 179
Thomas, Clare, 121–22
Togo, 194, 198, 222, 225
Tonga (ethnic group), 162–63
Tongu fishermen (Ghana), 125
torture, 55, 165, 173–74, 176
totalitarianism, 195
Traditional Councils (Ghana), 122
Trans African Forum (United States), 57
transitional justice mechanisms, 6
Tsvangirai, Morgan (MDC leader), 161–62, 175–78
Tunisia, 194, 198, 222–23, 225
Tutsi (ethnic group), 13, 28–50, 240n3, 241n15; in 1993 elections, 31–32, 38, 243n33; in 2005 elections, 40–45, 243n33; in 2010 elections, 48; accommodation of, 20; after 2005, 46–49; Arusha Accord and, 36, 39, 41; in civil war, 32–33, 35; before independence, 28–29; Pretoria Accord and, 37–38; reforms in Burundi and, 29–30; in Rwanda, 50. *See also* Burundi; Hutu
Twa (ethnic group), 38, 44–45, 48, 242n23
two-party systems, 17, 31, 131, 133. *See also* multi-party systems; one-party systems

Uganda, 36, 39, 104, 194, 195, 198, 223, 225
Ugborodo community (Nigeria), 250n34
unemployment, 58, 68, 143, 248n24
unicameralism, 101
Union Party (Ghana), 119
Union pour le Progrès National (UPRONA, Burundi), 28–33, 241n15, 242nn25–26; in 1993 elections, 31, 38, 243n33; in 2005

Union pour le Progrès National (*Continued*)
 elections, 40–45, 243n33; in 2010
 elections, 48; Arusha Accord and, 36
unitarism, 21, 186, 188, 190, 192, 226; in
 Ghana, 119, 121; in Sudan, 100. *See also*
 federalism
United Kingdom (UK). *See* Britain
United Nations (UN), 38–39, 108, 242n20
United Nations Development Programme
 (UNDP), 150
United Nations Environment Programme
 (UNEP), 73
United Nations Interim Security Force for
 Abyei (UNISFA), 105, 108
United Nations Security Council, 109
United States, 57, 80, 105, 174, 249n25;
 bicameralism in, 191; power of president
 in, 119
United States Agency for International
 Development (USAID), 228
United States Institute of Peace, 228
Unity Accord (1987, Zimbabwe), 161, 177
Unity, Sudan, 15, 99, 111
universal suffrage, 48
Upper Nile, Sudan, 15, 99

Vandeginste, Stefaan, 28, 38
variables, 4, 9–12
Venda (ethnic group), 162–63
veto power, 2–3, 6, 188, 229, 232; in Burundi,
 37; in Ghana, 119; minority, 185
Vieira, João Bernardo (president of
 Guinea-Bissau), 146
vigilantism, 62–63
violence, 1–5, 7, 9–11, 19–20, 230, 234; in
 Burundi, 27–29, 33, 35, 42, 45–46, 49–50;
 in Ghana, 118, 127–32; in Kenya, 14, 51–52,
 55–56, 59, 61–63, 65–69; in Nigeria, 71–72,
 84–85, 88, 90; in Senegal, 17, 135–36, 144,
 148, 152; in Sudan, 15–16, 97–100, 104–9,
 111; in Zimbabwe, 18, 159–62, 165–70,
 172–77, 179
Virginia, United States, 80
Volta Basin Area Development Plan
 (Ghana), 125
Volta Dam (Ghana), 7, 16, 118, 123–26
Volta River Authority (VRA, Ghana),
 124–25
Volta River Development Act (1961, Ghana),
 124

Volta River Project (VRP, Ghana), 123–24
Volta, Ghana, 127, 130
votes of no confidence, 192
voting systems, 21, 185–87, 190–92, 199;
 closed-list, 30, 46; plurality, 226; qualified,
 6, 102. *See also* electoral systems

Wade, Abdoulaye (president of Senegal),
 139–40, 145–48, 150–55, 157
Waki, Philip (Kenyan justice), 246n41
Walter, Barbara, 229–30
Wamalwa, Michael (Kenyan political
 figure), 64
war. *See* civil war
War Veterans Association (Zimbabwe), 170
warlords, 82, 87–88, 90, 250n42
Warrap, Sudan, 15, 99, 252n9
Washington, D.C., 57, 106
Waterbury, John, 139
Wealth Sharing Group (Sudan), 105
wealth-sharing agreements, 102, 106
West, 20, 35. *See also under* specific
 countries
Western Bahr el-Ghazal, Sudan, 106
Western Sahara, 113
Westminster system, 52, 160
wetlands, 80
whites in Zimbabwe, 7, 18, 160–64, 178–79;
 in Gukurahundi Massacres, 165–66, 169;
 land seizures and, 170–75; white flight of,
 158, 164
Wildlife and Environment Zimbabwe, 174
Windcrest Farm (Zimbabwe), 173
winner-take-all elections, 160, 177
Wiseman, John, 121
Wolof, Senegal, 139
Wolpe, Howard (US political figure), 47
women: in office, 37–38, 43, 45–46, 48, 61;
 quotas for, 243n31, 268n23
World Bank, 174
world commodity prices, 11
World Health Organization (WHO),
 73–74

youth: in Burundi, 29, 32, 42; in Kenya,
 68–69; in Nigeria, 76, 82, 90–91; in
 Zimbabwe, 168

Zaire. *See* Democratic Republic of the Congo
Zambia, 174, 194, 198, 223–25

Zezuru (ethnic group), 162–63
Ziguinchor Accord (2004, Senegal), 145–47
Ziguinchor, Casamance, 142, 144
Zimbabwe, 7, 10, 17–19, 117, 158–79, 194, 198, 224–25, 240n28; Commonwealth summit in, 57–58; demography, 162–64; elections of 2008 in, 175–77; Gukurahundi massacres, 165–69; history of constitution, 159–62; land seizures in, 169–75
Zimbabwe African People's Union (ZAPU), 161, 163–65, 168
Zimbabwe Environmental Law Association, 174
Zimbabwe People's Revolutionary Army (ZIPRA), 165–66
Zimbabwean African National Liberation Army (ZANLA), 165–66
Zimbabwean African National Union (ZANU), 160–63, 178–79; in 2008 election, 176–77; in Gukurahundi Massacres, 165, 168; land seizures and, 170, 172–74
Zimbabwean National Army (ZNA), 165–66
Zulu (ethnic group), 163
Zuma, Jacob (vice president of South Africa), 36–37
Zvimba, Zimbabwe, 173

ACKNOWLEDGMENTS

This volume culminates a five-year research project spanning three continents, so I can individually acknowledge only a fraction of those who helped along the way. For initial encouragement, I thank James Lindsay, founding director of the Robert Strauss Center for International Security and Law, who persuaded me to draft the grant proposal that enabled this project. The book is based mainly on work supported by the U.S. Army Research Office grant number W911NF-09-1-0077 under the Minerva Initiative of the U.S. Department of Defense. I am also grateful for financial support from the Jennings Randolph Senior Fellowship of the U.S. Institute of Peace, and the Policy Research Institute of the LBJ School of Public Affairs. The Strauss Center staff, notably Ashley Moran and Dominique Thuot, provided invaluable logistical and administrative aid.

For helpful comments at various stages of preparation of this book, I thank Joel Barkan, Cathy Boone, Herman J. Cohen, Gordon Crawford, Abdelwahab El-Effendi, Zachary Elkins, Pierre Englebert, Alan Goulty, Bernard Grofman, Christof Hartmann, Donald Horowitz, Rene LeMarchand, Carl LeVan, Peter Lewis, Terrence Lyons, Eliezer Poupko, H. Kwasi Prempeh, Mohamed Salih, Michael Schatzberg, Tim Sisk, Lahra Smith, Nicolas Van de Walle, and Jennifer Widner. I am also grateful for feedback on the work in progress at the following events: Jan Tinbergen European Peace Science Conference, Milan, Italy; Conference on Climate Change and Security at the Crossroads: Pathways to Conflict or Cooperation, Kristiansand, Norway; Association for the Study of Nationalities, Columbia University; Conference on Shifting Conflict Patterns in Africa: Drivers of Instability and Strategies for Cooperation, University of Texas at Austin; International Studies Association, San Francisco; Conference on Constitutional Design and Ethnic Conflict, New York University Law School; Conference on Rethinking Climate Change, Conflict and Security, University of Sussex; Minerva Meeting and Program Review.

For intellectual inspiration, I thank I. William Zartman, Stephen Stedman, and the late Saadia Touval, who as my first professors of conflict management introduced me to the policy challenges this volume aims to address. For helping keep me relatively sane, *grazie* to the members of BC Fuzz and The Elroys. Last but not least, I am very grateful to my parents. Carmel Kuperman and the late Abraham S. Kuperman, for their patient love and support. Dad, I miss you. Mom, please cross at the light.